S0-BDN-441

GUN of LAWS AMERICA

Every Federal Gun Law on the books.

WITH PLAIN ENGLISH SUMMARIES

by *Alan Korwin*
with Attorney Michael P. Anthony

BLOOMFIELD PRESS
Phoenix, Arizona

Copyright © 2005–2007 Alan Korwin
All rights reserved

No part of the original content of this book may be reproduced or transmitted in any form or by any means now known or which will become known, without written permission from the publisher. Permission is granted for reviewers and others to quote brief passages for use in newspapers, periodicals, or broadcasts provided credit is given to *Gun Laws of America*, published by Bloomfield Press.

For information contact:

BLOOMFIELD PRESS

4848 E. Cactus #505-440
Scottsdale, AZ 85254
602-996-4020 Offices
602-494-0679 Fax
1-800-707-4020 Order Hotline
info@gunlaws.com

GunLaws.com

ISBN-13: 978-1-889632-14-8   ISBN-10: 1-889632-14-7
Library of Congress Catalog Card Number: 95-77339
352 pgs.

ATTENTION

Firearms Training Instructors, Clubs, Organizations, Educators, Schools and all other interested parties: Call us for information on quantity discounts!

To Order Retail or Wholesale Quantities
just call, write, fax or click!

NOTE: Was a new law passed yesterday?
FOR UPDATES: Send us a self-addressed stamped envelope, or just click "Updates" on our website.

"It doesn't make sense to own a gun and not know the rules."

Printed in the United States of America
at McNaughton and Gunn, Saline, Michigan

Fifth Edition – 2nd Printing

TABLE OF CONTENTS

The Federal Gun Laws: "United States Code"

Some titles shortened for formatting; precise titles precede each law in the text

ACKNOWLEDGMENTS

Once again a book has demonstrated to me with brilliant clarity that nothing happens in a vacuum. Everyone who's path I cross while a book is underway has some impact on the final product. Hey, everyone I've ever met has had an effect on me and what I do. In fact, when I began this research, I didn't know it would lead to a book. So please don't fault me if we're friends or acquaintances and your name is not here. I feel like I'm preparing a wedding invitations list, the most lasting effect of which may be to tick off the people who aren't on it. Here I pay tribute to those people without whom this book simply would not have happened as it did.

Landis Aden, Brad Beebe, Kermit Burton, Susan Carley, Bob Corbin, Jim Cowlin, Mike Dillon, Sandy Froman, Fred Griisser, Charly Gullett, Stephen P. Halbrook, Ph.D., Brad Harper, Robb Itkin, Cheryl Korwin, Tyler Korwin, Harold Lawsky, Georgene Lockwood, Mark Moritz, Ted Parod, Mark Pixler, Terrence Plas, Richard Shaw, Dean Weingarten, Jim Willinger and of course my parents.

The Society for Technical Communication taught me many things that made my task easier and improved the results. This is as technical a document as ever there was.

Research Assistance by
Candice M. DeBarr and Jason Maxwell

Editing by
Gwen A. Henson

Cover design by
Ralph Richardson

Book design and charts by
Alan Korwin

FOREWORD
WARNING! • DON'T MISS THIS!

This book is not "the law," and is not a substitute for the law. The law includes all the legal obligations imposed on you, a much greater volume of work than the mere federal firearms statutes contained in this book. You are fully accountable under the exact wording and current official interpretations of all applicable laws, regulations, court precedents, executive orders and more, when you deal with firearms under any circumstances.

Many people find laws hard to understand, and gathering all the relevant ones is a lot of work. This book helps you with these chores. Collected in one volume are copies, reproduced with great care, of the principal written federal statutes controlling gun use in America.

In addition, capsule summaries called *Gists* appear throughout the text, expressed in regular conversational terms for your convenience. While great care has been taken to accomplish this with a high degree of accuracy, **no guarantee of accuracy is expressed or implied, and the explanatory sections of this book are not to be considered as legal advice or a restatement of law.**

In explaining the general meanings of the laws, using plain English, differences inevitably arise, so **you must always check the actual laws. This book only contains edited excerpts of federal statutes related to firearms.** The actual and complete set of federal statutes are published by The U.S. Government Printing Office and by commercial publishers. The author and publisher of this book expressly disclaim any liability whatsoever arising out of reliance on information contained in this book.

New laws and regulations may be enacted at any time by the authorities, and courts are constantly interpreting the laws and regulations. **The author and publisher make no representation that this book includes all requirements, prohibitions and rules which may exist.**

12

FIREARMS LAWS ARE CONSTANTLY CHANGING. You are strongly urged to consult with a qualified attorney and local authorities to determine the current status and applicability of the law to specific situations which you may encounter. Guns are deadly serious business and require the highest level of responsibility from you. Firearm ownership, possession and use are rights that carry awesome responsibility. Unfortunately, **what the law says and what the authorities and courts do aren't always an exact match.** You must remember that each legal case is different and may lack prior court precedents. A decision to prosecute a case and the charges brought may involve a degree of discretion from the authorities involved. Sometimes, there just isn't a plain, clear-cut answer you can rely upon. Abuses, ignorance, carelessness, human frailties and plain fate subject you to legal risks, which can be exacerbated when firearms are involved. Take nothing for granted, recognize that legal risk is attached to everything you do, and **ALWAYS ERR ON THE SIDE OF SAFETY.**

The One-Glaring-Error theory says there's at least
one glaring error hidden in any complex piece of work.
This book is no different. Watch out for it.

"It will be of little avail to the people that the laws are made by men of their own choice, if the laws be so voluminous that they cannot be read, or so incoherent that they cannot be understood; if they be repealed or revised before they are promulgated, or undergo such incessant changes that no man who knows what the law is to-day can guess what it will be to-morrow." –James Madison, The Federalist Papers, #62

13

PREFACE

(Phoenix, 1995) Until now, getting the gun laws—or any set of laws—was expensive. You could go to a library, which is free, and just look at a copy—but only certain libraries carry the law, and they're not usually next door. Photocopying a portion becomes costly quickly, and you end up, often enough, with poor quality library copies. Your time spent traveling, and the inconvenience of library-hours-only access, adds to the expense of "getting" the law. Top it all off with the cost of learning how to research and find anything.

You can hire an attorney to get it for you, and we all know what price range that falls into. Buying your own printed copies and maintaining them is priced in the low thousands of dollars. Even the cost to store a set in your home, with all the different sets needed, is no small price to pay.

Newly available CDs are the least expensive method (if you can call $1,000 cheap) and of course you need a computer to use one. Professional on-line services are pricey—charging dollars per minute. Internet proponents say that will drop to near zero, but what else has ever done that. The leatherbound set of federal laws that Senators and Representatives can order (and take with them when they leave office) is $2,500 worth of books.

The law of the land should be easily accessible and inexpensive in the best of all worlds, but this is just not the case. And free speech isn't free, freedom isn't free, and the law, when you get right down to it, is expensive. The cost of an informed democracy is exorbitant. And, by the way, worth it.

Eternal vigilance is a price of freedom.

Special Note on Pending Legislation

Many new bills have been proposed by legislators who would:
- Outlaw specific or classes of firearms by price range, melting point, operating characteristics, accuracy, type of safety mechanism, type of sighting mechanism, point of origin, appearance and by name.
- Restrict the amount of ammunition a gun can hold and the devices for feeding ammunition
- Restrict the number of firearms and the amount of ammunition a person may buy or own
- Require proficiency testing and periodic licensing
- Register firearms and owners nationally
- Use taxes to limit firearm and ammunition ownership
- Create new liabilities for firearm owners, manufacturers, dealers, parents and persons involved in firearms accidents
- Outlaw keeping firearms loaded or not locked away
- Censor classified ads for firearms, eliminate firearms publications and outlaw any dangerous speech or publication
- Melt down firearms that are confiscated by police
- Prohibit gun shows and abolish hunting
- Deny or criminalize civil rights for government-promised security
- Repeal the Second Amendment to the Constitution

In contrast, less attention has been paid to laws that would:
- Mandate school-based safety training
- Provide general self-defense awareness and training
- Encourage personal responsibility in resisting crime
- Protect people who stand up and act against crime
- Guarantee people's right to travel legally armed for personal safety
- Fix the conditions which generate hard-core criminals
- Assure sentencing of serious criminals, increase the percentage of sentences which are actually served, provide more prison space and permanently remove habitual criminals from society
- Improve rehabilitation and reduce repeat offenses
- Reduce plea bargaining and parole abuses
- Close legal loopholes and reform criminal justice malpractice
- Reform the juvenile justice system
- Improve law enforcement quality and efficiency
- Establish and strengthen victims' rights and protection
- Hold the rights of all American citizens in unassailable esteem
- Provide for the common defense and buttress the Constitution

Some experts have noted that easy-to-enact but ineffectual "feel good" laws are being pursued instead of the much tougher course of laws and social changes that would reduce crime and its root causes. Many laws aim at disarming honest people while ignoring the fact that gun possession by criminals is already strictly illegal and largely unenforced. Increasing attacks on the Constitution and civil liberties are threatening freedoms Americans have always had. You are advised to become aware of any new laws which may be enacted. Contact your legislators to express your views on proposed legislation.

To the mastermind

Overview

Anyone who has ever speculated that America's laws are written in secret code can simply look at the title of the laws to find the truth. *United States Code.* There's no "The" and no indication, for newcomers at least, of what's inside.

Welcome to the sometimes unusual world of the law.

Gun laws come in all shapes and sizes. At the top of the list is the U.S. Constitution. This is the agreement that people of free states came to ("We the people..."), the creed adopted when founding this nation, and upon which federal statutes are based. (The whole law has some roots deeper in history than the Constitution, and in civil, common and natural law). The Constitution has a number of parts that directly relate to the historical record of Americans keeping and bearing arms; these are reproduced as the first laws in this text.

Among many other things, the Constitution authorizes an assemblage, a "congress," of the citizenry's representatives. This Congress is empowered by the Constitution, within specific limits, to pass laws that are binding on all citizens. A quite complex mechanism has evolved since the nation's founding for passing laws, and moving the proposed drafts, called bills, through the legislative process.

The Written Laws

When a bill is approved by both houses of the Congress and signed by the President, it becomes a public law—the law of the land. After passage, the public laws are divided into more-or-less logical groups and inserted into a set of 50 numbered "Titles." These written laws, called *statutes*, are the framework of U.S. law.

It is important to note that many of the laws passed by Congress do not become numbered statutes. While "gun law" may grow in a given enactment, some parts can be thought of as merely current events, do not get statute numbers, and so the actual statutes grow more slowly than the total federal output of gun law. Examples include funding measures for gun-oriented agencies, studies to be conducted, various crime control initiatives of limited duration, training programs and more.

The compiled written laws are the U.S. Code. Putting the laws into the code is called *codification*. The official version has been produced by the Government Printing Office once every six years since 1926, annual updates are made available, and it is widely known by its acronym, U.S.C.

Private companies produce bound versions of the U.S.C. and sell it to a fairly broad market. The private versions include fascinating and extremely valuable historical notes and legal opinions, cross references, and summaries of sample court cases that affect how the statutes are now interpreted. The West Publishing Co. of St. Paul, Minn., produces a version called United States Code Annotated (U.S.C.A.) and Bancroft Whitney of San Francisco, Calif., calls their edition United States Code Service (U.S.C.S.).

Although the versions should be identical, tiny differences exist, and there is always the issue of typographical errors. Incredibly intertwined cross-referencing systems and indexes make various sets substantially different, and researchers often develop a preference for one set over another.

An annotated set of the complete federal law is well over 200 books, with dozens of supplements, more than 10,000 pages of index, and must be updated regularly. The criminal laws alone (Title 18) fill 11 volumes, two supplements, five books of rules and more than 1,200 pages of sentencing guidelines. Today, the laws are also available on quite small CD-ROM discs, and the entire set can be found on several Internet-based services, which are linked from the National Directory at gunlaws.com.

The Gun Laws

Over the years, a sizable body (though a tiny percentage) of federal law has evolved around firearms. The earliest federal gun statute (not including the Constitution) still in effect today appears to be a firearm forfeiture law for illegal hunting in Yellowstone National Park, passed on May 7, 1894, part of Title 16. A handful of similar laws passed early in the 20th century.

Since 1910 a decade hasn't gone by without the federal government enacting at least some gun laws. The enactment date is at the end of every statute in *Gun Laws of America*, along with a word count in parentheses. These have been used to make the charts showing the growth in federal gun law.

In 1934, the first major piece of federal gun legislation was enacted, the National Firearms Act, or NFA. The NFA was prompted by the St. Valentine's Day massacre, a machine-gun massacre of one criminal gang by another. The new law was codified in Title 26, the Internal Revenue tax laws. Basically, the NFA regulated firearms through tax requirements. Congress at the time understood it lacked authority to pass such laws, and held its collective breath to see if this novel approach would make it through the courts. The judiciary was cooperative.

The second major piece of federal gun law came in 1968, the Gun Control Act, in response to political assassinations of the 1960s. It, and most subsequent gun law, relies upon Congress' interstate commerce power to regulate guns. GCA created large bodies of law in Title 18, the criminal laws. These regulated private gun ownership in a manner unprecedented in America.

Before the GCA firearms were essentially unregulated at the federal level and availability was greater than it is today—guns were sold by mail order, and magazines and department stores routinely offered handguns and long guns.

Society was different then; it was unthinkable to bring a weapon to school for criminal purpose—but millions of kids did for legitimate reason. Crime wasn't the problem it is today, random senseless violence was virtually unheard of, and people pretty much took gun ownership for granted. Those days are gone.

Since those days, gun laws and crime have steadily grown. No one knows for sure what the problem is.

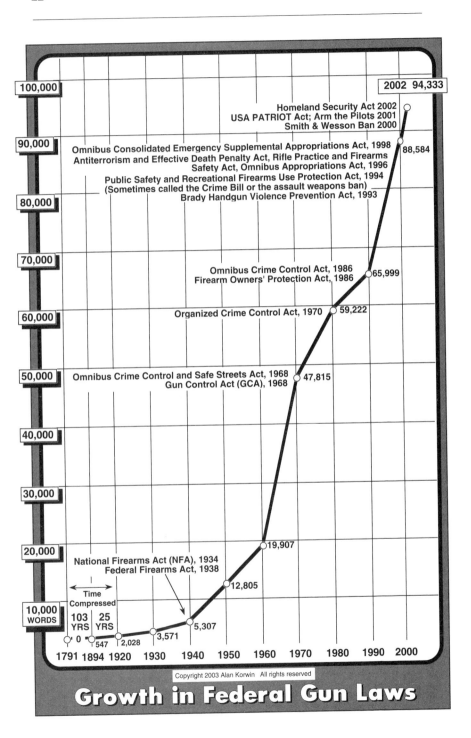

Growth in Federal Gun Laws

Copyright 2003 Alan Korwin   All rights reserved

GROWTH IN FEDERAL GUN LAWS: THE NUMBERS

DATE	Words added	New USC sections	% increase at the time	% of total thru 2002
1791	0*	0	—	0
1894	547	1	—	0.6
1910s	1,481	7	271.0	1.6
1920s	1,543	8	43.2	1.6
1930s	1,736	9	32.7	1.8
1940s	7,498	37	58.6	7.9
1950s	7,102	42	35.7	7.5
1960s	27,908	51	58.4	29.6
1970s	11,407	26	19.3	12.1
1980s	6,777	28	10.3	7.2
1990–95	7,870	22	11.9	8.3
1996	9,898	not codified	13.4	10.5
1998	4,817	not codified	5.8	5.1
1999	0	–	0.0	0.0
2000	90	not codified	0.1	0.1
2001	1,522	not codified	1.7	1.6
2002	4,120	not codified	4.6	4.7
Totals	**94,333**	**231** (codified thru 1995)		

*The 27 words of the Second Amendment (and other Constitutional provisions)
are not statutes and are not counted for the purposes of this chart.
The chart above reflects tabulations completed through 1995.

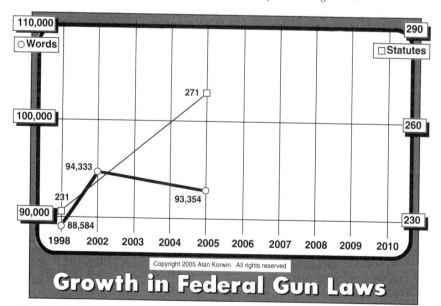

Growth in Federal Gun Laws

Copyright 2005 Alan Korwin   All rights reserved

The net reduction in words since 2002 results mainly from losses during codification of the Public Laws for this tenth anniversary edition, plus repeals, expirations and amendments. In several cases amendments expand a law's scope but reduce its word count (e.g., 610 words less in 18 1114). Expiration of the assault-weapon law removed 1,105 words, and the 3,710-word list of approved guns. The increase in numbered statutes is a net gain, accounting for repeals and new enactments. New statutes since 2002 added 4,339 words.

Many new federal gun laws are placed in Title 18, and contrary to popular reports, are typically minor, especially in light of the NFA or the GCA. A typical example is the so-called assault-weapons ban, part of the 1994 Crime Bill, codified as 18-922(v) and (w), now expired. Nothing was actually banned—Americans could still buy, own, sell, trade, have and use any of the millions of affected firearms and accessories while the law was in effect.

What the law did was to prohibit *manufacturers and importers* from selling newly made goods of that type to the public (and it was a crime for the public to get them). Maybe that is a ban, but not in the sense that was popularized. Contrary to news reports, the law did nothing about the very real problem of getting armed criminals off the street.

The net effect of the law was to motivate manufacturers to create stockpiles before the ban took affect, then to introduce new products that were not affected, by making minor cosmetic changes, and to step up marketing efforts overseas for affected products. In addition, demand and prices skyrocketed for the then fixed supply of goods domestically, and then adjusted downward when it became obvious that supplies were still available. None of this applies now since the law expired in 2004. No effect on criminal activity has been reported by any observers, all of whom now admit that these heavy, bulky guns are not the kind favored by hoodlums. If this is all news to you, it's time to question your source of news. News accuracy on gun issues is known to be quite low.

Gun Use

Firearm violations have criminal consequences, but placing the gun laws in the criminal code sets a tone that is not necessarily appropriate. A criminal can violate many laws that put people's lives at risk and go to jail for it, but that doesn't mean that, say, construction standards, belong in the criminal code.

Some gun use is obviously criminal and despicable. Other uses are noble, appeal to the highest ideals our society holds, and are enshrined in and ensured by the statutes on the books:

- Protecting your family in emergencies
- Personal safety and self defense
- Preventing and deterring crime
- Detaining criminals for arrest
- Guarding our national borders
- Deterring and resisting terrorism
- Preserving our interests abroad
- Helping defend our allies
- Overcoming tyranny
- International trade
- Emergency preparedness
- Obtaining food by hunting
- Commerce and employment
- Historical preservation and study
- Olympic competition
- Collecting
- Sporting pursuits
- Target practice
- Recreational shooting

Perhaps Title 42, public health and welfare, would better reflect the fact, recognized by the Framers and embodied throughout the law, that in the good guys' hands, guns are OK. Guns save lives. Guns stop crime. Guns are why America is still free.

In addition to regulating firearms for people (and not just the citizens) in the United States, federal laws regulate firearms in other categories not often recognized.

Gun Laws of America covers laws that affect:

- The public and the government
- Manufacturers and importers
- Collectors
- International commercial trade
- Military applications
- International military trade
- Domestic commerce and transportation
- Exclusions for the proper authorities—CIA, FBI, NASA, DIA, DEA, IRS, USPS, BIA, BATFE, GSA, TSA, HSD, etc. So many groups have special firearms privileges it would be interesting to see a study of how much of the population falls into this unusual category. At least nine new federal agencies have been added to the list since our first edition.
- Local law enforcement
- Domestic and international hunting
- Government aministrators

Firearm Requirements That Are Not Statutory

One of the main effects of the federal gun statutes is to authorize federal gun regulations. In many cases the statutes don't describe required actions or prohibitions. They merely assign the details to an agency, or often to the Attorney General, who then assigns it to the Bureau of Alcohol, Tobacco, Firearms and Explosives. Prior to 2002, all that activity went through the Treasury Dept., which reflected recognition, dating back to 1934, that the government was powerless under the Second Amendment to regulate firearms, but could circumvent that by using its taxing authority to exercise control over gun issues. Through a hopefully careful and fair deliberative process, the bureaucracy issues guidelines, called regulations, which have the force of law. None of the people doing this are elected.

The power to issue regulations is a great source of power. As anyone who has recently sought to restore lost civil rights can attest, the entire game can start and end with regulations. If an agency doesn't have the budget from Congress to implement regulations (as BATFE has not had, for rights-restoration, since 1992), your options are pretty much reduced to suing the federal government, a wholly unsavory thought.

Regulations are published in draft and final form in the Federal Register (the official record of federal proceedings), and assembled into the "Code of Federal Regulations." The CFR is at least as complex as the USC.

Within any given segment of government you may find agencies with their own special procedures, guidelines, policies, operations and attitudes, which may or may not completely agree with statutes, regulations or previously established precedents. A person can be unduly subject to obligations quite far removed from that intended by Congress when it passed its laws. Agency policies and procedures have no force of law, but can be a very real element of dealing within the system. For example, National Parks ban possession of operable firearms, but no legitimate delegated authority for this ban can be found.

State Laws and Travel

Parallel with federal laws and regulations (and the maze of systems that generate official interpretations) come the State Constitutions and statutes. Each state has its own Constitution and laws, and although these are sometimes modeled after one another and are quite similar, in many cases, and specifically with respect to guns, the laws are sometimes widely divergent. This is critical because the main, day-to-day operational aspects of bearing arms are regulated by the states and *not* the federal government.

You can't take a good understanding of your state's gun laws and hope it applies to firearms possession or use in another state, even an adjoining state that you travel to all the time. Such an approach can easily lead to arrest and severely unpleasant results, even if innocently performed.

Federal law generally does not control the details of how you can carry a firearm in your state, the rules for self defense and crime resistance, or where you can go for target practice on state property. Your individual state does. Federal laws aren't "higher" than state laws, as many people mistakenly believe. They control different things.

If you're used to the fact that federal laws are labyrinthine and obfuscatory (twisted and confusing), you'll feel right at home among state statutes.

In Arizona, a loaded personal firearm in the glove box of a private car is perfectly legal. Drive 50 feet across the border into California and you now have a loaded gun and a concealed gun—one gun, two crimes—and if "they" catch you, you could get a permanent criminal record and go to jail.

The bottom line is that the civil right and historical record of law-abiding citizens traveling with firearms for their own safety has evaporated, due to laws at the state level. People typically have no idea of what the gun laws are in any state but their own (and rarely enough that), getting a complete set of the relevant ones is hard work (they are all linked from gunlaws.com), understanding the laws runs from difficult to nearly impossible, and you can be arrested for making a simple mistake.

The legal risk created by our own government for a family traveling interstate with a firearm may be greater than the actual risk of a criminal confrontation. Because of this, the days of traveling armed and being responsible for your own safety and protection have all but ended for people who leave their home state. The proper authorities are generally exempt from these restrictions.

At least 39 states have a statute known as *preemption*. This, in theory, prohibits local governmental bodies within a state from passing their own gun laws in conflict with state statutes. Not all states adhere to their own preemption rules, and 11 states don't have any to help support uniform and comprehensible firearms policy within their borders.

Without preemption, a city or county may have a rule on its books, which they will enforce, in conflict with a state statute. This puts citizens under a severe jeopardy, where adherence to a statute may not protect them from a prosecution.

Those readers who purchased this book hoping it would somehow enable or empower them to travel interstate with a loaded personal firearm must contact their representatives and begin to ask about the lost National Right to Carry. That right has a name, the Second Amendment, and it has quietly disappeared for interstate travelers.

The
**Democracy
Clock**

Half an hour to midnight

Readers are invited to send us an old-fashioned stamped, self-addressed envelope which we will fill and return when there is news about new federal gun laws...

This is the Fifth Edition, issued July 2005.

Delegated Authority

Statutes authorizing the proper authorities to carry firearms are usually very long, and include details on what such people can do related to arrest, search and seizure, and other responsibilities. Although interesting, delegation of authority is not inherently a gun law and the decision was made to edit these details. Interestingly, this then pointed out a list of "proper authorities" who are beyond some firearms laws that bind the public. More than 20% of the numbered federal gun laws describe "official" groups that are exempt from the gun laws the rest of us face daily.

In at least one statute, 49-2428, the delegated responsibilities are what determine who is authorized for firearms carry, and so that list of responsibilities proved valuable. By including it you get a peek into the sorts of responsibilities frequently conveyed in the lengthy "may carry" statutes, many of which are much longer than this example.

The Proper Authorities

One of the unexpected results of compiling all the federal gun laws was discovering the subset of statutes that exempt many people from the gun laws. These people are referred to throughout this text as *proper authorities*. It's important to check the law when that phrase is used, to clearly identify who is authorized, under what circumstances and for what purposes. The purposes may be very narrow or extremely broad.

Only three U.S. organizations are described that simply "may carry firearms." These are the FBI, the Secret Service and U.S. Marshals and deputies. All others "may be authorized to carry" or have some other limiting factors applied.

A few of the statutes exempt certain activities for the proper authorities (such as boarding an airplane with a loaded firearm) as opposed to merely describing a group of people who may bear arms despite laws restricting ordinary people.

The list that follows is designed to show the related sections of law, not the complete descriptions of eligible personnel or the conditions under which these people are exempt from gun laws.

Chart of Government Exemptions from the Gun Laws

STATUTE	FIREARMS-EXEMPT GROUP OR EXEMPT CONDITION
5-App.	Inspectors General and specified staff
7-2270	Dept. of Agriculture Office of Inspector General
7-2274	Certain workers at the Dept. of Agriculture
10-1585	Dept. of Defense civilians
12-248	Federal Reserve Board law enforcement agents
14-95	Coast Guard civilians
16-1a-6	National Parks employees; any federal employee selected by the Secretary of the Interior, with that employee's agency approval
16-559c	Forest Service law enforcement officers and agents
16-670j	Dept. of Interior, Dept. of Agriculture, and state employees by agreement
16-3375	Anyone in federal or state government, or in an Indian tribe, to enforce hunting and fishing laws
18-922	Federally licensed manufacturers, importers, dealers, museums, researchers and others are exempt for firearms testing and evaluation, per subsection (b); all government authorities are exempt from the assault-weapons descriptions in subsections (v) and (w).
18-925	Federal and state governments are exempt from Title 18 Chapter 44 (the main gun laws)
18-930	Restrictions at federal facilities and federal courts do not apply to proper authorities
18-1715	Authorities exempt from mailing restrictions
18-2277	Possession of firearms on a vessel are at the control of the ship's master or owner; proper authorities are exempt
18-3050	Bureau of Prisons officers and employees
18-3051	Bureau of Alcohol, Tobacco, Firearms and Explosives
18-3052	Federal Bureau of Investigation
18-3053	U.S. marshals and their deputies
18-3056	Secret Service
18-3061	United States Postal Service
18-3063	Environmental Protection Agency
19-2072	Customs officials
20-60	Smithsonian Institution curators (for display)
21-372	Health and Human Services Dept.
21-878	Drug Enforcement Administration; any local law enforcement officer authorized by Atty. General
22-277d-3	International Boundary and Water Commission
22-2709	Dept. of State and the Foreign Service
22-2778	Government people who are not restricted by the U.S. Munitions List
25-2803	Bureau of Indian Affairs

26-4182	Armed forces are exempt from firearms taxes
26-5844	NFA weapons can only be imported for proper authorities or research and testing
26-5851	People working with proper authorities may be exempted from certain firearms taxes and other requirements
26-5852	Certain taxes are waived for proper authorities and the military
26-5853	Certain taxes are waived for proper authorities and the military
26-5872	Proper authorities can get confiscated firearms
26-7608	Internal Revenue Service agents
28-566	U.S. Marshals, deputies and officials of the Marshal's Svc.
31-321	Treasury Dept.
38-902	Dept. of Veterans Affairs
39-3001	Proper authorities are exempt from nonmailable firearms provisions
40-13n	Supreme Court Marshal and Police
40-193t	Smithsonian Institution police
40-210	Capitol Police
40-318d	General Services Admin. officers and employees
40-490	GSA protection force
40-1315	Dept. of Homeland Security; Federal Protective Service
42-2201	Atomic Energy Commission and contractors
42-2456	National Aeronautics and Space Administration and contractors
42-7270a	Dept. of Energy
43-1733	Dept. of the Interior
44-317	Government Printing Office employees
49-114	Transportation Security Administration
49-44903	Air transportation security personnel
49-44921	Federal Flight Deck Officers (deputized pilots)
49-46303	Proper authorities may have firearms on aircraft
49-46505	Proper authorities may have firearms on aircraft
49 App 2404	Dept. of Transportation employees at Washington National Airport
49 App 2428	Dept. of Transportation employees at Dulles International Airport
50-403f	Central Intelligence Agency
50 App 2411	Dept. of Commerce Office of Export Enforcement

61 statutes: 3 unconditional bear arms, 38 bear arms by rule, 6 any government employee may bear arms as specified, 14 special conditions apply (e.g., tax-free status, deputized pilots, etc.).

What exactly is "a" law?

A written law, a *statute*, is an agreement among the citizens to behave in a described way. In America, laws are established through indirect representation of the citizens' wishes, in Congress. Provisions are usually included for enforcement of the agreement, such as jail time or fines, imposed by a court system.

The agreement itself is drafted and approved by a legislature—a group of people hired and elected by the citizens to take care of this complex business. If you chose to live among the citizens as a full member of the community, in theory at least, you have agreed to abide by the entire set of agreements passed.

In contrast, *the* law is the entire set of legal obligations imposed on you. It includes federal, state and local requirements issued by legislatures, the judiciary, the executive branch and the many bureaucratic organs of government. The law is so vast and immane it has been said that it is impossible to comply with it all just based on the sheer size. If that's true, then every American is a law breaker. And will the people who never exceed the speed limit please raise their hands.

A law can't physically control how you act. A law instead provides guidelines for evaluating your actions after the fact. This explains why, though guns are outlawed for criminals, many remain armed. Enacting a law does not guarantee a result.

What does a law "mean"?

The courts decide what the laws mean. The words of Congress are less important, strangely enough, than the pronouncements of a court of competent jurisdiction. A statute means what a court says it means. In some courts, a statute means what a judge says it means. Sometimes, the law means what the cop with the gun in your ear says it means—until the judge gets you.

Do not confuse this with what a law *says*. The people who write these laws are in fact trying to say something, results notwithstanding. The *Gists* in *Gun Laws of America* attempt to strip away the fog from their legalese, so a regular person can more easily see what a law says. This is done by simplifying syntax, removing the effects of the Department of Redundancy Dept., weaving in cross-references instead of leaving them out, and using plain words instead of obscure ones. What a law actually says is a valuable thing to know.

Once you cross the line from law-abiding (or unnoticed) to law breaking (or at least charged as such), the meaning of the law is a whole new game. Injected into the court system, the law plays only a small role in your fate. Rules of evidence, procedural rules, get-tough policies which may be in effect just then—or not, how crowded the courts are and with what, deals you can make in the hallways and back rooms (called plea bargains), the personalities of the players—from the arresting officer to the clerks, to your defense team, if any... the law, what it says, what it means, and how it is enforced and interpreted in light of every court precedent currently set, these all affect you in concert to comprise "the law."

No matter how laws are written, circumstances arise which aren't covered. Violations occur, or the authorities believe violations have occurred, or the authorities single a person out for whatever reason, and the court system passes judgment, setting precedent for future occurrences and sealing your fate.

That seemingly innocent word *precedent* describes a body of information so immense and intertwined that it defies description. And it's required for a complete definition of what the laws mean. The statutes without the precedents, when the chips are down, are nearly worthless. What a system.

New laws are constantly passed, and new meanings are continually found by the courts. It's beyond difficult to remain current on even a single subject, let alone be reasonably versed across the board. The nation's founders envisioned an informed populace. The nature of the law makes this next to impossible.

Consider the commentary by William Godwin:

> "Law is an institution of the most pernicious tendency. The institution, once begun, can never be brought to a close. No action of any man was ever the same as any other action, had ever the same degree of utility of injury. As new cases occur, the law is perpetually found to be deficient. It is therefore perpetually necessary to make new laws. *The volume in which justice records her prescriptions is forever increasing, and the world would not contain the books that might be written.* The consequences of the infinitude of law is its uncertainty."

The Laws Are Generally Excellent

It's important to remember that the federal laws, in addition to regulating the bearing of arms, prohibit and penalize using guns for criminal purposes, a much needed feature. The well regulated legal uses of guns contain no tolerance for criminal misuse. Using a firearm for any evil deed is strictly illegal, reprehensible and can incur extreme punishments (though courts don't always mete out the full extent of the law).

It is completely prohibited in America to criminally use a gun to threaten or intimidate, harm, kidnap, hijack, rob, rape, pillage, plunder or murder. Reckless display of a gun is a crime. Delivering guns to felons, use of guns by felons, smuggling guns, using guns in the furtherance of any crime, these things are illegal, prohibited, absolutely against the law and subject a person to arrest or even death. Some of this is federal law, much of it is controlled individually by the states.

Using a gun to rob a store *ought* to be illegal. Who in the firearms debate disagrees with that? *That's* true gun control, and makes sense. When laws attempt to restrict what law-abiding citizens can and cannot do, in the *name* of gun control, and especially if there's no effect on criminals, ah, there's the rub.

People have come to realize that attempting to disarm the American public is not gun control, it's disarming the American public. *Gun control* means keeping guns out of the hands of the bad guys. This is good public policy. Rational people agree it's desirable. It deserves and earns the broadest support.

Unfortunately, because the term *gun control* has been so perverted it can barely be applied to its noble cause—controlling the truly criminal use of firearms. America *needs* better gun control—more criminals must be disarmed. Disarming honest citizens does not accomplish that. Need this even be said?

Favoring gun control yet staunchly resisting the gradualism of citizen disarmament is a coherent position. It is Orwellian to call citizen control crime control. The big question for America, perhaps, is can gradualism do what a century of Communism could not—dismember the greatest system for human government yet devised.

Authors note: Some people are actively working hard to take away or limit rights Americans currently have and exercise.

As a writer I see this threat ("actively working hard to take away or limit rights Americans currently have") brazenly at the First Amendment's door with alarming frequency. As a home owner I see a shadow growing over Fourth Amendment protections against unreasonable search and seizure. I have Fifth Amendment concerns about the likelihood of settling anything at a single trial and Sixth Amendment concerns about speedy trials and the cost of justice. I'm not alone. In my home state of Arizona, Governor Symington had set up a million-dollar legal trust fund to help defend the state itself against federal encroachments prohibited by the Tenth Amendment.

These rights in contention didn't spring up yesterday—they were here yesterday, and all the days before yesterday, tracing right back to the American war for independence. In the case of firearms, the existence of these unalienable rights leads right up to the armed citizenry we observe today.

The people who would remove or curtail our long-held rights, these "anti-rights activists," might seem sincere and well intentioned, but they are misdirected, and they are not necessarily all harmless idealistic do-gooders. Some suffer from *hoplophobia*, a terrible morbid fear of weapons. They need medical attention, and our sympathy, and have no place being involved in setting firearm policy. Some of the activists may go by sanitized, politically correct names, exude charm or credibility, and promote superficially appealing policies. But the people who would correct your politics by infringing your creed deserve scorn at best, and their motives warrant scrutiny. Americans continually need to stand fast and protect our constitutional rights from encroachment and infringement.

The battle between the anti-rights and pro-rights forces raged as hotly in the 1990s, when this book was first released, as at any time in decades. The battle rages on as this edition emerges ten years later. America's future hangs in the balance.

Room for Change

The passion for change is high in America. It seems that everyone has strongly held opinions on what ought to change.

Here are some ideas for the mix.

1. Under current law, the militia only includes all able-bodied American men and women from 17 to 45 years of age (with the exception of postal workers and a few similar groups... the mail must go through!). As citizens, they are subject to call by the President in the most dire social emergencies. If the country is about to flood and the President calls the people to the dikes, everyone is obliged to go. Which is as it should be. All is lost if we let anything come before the preservation of the nation. So it seems it would be reasonable to amend this law (10-311) and remove the age limitation, requiring virtually every able-bodied person to respond if the need ever arises.

2. People sometimes enthusiastically create so-called gun-free zones, by posting signs or passing local laws. With no enforcement or controls of any kind, armed criminals simply come and go through such zones. The whole approach seems negligent, and is known to be dangerous, since the only people disarmed are the honest ones. People who recklessly create such zones should be held liable for any harm they cause.

3. We know children get into trouble with guns, and typically have no gun-safety training at all. Recent federal law has sought to remove any connection to firearms from the classroom, increasing the ignorance and unfairly vilifying guns. Perhaps it is time to reintroduce widespread gun-safety classes, as America used to have until the 1960s, when political correctness eradicated it. Arizona has taken unique steps in this direction, see the new High School Marksmanship law on our website.

Coming Soon

Bloomfield Press embarks on a new journey with this book. Where it takes us ultimately is impossible to guess. In the short term, it seems obvious that update editions are in order, and we fully plan to issue revised editions (**this is now the fifth edition**). Based on experience, the second edition will include changes, adjustments, additions, and of course, any new gun laws that make it through the legislative process. That makes the first edition, issued on July 14, 1995. a piece of history—the earliest extant copy of the compiled gun laws, issued at a height of gun-law fever in the country.

How This Book Works

This book is an excerpt.

How big would it be if nothing was cut out?

What was cut out?

The primary editorial guideline for including statutes

If it's a numbered section of law in the United States Code and it relates to keeping and bearing arms include it. When in doubt, lean toward including extra, but eliminate anything that dilutes the essence.

Because this book includes only a *partial excerpt* from the federal codes, you should never rely on the information contained here for any legal purpose whatsoever.

If all goes as planned, this book will weigh under one pound when it's done. The light weight has an ecological impact but that is not the purpose. The reason for keeping this book as small as practical is to make it useful—to allow something that could never be done before—namely, to be able to hold all the federal firearms statutes in one hand, in a single handy volume.

In contrast, the complete annotated federal statutes take up an entire wall (about 35 feet) of bookcase space. You can buy a decent used car for the same four-figure price. The size and complexity of federal law has effectively sealed it off to the average citizen. This is not good.

One of my goals in creating *Gun Laws of America* was to present a portion of the federal laws, on a subject of interest to the nation, in a way the public could easily handle—to add light to the darkness where some discussions take place; to inject facts into the debates; to bring us a bit closer to the enlightened electorate our founders envisioned.

The process required non-stop editorial decisions, some easy, some extremely tough. Almost everything had to be cut away to leave the tiny kernel of what I believed an average person would call gun laws. I took nearly a quarter ton of fruit and boiled it down to one full glass of juice.

You may very well disagree with some of my choices, wish something were included that's not, or wonder why something else got space. In the final analysis, completeness is the function of the United States Code, and I suppose a responsible citizen should have a copy, even if it does cost two grand. Yes, you can now get the statutes on a CD-ROM disc—smaller in size but just as large. And now you can just download the entire thing from the Internet, in tens of thousands of individual increments.

So what would an average person think is *not* a gun law, and leave out of this text? Some things are obvious (crop subsidies, construction standards, copyrights) others are much less clear. See if you agree with my choices, because for better or worse, here's how it's been done.

Civil Rights

It is worth noting that four laws in particular have been added to this tenth anniversary edition, after lengthy thought and debate. (Numerous other laws have been added through the routine and inexhorable expansion of federal gun law.)

Laws protecting civil rights have not traditionally been viewed as gun laws, and have not appeared here before. As the debate and struggle intensifies to secure the right to keep arms and the right to bear arms to all people, these laws seem increasingly relevant. Are basic civil rights protections, in and of themselves, gun laws? Courts address the point with mixed vigor, and have been inconsistent over the years, but the plain language of these laws certainly implies that courts could, or even should, pursue such a course when dealing with gun ownership. For example:

> "If two or more persons conspire to injure, oppress, threaten, or intimidate any person in any State, Territory, Commonwealth, Possession, or District in the free exercise or enjoyment of any right or privilege secured to him by the Constitution or laws of the United States... They shall be fined under this title or imprisoned not more than ten years, or both..." (from 18-241)

For this reason, we have chosen to finally include 18-241, 18-242, 18-1001, and the granddaddy of them all, 42-1983, whose roots trace back to the original Civil Rights Act of Apr. 20, 1871, just after The Civil War ended. This adds 750 words to the total.

The following describes material that is not included in the text.

Regulations

More than anything else, maybe, federal regulations exert practical control over firearms matters, and are completely missing from this text. Many statutes simply authorize an agency to pass regulations, which are then churned out in large quantities. On a day-to-day operational basis, you need the regs. Dealers, manufacturers, importers and collectors live by the regs, fight over the regs, have a love-hate relationship with the regs. On one hand there's an attempt to be practical and functional in regulations, and on the other hand every negative aspect of government can turn up in the practically arbitrary pronouncements, which have the force of law right down to jail terms, made mandatory by bureaucratic process.

The Bureau of Alcohol, Tobacco, Firearms and Explosives publishes an edition of many of the more obvious federal gun regulations—primarily the ones they are responsible for. It is a good starting point but not a complete set, and notably omits material if it regulates them. The complete set is compiled in the *Code of Federal Regulations*, a set of books roughly the size and complexity of the U.S.C.

War
War and guns go hand in hand, but the laws for conducting war are so far removed from a citizen's daily life that it didn't make sense to include most war laws. More than 2,400 section numbers fill *Title 50 War and National Defense*, deal with appropriations of, say, $600 million at a clip, and are for armaments, materiel, ordnance and other things you will likely never see. It is not for lack of interest that wartime sabotage, sustainable firepower, tanks, nukes, nerve gas and more are missing—it's for lack of relevance to the editorial guideline.

The Armed Forces
Although laws governing the military are plentiful (the section numbers go past 18,000), they generally fall outside the scope of this book. Also, specifics about military arms and munitions are typically included in regulations, not statutes, and hence don't meet the editorial guidelines. However, some military statutes are quite relevant to bearing arms, such as laws on the Militia, the National Guard and the Civilian Marksmanship Program. These are covered in depth.

Cross References
Many laws include cross references to other laws, in this fashion: "Anyone who violates law X shall be imprisoned according to law B." To make sense of this you need the other laws.

The problem is that if you include *every* internal cross reference you quickly end up with the entire federal code—it is totally cross referenced to itself, a pretty neat trick. Look at statute 18-3050. It references entire Titles of law—along with paragraphs or subsections, which is more common. Those full Titles (as well as most subsections or paragraphs) are jammed with their own cross references. Smart money says you could start with one piece of law and travel to every other statute on a bridge of references. It would make a good board game.

If a cross-referenced law is about firearms, it is included. If not, not. If a law that's not about firearms is needed to make sense of another law, it is typically described in the *Gist*. The example above would then say: "Using a gun while breaking drug-running laws carries a prison sentence penalty." Law X, since it's a gun law, would be found in its numerical spot, and law B would probably not appear, bringing us to the next point.

Sentencing Guidelines

You can make a good case that no single person truly understands federal sentencing guidelines. At any rate, it is a subject generally beyond the scope of this book. Violating gun laws carries penalties. Once you're into the penalties, in most cases, you've entered a whole 'nother world and you need a lot more than this book, starting with an attorney. Note however that penalty statutes that are part and parcel of gun laws are included in depth—see 18–924 for an example.

Judicial and Administrative Procedure

When a gun is used illegally it may be seized by the authorities. What then? What becomes of the property? Unless procedural laws specifically include firearms they do not appear in the text. Forfeiture laws generally treat property regardless of what the property is. You'll need other source material, and probably professional help, to discover how the government works in such matters.

This guideline edits a lot: procedures to review and appeal government actions (unless specifically gun-related, which several are), penalties for failure to pay taxes (though gun taxes are included), how Customs officials (and many others) handle confiscated property, descriptions of the duties of various proper authorities (who have immunity from many firearms laws), and much more. The primary rule applies—if a law is about bearing arms, it's in there. If it could be indirectly applied to guns as well as other things, it's probably omitted. Note however that the procedural laws that are part and parcel of gun laws are included in depth—see 18–925 for an example.

Things That Have The Effect of Law
But Are Not Laws Passed By Congress

This category of edits has just a few components, but the components are gigantic. Described in detail below, they are Case Law, Executive Orders, Historical Notes, Law Review Articles, Attorney General Opinions, and Regulations (which were discussed earlier). These affect all citizens, have direct bearing on gun statutes, and begin to give you a sense of just how incomplete an excerpt this book really is. It should also make you realize the importance of getting competent professional assistance whenever you deal with the law for any official purpose. "The law," when you look at the whole ball of string, gives you a stupefying sense of the essentially incomprehensible knot the American jurisprudence system has evolved into.

Case Law and Precedents

When a court makes a decision and the decision is officially published, it becomes a *precedent*. All Supreme Court and Federal Circuit Court decisions set precedents, and some Federal District Court decisions do also, if the powers that be decide a case merits publication. Precedents tell future courts—upper and lower—how to act in similar cases. Some court somewhere may have reached totally different conclusions, but only the published cases count.

State courts set precedents too, at the state level. A case that is appealed out of the state to the federal level acquires new precedents to deal with.

Case law can stray so far from the original words passed by Congress that you can't recognize any similarity between the two. Many observers disparagingly call this "legislating from the bench," it's known as "judge-made law" in legal circles, and it happens with some frequency.

The bottom line is that you cannot legally count on what a law *says* (which ironically is the only thing addressed by this book) to know what the law *means*. A lawyer who counseled you based solely on the statutes would be guilty of malpractice.

To be sure, studying the words passed by Congress has value, and this book facilitates that process. Courts, however, decide what the laws mean, the meaning is constantly evolving, and you won't find any of that between these covers. To read some case law, go to a law library or most law offices and look at books called *Court Reporters* for the various court systems, or read the case law summaries provided in the two commercial versions of the U.S. Code. Substantial amounts of case law are available on line, and may be found through the National Directory link at gunlaws.com.

Executive Orders

The Constitution grants powers to the President to independently issue rules with the force of law, in carefully described areas. President George H. W. Bush used this power during his administration to ban the importation of certain types of firearms (and the edict stands as law unless rescinded or removed by legal process). Military law has many Executive Orders in place and operating, which is understandable since the President is the Commander-in-Chief of the armed forces. Executive Orders are sometimes included as notes in published law books.

Historical Notes and Congressional Intent

When people in the legal system can't tell what a law means (this does occur), they may look back on the legislative history to glean the intent of the legislature. This is often revealing, helpful and compelling, though it is sometimes abused or ignored. For the most part you won't find such information in these pages.

Historical files may be obscure or non-existent, and some discussions of Congress have been clearly preserved while others are partial or have been lost. Occasionally Congress includes a statement of intent at the head of a new law. Look at 10–2579 or 20–5812 for examples of an included intent. Such statements are often filled with political rhetoric and their value in interpreting a law is subject to debate, but then, what isn't.

Perhaps the most contentious topic currently raging in firearms-policy debates is the historical question of intent behind the Second Amendment itself, entitled The Right To Keep and Bear Arms. Some people have actually taken to saying that the Second Amendment doesn't mean what it always used to mean.

Until recently there simply was no debate on this point at all, and the commonly understood right to bear arms—embodied in the Second Amendment and fully operational since the founding days—is the reason why so many Americans are in fact, and have always been, armed. How else could half the populace bear arms if it weren't endemic.

The entire body of federal firearms law is built on and reflects the premise that people in the United States bear arms if they so choose.

Those who study the origination of the Second Amendment reach similar conclusions. The thinking back then was surprisingly uniform and resolute. A few brief quotes typical of the rhetoric of the day demonstrate this clearly, and show the value of historical notes in clarifying issues:

No free man shall be debarred the use of arms.
–Thomas Jefferson

The Constitution shall never be construed to authorize Congress
to prevent the people of the United States, who are peaceable
citizens, from keeping their own arms.
–Samuel Adams

Little more can reasonably be aimed at with respect to the
people at large than to have them properly armed.
–Alexander Hamilton

Americans have the right and advantage of being armed.
–James Madison

The great object is that every man be armed.
Everyone who is able may have a gun.
–Patrick Henry

Stephen Halbrook's extensive historical research lead him to this interesting conclusion:

> "In recent years it has been suggested that the Second Amendment protects the "collective" right of states to maintain militias, while it does not protect the right of "the people" to keep and bear arms. If anyone entertained this notion in the period during which the Constitution and Bill of Rights were debated and ratified, it remains one of the most closely guarded secrets of the eighteenth century, for no known writing surviving from the period between 1787 and 1791 states such a thesis. The phrase "the people" meant the same thing in the Second Amendment as it did in the First, Fourth, Ninth and Tenth Amendments—that is, each and every free person."

The closest thing to opposition in the historical record seems to be the belief held by some that the Bill of Rights rights were so basic that writing them down was unessential and in fact restricted them (an idea addressed in the Ninth Amendment). Other thinkers won out and the rules were reduced to writing, just in case future generations needed to refresh themselves once in a while.

The entire Constitution is fully subject to change through ordered legal process, which is as it should be and bolsters the very concepts embodied in the Constitution. However, attempting to change the meaning of the fundamental creed by deliberate and repetitious subterfuge is the abhorrent method of Orwellian fascists, to be quickly identified at its roots, and vigorously weeded out as the pernicious freedom-squelching plant that it is.

Law Journal Articles

Scholarly treatises on the law, published by recognized authorities at prestigious institutions, are frequently used in arriving at court decisions. Such documents may be considered by courts because they contain useful analytical examinations of discrete legal topics.

Articles that run in the popular press, especially when written by noted authorities, reach large audiences and may sway public opinion, but the little known Journal entries carry more weight in court and are cited in decisions. Compare former Chief Justice Warren Berger's rhetoric for *Parade* magazine, which has become a bulwark for the anti-rights side of the firearms debate, with the measured studiousness of the Duke Law Journal on "The Second Amendment and the Personal Right to Arms" by William Van Alstyne (43 Duke L.J. 1236 (1994)).

Attorney General Opinions

When there is nothing else to go by, the federal authorities may ask the U.S. Attorney General for guidance. Opinions issued by that office can be very useful and may remain unchallenged for long periods, or they may be quickly dismissed as unacceptable. They are not found in this text. They cannot be ignored but do have the least effect in the various precedent-setting priorities of the legal system.

Editing

If you've read the overview this far you must be convinced by now that this book is an excerpt. In fact, 20 entire Titles have been omitted. It's important to note that law sections that do appear may have themselves been edited or truncated.

Section 7–2015 is used in the text to show precisely how the *Gun Laws of America* editing process works. To meet the editorial guidelines of presenting only those laws that relate directly to bearing arms, unrelated portions of many statutes are not printed. This sometimes amounts to many pages of deleted text.

The 7-2015 example shows first the unedited and then the edited version of the beginning of this section of law. The remaining text of this law (there are some 420 additional lines) has no bearing on the subject and does not appear at all.

This leads to sequential though uncontiguous numbering, eliminates material which is not germane (though frequently interesting), preserves the meaning of the law as it concerns firearms, and allows the text to fit in a single volume.

Completeness, which is usually a virtue, here would dilute the essence and reduce the value of this book.

Accurate citations may still be made, since care was taken to preserve the necessary elements of outline hierarchy.

Oversights

Considering all the work that went into this book, it's tough for me to accept the fact that some things most likely slipped through the cracks. There may be some laws out there that we just didn't find. If you should ever happen to find one, call the publisher immediately. If you are the first to identify a statute that we include in a later edition, Bloomfield Press will send you a free copy of *Gun Laws of America* for your trouble. Makes a great gift. The phone number is on page two.

The search process is more difficult than you can imagine. Indexes are only partially accurate, with missing, inaccurate and bogus entries common. Erroneous entries are the worst, forcing you to pore over them desperately seeking something that justifies inclusion until, in frustration, you cross it off the list as apparently irrelevant and move on. Each Title of the U.S.C. has its own index, and one overall index for the federal statutes is more than *10,000* pages long.

An open-ended on-line search chokes up a "list too long" message from the computer. Attempting to limit a computer search has its own plusses and minuses. Anything you choose to omit from the search may hide relevant details. However you proceed, all identified statutes have to be laboriously studied to determine if they're relevant, which they often aren't. A "weapon" against hunger gets found while searching, along with "weapons of mass destruction," but obviously neither belongs here. See 16–425 for a provocative example of the problem. Through luck, *nonmailable matter* turned up; so did *civilian marksmanship;* these were not keywords we had the foresight to use. Is anything else still out there?

The Cop Nearby

More law gets enforced, as a practical matter, in the way the officer says it gets enforced, than in any other way. If an officer has a mistaken impression, or simply wants to exert authority, you are typically under the law as the officer says it exists, from being stopped at some activity, physically detained, or killed on the spot. Such active expressions of what the law "is" are infinitely more common than the number of laws that move forward to be decided in a courthouse.

Policy

Increasingly, police and government policies do not precisely or always match the wording of the law. Unless there is someone to hold the authorities' feet to the fire, policies can for periods of time set law more firmly than Congress can.

Typos

Life being what it is, typographical errors are a reality. How bad is the worst typo hidden in this text? Don't I wish I knew before going to press. Is it a missing word, line, worse? Is a citation number wrong? Is there a gross inaccuracy or an insignificant one, a misleading phrase, an incorrect *Gist*? Whatever it is, it's most probably in there despite all attempts to get it out, so watch out for it. (I do know of one typo I used for effect in the intro, but I forget what it is.)

If you find a typo, from a spelling error to a bad indent to the most horrendous oversight, please contact the publisher immediately. If you are the first to detect a true typo, Bloomfield Press will send you a free copy of *Gun Laws of America* for your trouble. Makes a great gift. The phone number is on page two.

Notes on Form

Misuse of Gender

Statutes make prolific use of the word *he* to mean a person. Beginning around the 1990s, statutes begin using the awkward construction *he or she* to mean a person. Both of these are unnecessary inaccuracies. The English language is sufficiently flexible to allow expression without gender-specific references where they don't apply. Good English refers to a man as *he*, a woman as *she*, and when specificity isn't needed, calls a person a person. Writers reading this may want to look at the *Gists* with a third eye to glean how it's done. Why resort to aberrant showstoppers (*she or he* is a roadblock, *s/he* is an immovable object) when neutral (neutered?) prose can be achieved without notice.

The very first statute in federal law, 1 USC § 1, points out that where masculine gender is used in the law the feminine is included, singular includes plural and vice versa, present tense includes the future, *person* and *whoever* includes most businesses, associations and other groups, and the words *insane* and *lunatic* include every idiot, lunatic, insane person and anyone who is non compos mentis. (Section 3 of Title 1 goes on to point out that *vessel* includes all watercraft, section 4 adds that *vehicle* includes all forms of land transportation, and section 5 says *company* or *association* includes their successors and assigns.)

Convolutivity

The law is convoluted deliberately and don't ever let anyone convince you otherwise. Recognize the problem and stop taking it for granted. Bureaucratic bafflegab must be eradicated for the good of the country. The idea that these bizarre and arcane forms are needed for precision is pure baloney. Here's a perfect example, a remarkably short statute, with blaringly bad elements designed only to confuse and obfuscate:

> 39 3001: "Matter the deposit of which in the mails is punishable under section 1302, 1341, 1342, 1461, 1463, 1715, 1716, 1717, or 1738 of title 18, or section 26 of the Animal Welfare Act is nonmailable."

What would be wrong with: "Putting anything in the mail which is punishable under sections X, X, X and X is illegal." The heart of the Brady Law, embodied in 18-922(s), is probably the worst case of tortured English currently on the books.

Language Abuse

Little in the known universe is more confusing than the convoluted language, the *legalese*, used to write the law. Although proponents of the present system argue that the complexity is necessary to achieve the needed precision, this is nonsense. Every element of law can be expressed in clear terms without sacrificing accuracy or detail.

The idea of precision is a myth in the first place. Debate about what laws mean is a staple of every court system in the land. Courts issue rulings on what laws mean on a non-stop basis. If laws weren't so totally imprecise and open to interpretation, courts would have little to do.

To be fair, this is not the fault of the laws or the courts. It is the nature of the human condition. Precious little if anything in life is black and white. Life is a gray area. Pursue excellence and not perfection. You'll be happier, and you can get there. Recognize that no system is foolproof or immune from debate.

The only problem then is that the legal system presents itself as above the vagaries of humanity, which is, basically, ridiculous. A good part of the reason for this is to promote job security for the ministers of the system. Jargon is a time-honored method for creating dependency between an industry and its market. The judicial system has always been a huge employer. Where jargon is insufficient to ensure dependence, the legal community uses Latin. Very effective.

Efforts are being made to simplify the secretive nature of legalese, but progress is slow, the task is enormous, and we're likely to be stuck with the existing system for a long time to come. Fixing the verbiage can be done with every new law passed, but the percent of change is minuscule. The numbering system, because it is imbedded universally, holds less promise for undergoing change.

Plain English

Ah, plain English. What defines thee? Plain English is language you don't have to chew hard to get out the juice. It is words used in a way that a regular person would take for granted.

Every user of plain English makes unique judgment calls to get the desired result—easy unambiguous communication. Some have better luck with it than others.

Plain English by its very nature is subject to debate, just like everything else. But in the end, plain English is plainly evident, unless you conduct an opinion poll.

Gun Laws of America uses plain-English guidelines for *Gists* that appear throughout the text.

Word Counts and Dates

Each statute's word count appears in parentheses, following the original date of enactment, which concludes every law in this book. Modern technology supported the simple (though incredibly repetitious) task of determining the approximate size of each section of the law. What you see is what the word processor counted. Undoubtedly, the perfect English-language word count is slightly smaller than the numbers shown and used in the charts. The computer picks up "(a)" and "(1)" as words (is that fair?) and makes other decisions which tend to adjust the true word count slightly. Excluded are any words which have been truncated or edited from statutes, and there are no word counts provided for Statutes at Large, since only some of these appear. Anyone eager to manually correct the aberrations is welcome to call and please hold for the next available operator.

Word count is an imprecise method for measuring gun law for the reasons above, and because enacted public laws are typically longer than the mere statutory parts found in *Gun Laws of America*. It is far better, however, than the widely circulated, yet unattributable "numbers of laws" you frequently see bandied about. For a full discussion of "How many gun laws are there?" see our FAQ file at gunlaws.com.

Only the origination date is given for each statute. This can be misleading, but was a necessary expedient. Many of these laws are amended incessantly. Tracking it all, and listing it, would not make this a better book.

A law like 18 USC 922, the main federal prohibitions, was amended in 1994 to add the Brady law. In 1995 the Gun Free School Zones law was amended into it (which was then declared unconstitutional and removed, and then reenacted back in). The Undetectable Firearms law entered in 1988 (and has been extended by amendment three times, so far). Dozens of similar changes have been made, but the statute shows 1968 as its date, when the Gun Control Act first introduced it. If you really want to see the amendment lists, which can be many pages long and filled with arcane legal technicalities, they are available online, linked from our National Directory.

Gists

The commentary notes called *Gists* are provided for your convenience only, to help you find your way through the federal laws. They give partial, indirect, conversational expression to the kernel of the laws, and are not intended in any way to be restatements of law or an explanation of the laws. They deal solely with legislative enactments—the words of the law—and do not account at all for regulatory and judicial aspects which enforce and interpret the law and may, in many cases, differ widely from the words passed by Congress. **Do not rely on the *Gists* for any legal purposes whatsoever.**

I wrestled for a long time with what to call the plain-English segments that accompany each law. *Summary* is good because it's easy, but it isn't really accurate. The *Gists* aren't summaries, they're expressions of the essence. I considered *kernel, core, abstract,* even *meat. Gist* won because of its meaning; the "G" is pronounced as a "J."

AG

The acronym for United States Attorney General. A minor player in gun policy until 2002, significant authority was transferred to this office, and away from the Treasury Dept., where it had been since 1934, until the Arab muslim attacks in 2001.

FFL

The acronym for a Federal Firearms License (or Licensee) is widely used.

NFA

The acronym for National Firearms Act is a widely used term in this book and among people involved in firearms issues.

<Bracketed Notes>

When it was necessary to interject comments directly within the body of a statute, the words of the comment appear in <pointed brackets>. This was typically needed to make cross references, note laws that had been repealed or replaced, and to point out the few minor typos within the laws themselves. Federal laws are surprisingly free of apparent typos.

Obfuscate

To obfuscate (**ob**-fiss-kate) means to bamboozle with high-falootin' language. To obscure, confuse. It comes from the Latin word *fuscus*, which means dark brown. Modern law is ob**fus**catory to an extraordinary degree. A wise person seeking to communicate clearly eschews obfus**ca**tion perfunctorily.

Notwithstanding

This word means *despite*.

The Proper Authorities

Be mindful of the proper authorities, a catch-all phrase used for people who are, at least in some instances, exempt from certain laws. The laws define such people in numerous ways and with intricate detail (though the phrase *proper authorities* is never used in statutes). Latitudes may sometimes be taken by these people, to do their legitimate work and for other reasons.

Typically, a law will define certain federal employees, departments or agencies in a way that grants them immunities, special powers, or privileges not generally available to the public. In the context of this book, that generally means the right to bear arms where or when a regular citizen could not. It also includes people who judge the validity of a private person's bearing of arms, such as peace officers, members of the judiciary, and employees of the government and its agencies.

The Index You Can't Find

Gun Laws of America features a detailed Table of Contents and has no index at this time. To put it bluntly, producing this book has taxed the capabilities of our company to the max, and an index was simply beyond those capabilities for this edition.

A good index is a greater undertaking than most people realize, according to the American Society of Indexers. Before you jump and say, "Just use the automated index maker in the word processor," you must realize that a key word like *firearm* appears more than 800 times in the statutes and *Gists*. Such an automated listing would consume space and be less than worthless. In order to work, an index must anticipate the words and phrases you would use to seek information, not just the words that appear in the text. The time and systems needed to do this were simply not available.

How the Federal Law-Numbering System Works

Don't feel bad if you find the legal numbering system hard to read. It's hard to read. The book that describes it is more than 200 pages long.

Once you get used to it, you'll find that the legal numbering system works with great precision and handles every labeling task necessary to make accurate citations—that is, to refer to laws, verbally or in writing, by their code numbers.

However, once you get used to it, you'll also begin to realize how unnecessarily complicated the system is. This deliberate complexifying works to keep the average citizen distanced from the law, and serves little other purpose. Like it or not, though, you had better learn the existing system if you want a fair chance at gaining command of your own laws.

Check the chart "How Federal Law Is Structured" for the big picture of the whole system. The following describes how the actual citation numbers work. Gluttons for this sort of information should read the definitive text, *A Uniform System of Citation* by the Harvard Law Review Association.

How to Read the
Legal Numbering System

❶ The Title Number **18** USC § 922

All federal laws are placed under one of 50 different headings called "Titles." The Title number is the first element of a federal law's citation number. Each Title number has a name associated with it, in this case, it is Title 18 Crimes & Criminal Procedure.

❷ Source Code 18 **USC** § 922

USC is the abbreviation for "United States Code," the official name of the federal laws, and it is the second element of a law's citation number. Yes, it would make sense to put the source code before the Title number (after all, you have to find the set of books before you can look up a particular Title), but that would make things logical and so was rejected when the system was established.

USC is often abbreviated U.S.C. It's the same thing. Do not confuse it with USCA or USCS, the proprietary and trademarked acronyms for privately published sets of the USC. For most intents and purposes, 18 USC is identical to 18 USCA and 18 USCS, with or without the periods.

❸ The Dreaded "§" Section Symbol   18 USC § 922

The character "§" means "section." You read it aloud (or to yourself) as "section" whenever it appears. Every individually named chunk of law is called a section and has a section number, so you see this symbol a lot. It's an integral part of the written name for every statute on the books.

A section may be just a few words or extremely long. Section 20-5811 is the shortest with a mere 11 words; 18-922 runs on for 8,084 words to claim the longest-law prize by a substantial margin.

The section "§" symbol intimidates many people and as such it's valuable for keeping law mysterious and somehow unknowable to the general public. Don't let it scare you. Just think "section" whenever you see "§." To write a section symbol, make a small capital "S" on top of another small capital "S."

To make a "section" symbol
draw an "S" over another "S"

❹ Section Number   18 USC § 922

The final element of a law's citation is a simple number, almost. All laws within a Title are given sequential numbers to keep track of them.

A series of numbers may be dedicated to a particular subject, making things easier. In Title 18 the 840s cover explosives and the 920s cover firearms.

It can get even easier (an oversight, no doubt) when chapters and numbers match. In Title 32 National Guard statutes, for example, the 100s are in Chapter 1 and the 500s are in Chapter 5 (in contrast, the 920s of Title 18 are conveniently located in Chapter 44).

New laws are typically added at the end of an appropriate series, making things quite simple, although a number of exceptions apply, to help ensure complexity.

In some cases, a law logically belongs near other related laws. If the other laws are already in numerical order, you can't just insert a new number in the series, so a letter will often be attached to the end of the section number. Thus 926 becomes followed by 926A, as it does in Title 18. Do not, however, confuse 926A which guarantees the private interstate transportation of firearms, for example, with 926(a), the subsection of 18-926 which authorizes the Attorney General (formerly the Treasury Dept.) to make firearms regulations.

Alphabetical extensions to section numbers can go on at length—Title 40 has a law that goes to 193t (inconsistently using a lower case letter as some statutes do, but fortunately leaving off the parentheses that connotes a subsection). In Title 16, law number 669c refers you to 669b(b) for clarity. Title 42 has a gun law numbered 3796ii—they used up the alphabet and conveniently just started over with "aa." To keep things exciting, (ii) is also used as a lower-case Roman numeral subparagraph heading in many statutes. Got it?

Subsections (indicated with lower case letters in parenthesis) can get up there as well—for example, Title 18 has 922(x), which is a subsection of the 1994 Crime Bill that deals with armed juveniles. Be sure not to confuse "(x)" which is a subsection, with "(x)" which is a lower case Roman numeral for a subparagraph. What could be simpler.

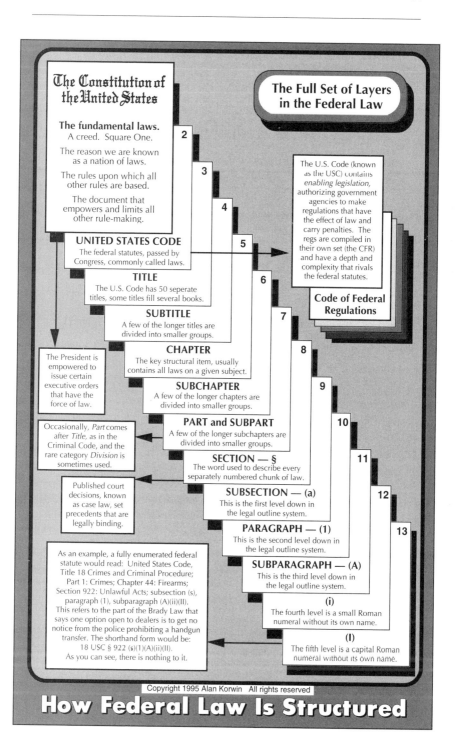

The Constitution of the United States

The fundamental laws.
A creed. Square One.

The reason we are known as a nation of laws.

The rules upon which all other rules are based.

The document that empowers and limits all other rule-making.

The Full Set of Layers in the Federal Law

The U.S. Code (known as the USC) contains *enabling legislation*, authorizing government agencies to make regulations that have the effect of law and carry penalties. The regs are compiled in their own set (the CFR) and have a depth and complexity that rivals the federal statutes.

Code of Federal Regulations

UNITED STATES CODE
The federal statutes, passed by Congress, commonly called laws.

TITLE
The U.S. Code has 50 seperate titles, some titles fill several books.

SUBTITLE
A few of the longer titles are divided into smaller groups.

CHAPTER
The key structural item, usually contains all laws on a given subject.

SUBCHAPTER
A few of the longer chapters are divided into smaller groups.

PART and SUBPART
A few of the longer subchapters are divided into smaller groups.

SECTION — §
The word used to describe every separately numbered chunk of law.

SUBSECTION — (a)
This is the first level down in the legal outline system.

PARAGRAPH — (1)
This is the second level down in the legal outline system.

SUBPARAGRAPH — (A)
This is the third level down in the legal outline system.

(i)
The fourth level is a small Roman numeral without its own name.

(I)
The fifth level is a capital Roman numeral without its own name.

The President is empowered to issue certain executive orders that have the force of law.

Occasionally, *Part* comes after *Title,* as in the Criminal Code, and the rare category *Division* is sometimes used.

Published court decisions, known as case law, set precedents that are legally binding.

As an example, a fully enumerated federal statute would read: United States Code, Title 18 Crimes and Criminal Procedure; Part 1: Crimes; Chapter 44: Firearms; Section 922: Unlawful Acts; subsection (s), paragraph (1), subparagraph (A)(ii)(II). This refers to the part of the Brady Law that says one option open to dealers is to get no notice from the police prohibiting a handgun transfer. The shorthand form would be:
18 USC § 922 (s)(1)(A)(ii)(II).
As you can see, there is nothing to it.

Copyright 1995 Alan Korwin   All rights reserved

How Federal Law Is Structured

How Federal Law
Is Structured

1. The Constitution
This provides the foundation for everything else. By writing down and adhering to the conditions in a constitution, we enjoy a stable basis for defining the leadership, judicial and legislative elements of our government. The Constitution describes, empowers and limits the powers of a Congress of the people's representatives to enact fair laws.

2. United States Code
When Congress enacts a "public law," some of the language is inserted into a set of 50 numbered "Titles," organized to fit the federal bureaucracy. This process, called *codification*, produces the *United States Code*, the official written federal statutes. The public laws themselves are available, but for all sorts of practical purposes, the codified version is the one everyone uses. The uncodified parts are called Statutes at Large.

3. Title
The name of each "book" of the U.S. Code is its *Title*, and is usually referred to by number and name. Some Titles are long enough to fill several books (Title 18 fills 11), so it's not really accurate to think of a Title as a book; it's more like a segment. The more important Titles with respect to gun law are Title 18 Crimes and Criminal Procedure and Title 26 Internal Revenue Code. Material on firearms is found in 30 different Titles.

Something about the way the legal system uses the word *title* makes it seem awkward and difficult, in part helping to create the cloak of distance many people feel about the law. Once your ear gets used to the sound it begins to seem more natural and comprehensible.

4. Subtitle

Occasionally a Title is divided into large, discrete chunks, called *subtitles*, within itself. This occurs in gun law, for example, in Title 26 Internal Revenue Code.

5. Chapter

This is a key structural element within the body of the law. Typically, laws related to a single subject appear within a chapter. Penalties are frequently described once for a chapter, and applied to all violations within the chapter. Definitions also often apply only to the laws within a given chapter.

6. Subchapter

A few longer chapters are divided into smaller *subchapters*, or the rare *Division* grouping may be seen after *chapter*.

7. Part

A few of the longer subchapters are divided into smaller *parts*. Occasionally a *part* will be divided into subparts. To help prevent uniformity, in some older statutes, *part* comes right after *Title* in the hierarchy. The criminal code is set up this way.

Items 2 to 7 (above)
describe a location in the law books.

In the main text of this book, items 2 through 7 appear in small capital letters at the end of each entry. Here is an example from statute 26-4182:

TITLE 26. INTERNAL REVENUE CODE • SUBTITLE D: MISCELLANEOUS EXCISE TAXES • CHAPTER 32: MANUFACTURERS EXCISE TAX • SUBCHAPTER D: RECREATIONAL EQUIPMENT • PART III: FIREARMS

Items 8 to 13 (below)
are used to number the individual statutes.

Items 8 through 13 comprise each law's section number and the left-margin characters that index each law. A fully enumerated section number takes this format:

18 USC § 922(s)(1)(A)(i)(I)

8. Section

This is where the rubber meets the road—the section number is the main identifier of every numbered statute on the books. Every statute has an official name, which appears in this book in bold type after the section number.

Although you refer to each statute with the word *section*, it is customary to use the section symbol, the unusual "§" character when writing. If there is one thing which distances more people from the law it is the imperious, Latin-oid nature of this small curlicue. As a piece of written English, *18 USC § 922* defies every basic school principle you were taught. Once mastered though, it flows euphonically from the tongue, inspiring awe and deference to those in earshot, "I'm sure you'll find that in Title 18 U-S-C section nine twenty two." For brevity, statutes are often voiced simply as, "eighteen nine twenty two." In the non-statutory parts of this text (essentially the overview and the *Gists*) 18-922 means 18 USC § 922.

9, 10, 11, 12 and 13. The Numbering Scheme

Statutes are organized in a standard outline system, with non-standard (some would say mind-numbing) numbering. It's almost as if they said, "Let's take the intuitively lowest character, put it in parenthesis, and give it the highest ranking." And so the lower case letter "a" is always the first subsection under any section of law. Capital Roman numerals (the school system's choice for the first element in an outline) is dead last. A lower case Roman number is higher than a capital Roman number. I'm not making this up.

Look at the chart below to see how the system is ordered and the names of the groups. The names are *critical*, because laws often refer back to everything in "this paragraph" or "this subsection" and you must be able to identify the scope of the reference to make sense of the law. No one ever said this would be easy.

SYMBOL	NAME	CHARACTER USED	HIERARCHY
§	**Section**	**unique symbol**	**Highest level**
(a)	**Subsection**	**lower-case letter**	**1st rank**
(1)	**Paragraph**	**Arabic number**	**2nd rank**
(A)	**Subparagraph**	**capital letter**	**3rd rank**
(i)	unnamed	**small Roman**	**4th rank**
(I)	unnamed	**capital Roman**	**Lowest rank**

When writing the citation number for a piece of law, you simply stack the symbols after the section number with no spaces.

Some statutes have no subgroups and are easy:
22 USC § 2561 or 26 USC § 4181

Some statutes only have subsections:
22 USC § 2552(a) or 22 USC § 2552(c)

Some statutes go the distance:
18 USC § 922(s)(1)(A)(i)(I) or 18 USC § 923 (d)(1)(F)(ii)(I)

To help you remember the legal outline hierarchy,
copy this summary and use it as a book mark:

Gun Laws of America

Constitution • U.S. Code • Title • Subtitle • Chapter • Subchapter • Part • Subpart

Section (§) • Subsection (a) • Paragraph (1) • Subparagraph (A) • (i) • (I)
Full citation: **18 USC § 922 (s)(1)(A)(i)(I)**

THE 50 TITLES OF THE UNITED STATES CODE

The 271 federal firearm statutes are spread through 30 of the 50 Titles of the U.S.Code. This represents an increase of four Titles (13%) and 40 statutes (17%), since our first edition appeared in 1995, and provides one more measurement of federal gun law. Titles containing gun law appear in **bold** type.

1. General Provisions.
2. **The Congress.**
3. The President.
4. Flag and Seal, Seat of Government, and the States.
5. **Government Organization and Employees; and Appendix.**
6. **Domestic Security**
7. **Agriculture.**
8. **Aliens and Nationality.**
9. Arbitration.
10. **Armed Forces; and Appendix.**
11. Bankruptcy; and Appendix.
12. **Banks and Banking.**
13. Census.
14. **Coast Guard.**
15. **Commerce and Trade.**
16. **Conservation.**
17. Copyrights.
18. **Crimes and Criminal Procedure; and Appendix.**
19. **Customs Duties.**
20. **Education.**
21. **Food and Drugs.**
22. **Foreign Relations and Intercourse.**
23. Highways.
24. Hospitals and Asylums.
25. **Indians.**
26. **Internal Revenue Code.**
27. Intoxicating Liquors.
28. **Judiciary and Judicial Procedure; and Appendix.**
29. Labor.

Excerpts from the Constitution of the United States of America

Preamble

We the People of the United States, in Order to form a more perfect Union, establish Justice, insure domestic Tranquillity, provide for the common defence, promote the general Welfare, and secure the Blessings of Liberty to ourselves and our Posterity, do ordain and establish this Constitution for the United States of America.

Article I.

Section 1.

All legislative Powers herein granted shall be vested in a Congress of the United States, which shall consist of a Senate and a House of Representatives.

Section 8. Clause 1

The Congress shall have Power To lay and collect Taxes, Duties, Imposts and Excises, to pay the Debts and provide for the common Defence and general Welfare of the United States; but all Duties, Imposts and Excises shall be uniform throughout the United States;

Section 8. Clause 3
To regulate Commerce with foreign Nations, and among the several States, and within the Indian Tribes;

Section 8. Clause 12
To raise and support Armies, but no Appropriation of Money to that Use shall be for a longer Term than two Years;

Section 8. Clause 13
To provide and maintain a Navy;

Section 8. Clause 14
To make Rules for the Government and Regulation of the land and naval Forces;

Section 8. Clause 15
To provide for calling forth the Militia to execute the Laws of the Union, suppress Insurrections and repel Invasions;

Section 8. Clause 16
To provide for organizing, arming and disciplining, the Militia, and for governing such Part of them as may be employed in the Service of the United States, reserving to the States respectively, the Appointment of the Officers, and the Authority of training Militia according to the discipline prescribed by Congress;

Article II.

Section 2. Clause 1
The President shall be the Commander in Chief of the Army and Navy of the United States, and of the Militia of the several States when called into the actual Service of the United States;

AMENDMENTS
TO THE CONSTITUTION OF
THE UNITED STATES OF AMERICA

(As related to the subject of this book)

Second Amendment

A well regulated Militia, being necessary to the security of a free State, the right of the people to keep and bear Arms, shall not be infringed.

Fourth Amendment

The right of the people to be secure in their persons, houses, papers, and effects, against unreasonable searches and seizures, shall not be violated, and no Warrants shall issue, but upon probable cause, supported by Oath or affirmation, and particularly describing the place to be searched, and the persons or things to be seized.

Ninth Amendment

The enumeration in the Constitution of certain rights shall not be construed to deny or disparage others retained by the people.

Tenth Amendment

The powers not delegated to the United States by the Constitution, nor prohibited by it to the States, are reserved to the States respectively, or to the people.

Fourteenth Amendment. Section 1

All persons born or naturalized in the United States and subject to the jurisdiction thereof, are citizens of the United States and of the State wherein they reside. No State shall make or enforce any law which shall abridge the privileges or immunities of citizens of the United States; nor shall any State deprive any person of life, liberty or property, without due process of law; nor deny to any person within its jurisdiction the equal protection of the laws.

THE FEDERAL GUN LAWS

OFFICIALLY KNOWN AS

"United States Code"

Excerpts Related to Firearms

2005–2007 Edition

Main text is complete through midterm in the 109th Congress.
Check our website for latest statutes.

High-profile gun laws included in this edition, added since
the first edition of *Gun Laws of America* came out in 1995:

Rifle Practice and Firearms Safety Act
P.L. 104-106, Enacted Feb. 10, 1996

Antiterrorism And Effective Death Penalty Act
P.L. 104-132, Enacted April 24, 1996

Omnibus Consolidated Appropriations Act for Fiscal Year 1997
P.L. 104-208 Enacted Sep. 30, 1996

**Omnibus Consolidated and Emergency
Supplemental Appropriations Act, 1999**
P.L. 105-277, Enacted Oct. 21, 1998

Floyd D. Spence National Defense Authorization Act for FY 2001
P.L. 106-398, Enacted Oct. 30, 2000

**Uniting and Strengthening America by Providing Appropriate Tools Required
to Intercept and Obstruct Terrorism (USA PATRIOT ACT) Act of 2001**
P.L. 107-56, Enacted Oct. 26, 2001

Aviation and Transportation Security Act
P.L. 107-71, Enacted Nov. 19, 2001

Homeland Security Act of 2002
P.L. 107-296, Enacted Nov. 25, 2002

Law Enforcement Officers Safety Act of 2004
P.L. 108-277, Enacted July 22, 2004

Numerous other laws made scores of changes, large and small,
and are in this text, but received little public attention (e.g., 14 USC §95).

POSTED AS UPDATES AT GUNLAWS.COM:
P.L. 109-92: Protection of Lawful Commerce in Arms Act (3,437) 2005
P.L. 109-203: Small Manufacturers Exempt From Firearms Excise Tax (173) 2006
P.L. 109-596: Disaster Recovery Personal Protection Act (878) 2006

Statute at Large

Note: The following is a Statute at Large; it received no section number after it was passed by Congress. As such, it does not appear in the regular numbered sections of the U.S. laws. The result is that, although this is law passed by Congress, with the full weight and effect of any other statute, it is not widely known.

This is the somewhat troublesome case with so-called Statutes at Large. Often, it seems items that place limits on the government, or protect rights of individuals, find their way to this somewhat nebulous world. The language here is originally part of the Firearms Owners' Protection Act of 1986.

Since it has no number and applies so broadly to the Constitution, it seemed logical to include it at the beginning. Other Statutes at Large have been included near the sections they affect, or at the end.

The language of this statute is surprisingly clear. It is worth reading as a prelude to the other statutes in this book.

(a) Short Title.—This Act may be cited as the "**Firearms Owners' Protection Act**".

(b) Congressional Findings.—

The Congress finds that—
(1) the rights of citizens—
    (A) to keep and bear arms under the second amendment to the United States Constitution;
    (B) to security against illegal and unreasonable searches and seizures under the fourth amendment;
    (C) against uncompensated taking of property, double jeopardy, and assurance of due process of law under the fifth amendment; and
    (D) against unconstitutional exercise of authority under the ninth and tenth amendments;
    require additional legislation to correct existing firearms statutes and enforcement policies; and

(2) additional legislation is required to reaffirm the intent of the Congress, as expressed in section 101 of the Gun Control Act of 1968, that "it is not the purpose of this title to place any undue or unnecessary Federal restrictions or burdens on law-abiding citizens with respect to the acquisition, possession, or use of firearms appropriate to the purpose of hunting, trap-shooting, target shooting, personal protection, or any other lawful activity, and that this title is not intended to discourage or eliminate the private ownership or use of firearms by law-abiding citizens for lawful purposes.".

Title 2 • The Congress

This law is used to show how
Gun Laws of America is annotated.

---

2 USC § 167d. Firearms or fireworks; speeches; objectionable language in Library buildings and grounds <Official section numbers and names appear in bold. The "§" mark means "section." When editorial notes are embedded they appear in pointed brackets as seen here.>

The Gist: You must act in a safe and civilized manner at the Library of Congress.

The commentary notes called Gists are provided for your convenience only, to help you find your way through the federal laws. They give partial, indirect, conversational expression to the kernel of the laws, and are not intended in any way to be restatements of law or an explanation of the laws. They deal solely with legislative enactments—the words of the law—and do not account at all for regulatory and judicial aspects that enforce and interpret the law and may, in many cases, differ widely from the words passed by Congress. Do not rely on the gists for any legal purposes whatsoever. Do not rely on the gists for any legal purposes whatsoever.

It shall be unlawful to discharge any firearm, firework or explosive, set fire to any combustible, make any harangue or oration, or utter loud, threatening, or abusive language in the Library of Congress buildings or grounds. <The actual words of the law appear in plain type.>

Aug. 4, 1950 (36) The date indicates when the law was originally passed. Amendment dates, if any, are not shown. The number in parentheses is the current word count.

TITLE 2. THE CONGRESS • CHAPTER 5: LIBRARY OF CONGRESS <The precise location of each section of the law appears in small capital letters at the end. These are used when a statute refers to "all laws" in this chapter, title, etc.>

2 USC § 167g. Prosecution and punishment of offenses in Library buildings and grounds

> The Gist: Acting in an unsafe and uncivilized manner at the Library of Congress is a misdemeanor, unless you damage public property in excess of $100, in which case it's a felony.

Whoever violates any provision of sections 167a to 167e of this title, or of any regulation prescribed under section 167f of this title commits a Class B misdemeanor, prosecution for such offenses to be had in the Superior Court of the District of Columbia, upon information by the United States attorney or any of his assistants: Provided, That in any case where, in the commission of any such offense, public property is damaged in an amount exceeding $100, the person commits a Class D felony.

Aug. 4, 1950 (85)
TITLE 2. THE CONGRESS • CHAPTER 5: LIBRARY OF CONGRESS

Title 5 • Government Organization and Employees; and Appendix

5 USC App. Law Enforcement Powers Of Inspector General Agents

> The Gist: A new federal force, comprised of Inspectors General, their assistants, and any special agent supervised by them, is authorized to carry firearms while on duty or as approved by the Attorney General, at the discretion of and under guidelines issued by the Attorney General.

(e)(1) In addition to the authority otherwise provided by this Act, each Inspector General appointed under section 3, any Assistant Inspector General for Investigations under such an Inspector General, and any special agent supervised by such an Assistant Inspector General may be authorized by the Attorney General to—

(A) carry a firearm while engaged in official duties as authorized under this Act or other statute, or as expressly authorized by the Attorney General;

(4) The Attorney General shall promulgate, and revise as appropriate, guidelines which shall govern the exercise of the law enforcement powers established under paragraph (1).

Nov. 25, 2002 (98)

TITLE 5. GOVERNMENT ORGANIZATION AND EMPLOYEES; AND APPENDIX

Title 6 • Domestic Security

6 USC § 161. Establishment Of Office; Director

> The Gist: A new office for, among other duties, specialized gun research, called the Office of Science and Technology, is established within the Dept. of Justice.

(a) Establishment—
(1) In General—There is hereby established within the Department of Justice an Office of Science and Technology (hereinafter in this title referred to as the "Office").
(2) Authority—The Office shall be under the general authority of the Assistant Attorney General, Office of Justice Programs, and shall be established within the National Institute of Justice.
(b) Director—The Office shall be headed by a Director, who shall be an individual appointed based on approval by the Office of Personnel Management of the executive qualifications of the individual.

Nov. 25, 2002 (90)
TITLE 6. DOMESTIC SECURITY • CHAPTER 1: HOMELAND SECURITY ORGANIZATION • SUBCHAPTER II: INFORMATION ANALYSIS AND INFRASTRUCTURE PROTECTION • PART D: OFFICE OF SCIENCE AND TECHNOLOGY

6 USC § 162. Mission Of Office; Duties

> The Gist: The Office of Science and Technology shall carry out wide range research and development of: 1–personalized guns that can only be operated by an authorized user, 2–bullet- and explosion-resistant glass, and 3–protective apparel. All contracts for this work must be competitively bid. Reports on the research may be withheld at the discretion of the Director of the office.

(b) Duties
In carrying out its mission, the Office shall have the following duties:
(6) To carry out research, development, testing, evaluation, and cost-benefit analyses in fields that would improve the safety, effectiveness, and efficiency of law enforcement technologies used by Federal, State, and local law enforcement agencies, including, but not limited to—
(A) weapons capable of preventing use by unauthorized persons, including personalized guns;
(B) protective apparel;
(C) bullet-resistant and explosion-resistant glass;
(D) monitoring systems and alarm systems capable of providing precise location information;

(c) Competition Required—Except as otherwise expressly provided by law, all research and development carried out by or through the Office shall be carried out on a competitive basis.

Nov. 25, 2002 (114)

TITLE 6. DOMESTIC SECURITY • CHAPTER 1: HOMELAND SECURITY ORGANIZATION • SUBCHAPTER II: INFORMATION ANALYSIS AND INFRASTRUCTURE PROTECTION • PART D: OFFICE OF SCIENCE AND TECHNOLOGY

6 USC § 531. Bureau Of Alcohol, Tobacco, Firearms, And Explosives

> The Gist: After years of speculation and Capitol Hill wrangling, the venerable Bureau of Alcohol, Tobacco and Firearms is closed out of the Treasury Dept. and rolled into the Justice Dept., where it will operate alongside and coordinate with the nation's main law enforcement arm, the FBI. Although the chain of command is radically altered, granting significant new powers to the Attorney General and away from the Secretary of the Treasury, most employees will still report to work in the same places and perform similar functions.
>
> A new office called the Bureau of Alcohol, Tobacco, Firearms and Explosives (BATFE) is established within the Dept. of Justice. The Director of BATFE is appointed by and answers to the Attorney General, and is to coordinate all firearm-related enforcement functions within the Department. The BATFE is responsible for investigating all criminal and regulatory violations of firearms requirements, essentially doing the work formerly performed by BATF, plus any other function related to violent crime or domestic terrorism, as determined by the Attorney General. Specified tax, financial and enforcement functions of the former BATF remain with Treasury in a new office called the Tax and Trade Bureau. A new headquarters for BATFE, based on prior approval for BATF, is authorized.

(a) Establishment—

(1) In General—There is established within the Department of Justice under the general authority of the Attorney General the Bureau of Alcohol, Tobacco, Firearms, and Explosives (in this section referred to as the "Bureau").

(2) Director—There shall be at the head of the Bureau a Director, Bureau of Alcohol, Tobacco, Firearms, and Explosives (in this subtitle referred to as the "Director"). The Director shall be appointed by the Attorney General and shall perform such functions as the Attorney General shall direct. The Director shall receive compensation at the rate prescribed by law under section 5314 of title V, United States Code, for positions at level III of the Executive Schedule.

(3) Coordination—The Attorney General, acting through the Director and such other officials of the Department of Justice as the Attorney General may designate, shall provide for the coordination of all firearms, explosives, tobacco enforcement, and arson enforcement functions vested in the Attorney General so as to assure maximum cooperation between and among any officer, employee, or agency of the Department of Justice involved in the performance of these and related functions.

(4) Performance Of Transferred Functions—The Attorney General may make such provisions as the Attorney General determines appropriate to authorize the performance by any officer, employee, or agency of the Department of Justice of any function transferred to the Attorney General under this section.

(b) Responsibilities—Subject to the direction of the Attorney General, the Bureau shall be responsible for investigating—

(1) criminal and regulatory violations of the Federal firearms, explosives, arson, alcohol, and tobacco smuggling laws;

(2) the functions transferred by subsection (c); and

(3) any other function related to the investigation of violent crime or domestic terrorism that is delegated to the Bureau by the Attorney General.

(c) Transfer Of Authorities, Functions, Personnel, And Assets To The Department Of Justice—

(1) IN GENERAL—Subject to paragraph (2), but notwithstanding any other provision of law, there are transferred to the Department of Justice the authorities, functions, personnel, and assets of the Bureau of Alcohol, Tobacco and Firearms, which shall be maintained as a distinct entity within the Department of Justice, including the related functions of the Secretary of the Treasury.

(2) Administration And Revenue Collection Functions—There shall be retained within the Department of the Treasury the authorities, functions, personnel, and assets of the Bureau of Alcohol, Tobacco and Firearms relating to the administration and enforcement of chapters 51 and 52 of the Internal Revenue Code of 1986, sections 4181 and 4182 of the Internal Revenue Code of 1986, and title 27, United States Code.

(3) Building Prospectus—Prospectus PDC-98W10, giving the General Services Administration the authority for site acquisition, design, and construction of a new headquarters building for the Bureau of Alcohol, Tobacco and Firearms, is transferred, and deemed to apply, to the Bureau of Alcohol, Tobacco, Firearms, and Explosives established in the Department of Justice under subsection (a).

(d) Tax And Trade Bureau—

(1) Establishment—There is established within the Department of the Treasury the Tax and Trade Bureau.

(2) Administrator—The Tax and Trade Bureau shall be headed by an Administrator, who shall perform such duties as assigned by the Under Secretary for Enforcement of the Department of the Treasury. The Administrator shall occupy a career-reserved position within the Senior Executive Service.

(3) Responsibilities—The authorities, functions, personnel, and assets of the Bureau of Alcohol, Tobacco and Firearms that are not transferred to the Department of Justice under this section shall be retained and administered by the Tax and Trade Bureau.

Nov. 25, 2002 (591)
TITLE 6. DOMESTIC SECURITY • CHAPTER 1: HOMELAND SECURITY ORGANIZATION • SUBCHAPTER XI: DEPARTMENT OF JUSTICE DIVISIONS • PART B • TRANSFER OF THE BUREAU OF ALCOHOL, TOBACCO AND FIREARMS TO THE DEPARTMENT OF JUSTICE

Title 7 • Agriculture

7 USC § 2012. Definitions

> **The Gist:** In extremely remote parts of Alaska the food stamp program defines food to include implements for obtaining food by hunting or fishing, but not firearms or ammunition.

Definitions
As used in this chapter, the term:
(g) "Food" means
(6) in the case of certain eligible households living in Alaska, equipment for procuring food by hunting and fishing, such as nets, hooks, rods, harpoons, and knives (but not equipment for purposes of transportation, clothing, or shelter, and not firearms, ammunition, and explosives) if the Secretary determines that such households are located in an area of the State where it is extremely difficult to reach stores selling food and that such households depend to a substantial extent upon hunting and fishing for subsistence,
(h) "Food stamp program" means the program operated pursuant to the provisions of this chapter.
Aug. 31, 1964 (109)
TITLE 7. AGRICULTURE • CHAPTER 51: FOOD STAMP PROGRAM

7 USC § 2015. Eligibility disqualifications <without edits, see the Gist below and the next section for details>

> **The Gist:** Using food stamps to obtain firearms or ammunition is grounds for permanent disqualification from the food-stamps program.
>
> ———————————
>
> **This section has been used to show how the *Gun Laws of America* editing process works.**
>
> To meet the editorial guidelines of presenting only the laws that relate directly to guns, unrelated portions of many laws are not printed. This sometimes amounts to many pages of deleted text.
>
> Shown below is the unedited first portion of a lengthy law. Appearing in regular type are the portions that would normally remain after the editing process. Shown in *italics* are the portions that would normally be edited and *not* appear. The remaining text of this law (there are approximately

420 additional lines or about 3,300 more words) have no bearing on the subject and do not appear.

This leads to intermittent but sequential numbering, eliminates material which is not germane (though frequently interesting), preserves the meaning of the law as it concerns firearms and allows the text to fit in a single volume. Citations may still be made accurately, since care was taken to preserve the necessary elements of outline order. For example, the "law" that says you're permanently disbarred from the food stamps program for trading stamps for firearms is 7–2015(b)(1)(B)(iii)(III).

Following the unedited text is the text as it would appear in its edited form, saving nearly *23 times the space*, and helping to crystallize the meaning as it concerns firearms.

(a) Additional specific conditions rendering individuals ineligible
In addition to meeting the standards of eligibility prescribed in section 2014 of this title, households and individuals who are members of eligible households must also meet and comply with the specific requirements of this section to be eligible for participation in the food stamp program.
(b) Fraud and misrepresentation; disqualification penalties; ineligibility period; applicable procedures
(1) Any person who has been found by any State or Federal court or administrative agency to have intentionally
(A) *made a false or misleading statement, or misrepresented, concealed or withheld facts, or*
(B) committed any act that constitutes a violation of this chapter, the regulations issued thereunder, or any State statute, for the purpose of using, presenting, transferring, acquiring, receiving, or possessing coupons or authorization cards shall, immediately upon the rendering of such determination, become ineligible for further participation in the program—
(i) *for a period of six months upon the first occasion of any such determination;*
(ii) *for a period of 1 year upon—*
(I) *the second occasion of any such determination; or*
(II) *the first occasion of a finding by a Federal, State, or local court of the trading of a controlled substance (as defined in section 802 of Title 21) for coupons; and*
(iii) permanently upon—
(I) *the third occasion of any such determination;*
(II) *the second occasion of a finding by a Federal, State, or local court of the trading of a controlled substance (as defined in section 802 of Title 21) for coupons; or*
(III) the first occasion of a finding by a Federal, State, or local court of the trading of firearms, ammunition, or explosives for coupons.
During the period of such ineligibility, no household shall receive increased benefits under this chapter as the result of a member of such household having been disqualified under this subsection.
(2) *Each State agency shall proceed against an individual alleged to have engaged in such activity either by way of administrative hearings, after notice and an opportunity for a hearing at the State level, or by referring such matters to appropriate authorities for civil or criminal action in a court of law.*
(3) *Such periods of ineligibility as are provided for in paragraph (1) of this subsection shall remain in effect, without possibility of administrative stay, unless and until the finding upon which the ineligibility is based is subsequently reversed by a court of appropriate jurisdiction, but in no event shall the period of ineligibility be subject to review.*
(4) *The Secretary shall prescribe such regulations as the Secretary may deem appropriate to ensure that information concerning any such determination with respect to a specific individual is forwarded to the Office of the Secretary by any*

appropriate State or Federal entity for the use of the Secretary in administering the provisions of this section. No State shall withhold such information from the Secretary or the Secretary's designee for any reason whatsoever.

<Another 420 lines of text from this section are unrelated to the subject of this book and have been truncated.>

Aug. 31, 1964 (467)
TITLE 7. AGRICULTURE • CHAPTER 51: FOOD STAMP PROGRAM

7 USC § 2015 Eligibility disqualifications
<as edited, see the Gist above for explanation>

> The Gist: Using food stamps to obtain firearms or ammunition is grounds for permanent disqualification from the food-stamps program.

(a) Additional specific conditions rendering individuals ineligible
In addition to meeting the standards of eligibility prescribed in section 2014 of this title, households and individuals who are members of eligible households must also meet and comply with the specific requirements of this section to be eligible for participation in the food stamp program.
(b) Fraud and misrepresentation; disqualification penalties; ineligibility period; applicable procedures
(1) Any person who has been found by any State or Federal court or administrative agency to have intentionally
(B) committed any act that constitutes a violation of this chapter, the regulations issued thereunder, or any State statute, for the purpose of using, presenting, transferring, acquiring, receiving, or possessing coupons or authorization cards shall, immediately upon the rendering of such determination, become ineligible for further participation in the program—
(iii) permanently upon—
(III) the first occasion of a finding by a Federal, State, or local court of the trading of firearms, ammunition, or explosives for coupons;

Aug. 31, 1964 (159)
TITLE 7. AGRICULTURE • CHAPTER 51: FOOD STAMP PROGRAM

7 USC § 2021. Civil money penalties and disqualification of retail food stores and wholesale food concerns

> The Gist: A food-stamp approved food outlet may be disqualified permanently and fined for selling firearms or ammunition for food stamps.

(a) Disqualification or civil penalty
Any approved retail food store or wholesale food concern may be disqualified for a specified period of time from further participation in the food stamp program, or subjected to a civil money penalty of up to $10,000 for each violation if the Secretary determines that its disqualification would cause hardship to food stamp households, on a finding, made as specified in the regulations, that such store or concern has violated any of the provisions of this chapter or the regulations issued pursuant to this chapter.
(b) Period of disqualification
Disqualification under subsection (a) of this section shall be—
(3) permanent upon—

(C) a finding of the sale of firearms, ammunition, explosives, or controlled substance (as defined in section 802 of Title 21) for coupons, except that the Secretary shall have the discretion to impose a civil money penalty of up to $20,000 for each violation (except that the amount of civil money penalties imposed for violations occurring during a single investigation may not exceed $40,000) in lieu of disqualification under this subparagraph if the Secretary determines that there is substantial evidence (including evidence that neither the ownership nor management of the store or food concern was aware of, approved, benefited from, or was involved in the conduct or approval of the violation) that the store or food concern had an effective policy and program in effect to prevent violations of this chapter.

Aug. 31, 1964 (240)
TITLE 7. AGRICULTURE • CHAPTER 51: FOOD STAMP PROGRAM

7 USC § 2146. Administration and enforcement by Secretary

> The Gist: Special penalties are provided for anyone who uses a deadly weapon to interfere with animal inspectors on official business for the Dept. of Agriculture.

(a) Investigations and inspections
The Secretary shall make such investigations or inspections as he deems necessary to determine whether any dealer, exhibitor, intermediate handler, carrier, research facility, or operator of an auction sale subject to section 2142 of this title, has violated or is violating any provision of this chapter or any regulation or standard issued thereunder, and for such purposes, the Secretary shall, at all reasonable times, have access to the places of business and the facilities, animals, and those records required to be kept pursuant to section 2140 of this title of any such dealer, exhibitor, intermediate handler, carrier, research facility, or operator of an auction sale. The Secretary shall inspect each research facility at least once each year and, in the case of deficiencies or deviations from the standards promulgated under this chapter, shall conduct such follow-up inspections as may be necessary until all deficiencies or deviations from such standards are corrected. The Secretary shall promulgate such rules and regulations as he deems necessary to permit inspectors to confiscate or destroy in a humane manner any animal found to be suffering as a result of a failure to comply with any provision of this chapter or any regulation or standard issued thereunder if
(1) such animal is held by a dealer,
(2) such animal is held by an exhibitor,
(3) such animal is held by a research facility and is no longer required by such research facility to carry out the research, test, or experiment for which such animal has been utilized,
(4) such animal is held by an operator of an auction sale, or
(5) such animal is held by an intermediate handler or a carrier.
(b) Penalties for interfering with official duties
Any person who forcibly assaults, resists, opposes, impedes, intimidates, or interferes with any person while engaged in or on account of the performance of his official duties under this chapter shall be fined not more than $5,000, or imprisoned not more than three years, or both. Whoever, in the commission of such acts, uses a deadly or dangerous weapon shall be fined not more than $10,000, or imprisoned not more than ten years, or both. Whoever kills any person while engaged in or on account of the performance of his official duties under this chapter shall be punished as provided under sections 1111 and 1114 of Title 18.

Aug. 24, 1966 (398)
TITLE 7. AGRICULTURE • CHAPTER 54: TRANSPORTATION, SALE, AND HANDLING OF CERTAIN ANIMALS

7 USC § 2238. Use of field work funds for purchase of arms and ammunition

> **The Gist:** The Army may provide arms and ammunition to certain government entities upon request. The Dept. of Agriculture is authorized to purchase arms and ammunition commercially if the cost is under $50 or if the Army's terms are unacceptable.

Funds available for field work in the Department of Agriculture may be used for the purchase of arms and ammunition whenever the individual purchase does not exceed $50, and for individual purchases exceeding $50, when such arms and ammunition cannot advantageously be supplied by the Secretary of the Army pursuant to section 4655 of Title 10.

June 4, 1936 (56)

TITLE 7. AGRICULTURE • CHAPTER 55: DEPARTMENT OF AGRICULTURE

7 USC § 2270. Authority of Office of Inspector General

> **The Gist:** Certain employees of the Office of the Inspector General of the Dept. of Agriculture may be authorized to carry firearms.

Any person who is employed in the Office of the Inspector General, Department of Agriculture, who conducts investigations of alleged or suspected felony criminal violations of statutes, including but not limited to the Food Stamp Act of 1977 <7 USC § 2011 et seq.>, administered by the Secretary of Agriculture or any agency of the Department of Agriculture and who is designated by the Inspector General of the Department of Agriculture may—

(3) carry a firearm; in accordance with rules issued by the Secretary of Agriculture, while such employee is engaged in the performance of official duties under the authority provided in section 6, or described in section 9, of the Inspector General Act of 1978 (5 U.S.C. App. 6, 9). The Attorney General of the United States may disapprove any designation made by the Inspector General under this section.

Dec. 22, 1981 (141)

TITLE 7. AGRICULTURE • CHAPTER 55: DEPARTMENT OF AGRICULTURE

7 USC § 2274. Firearm authority of employees engaged in animal quarantine enforcement

> **The Gist:** Dept. of Agriculture employees may be authorized to carry and use firearms for self-protection with animals with communicable diseases.

Any employee of the United States Department of Agriculture designated by the Secretary of Agriculture and the Attorney General of the United States may carry a firearm and use a firearm when necessary for self-protection, in accordance with rules and regulations issued by the Secretary of Agriculture and the Attorney General of the United States, while such employee is engaged in the performance of the employee's official duties to

(1) carry out any law or regulation related to the control, eradication, or prevention of the introduction or dissemination of communicable disease of livestock or poultry into the United States or

(2) perform any duty related to such disease control, eradication, or prevention, subject to the direction of the Secretary.

Oct. 14, 1982 (120)

TITLE 7. AGRICULTURE • CHAPTER 55: DEPARTMENT OF AGRICULTURE

Title 8 • Aliens and Nationality

8 USC § 1101. Definitions

> The Gist: The serious crime known as *aggravated felony* is defined, with respect to laws concerning alien immigration, to include gun running, specified explosive and weapons offenses, specified NFA weapon offenses, and attempts or conspiracies to commit such offenses The term applies whether the crimes were committed at a federal or state level, or in a foreign nation.

(a) As used in this chapter—
(43) The term "aggravated felony" means—
(C) illicit trafficking in firearms or destructive devices (as defined in section 921 of title 18) or in explosive materials (as defined in section 841(c) of that title);
(E) an offense described in—
(i) section 842(h) or (i) of title 18, or section 844(d), (e), (f), (g), (h), or (i) of that title (relating to explosive materials offenses);
(ii) section 922(g)(1), (2), (3), (4), or (5), (j), (n), (o), (p), or (r) or 924(b) or (h) of title 18 (relating to firearms offenses); or
(iii) section 5861 of title 26 (relating to firearms offenses);
(U) an attempt or conspiracy to commit an offense described in this paragraph.
The term applies to an offense described in this paragraph whether in violation of Federal or State law and applies to such an offense in violation of the law of a foreign country for which the term of imprisonment was completed within the previous 15 years. Notwithstanding any other provision of law (including any effective date), the term applies regardless of whether the conviction was entered before, on, or after September 30, 1996.
June 27, 1952 (192)
TITLE 8. ALIENS AND NATIONALITY • CHAPTER 12: IMMIGRATION AND NATIONALITY • SUBCHAPTER I: GENERAL PROVISIONS

8 USC § 1182. Inadmissible aliens

> The Gist: The list of offenses that makes certain aliens ineligible for visas or for admission into the United States was increased in 2000 to include other weapons or dangerous devices An exception exists if the weapon was used, "for mere personal monetary gain."

(a) Classes of aliens ineligible for visas or admission
Except as otherwise provided in this chapter, aliens who are inadmissible under the following paragraphs are ineligible to receive visas and ineligible to be admitted to the United States:
(3) Security and related grounds
(B) Terrorist activities

(iii) "Terrorist activity" defined
(V) The use of any—
(b) explosive, firearm, or other weapon or dangerous device (other than for mere personal monetary gain), with intent to endanger, directly or indirectly, the safety of one or more individuals or to cause substantial damage to property.
(VI) A threat, attempt, or conspiracy to do any of the foregoing.

Oct. 30, 2000 (104)

TITLE 8. ALIENS AND NATIONALITY • CHAPTER 12: IMMIGRATION AND NATIONALITY • SUBCHAPTER II: IMMIGRATION • PART II: ADMISSION QUALIFICATIONS FOR ALIENS; TRAVEL CONTROL OF CITIZENS AND ALIENS

8 USC § 1227. Deportable aliens

> The Gist: An alien may be deported for any violation of any firearms law.

(a) Classes of deportable aliens
Any alien (including an alien crewman) in and admitted to the United States shall, upon the order of the Attorney General, be removed if the alien is within one or more of the following classes of deportable aliens:
(2) Criminal offenses
(C) Certain firearm offenses
Any alien who at any time after admission is convicted under any law of purchasing, selling, offering for sale, exchanging, using, owning, possessing, or carrying, or of attempting or conspiring to purchase, sell, offer for sale, exchange, use, own, possess, or carry, any weapon, part, or accessory which is a firearm or destructive device (as defined in section 921(a) of Title 18) in violation of any law is deportable.

June 27, 1952 (117)

TITLE 8. ALIENS AND NATIONALITY • CHAPTER 12: IMMIGRATION AND NATIONALITY • SUBCHAPTER II: IMMIGRATION • PART V: DEPORTATION; ADJUSTMENT OF STATUS

Title 10 • Armed Forces

10 USC § 311. Militia: composition and classes

> The Gist: All able-bodied Americans from 17 to 45 years of age are
> members of the militia. American women who are in the National Guard
> are members of the militia. Former members of the U.S. Army, Navy, Air
> Force and Marine Corps are members of the militia until they are 64 years
> old (described in 32-313). The National Guard and the Naval Militia are
> called the organized militia. The unorganized militia includes everyone in
> the militia who is not in the National Guard or the Naval Militia.
>
> Note: In federal law, use of male gender includes female, use of singular
> includes plural, and use of present tense includes the future (1 USC § 1).

(a) The militia of the United States consists of all able-bodied males at least 17 years
of age and, except as provided in section 313 of title 32, under 45 years of age who
are, or who have made a declaration of intention to become, citizens of the United
States and of female citizens of the United States who are members of the National
Guard.
(b) The classes of the militia are —
(1) the organized militia, which consists of the National Guard and the Naval Militia;
and
(2) the unorganized militia, which consists of the members of the militia who are not
members of the National Guard or the Naval Militia.

Aug. 10, 1956 (112)
TITLE 10. ARMED FORCES • SUBTITLE A: GENERAL MILITARY LAW • CHAPTER 13: THE MILITIA • PART 1.
ORGANIZATION AND GENERAL MILITARY POWERS

10 USC § 312. Militia duty: exemptions

> The Gist: Certain people are excused from militia duty, as listed below.

(a) The following persons are exempt from militia duty:
(1) The Vice President.
(2) The judicial and executive officers of the United States, the several States and
Territories, and Puerto Rico.
(3) Members of the armed forces, except members who are not on active duty.
(4) Customhouse clerks.
(5) Persons employed by the United States in the transmission of mail.
(6) Workmen employed in armories, arsenals, and naval shipyards of the United
States.
(7) Pilots on navigable waters.
(8) Mariners in the sea service of a citizen of, or a merchant in, the United States.
(b) A person who claims exemption because of religious belief is exempt from militia
duty in a combatant capacity, if the conscientious holding of that belief is

established under such regulations as the President may prescribe. However, such a person is not exempt from militia duty that the President determines to be noncombatant.

Aug. 10, 1956 (148)

TITLE 10. ARMED FORCES • SUBTITLE A: GENERAL MILITARY LAW • CHAPTER 13: THE MILITIA • PART 1. ORGANIZATION AND GENERAL MILITARY POWERS

10 USC § 331. Federal aid for State governments

The Gist: The President may call up the militia and the armed forces, if a state officially requests it, to stop a revolt. See 32-102 for separate rules concerning calling up the National Guard.

Whenever there is an insurrection in any State against its government, the President may, upon the request of its legislature or of its governor if the legislature cannot be convened, call into Federal service such of the militia of the other States, in the number requested by that State, and use such of the armed forces, as he considers necessary to suppress the insurrection.

Aug. 10, 1956 (64)

TITLE 10. ARMED FORCES • SUBTITLE A: GENERAL MILITARY LAW • CHAPTER 15: INSURRECTION • PART 1. ORGANIZATION AND GENERAL MILITARY POWERS

10 USC § 332. Use of militia and armed forces to enforce Federal authority

The Gist: The President may call up the militia and the armed forces when the President considers it necessary to enforce federal laws or suppress unlawful rebellion against the country.

Whenever the President considers that unlawful obstructions, combinations, or assemblages, or rebellion against the authority of the United States, make it impracticable to enforce the laws of the United States in any State or Territory by the ordinary course of judicial proceedings, he may call into Federal service such of the militia of any State, and use such of the armed forces, as he considers necessary to enforce those laws or to suppress the rebellion.

Aug. 10, 1956 (75)

TITLE 10. ARMED FORCES • SUBTITLE A: GENERAL MILITARY LAW • CHAPTER 15: INSURRECTION • PART 1. ORGANIZATION AND GENERAL MILITARY POWERS

10 USC § 333. Interference with State and Federal law

The Gist: The President must take whatever measures are necessary, including using the militia or the armed forces, to suppress an uprising in a state, if the uprising denies people their rights under the Constitution or under law, and if the state's authorities cannot or refuse to protect those rights. A state which doesn't or can't protect citizens' rights is deemed to have denied equal protection under the Constitution.

The President, by using the militia or the armed forces, or both, or by any other means, shall take such measures as he considers necessary to suppress, in a State, any insurrection, domestic violence, unlawful combination, or conspiracy, if it—

(1) so hinders the execution of the laws of that State, and of the United States within the State, that any part or class of its people is deprived of a right, privilege,

immunity, or protection named in the Constitution and secured by law, and the constituted authorities of that State are unable, fail, or refuse to protect that right, privilege, or immunity, or to give that protection; or

(23) opposes or obstructs the execution of the laws of the United States or impedes the course of justice under those laws.

In any situation covered by clause (1), the State shall be considered to have denied the equal protection of the laws secured by the Constitution.

Aug. 10, 1956 (156)
TITLE 10. ARMED FORCES • SUBTITLE A: GENERAL MILITARY LAW • CHAPTER 15: INSURRECTION • PART 1. ORGANIZATION AND GENERAL MILITARY POWERS

10 USC § 372. Use of military equipment and facilities

The Gist: The Dept. of Defense may supply equipment and facilities to local law enforcement authorities for law enforcement purposes.

The Secretary of Defense may, in accordance with other applicable law, make available any equipment (including associated supplies or spare parts), base facility, or research facility of the Department of Defense to any Federal, State, or local civilian law enforcement official for law enforcement purposes.

Sept. 29, 1988 (45)
TITLE 10. ARMED FORCES • SUBTITLE A: GENERAL MILITARY LAW • CHAPTER 18: MILITARY SUPPORT FOR CIVILIAN LAW ENFORCEMENT AGENCIES • PART 1. ORGANIZATION AND GENERAL MILITARY POWERS

10 USC § 373. Training and advising civilian law enforcement officials

The Gist: The Dept. of Defense may provide its personnel to train and advise local law enforcement authorities in the use of equipment, including equipment which the Defense Dept. provides to local law enforcement.

The Secretary of Defense may, in accordance with other applicable law, make Department of Defense personnel available—

(1) to train Federal, State, and local civilian law enforcement officials in the operation and maintenance of equipment, including equipment made available under section 372 of this title; and

(2) to provide such law enforcement officials with expert advice relevant to the purposes of this chapter.

Nov. 8, 1985 (63)
TITLE 10. ARMED FORCES • SUBTITLE A: GENERAL MILITARY LAW • CHAPTER 18: MILITARY SUPPORT FOR CIVILIAN LAW ENFORCEMENT AGENCIES • PART 1. ORGANIZATION AND GENERAL MILITARY POWERS

10 USC § 1585. Carrying of firearms

The Gist: Civilians in the Dept. of Defense may be authorized to carry firearms or other weapons.

Under regulations to be prescribed by the Secretary of Defense, civilian officers and employees of the Department of Defense may carry firearms or other appropriate weapons while assigned investigative duties or such other duties as the Secretary may prescribe.

July 31, 1958 (39)
TITLE 10. ARMED FORCES • SUBTITLE A: GENERAL MILITARY LAW • PART II: PERSONNEL • CHAPTER 81: CIVILIAN EMPLOYEES

10 USC § 2358. Research and development projects

> The Gist: The military may conduct research and development on weapons, and may contract with others for this work.

(a) Authority.—The Secretary of Defense or the Secretary of a military department may engage in basic research, applied research, advanced research, and development projects that—

(1) are necessary to the responsibilities of such Secretary's department in the field of research and development; and

(2) either—

(A) relate to weapon systems and other military needs; or

(B) are of potential interest to the Department of Defense.

(b) Authorized means.—The Secretary of Defense or the Secretary of a military department may perform research and development projects—

(1) by contract, cooperative agreement, or grant, in accordance with chapter 63 of title 31;

(2) through one or more military departments;

(3) by using employees and consultants of the Department of Defense; or

(4) by mutual agreement with the head of any other department or agency of the Federal Government.

(c) Requirement of potential Department of Defense interest.—Funds appropriated to the Department of Defense or to a military department may not be used to finance any research project or study unless the project or study is, in the opinion of the Secretary of Defense or the Secretary of that military department, respectively, of potential interest to the Department of Defense or to such military department, respectively.

(d) Additional provisions applicable to cooperative agreements.—Additional authorities, conditions, and requirements relating to certain cooperative agreements authorized by this section are provided in section 2371 and 2371a of this title.

Sept. 7, 1962 (233)

TITLE 10. ARMED FORCES • SUBTITLE A: GENERAL MILITARY LAW • PART IV: SERVICE SUPPLY, AND PROCUREMENT • CHAPTER 139: RESEARCH AND DEVELOPMENT

10 USC § 2576. Surplus military equipment: sale to State and local law enforcement and firefighting agencies

> The Gist: Certain surplus military firearms and related gear may be sold to state and local law enforcement and fire fighting agencies, at fair market value. The agency must make an official request, justify the necessity of the request, and may not resell the equipment.

(a) The Secretary of Defense, under regulations prescribed by him, may sell to State and local law enforcement and firefighting agencies, at fair market value, pistols, revolvers, shotguns, rifles of a caliber not exceeding .30, ammunition for such firearms, gas masks, and protective body armor which

(1) are suitable for use by such agencies in carrying out law enforcement and firefighting activities, and

(2) have been determined to be surplus property under subtitle I of title 40 and title III of the Federal Property and Administrative Services Act of 1949 (41 U.S.C. 251 et seq.)

(b) Such surplus military equipment shall not be sold under the provisions of this section to a State or local law enforcement or firefighting agency unless request therefor is made by such agency, in such form and manner as the Secretary of Defense shall prescribe, and such request, with respect to the type and amount of equipment so requested, is certified as being necessary and suitable for the operation of such agency by the Governor (or such State official as he may designate) of the State in which such agency is located. Equipment sold to a State or local law enforcement or firefighting agency under this section shall not exceed, in quantity, the amount requested and certified for such agency and shall be for the exclusive use of such agency. Such equipment may not be sold, or otherwise transferred, by such agency to any individual or public or private organization or agency.

Sept. 20, 1968 (247)
TITLE 10. ARMED FORCES • SUBTITLE A: GENERAL MILITARY LAW • PART IV: SERVICE SUPPLY, AND PROCUREMENT • CHAPTER 153: EXCHANGE OF MATERIAL AND DISPOSAL OF OBSOLETE, SURPLUS, OR UNCLAIMED PROPERTY

10 USC § 2579. War booty: procedures for handling and retaining battlefield objects

> The Gist: The United States recognizes that battlefield souvenirs have traditionally provided military personnel with a valued memento of service in a national cause. The Defense Dept. makes regulations for handling battlefield souvenirs, including enemy weaponry. Before a captured weapon may be turned over to a member of the armed forces who requests it, it must be made unserviceable, and the full cost of making it so may be charged.

(a) Policy.—The United States recognizes that battlefield souvenirs have traditionally provided military personnel with a valued memento of service in a national cause. At the same time, it is the policy and tradition of the United States that the desire for souvenirs in a combat theater not blemish the conduct of combat operations or result in the mistreatment of enemy personnel, the dishonoring of the dead, distraction from the conduct of operations, or other unbecoming activities.
(b) Regulations.—
(1) The Secretary of Defense shall prescribe regulations for the handling of battlefield objects that are consistent with the policies expressed in subsection (a) and the requirements of this section.
(2) When forces of the United States are operating in a theater of operations, enemy material captured or found abandoned shall be turned over to appropriate United States or allied military personnel except as otherwise provided in such regulations. A member of the armed forces (or other person under the authority of the armed forces in a theater of operations) may not (except in accordance with such regulations) take from a theater of operations as a souvenir an object formerly in the possession of the enemy.
(3) Such regulations shall provide that a member of the armed forces who wishes to retain as a souvenir an object covered by paragraph (2) may so request at the time the object is turned over pursuant to paragraph (2).
(4) Such regulations shall provide for an officer to be designated to review requests under paragraph (3). If the officer determines that the object may be appropriately retained as a war souvenir, the object shall be turned over to the member who requested the right to retain it.
(5) Such regulations shall provide for captured weaponry to be retained as souvenirs, as follows:
(A) The only weapons that may be retained are those in categories to be agreed upon jointly by the Secretary of Defense and the Secretary of the Treasury.
(B) Before a weapon is turned over to a member, the weapon shall be rendered unserviceable.
(C) A charge may be assessed in connection with each weapon in an amount sufficient to cover the full cost of rendering the weapon unserviceable.

Nov. 30, 1993 (367)
TITLE 10. ARMED FORCES • SUBTITLE A: GENERAL MILITARY LAW • PART II: PERSONNEL • CHAPTER 153: EXCHANGE OF MATERIAL AND DISPOSAL OF OBSOLETE, SURPLUS, OR UNCLAIMED PROPERTY

10 USC § 4308. (Repealed) Promotion of civilian marksmanship: authority of the Secretary of the Army <Historical Note>

Historical note: Enacted in 1956 during the height of Cold War tensions (Eisenhower), and repealed in 1996 under gun-control pressure (Clinton), **10 USC § 4308** used to provide that:

The Army is required to provide, for civilian use, rifle ranges, .22 and .30 caliber ammunition free of charge, and practice and instruction in firearm use for citizens and for youths in the Boy Scouts, 4-H and similar clubs. It must hold competitions, provide awards, make firearms and ammunition available for loan to, or purchase by, the public, and perform support functions to make everything run. Fees the Army may charge, and other funds, support the Civilian Marksmanship Program (CMP, this section).

The original language can be found on our website under Updates. Section 18-925(a)(2)(A) now provides an exemption from most federal laws to operate the marksmanship program in its current form, but the descriptive language 10-4308 included has been repealed.

Similarly, **10 USC § 4310,** repealed at the same time formerly provided: The President and the Army may appoint Army personnel as rifle range instructors for civilians. See Title 36, where the CMP laws now reside.

10 USC § 4309. Rifle ranges: availability for use by members and civilians

The Gist: Any rifle range built at least partially by federal money may be used by the military and the public. Regulations for use are written by whoever controls the range, fees may be charged, and the military has first call on use of the range. This is one of the few sections to survive the 1996 repeals of the Civilian Marksmanship provisions. The repealed sections have been changed somewhat and are now under Title 36.

(a) Ranges available.—All rifle ranges constructed in whole or in part with funds provided by the United States may be used by members of the armed forces and by persons capable of bearing arms.
(b) Military ranges.—
(1) In the case of a rifle range referred to in subsection (a) that is located on a military installation, the Secretary concerned may establish reasonable fees for the use by civilians of that rifle range to cover the material and supply costs incurred by the armed forces to make that rifle range available to civilians.
(2) Fees collected pursuant to paragraph (1) in connection with the use of a rifle range shall be credited to the appropriation available for the operation and maintenance of that rifle range and shall be available for the operation and maintenance of that rifle range.
(3) Use of a rifle range referred to in paragraph (1) by civilians may not interfere with the use of the range by members of the armed forces.
(c) Regulations.—Regulations to carry out this section with respect to a rifle range shall be prescribed, subject to the approval of the Secretary concerned, by the authorities controlling the rifle range.

Aug. 10, 1956 (199)
TITLE 10. ARMED FORCES • SUBTITLE B: ARMY • PART III: TRAINING • CHAPTER 401—TRAINING GENERALLY

10 USC § 4312. National rifle and pistol matches: small-arms firing school

> The Gist: Official firearms *National Matches* are held annually by the Army. The matches are open to military and civilian competitors, and a firing school and a National Rifle Association competition are held in connection with the matches. The National Matches also survived the 1996 repeals.

(a) An annual competition called the "National Matches" and consisting of rifle and pistol matches for a national trophy, medals, and other prizes shall be held as prescribed by the Secretary of the Army.
(b) The National Matches are open to members of the armed forces, National Guard, Reserve Officers' Training Corps, Air Force Reserve Officers' Training Corps, Citizens' Military Training Camps, Citizens' Air Training Camps, and rifle clubs, and to civilians.
(c) A small-arms firing school shall be held in connection with the National Matches.
(d) Competitions for which trophies and medals are provided by the National Rifle Association of America shall be held in connection with the National Matches.

Aug. 10, 1956 (112)
TITLE 10. ARMED FORCES • SUBTITLE B: ARMY • PART III: TRAINING • CHAPTER 401: TRAINING GENERALLY

10 USC § 4313. National Matches and small-arms school: expenses

> The Gist: The Army may subsidize the participation of youngsters under 18 and people active in the military reserves, in the National Matches and small-arms school.

(a) Allowances for participation of junior competitors.—
(1) Junior competitors at National Matches, small-arms firing schools, and competitions in connection with National Matches and special clinics under section 4312 of this title may be paid a subsistence allowance in such amount as the Secretary of the Army shall prescribe.
(2) A junior competitor referred to in paragraph (1) may be paid a travel allowance, in such amount as the Secretary of the Army shall prescribe, instead of travel expenses and subsistence while traveling. The travel allowance for the return trip may be paid in advance.
(b) Junior competitor defined—For the purposes of subsection (a) a junior competitor is a competitor who is under 18 years of age or is a member of a gun club organized for the students of a college or university.

Aug. 10, 1956 (203)
TITLE 10. ARMED FORCES • SUBTITLE B: ARMY • PART III: TRAINING • CHAPTER 401: TRAINING GENERALLY

10 USC § 4651. Arms, tentage, and equipment: educational institutions not maintaining units of R.O.T.C.

> The Gist: The Army may provide arms and other equipment to schools which meet certain military requirements.

Under such conditions as he may prescribe, the Secretary of the Army may issue arms, tentage, and equipment that he considers necessary for proper military training, to any educational institution at which no unit of the Reserve Officers' Training Corps is maintained, but which has a course in military training prescribed by the Secretary and which has at least 100 physically fit students over 14 years of age.

Aug. 10, 1956 (68)
TITLE 10. ARMED FORCES • SUBTITLE B: ARMY • PART IV: SERVICE, SUPPLY, AND PROCUREMENT • CHAPTER 441: ISSUE OF SERVICEABLE MATERIAL OTHER THAN TO ARMED FORCES

10 USC § 4655. Arms and ammunition: agencies and departments of the United States

> The Gist: If needed to protect public money or property, the Army may lend firearms and ammunition to any U.S. agency, on request. The requesting agency must pay for: 1–the ammunition issued; 2–repairs and replacements for damage; 3–incidental expenses, and 4–must return items when they are no longer needed.

(a) Whenever required for the protection of public money and property, the Secretary of the Army may lend arms and their accouterments, and issue ammunition, to a department or independent agency of the United States, upon request of its head. Property lent or issued under this subsection may be delivered to an officer of the department or agency designated by the head thereof, and that officer shall account for the property to the Secretary of the Army. Property lent or issued under this subsection and not properly expended shall be returned when it is no longer needed.

(b) The department or agency to which property is lent or issued under subsection (a) shall transfer funds to the credit of the Department of the Army to cover the costs of—

(1) ammunition issued:

(2) replacing arms and accouterments that have been lost or destroyed, or cannot be repaired:

(3) repairing arms and accouterments returned to the Department of the Army; and

(4) making and receiving shipments by the Department of the Army.

Aug. 10, 1956 (171)
TITLE 10. ARMED FORCES • SUBTITLE B: ARMY • PART IV: SERVICE, SUPPLY, AND PROCUREMENT • CHAPTER 441: ISSUE OF SERVICEABLE MATERIAL OTHER THAN TO ARMED FORCES

10 USC § 4683. Excess M-1 rifles: loan or donation for funeral and other ceremonial purposes

> The Gist: The Secretary of the Army can lend or donate M-1 rifles, slings, cartridges belts, blank ammunition and necessary accoutrements, to certain organizations, for use by honor guards at certain funerals, at no charge. Such organizations have limited liability for loss or damage of the rifles and supplies. The Army must set conditions for security, safety, and accountability of the materials, and any other conditions it deems necessary. Eligible organizations include national cemetery honor guards, law enforcement agencies, and recognized veteran's organizations.

(a) Authority To Lend or Donate.—

(1) The Secretary of the Army, under regulations prescribed by the Secretary, may conditionally lend or donate excess M-1 rifles (not more than 15), slings, and cartridge belts to any eligible organization for use by that organization for funeral ceremonies of a member or former member of the armed forces, and for other ceremonial purposes.

(2) If the rifles to be loaned or donated under paragraph (1) are to be used by the eligible organization for funeral ceremonies of a member or former member of the armed forces, the Secretary may issue and deliver the rifles, together with the necessary accoutrements and blank ammunition, without charge.

(b) Relief From Liability.—The Secretary may relieve an eligible organization to which materials are lent or donated under subsection (a), and the surety on its bond, from liability for loss or destruction of the material lent or donated, if there is conclusive evidence that the loss or destruction did not result from negligence.

(c) Conditions on Loan or Donation.—In lending or donating rifles under subsection (a), the Secretary shall impose such conditions on the use of the rifles as may be necessary to ensure security, safety, and accountability. The Secretary may impose such other conditions as the Secretary considers appropriate.

(d) Eligible Organization Defined.—In this section, the term "eligible organization" means—

(1) a unit or other organization of honor guards recognized by the Secretary of the Army as honor guards for a national cemetery;

(2) a law enforcement agency; or

(3) a local unit of any organization that, as determined by the Secretary of the Army, is a nationally recognized veterans' organization.

Oct. 5, 1999 (277)
TITLE 10: ARMED FORCES. SUBTITLE B: ARMY • PART III: TRAINING • CHAPTER 401: TRAINING GENERALLY

10 USC § 9652. Rifles and ammunition for target practice: educational institutions having corps of cadets

> The Gist: The Air Force may lend to a school with a uniformed cadet corps, excess non-current-model magazine rifles and appendages with up to 120 rounds of ammunition per cadet annually, for target practice. The school must take care of the materials, return them when requested, and the Air Force may make any rules it deems necessary to safeguard the interests of the United States.

(a) The Secretary of the Air Force may lend, without expense to the United States, magazine rifles and appendages that are not of the existing service models in use at the time, and that are not necessary for a proper reserve supply, to any educational institution having a uniformed corps of cadets of sufficient number for target practice. He may also issue 40 rounds of ball cartridges for each cadet for each range at which target practice is held, but not more than 120 rounds each year for each cadet participating in target practice.

(b) The institutions to which property is lent under subsection (a) shall use it for target practice, take proper care of it, and return it when required.

(c) The Secretary shall prescribe regulations to carry out this section, containing such other requirements as he considers necessary to safeguard the interests of the United States.

Aug. 10, 1956 (148)
TITLE 10: ARMED FORCES. SUBTITLE D: AIR FORCE • PART IV: SERVICE, SUPPLY, AND PROCUREMENT • CHAPTER 941: ISSUE OF SERVICEABLE MATERIAL OTHER THAN TO ARMED FORCES

Title 12 • Banks and Banking

12 USC § 248. Enumerated powers

> The Gist: A new federal police force was authorized in 2000 to protect the Federal Reserve Board, its banks, personnel, property and operations. Subject to successful completion of law enforcement training they are authorized to carry firearms. This made Title 12 of the U.S. Code the 27th Title to contain federal gun law.

(q) Uniform protection authority for Federal reserve facilities

(1) Notwithstanding any other provision of law, to authorize personnel to act as law enforcement officers to protect and safeguard the premises, grounds, property, personnel, including members of the Board, of the Board, or any Federal reserve bank, and operations conducted by or on behalf of the Board or a reserve bank.

(2) The Board may, subject to the regulations prescribed under paragraph (5), delegate authority to a Federal reserve bank to authorize personnel to act as law enforcement officers to protect and safeguard the bank's premises, grounds, property, personnel, and operations conducted by or on behalf of the bank.

(3) Law enforcement officers designated or authorized by the Board or a reserve bank under paragraph (1) or (2) are authorized while on duty to carry firearms and make arrests without warrants for any offense against the United States committed in their presence, or for any felony cognizable under the laws of the United States committed or being committed within the buildings and grounds of the Board or a reserve bank if they have reasonable grounds to believe that the person to be arrested has committed or is committing such a felony. Such officers shall have access to law enforcement information that may be necessary for the protection of the property or personnel of the Board or a reserve bank.

(4) For purposes of this subsection, the term "law enforcement officers" means personnel who have successfully completed law enforcement training and are authorized to carry firearms and make arrests pursuant to this subsection.

(5) The law enforcement authorities provided for in this subsection may be exercised only pursuant to regulations prescribed by the Board and approved by the Attorney General.

Oct. 30, 2000 (288)

TITLE 12. BANKS AND BANKING • CHAPTER 3: FEDERAL RESERVE SYSTEM • SUBCHAPTER II: BOARD OF GOVERNORS OF THE FEDERAL RESERVE SYSTEM

Title 14 • Coast Guard

14 USC § 95. Special agents of the Coast Guard Investigative Service law enforcement authority

> The Gist: A special agent of the Coast Guard Investigative Service may be authorized to carry firearms or other weapons under specified conditions.
>
> Historical note: Reduced by 168 words with little fanfare in 1998 (P.L. 105-383), previously, civilians working for the Coast Guard could be authorized to carry firearms or other weapons:
>
> Former 14 USC § 95: "Under regulations prescribed by the Secretary with the approval of the Attorney General, civilian special agents of the Coast Guard may carry firearms or other appropriate weapons while assigned to official investigative or law enforcement duties."

(a)(1) A special agent of the Coast Guard Investigative Service designated under subsection (b) has the following authority:
(A) To carry firearms.
(B) To execute and serve any warrant or other process issued under the authority of the United States.
(C) To make arrests without warrant for—
(i) any offense against the United States committed in the agent's presence; or
(ii) any felony cognizable under the laws of the United States if the agent has probable cause to believe that the person to be arrested has committed or is committing the felony.
(2) The authorities provided in paragraph (1) shall be exercised only in the enforcement of statutes for which the Coast Guard has law enforcement authority, or in exigent circumstances.
(b) The Commandant may designate to have the authority provided under subsection (a) any special agent of the Coast Guard Investigative Service whose duties include conducting, supervising, or coordinating investigation of criminal activity in programs and operations of the United States Coast Guard.
(c) The authority provided under subsection (a) shall be exercised in accordance with guidelines prescribed by the Commandant and approved by the Attorney General and any other applicable guidelines prescribed by the Secretary of Homeland Security or the Attorney General.

Sept. 28, 1988 (204)
TITLE 14. COAST GUARD • PART I: REGULAR COAST GUARD • CHAPTER 5: FUNCTIONS AND POWERS

Title 15 • Commerce and Trade

15 USC § 2052. Definitions

> The Gist: *Consumer product,* as used in this chapter (Chapter 15), does not include firearms.

(a) For purposes of this chapter:
(1) The term "consumer product" means any article, or component part thereof, produced or distributed
(i) for sale to a consumer for use in or around a permanent or temporary household or residence, a school, in recreation, or otherwise, or
(ii) for the personal use, consumption or enjoyment of a consumer in or around a permanent or temporary household or residence, a school, in recreation, or otherwise; but such term does not include—
(E) any article which, if sold by the manufacturer, producer, or importer, would be subject to the tax imposed by section 4181 of the Internal Revenue Code of 1954 (determined without regard to any exemptions from such tax provided by section 4182 or 4221, or any other provision of such Code), or any component of any such article

Oct. 27, 1972 (137)
TITLE 15. COMMERCE AND TRADE • CHAPTER 47: CONSUMER PRODUCT SAFETY

Statute at Large
15 USC § 2080 note. Limitations on jurisdiction of Consumer Products Safety Commission

> The Gist: The following is a *Statute at Large;* it received no section number after it was passed by Congress. As such, it does not appear in the regular numbered sections of the U.S. laws—it was enacted on May 11, 1976, and is found as a note to 15-2080. The result is that, although this is law passed by Congress, with the full weight and effect of any other statute, it is not widely known.
>
> This is the somewhat troublesome case with so-called Statutes at Large. Often, it seems items that place limits on government, or protect rights of individuals, find their way to this somewhat nebulous world.
>
> The language here prohibits the Consumer Product Safety Commission from regulating firearms or ammunition.

Manufacture or Sale of Firearms or Firearms Ammunition
P. L. 94-284, Sec. 3(e), May 11, 1976, 90 Stat. 504, provides that: "The Consumer Product Safety Commission shall make no ruling or order that restricts the manufacture or sale of firearms, firearms ammunition, or components of firearms ammunition, including black powder or gunpowder for firearms."

15 USC § 5001. Penalties for entering into commerce of imitation firearms

> The Gist: Toy guns must be clearly marked as toys, except for theater, movie and TV use. Toy guns are defined and do not include BB, pellet or similar air guns. States may not prohibit the sale of BB guns or certain non-firing replicas. The government is authorized to study the criminal misuse of toy guns and the effectiveness of the marking system in police combat situations.

(a) Acts prohibited
It shall be unlawful for any person to manufacture, enter into commerce, ship, transport, or receive any toy, look-alike, or imitation firearm unless such firearm contains, or has affixed to it, a marking approved by the Secretary of Commerce, as provided in subsection (b) of this section.
(b) Distinctive markings for toys, look-alikes, and imitation firearms; exception; waiver; adjustments and changes
(1) Except as provided in paragraph (2) or (3), each toy, look-alike, or imitation firearm shall have as an integral part, permanently affixed, a blaze orange plug inserted in the barrel of such toy, look-alike, or imitation firearm. Such plug shall be recessed no more than 6 millimeters from the muzzle end of the barrel of such firearm.
(2) The Secretary of Commerce may provide for an alternate marking or device for any toy, look-alike, or imitation firearm not capable of being marked as provided in paragraph (1) and may waive the requirement of any such marking or device for any toy, look-alike, or imitation firearm that will only be used in the theatrical, movie or television industry.
(3) The Secretary is authorized to make adjustments and changes in the marking system provided for by this section, after consulting with interested persons.
(c) "Look-alike firearm" defined
For purposes of this section, the term "look-alike firearm" means any imitation of any original firearm which was manufactured, designed, and produced since 1898, including and limited to toy guns, water guns, replica nonguns, and air-soft guns firing nonmetallic projectiles. Such term does not include any look-alike, nonfiring, collector replica of an antique firearm developed prior to 1898, or traditional B-B, paint-ball, or pellet-firing air guns that expel a projectile through the force of air pressure.
(d) Study of criminal misuse of toy, look-alike, and imitation firearms; report
The Director of the Bureau of Justice Statistics is authorized and directed to conduct a study of the criminal misuse of toy, look-alike and imitation firearms, including studying police reports of such incidences and shall report on such incidences relative to marked and unmarked firearms.
(c) <Note: enacted with two subsections "c", probably should be "(e)"> Technical evaluation of marking systems
The Director of National Institute of Justice is authorized and directed to conduct a technical evaluation of the marking systems provided for in subsection (b) of this section to determine their effectiveness in police combat situations. The Director shall begin the study within 3 months after November 5, 1988 and such study shall be completed within 9 months after November 5, 1988.
(f) Effective date
This section shall become effective on the date 6 months after November 5, 1988 and shall apply to toy, look-alike, and imitation firearms manufactured or entered into commerce after November 5, 1988.

(g) Preemption of State or local laws or ordinances; exceptions

The provisions of this section shall supersede any provision of State or local laws or ordinances which provide for markings or identification inconsistent with provisions of this section provided that no State shall—

(i) prohibit the sale or manufacture of any look-alike, nonfiring, collectorreplica of an antique firearm developed prior to 1898, or

(ii) prohibit the sale (other than prohibiting the sale to minors) of traditional B-B, paint ball, or pellet-firing air guns that expel a projectile through the force of air pressure.

Nov. 5, 1988 (598)

TITLE 15. COMMERCE AND TRADE • CHAPTER 76: IMITATION FIREARMS

Title 16 • Conservation

16 USC § 1a-6. Law enforcement personnel within National Park System

> The Gist: The Secretary of the Interior can allow specified employees of the National Park System to carry firearms. The Secretary may also designate members of any other federal agencies to bear arms as special police in the National Parks System, when needed and with the other agency's agreement.

(b) Designation authority of Secretary; powers and duties of designees
In addition to any other authority conferred by law, the Secretary of the Interior is authorized to designate, pursuant to standards prescribed in regulations by the Secretary, certain officers or employees of the Department of the Interior who shall maintain law and order and protect persons and property within areas of the National Park System. In the performance of such duties, the officers or employees, so designated, may—
(1) carry firearms and make arrests without warrant for any offense against the United States committed in his presence, or for any felony cognizable under the laws of the United States if he has reasonable grounds to believe that the person to be arrested has committed or is committing such felony, provided such arrests occur within that system or the person to be arrested is fleeing therefrom to avoid arrest:
(2) execute any warrant or other process issued by a court or officer of competent jurisdiction for the enforcement of the provisions of any Federal law or regulation issued pursuant to law arising out of an offense committed in that system or, where the person subject to the warrant or process is in that system, in connection with any Federal offense; and
(3) conduct investigations of offenses against the United States committed in that system in the absence of investigation thereof by any other Federal law enforcement agency having investigative jurisdiction over the offense committed or with the concurrence of such other agency.
(c) Supplemental special policemen; designation authority of Secretary; cooperation with State officials in enforcement of State law; reimbursement to State; concurrent jurisdiction; delegation of enforcement responsibilities
The Secretary of the Interior is hereby authorized to—
(1) designate officers and employees of any other Federal agency or law enforcement personnel of any State or political subdivision thereof, when deemed economical and in the public interest and with the concurrence of that agency or that State or subdivision, to act as special policemen in areas of the National Park System when supplemental law enforcement personnel may be needed, and to exercise the powers and authority provided by paragraphs (1), (2), and (3) of subsection (a) of this section;
(2) cooperate, within the National Park System, with any State or political subdivision thereof in the enforcement of supervision of the laws or ordinances of that State or subdivision;

(3) mutually waive, in any agreement pursuant to paragraphs (1) and (2) of this subsection or pursuant to subsection (b)(1) of this section with any State or political subdivision thereof where State law requires such waiver and indemnification, any and all civil claims against all the other parties thereto and, subject to available appropriations, indemnify and save harmless the other parties to such agreement from all claims by third parties for property damage or personal injury, which may arise out of the parties' activities outside their respective jurisdictions under such agreement; and

(4) provide limited reimbursement, to a State or its political subdivisions, in accordance with such regulations as he may prescribe, where the State has ceded concurrent legislative jurisdiction over the affected area of the system, for expenditures incurred in connection with its activities within that system which were rendered pursuant to paragraph (1) of this subsection.

Oct. 7, 1976 (544)

TITLE 16. CONSERVATION • CHAPTER 1: NATIONAL PARKS, MILITARY PARKS, MONUMENTS, AND SEASHORES • SUBCHAPTER I: NATIONAL PARK SERVICE

16 USC § 26. Regulations for hunting and fishing in park; punishment for violations; forfeitures

> The Gist: Any firearm used in hunting in Yellowstone National Park may be seized and held by the authorities. If the user is convicted, the firearm is forfeited to the Dept. of the Interior.
>
> This appears to be the oldest federal firearms statute on the books.

All hunting, or the killing, wounding, or capturing at any time of any bird or wild animal, except dangerous animals, when it is necessary to prevent them from destroying human life or inflicting an injury, is prohibited within the limits of said park; nor shall any fish be taken out of the waters of the park by means of seines, nets, traps, or by the use of drugs or any explosive substances or compounds, or in any other way than by hook and line, and then only at such seasons and in such times and manner as may be directed by the Secretary of the Interior. The Secretary of the Interior shall make and publish such rules and regulations as he may deem necessary and proper for the management and care of the park and for the protection of the property therein, especially for the preservation from injury or spoliation of all timber, mineral deposits, natural curiosities, or wonderful objects within said park; and for the protection of the animals and birds in the park, from capture or destruction, or to prevent their being frightened or driven from the park; and he shall make rules and regulations governing the taking of fish from the streams or lakes in the park. Possession within the said park of the dead bodies, or any part thereof, of any wild bird or animal shall be prima facie evidence that the person or persons having the same are guilty of violating this Act. <refers to "Act May 7, 1894"> Any person or persons, or stage or express company or railway company, receiving for transportation any of the said animals, birds, or fish so killed, taken, or caught shall be deemed guilty of a misdemeanor, and shall be fined for every such offense not exceeding $300. Any person found guilty of violating any of the provisions of this Act or any rule or regulation that may be promulgated by the Secretary of the Interior with reference to the management and care of the park, or for the protection of the property therein, for the preservation from injury or spoliation of timber, mineral deposits, natural curiosities, or wonderful objects within said park, or for the protection of the animals, birds, and fish in the said park, shall be deemed guilty of a misdemeanor, and shall be subjected to a fine of not more than $500 or imprisonment not exceeding six months, or both, and be adjudged to pay all costs of the proceedings.

All guns, traps, teams, horses, or means of transportation of every nature or description used by any person or persons within said park limits when engaged in killing, trapping, ensnaring, or capturing such wild beasts, birds, or wild animals shall be forfeited to the United States, and may be seized by the officers in said park and held pending the prosecution of any person or persons arrested under charge of violating the provisions of this Act, and upon conviction under this Act of such person or persons using said guns, traps, teams, horses, or other means of transportation such forfeiture shall be adjudicated as a penalty in addition to the other punishment provided in this Act. Such forfeited property shall be disposed of and accounted for by and under the authority of the Secretary of the Interior.

May 7, 1894 (547)
TITLE 16. CONSERVATION • CHAPTER 1: NATIONAL PARKS, MILITARY PARKS, MONUMENTS, AND SEASHORES • SUBCHAPTER V: YELLOWSTONE NATIONAL PARK

16 USC § 65. Seizure and forfeiture of guns, traps, teams, horses, etc.

The Gist: Any firearm used in hunting in Sequoia and Yosemite National Parks may be seized and held by the authorities. If the user is convicted, the firearm is forfeited to the Dept. of the Interior.

All guns, traps, teams, horses, or means of transportation of every nature or description used by any person or persons within the limits of said parks, or either of them, when engaged in killing, trapping, ensnaring, or capturing such wild beasts, birds, or animals, shall be forfeited to the United States and may be seized by the officers in said parks, or either of them, and held pending prosecution of any person or persons arrested under the charge of violating the provisions of sections 57, 58, and 60 to 65 of this title, and upon conviction such forfeiture shall be adjudicated as a penalty in addition to the other punishment prescribed therein. Such forfeited property shall be disposed of and accounted for by and under the authority of the Secretary of the Interior.

June 2, 1920 (133)
TITLE 16. CONSERVATION • CHAPTER 1: NATIONAL PARKS, MILITARY PARKS, MONUMENTS, AND SEASHORES • SUBCHAPTER VI: SEQUOIA AND YOSEMITE NATIONAL PARKS

16 USC § 99. Forfeitures and seizures of guns, traps, teams, etc.

The Gist: Any firearm used in hunting in Mount Rainier National Park may be seized and held by the authorities. If the user is convicted, the firearm is forfeited to the Dept. of the Interior.

All guns, traps, teams, horses, or means of transportation of every nature or description used by any person or persons within said park limits when engaged in killing, trapping, ensnaring, or capturing such wild beasts, birds, or animals shall be forfeited to the United States and may be seized by the officers in said park and held pending the prosecution of any person or persons arrested under charge of violating the provisions of this Act, and upon conviction under this Act of such person or persons using said guns, traps, teams, horses, or other means of transportation, such forfeiture shall be adjudicated as a penalty in addition to the other punishment provided in this Act. Such forfeited property shall be disposed of and accounted for by and under the authority of the Secretary of the Interior.

June 30, 1916 (136)
TITLE 16. CONSERVATION • CHAPTER 1: NATIONAL PARKS, MILITARY PARKS, MONUMENTS, AND SEASHORES • SUBCHAPTER XI: MOUNT RAINIER NATIONAL PARK

16 USC § 117d. Forfeiture of property used for unlawful purpose

> **The Gist:** Any firearm used in hunting in Mesa Verde National Park may be seized and held by the authorities. If the user is convicted, the firearm is forfeited to the Dept. of the Interior.

All guns, traps, teams, horses, or means of transportation of every nature or description used by any person or persons within said park limits when engaged in killing, trapping, ensnaring, or capturing such wild beasts, birds, or animals shall be forfeited to the United States and may be seized by the officers in said park and held pending the prosecution of any person or persons arrested under charge of violating the provisions of this Act, and upon conviction under this Act of such person or persons using said guns, traps, teams, horses, or other means of transportation, such forfeiture shall be adjudicated as a penalty in addition to the other punishment provided in this Act. Such forfeited property shall be disposed of and accounted for by and under the authority of the Secretary of the Interior.

Apr. 25, 1928 (136)

TITLE 16. CONSERVATION • CHAPTER 1: NATIONAL PARKS, MILITARY PARKS, MONUMENTS, AND SEASHORES • SUBCHAPTER XII: MESA VERDE NATIONAL PARK

16 USC § 128. Forfeitures or seizures of guns, traps, teams, etc., for violating regulations

> **The Gist:** Any firearm used in hunting in Wind Cave National Park may be seized and held by the authorities. If the user is convicted, the firearm is forfeited to the Dept. of the Interior.

All guns, traps, teams, horses, or means of transportation of every nature or description used by any person or persons within said park limits when engaged in killing, trapping, ensnaring, or capturing such wild beasts, birds, or animals shall be forfeited to the United States and may be seized by the officers in said park and held pending the prosecution of any person or persons arrested under charge of violating the provisions of this Act and upon conviction under this Act of such person or persons using said guns, traps, teams, horses, or other means of transportation, such forfeiture shall be adjudicated as a penalty in addition to the other punishment provided in this Act. Such forfeited property shall be disposed of and accounted for by and under the authority of the Secretary of the Interior.

Aug. 21, 1916 (136)

TITLE 16. CONSERVATION • CHAPTER 1. NATIONAL PARKS, MILITARY PARKS, MONUMENTS, AND SEASHORES • SUBCHAPTER XV: WIND CAVE NATIONAL PARK

16 USC § 171. Forfeitures and seizures of guns, traps, teams, etc.

> **The Gist:** Any firearm used in hunting in Glacier National Park may be seized and held by the authorities. If the user is convicted, the firearm is forfeited to the Dept. of the Interior.

All guns, traps, teams, horses, or means of transportation of every nature or description, used by any person or persons within said park limits when engaged in killing, trapping, ensnaring, or capturing such wild beasts, birds, or wild animals shall be forfeited to the United States and may be seized by the officers in said park and held pending the prosecution of any person or persons arrested under charge of violating the provisions of this Act, and upon conviction under this Act of such person or persons using said guns, traps, teams, horses, or other means of transportation, such forfeiture shall be adjudicated as a penalty in addition to the other punishment provided under this Act. Such forfeited property shall be disposed of and accounted for by and under the authority of the Secretary of the Interior.

Aug. 22, 1914 (137)

TITLE 16. CONSERVATION • CHAPTER 1: NATIONAL PARKS, MILITARY PARKS, MONUMENTS, AND SEASHORES • SUBCHAPTER XX: GLACIER NATIONAL PARK

16 USC § 198d. Forfeiture of property used in commission of offenses

> The Gist: Any firearm used in hunting in Rocky Mountain National Park may be seized and held by the authorities. If the user is convicted, the firearm is forfeited to the Dept. of the Interior.

All guns, traps, teams, horses, or means of transportation of every nature or description used by any person or persons within said park limits when engaged in killing, trapping, ensnaring, or capturing such wild beasts, birds, or animals shall be forfeited to the United States and may be seized by the officers in said park and held pending the prosecution of any person or persons arrested under charge of violating the provisions of this Act, and upon conviction under this Act of such person or persons using said guns, traps, teams, horses, or other means of transportation, such forfeiture shall be adjudicated as a penalty in addition to the other punishment provided in this Act. Such forfeited property shall be disposed of and accounted for by and under the authority of the Secretary of the Interior.

Mar. 2, 1929 (136)

TITLE 16. CONSERVATION • CHAPTER 1: NATIONAL PARKS, MILITARY PARKS, MONUMENTS, AND SEASHORES • SUBCHAPTER XXI: ROCKY MOUNTAIN NATIONAL PARK

16 USC § 204d. Forfeiture of property used for unlawful purposes

> The Gist: Any firearm used in hunting in Lassen Volcanic National Park may be seized and held by the authorities. If the user is convicted, the firearm is forfeited to the Dept. of the Interior.

All guns, traps, teams, horses, or means of transportation of every nature or description, used by any person or persons within the limits of said park when engaged in killing, trapping, ensnaring, or capturing such wild beasts, birds, or animals, shall be forfeited to the United States and may be seized by the officers in said park, and held pending prosecution of any person or persons arrested under the charge of violating the provisions of this Act, and upon conviction under this Act of such person or persons using said guns, traps, teams, horses, or other means of transportation, such forfeiture shall be adjudicated as a penalty in addition to the other punishment prescribed in this Act. Such forfeited property shall be disposed of and accounted for by and under the authority of the Secretary of the Interior.

Apr. 26, 1928 (138)

TITLE 16. CONSERVATION • CHAPTER 1: NATIONAL PARKS, MILITARY PARKS, MONUMENTS, AND SEASHORES • SUBCHAPTER XXII: LASSEN VOLCANIC NATIONAL PARK

16 USC § 256c. Forfeiture of property used in hunting, fishing, etc.

> The Gist: Any firearm illegally used in hunting in Olympic National Park may be seized and held by the authorities. If the user is convicted, the firearm is forfeited to the Dept. of the Interior.

All guns, bows, traps, nets, seines, fishing tackle, clothing, teams, horses, machinery, logging equipment, motor vehicles, aircraft, boats, or means of transportation of every nature or description used by any person or persons or organizations within the limits of the park when engaged in or attempting to engage in killing, trapping, ensnaring, taking or capturing such wild birds, fish or animals, or taking, destroying or damaging such trees, plants, or mineral deposits contrary to the provisions of this Act or the rules and regulations promulgated by the Secretary of the Interior shall be forfeited to the United States and may be seized by the officers in the park and held pending prosecution of any person or persons or organization arrested under or charged with violating the provisions of this Act, and upon conviction under this Act of such persons or organizations using said guns, bows, traps, nets, selnes, fishing tackle, clothing, teams, horses, machinery, logging equipment, motor vehicles, aircraft, boats, or other means of transportation of every nature and description used by any person or persons or organization, such forfeiture shall be adjudicated as a penalty in addition to the other punishment prescribed in this Act. Such forfeited property shall be disposed of and accounted for by and under the authority of the Secretary of the Interior: Provided, That the forfeiture of teams, horses, machinery, logging equipment, motor vehicles, aircraft, boats, or other means of transportation shall be in the discretion of the Court.

Mar. 6, 1942 (244)

TITLE 16. CONSERVATION • CHAPTER 1: NATIONAL PARKS, MILITARY PARKS, MONUMENTS, AND SEASHORES • SUBCHAPTER XXVII: OLYMPIC NATIONAL PARK

16 USC § 395d. Forfeiture of property used for unlawful purposes

The Gist: Any firearm used in hunting in Hawaii National Park may be seized and held by the authorities. If the user is convicted, the firearm is forfeited to the Dept. of the Interior.

All guns, traps, teams, horses, or means of transportation of every nature or description used by any person or persons within said park limits when engaged in killing, trapping, ensnaring, or capturing such wild beasts, birds, or animals shall be forfeited to the United States and may be seized by the officers in said park and held pending the prosecution of any person or persons arrested under charge of violating the provisions of this Act, and upon conviction under this Act of such person or persons using said guns, traps, teams, horses, or other means of transportation, such forfeiture shall be adjudicated as a penalty in addition to the other punishment provided in this Act. Such forfeited property shall be disposed of and accounted for by and under the authority of the Secretary of the Interior.

Apr. 19, 1930 (136)

TITLE 16. CONSERVATION • CHAPTER 1: NATIONAL PARKS, MILITARY PARKS, MONUMENTS, AND SEASHORES • SUBCHAPTER XLI: HAWAII NATIONAL PARK

16 USC § 403c-4. Forfeiture of property used in commission of offenses

The Gist: Any firearm used in hunting in Shenandoah or Great Smoky Mountains National Park may be seized and held by the authorities. If the user is convicted, the firearm is forfeited to the Dept. of the Interior.

All guns, traps, nets, seines, teams, horses, or means of transportation of every nature or description, used by any person or persons within the limits of said park when engaged in killing, trapping, ensnaring, taking, or capturing such wild beasts, birds, fish, or animals, shall be forfeited to the United States and may be seized by the officers in said park and held pending prosecution of any person or persons arrested under the charge of violating the provisions of this Act, and upon conviction under this Act of such person or persons using said guns, traps, nets, seines, teams, horses, or other means of transportation, such forfeiture shall be adjudicated as a penalty in addition to the other punishment prescribed in this Act. Such forfeited property shall be disposed of and accounted for by and under the authority of the Secretary of the Interior.

Aug. 19, 1937 (144)

TITLE 16. CONSERVATION • CHAPTER 1: NATIONAL PARKS, MILITARY PARKS, MONUMENTS, AND SEASHORES • SUBCHAPTER XLVI: SHENANDOAH NATIONAL PARK AND GREAT SMOKY MOUNTAINS NATIONAL PARK

16 USC § 403h-4. Forfeiture of property used in commission of offenses

The Gist: Similar to the requirements of 16–403c 4, above, this section includes firearms forfeiture in Shenandoah or Great Smoky Mountains National Park for hunting in violation of this act or any Dept. of the Interior rule or regulation, and allocates any proceeds to the U.S. Treasury.

All guns, traps, nets, seines, fishing tackle, teams, horses, or means of transportation of every nature or description used by any person or persons within the limits of said park when engaged in killing, trapping, ensnaring, taking, or capturing such wild birds, fish, or animals contrary to the provisions of this Act or the rules and regulations promulgated by the Secretary of the Interior, shall be forfeited to the United States and may be seized by the officers in said park and held pending prosecution of any person or persons arrested under the charge of violating the provisions of this Act, and upon conviction under this Act of such person or persons using said guns, traps, nets, seines, fishing tackle, teams, horses, or other means of transportation, such forfeiture shall be adjudicated as a penalty in addition to the other punishment prescribed in this Act. Such forfeited property shall be disposed of and accounted for by and under the authority of the Secretary of the Interior and the proceeds paid into the Treasury of the United States: Provided, That the forfeiture of teams, horses, or other means of transportation shall be in the discretion of the court.

Apr. 29, 1942 (197)

TITLE 16. CONSERVATION • CHAPTER 1: NATIONAL PARKS, MILITARY PARKS, MONUMENTS, AND SEASHORES • SUBCHAPTER XLVI: SHENANDOAH NATIONAL PARK AND GREAT SMOKY MOUNTAINS NATIONAL PARK

16 USC § 404c-4. Forfeiture of property used in commission of offenses

The Gist: Any firearm used in hunting in violation of this act or any other Dept. of the Interior rule or regulation, in Mammoth Cave National Park, may be seized and held by the authorities. If the user is convicted, the firearm is forfeited to the Dept. of the Interior.

All guns, traps, nets, seines, fishing tackle, teams, horses, or means of transportation of every nature or description used by any person or persons within the limits of the park when engaged in killing, trapping, ensnaring, taking, or capturing such wild birds, fish, or animals contrary to the provisions of this Act or the rules and regulations promulgated by the Secretary of the Interior shall be forfeited to the United States and may be seized by the officers in the park and held pending prosecution of any person or persons arrested under the charge of violating the provisions of this Act, and upon conviction under this Act of such person or persons using said guns, traps, nets, seines, fishing tackle, teams, horses, or other means of transportation, such forfeiture shall be adjudicated as a penalty in addition to the other punishment prescribed in this Act. Such forfeited property shall be disposed of and accounted for by and under the authority of the Secretary of the Interior: Provided, That the forfeiture of teams, horses, or other means of transportation shall be in the discretion of the court.

June 5, 1942 (186)
TITLE 16. CONSERVATION • CHAPTER 1: NATIONAL PARKS, MILITARY PARKS, MONUMENTS, AND SEASHORES • SUBCHAPTER XLVII: MAMMOTH CAVE NATIONAL PARK

16 USC § 408l. Forfeiture of property used in hunting, fishing, etc. <the section number is 408 "L">

> The Gist: Any firearm used in hunting in Isle Royale National Park, in violation of this act or any Dept. of the Interior regulation in the park, may be seized and held by the authorities. If the user is convicted, the firearm is forfeited to the United States.

All guns, traps, nets, seines, fishing tackle, teams, horses, or means of transportation of every nature or description used by any person or persons within the limits of said park when engaged in killing, trapping, ensnaring, taking, or capturing such wild birds, fish, or animals contrary to the provisions of this Act <16 USC § 408i et seq.> or the rules and regulations promulgated by the Secretary of the Interior, shall be forfeited to the United States and may be seized by the officers in said park and held pending prosecution of any person or persons arrested under the charge of violating the provisions of this Act, and upon conviction under this Act of such person or persons using said guns, traps, nets, seines, fishing tackle, teams, horses, or other means of transportation, such forfeiture shall be adjudicated as a penalty in addition to the other punishment prescribed in this Act. Such forfeited property shall be disposed of and accounted for by and under the authority of the Secretary of the Interior: Provided, That the forfeiture of teams, horses, or other means of transportation shall be in the discretion of the court.

Mar. 6, 1942 (195)
TITLE 16. CONSERVATION • CHAPTER 1: NATIONAL PARKS, MILITARY PARKS, MONUMENTS, AND SEASHORES • SUBCHAPTER LII: ISLE ROYALE NATIONAL PARK

16 USC § 410y-3. Access

> The Gist: People may cross the Chesapeake and Ohio Canal National Park on foot to get to the Potomac River or non-federal hunting areas, for the purpose of hunting, but their firearms must be unloaded.

(a) Pre-existing rights and permits
The enactment of this subchapter shall not affect adversely any valid rights heretofore existing, or any valid permits heretofore issued, within or relating to areas authorized for inclusion in the park.
(b) Issuance of permits by Secretary for use of park lands and utility, highway, and railway crossings
Other uses of park lands, and utility, highway, and railway crossings, may be authorized under permit by the Secretary, if such uses and crossings are not in conflict with the purposes of the park and are in accord with any requirements found necessary to preserve park values.
(c) Crossing by foot at designated locations; purposes; conduct
Authority is hereby granted for individuals to cross the park by foot at locations designated by the Secretary for the purpose of gaining access to the Potomac River or to non-Federal lands for hunting purposes: Provided, That while such

individuals are within the boundaries of the park firearms shall be unloaded, bows
unstrung, and dogs on leash.

Jan. 8, 1971 (168)
TITLE 16. CONSERVATION • CHAPTER 1: NATIONAL PARKS, MILITARY PARKS, MONUMENTS, AND
SEASHORES • SUBCHAPTER LVI: CHESAPEAKE AND OHIO CANAL NATIONAL HISTORICAL PARK

16 USC § 425. Fredericksburg and Spotsylvania County Battle Fields Memorial; establishment

The Gist: This law establishes a national military park to commemorate
certain battles of the Civil War.

Section 16-425 helps demonstrate the difficulties in determining what
constitutes a "gun law." Under this law, certain historical *gun
emplacements* are protected. Gun emplacements are typically immovable
structures made of stone and cement and wood. Is this a gun law? The
question is complicated by an indexing error in a published edition of this
law, which refers mistakenly to *gun implements*. Index and cross-
reference errors occur with some frequency in published law, and can
result in finding irrelevant or nearly irrelevant entries, and, perhaps more
important, it leads to overlooked entries which would be relevant and
included if found.

As a matter of policy, laws related to deadly weapons are included, even
if they don't specifically mention firearms, and would therefore include a
wide variety of things that firearms laws *per se* would not. Explosives, a
word generally used in the sense of demolition supplies, can and
specifically does in many cases include ammunition and its components,
leading to inclusion of many statutes outside a narrow definition of
firearms law.

In some cases, a law or paragraphs within a law are not truly related to
firearms but are so close it might interest readers. The editorial policy is to
lean toward inclusion, which means you may find portions that you, with
the editor's cursor in hand, would not have included. Anyone identifying
a relevant federal gun law that is missing from this book is encouraged to
notify the publisher.

In order to commemorate the Civil War battles of Fredericksburg, Spotsylvania Court
House, Wilderness, and Chancellorsville, including Salem Church, all located at or
near Fredericksburg, Virginia, and to mark and preserve for historical purposes the
breastworks, earthworks, gun emplacements, walls, or other defenses or shelters
used by the armies in said battles, so far as the marking and preservation of the
same are practicable, the land herein authorized to be acquired, or so much thereof
as may be taken, and the highways and approaches herein authorized to be
constructed, are declared to be a national military park to be known as the
Fredericksburg and Spotsylvania County Battle Fields Memorial whenever the title
to the same shall have been acquired by the United States, the said land so to be
acquired being the land necessary for a park of the plan indicated on the index map
sheet filed with the report of the Battle Field Commission appointed pursuant to an
Act entitled "An Act to provide for the inspection of the battle fields in and around
Fredericksburg and Spotsylvania Court House, Virginia," approved on the 7th day
of June 1924, said index map sheet being referred to in said report, and particularly
in the "Combined Plan—Antietam system," described in said report, the first of the
plans mentioned in said report under the heading "Combined Plan—Antietam

system" being the plan which is adopted, the said land herein authorized to be acquired being such land as the Secretary of the Interior may deem necessary to establish a park on the combined plan, Antietam system, above referred to, the particular boundaries of such land to be fixed by surveys made previous to the attempt to acquire the same, and authority is given to the Secretary of the Interior to acquire for the purposes of sections 425 to 425j of this title the land above mentioned, or so much thereof as he may deem necessary, together with all such existing breastworks, earthworks, gun emplacements, walls, defenses, shelters, or other historical points as the Secretary of the Interior may deem necessary, whether shown on said index map sheet or not, and together also with such additional land as the Secretary of the Interior may deem necessary for monuments, markers, tablets, roads, highways, paths, approaches, and to carry out the general purposes of said sections. As title is acquired to parts of the land herein authorized to be acquired, the Secretary of the Interior may proceed with the establishment of the park upon such portions so acquired, and the remaining portions of the lands desired shall be respectively brought within said park as titles to said portions are severally acquired.

Feb. 14, 1927 (445)

TITLE 16. CONSERVATION • CHAPTER 1: NATIONAL PARKS, MILITARY PARKS, MONUMENTS, AND SEASHORES • SUBCHAPTER LX: NATIONAL MILITARY PARKS

16 USC § 559c. Powers of special agents and law enforcement officers of Forest Service

The Gist: Special agents and law enforcement officers of the Forest Service may be authorized to carry firearms. In an unprecedented requirement, the Forest Service is prohibited from authorizing more than 1,000 people to carry firearms.

For the purposes of sections 559b to 559g of this title, if specifically designated by the Secretary and specially trained, not to exceed 1,000 special agents and law enforcement officers of the Forest Service when in the performance of their duties shall have authority to—
(1) carry firearms

Oct. 27, 1986 (49)

TITLE 16. CONSERVATION • CHAPTER 3: FORESTS; FOREST SERVICE; REFORESTATION; MANAGEMENT • SUBCHAPTER I: GENERAL PROVISIONS

16 USC § 669c. Apportionment of funds; expenses of Secretary

The Gist: A portion of any tax on pistols, revolvers and bows and arrows is divided among the states within 60 days of the end of the fiscal year (October 1), by the Secretary of the Interior. The division of monies is based on a complex ratio of land area of the states, and hunter licenses issued, as certified by state game and fish departments. Prior to 2000, the division was based simply on population. No state may receive less than 1/2% or more than 5% of the funds available. A formula for limiting the amount that government may spend on its administrative costs is included. Monies that go into the Federal Aid to Wildlife Restoration Fund are apportioned under a separate complex formula, which is described. States that apply for monies from Federal Aid to Wildlife Restoration Fund must comply with detailed requirements, run by the state's game and fish department, for wildlife management, restoration, conservation, education, recreation projects, public input, strategy, reporting, use and periodic updates.

Allocation and apportionment of available amounts
(a) Set-aside for expenses for administration of this chapter
(1) In general
(A) Set-aside—For fiscal year 2001 and each fiscal year thereafter, of the revenues (excluding interest accruing under section 669b(b) of this title) covered into the fund for the fiscal year, the Secretary of the Interior may use not more than the available amount specified in subparagraph (B) for the fiscal year for expenses for administration incurred in implementation of this chapter, in accordance with this subsection and section 669h of this title.
(B) Available amounts—The available amount referred to in subparagraph (A) is—
(i) for each of fiscal years 2001 and 2002, $9,000,000;
(ii) for fiscal year 2003, $8,212,000; and
(iii) for fiscal year 2004 and each fiscal year thereafter, the sum of—
(I) the available amount for the preceding fiscal year; and
(II) the amount determined by multiplying—
(aa) the available amount for the preceding fiscal year; and
(bb) the change, relative to the preceding fiscal year, in the Consumer Price Index for All Urban Consumers published by the Department of Labor.
(2) Period of availability; apportionment of unobligated amounts
(A) Period of availability—For each fiscal year, the available amount under paragraph (1) shall remain available for obligation for use under that paragraph until the end of the fiscal year.
(B) Apportionment of unobligated amounts—Not later than 60 days after the end of a fiscal year, the Secretary of the Interior shall apportion among the States any of the available amount under paragraph (1) that remains unobligated at the end of the fiscal year, on the same basis and in the same manner as other amounts made available under this chapter are apportioned among the States for the fiscal year.
(b) Apportionment to States
The Secretary of the Interior, after deducting the available amount under subsection (a) of this section, the amount apportioned under subsection (c) of this section, any amount apportioned under section 669g-1 of this title, and amounts provided as grants under sections 669h-1 and 669h-2 of this title, shall apportion the remainder of the revenue in said fund for each fiscal year among the several States in the following manner:
One-half in the ratio which the area of each State bears to the total area of all the States, and one-half in the ratio which the number of paid hunting-license holders of each State in the second fiscal year preceding the fiscal year for which such apportionment is made, as certified to said Secretary by the State fish and game departments, bears to the total number of paid hunting-license holders of all the States. Such apportionments shall be adjusted equitably so that no State shall receive less than one-half of 1 per centum nor more than 5 per centum of the total amount apportioned. The term fiscal year as used in this chapter shall be a period of twelve consecutive months from October 1 through the succeeding September 30, except that the period for enumeration of paid hunting-license holders shall be a State's fiscal or license year.
(c) Apportionment of certain taxes
One-half of the revenues accruing to the fund under this chapter each fiscal year (beginning with the fiscal year 1975) from any tax imposed on pistols, revolvers, bows, and arrows shall be apportioned among the States in proportion to the ratio that the population of each State bears to the population of all the States: Provided, That each State shall be apportioned not more than 3 per centum and not less than 1 per centum of such revenues and Guam, the Virgin Islands, American Samoa, Puerto Rico, and the Northern Mariana Islands shall each be apportioned one-sixth of 1 per centum of such revenues. For the purpose of this subsection, population shall be determined on the basis of the latest decennial census for which figures are available, as certified by the Secretary of Commerce.
(c) Apportionment of Wildlife Conservation and Restoration Account <Enacted with two subsections "(c)">
(1) The Secretary of the Interior shall make the following apportionment from the Wildlife Conservation and Restoration Account:

(A) to the District of Columbia and to the Commonwealth of Puerto Rico, each a sum equal to not more than one-half of 1 percent thereof.

(B) to Guam, American Samoa, the Virgin Islands, and the Commonwealth of the Northern Mariana Islands, each a sum equal to not more than one-fourth of 1 percent thereof.

(2)(A) The Secretary of the Interior, after making the apportionment under paragraph (1), shall apportion the remaining amount in the Wildlife Conservation and Restoration Account for each fiscal year among the States in the following manner:

(i) one-third of which is based on the ratio to which the land area of such State bears to the total land area of all such States; and

(ii) two-thirds of which is based on the ratio to which the population of such State bears to the total population of all such States.

(B) The amounts apportioned under this paragraph shall be adjusted equitably so that no such State shall be apportioned a sum which is less than one percent of the amount available for apportionment under this paragraph for any fiscal year or more than five percent of such amount.

(3) Of the amounts transferred to the Wildlife Conservation and Restoration Account, not to exceed 3 percent shall be available for any Federal expenses incurred in the administration and execution of programs carried out with such amounts.

(d) Wildlife conservation and restoration programs

(1) Any State, through its fish and wildlife department, may apply to the Secretary of the Interior for approval of a wildlife conservation and restoration program, or for funds from the Wildlife Conservation and Restoration Account, to develop a program. To apply, a State shall submit a comprehensive plan that includes—

(A) provisions vesting in the fish and wildlife department of the State overall responsibility and accountability for the program;

(B) provisions for the development and implementation of—

(i) wildlife conservation projects that expand and support existing wildlife programs, giving appropriate consideration to all wildlife;

(ii) wildlife-associated recreation projects; and

(iii) wildlife conservation education projects pursuant to programs under section 669g(a) of this title; and

(C) provisions to ensure public participation in the development, revision, and implementation of projects and programs required under this paragraph.

(D) Wildlife conservation strategy.—Within five years of the date of the initial apportionment, develop and begin implementation of a wildlife conservation strategy based upon the best available and appropriate scientific information and data that—

(i) uses such information on the distribution and abundance of species of wildlife, including low population and declining species as the State fish and wildlife department deems appropriate, that are indicative of the diversity and health of wildlife of the State;

(ii) identifies the extent and condition of wildlife habitats and community types essential to conservation of species identified under paragraph (1);

(iii) identifies the problems which may adversely affect the species identified under paragraph (1) or their habitats, and provides for priority research and surveys to identify factors which may assist in restoration and more effective conservation of such species and their habitats;

(iv) determines those actions which should be taken to conserve the species identified under paragraph (1) and their habitats and establishes priorities for implementing such conservation actions;

(v) provides for periodic monitoring of species identified under paragraph (1) and their habitats and the effectiveness of the conservation actions determined under paragraph (4), and for adapting conservation actions as appropriate to respond to now information or changing conditions;

(vi) provides for the review of the State wildlife conservation strategy and, if appropriate, revision at intervals of not more than ten years;

(vii) provides for coordination to the extent feasible the State fish and wildlife department, during the development, implementation, review, and revision of the wildlife conservation strategy, with Federal, State, and local agencies and Indian tribes that manage significant areas of land or water within the State, or administer programs that significantly affect the conservation of species identified under paragraph (1) or their habitats.

(2) A State shall provide an opportunity for public participation in the development of the comprehensive plan required under paragraph (1).

(3) If the Secretary finds that the comprehensive plan submitted by a State complies with paragraph (1), the Secretary shall approve the wildlife conservation and restoration program of the State and set aside from the apportionment to the State made pursuant to subsection (c) of this section an amount that shall not exceed 75 percent of the estimated cost of developing and implementing the program.

(4)(A) Except as provided in subparagraph (B), after the Secretary approves a State's wildlife conservation and restoration program, the Secretary may make payments on a project that is a segment of the State's wildlife conservation and restoration program as the project progresses. Such payments, including previous payments on the project, if any, shall not be more than the United States pro rata share of such project. The Secretary, under such regulations as he may prescribe, may advance funds representing the United States pro rata share of a project that is a segment of a wildlife conservation and restoration program, including funds to develop such program.

(B) Not more than 10 percent of the amounts apportioned to each State under this section for a State's wildlife conservation and restoration program may be used for wildlife-associated recreation.

(5) For purposes of this subsection, the term "State" shall include the District of Columbia, the Commonwealth of Puerto Rico, the Virgin Islands, Guam, American Samoa, and the Commonwealth of the Northern Mariana Islands.

Sept. 2, 1937 (1,600)
TITLE 16. CONSERVATION • CHAPTER 5B: WILDLIFE RESTORATION

16 USC § 670j. Enforcement provisions

> The Gist: To enforce the provisions against hunting on certain restricted public lands, Dept. of Interior and Dept. of Agriculture employees, and certain state employees, may be allowed to carry firearms. Any firearm used in violating the hunting restrictions may be seized and held by the authorities. If the user is convicted, the firearm is forfeited to the United States.

(a) Violations and penalties

(1) Any person who hunts, traps, or fishes on any public land which is subject to a conservation and rehabilitation program implemented under this subchapter without having on his person a valid public land management area stamp, if the possession of such a stamp is required, shall be fined not more than $1,000, or imprisoned for not more than six months, or both.

(2) Any person who knowingly violates or fails to comply with any regulations prescribed under section 670h(c)(5) of this title shall be fined not more than $500, or imprisoned not more than six months, or both.

(b) Designation of enforcement personnel powers; issuance of arrest warrants; trial and sentencing by United States magistrates

(1) For the purpose of enforcing subsection (a) of this section, the Secretary of the Interior and the Secretary of Agriculture may designate any employee of their respective departments, and any State officer or employee authorized under a cooperative agreement to enforce subsection (a) of this section, to

(i) carry firearms;

(ii) execute and serve any warrant or other process issued by a court or officer of competent jurisdiction;

(iii) make arrests without warrant or process for a misdemeanor he has reasonable grounds to believe is being committed in his presence or view;

(iv) search without warrant or process any person, place, or conveyance as provided by law; and

(v) seize without warrant or process any evidentiary item as provided by law.

(2) Upon the sworn information by a competent person, any United States magistrate or court of competent jurisdiction may issue process for the arrest of any person charged with committing any offense under subsection (a) of this section.

(3) Any person charged with committing any offense under subsection (a) of this section may be tried and sentenced by any United States magistrate designated for that purpose by the court by which he was appointed, in the same manner and subject to the same conditions as provided for in section 3401 of Title 18.

(c) Seizure and forfeiture of equipment and vessels

All guns, traps, nets, and other equipment, vessels, vehicles, and other means of transportation used by any person when engaged in committing an offense under subsection (a) of this section shall be subject to forfeiture to the United States and may be seized and held pending the prosecution of any person arrested for committing such offense. Upon conviction for such offense, such forfeiture may be adjudicated as a penalty in addition to any other provided for committing such offense.

Oct. 18, 1974 (425)

TITLE 16. CONSERVATION • CHAPTER 5C: CONSERVATION PROGRAMS ON GOVERNMENT LANDS • SUBCHAPTER II: CONSERVATION PROGRAMS ON PUBLIC LANDS

16 USC § 809. Temporary use by Government of project works for national safety; compensation for use

> The Gist: The United States may, in time of crisis, take possession of a project licensed under this chapter (Chapter 12), to make nitrates, explosives, war munitions or for any other purpose involving the safety of the nation. The government must return control and pay reasonable compensation when the crisis is ended.

When in the opinion of the President of the United States, evidenced by a written order addressed to the holder of any license under this chapter, the safety of the United States demands it, the United States shall have the right to enter upon and take possession of any project, or part thereof, constructed, maintained, or operated under said license, for the purpose of manufacturing nitrates, explosives, or munitions of war, or for any other purpose involving the safety of the United States, to retain possession, management, and control thereof for such length of time as may appear to the President to be necessary to accomplish said purposes, and then to restore possession and control to the party or parties entitled thereto; and in the event that the United States shall exercise such right it shall pay to the party or parties entitled thereto just and fair compensation for the use of said property as may be fixed by the commission upon the basis of a reasonable profit in time of peace, and the cost of restoring said property to as good condition as existed at the time of the taking over thereof, less the reasonable value of any improvements that may be made thereto by the United States and which are valuable and serviceable to the licensee.

June 10, 1920 (218)

TITLE 16. CONSERVATION • CHAPTER 12: FEDERAL REGULATION AND DEVELOPMENT OF POWER • SUBCHAPTER I: REGULATION OF DEVELOPMENT OF WATER POWER AND RESOURCES

16 USC § 1153. Sealing permitted by Aleuts, Eskimos, and Indians

> The Gist: Certain natives of the North Pacific coast may take fur seals for subsistence, from traditional canoes with five people or less, not under contract, as they always had before this law, without firearms.

(a) Indians, Aleuts, and Eskimos who dwell on the coasts of the North Pacific Ocean are permitted to take fur seals and dispose of their skins after the skins have been officially marked and certified by a person authorized by the Secretary: Provided, That the seals are taken for subsistence uses as defined in section 1379(f)(2) of this title, and only in canoes not transported by or used in connection with other vessels, and propelled entirely by oars, paddles, or sails, and manned by not more than five persons each, in the way hitherto practiced and without the use of firearms. This authority shall not apply to Indians, Aleuts, and Eskimos while they are employed by any person for the purpose of taking fur seals or are under contract to deliver the skins to any person.

Nov. 2, 1966 (138)
TITLE 16. CONSERVATION • CHAPTER 24: CONSERVATION AND PROTECTION OF NORTH PACIFIC FUR SEALS • SUBCHAPTER I: FUR SEAL MANAGEMENT

16 USC § 2409. Enforcement

> The Gist: Any firearm used in violating the Antarctic Conservation law may be seized and held by the authorities. If the user is convicted, the firearm is forfeited to the United States.

(d) Forfeiture
(2) All guns, traps, nets, and other equipment, vessels, vehicles, aircraft, and other means of transportation used in the commission of any act prohibited by section 2403(a) of this title shall be subject to forfeiture to the United States.

Oct. 28, 1978 (42)
TITLE 16. CONSERVATION • CHAPTER 44: ANTARCTIC CONSERVATION

16 USC § 3375. Enforcement

> The Gist: The Departments of the Interior, Transportation and the Treasury may authorize anyone in federal or state government, or from any Indian tribe, to carry firearms to enforce the laws in this chapter, which relate to fish and wildlife (Chapter 53).

(a) In general
The provisions of this chapter and any regulations issued pursuant thereto shall be enforced by the Secretary, the Secretary of Transportation, or the Secretary of the Treasury. Such Secretary may utilize by agreement, with or without reimbursement, the personnel, services, and facilities of any other Federal agency or any State agency or Indian tribe for purposes of enforcing this chapter.
(b) Powers
Any person authorized under subsection (a) of this section to enforce this chapter may carry firearms

Nov. 16, 1981 (81)
TITLE 16. CONSERVATION • CHAPTER 53: CONTROL OF ILLEGALLY TAKEN FISH AND WILDLIFE

Title 18 • Crimes and Criminal Procedure

18 USC § 13. Laws of states adopted for areas within federal jurisdiction

> **The Gist:** If a person commits a crime on federal land within a state, and no federal penalties exist for the crime, then the law of the state is used by federal authorities to determine the offense and set punishment. This is known as the Assimilative Crimes Act. Increased penalties are provided for certain offenses. In 1996, the physical boundaries of the U.S. were described in greater detail, encompassing a greater area—"territorial seas" in (a), and all of (c).

(a) Whoever within or upon any of the places now existing or hereafter reserved or acquired as provided in section 7 of this title, or on, above, or below any portion of the territorial sea of the United States not within the jurisdiction of any State, Commonwealth, territory, possession, or district is guilty of any act or omission which, although not made punishable by any enactment of Congress, would be punishable if committed or omitted within the jurisdiction of the State, Territory, Possession, or District in which such place is situated, by the laws thereof in force at the time of such act or omission, shall be guilty of a like offense and subject to a like punishment.

(b)(1) Subject to paragraph (2) and for purposes of subsection (a) of this section, that which may or shall be imposed through judicial or administrative action under the law of a State, territory, possession, or district, for a conviction for operating a motor vehicle under the influence of a drug or alcohol, shall be considered to be a punishment provided by that law. Any limitation on the right or privilege to operate a motor vehicle imposed under this subsection shall apply only to the special maritime and territorial jurisdiction of the United States.

(2)(A) In addition to any term of imprisonment provided for operating a motor vehicle under the influence of a drug or alcohol imposed under the law of a State, territory, possession, or district, the punishment for such an offense under this section shall include an additional term of imprisonment of not more than 1 year, or if serious bodily injury of a minor is caused, not more than 5 years, or if death of a minor is caused, not more than 10 years, and an additional fine under this title, or both, if—

(i) a minor (other than the offender) was present in the motor vehicle when the offense was committed; and

(ii) the law of the State, territory, possession, or district in which the offense occurred does not provide an additional term of imprisonment under the circumstances described in clause (i).

(B) For the purposes of subparagraph (A), the term "minor" means a person less than 18 years of age.

(c) Whenever any waters of the territorial sea of the United States lie outside the territory of any State, Commonwealth, territory, possession, or district, such waters (including the airspace above and the seabed and subsoil below, and artificial islands and fixed structures erected thereon) shall be deemed, for purposes of subsection (a), to lie within the area of the State, Commonwealth, territory, possession, or district that it would lie within if the boundaries of such State, Commonwealth, territory, possession, or district were extended seaward to the outer limit of the territorial sea of the United States.

June 25, 1948 (470)
TITLE 18. CRIMES AND CRIMINAL PROCEDURE • PART I: CRIMES • CHAPTER 1: GENERAL PROVISIONS

18 USC § 111. Assaulting, resisting, or impeding certain officers or employees

> The Gist: An increased penalty is provided for using a deadly weapon (including a weapon that won't operate due to a defective part) to assault or interfere with special classes of proper authorities (described in 18–1114) while they are performing official duties.

(a) In general.—Whoever—
(1) forcibly assaults, resists, opposes, impedes, intimidates, or interferes with any person designated in section 1114 of this title while engaged in or on account of the performance of official duties; or
(2) forcibly assaults or intimidates any person who formerly served as a person designated in section 1114 on account of the performance of official duties during such person's term of service, shall, where the acts in violation of this section constitute only simple assault, be fined under this title or imprisoned not more than one year, or both, and in all other cases, be fined under this title or imprisoned not more than 8 years, or both.
(b) Enhanced penalty.—Whoever, in the commission of any acts described in subsection (a), uses a deadly or dangerous weapon (including a weapon intended to cause death or danger but that fails to do so by reason of a defective component) or inflicts bodily injury, shall be fined under this title or imprisoned not more than ten years, or both.

June 25, 1948 (173)
TITLE 18. CRIMES AND CRIMINAL PROCEDURE • PART I: CRIMES • CHAPTER 7: ASSAULT

18 USC § 112. Protection of foreign officials, official guests, and internationally protected persons

> The Gist: An increased penalty is provided for using a deadly weapon against foreign dignitaries and (added in 1996) nationals of the United States.

(a) Whoever assaults, strikes, wounds, imprisons, or offers violence to a foreign official, official guest, or internationally protected person or makes any other violent attack upon the person or liberty of such person, or, if likely to endanger his person or liberty, makes a violent attack upon his official premises, private accommodation, or means of transport or attempts to commit any of the foregoing shall be fined under this title or imprisoned not more than three years, or both. Whoever in the commission of any such act uses a deadly or dangerous weapon, or inflicts bodily injury, shall be fined under this title or imprisoned not more than ten years, or both.
(c) For the purpose of this section "foreign government", "foreign official", "internationally protected person", "international organization", national of the United States and "official guest" shall have the same meanings as those provided in section 1116(b) of this title.

June 25, 1948 (146)
TITLE 18. CRIMES AND CRIMINAL PROCEDURE • PART I: CRIMES • CHAPTER 7: ASSAULT

18 USC § 231. Civil disorders

> The Gist: Making, transporting or teaching someone to make or use firearms, knowing they will be used for a civil disorder which interferes with commerce or any other federal function, is illegal.

(a)(1) Whoever teaches or demonstrates to any other person the use, application, or making of any firearm or explosive or incendiary device, or technique capable of causing injury or death to persons, knowing or having reason to know or intending that the same will be unlawfully employed for use in, or in furtherance of, a civil disorder which may in any way or degree obstruct, delay, or adversely affect commerce or the movement of any article or commodity in commerce or the conduct or performance of any federally protected function; or

(2) Whoever transports or manufactures for transportation in commerce any firearm, or explosive or incendiary device, knowing or having reason to know or intending that the same will be used unlawfully in furtherance of a civil disorder; or

(3) Whoever commits or attempts to commit any act to obstruct, impede, or interfere with any fireman or law enforcement officer lawfully engaged in the lawful performance of his official duties incident to and during the commission of a civil disorder which in any way or degree obstructs, delays, or adversely affects commerce or the movement of any article or commodity in commerce or the conduct or performance of any federally protected function—

Shall be fined under this title or imprisoned not more than five years, or both.

(b) Nothing contained in this section shall make unlawful any act of any law enforcement officer which is performed in the lawful performance of his official duties.

Apr. 11, 1968 (245)
TITLE 18. CRIMES AND CRIMINAL PROCEDURE • PART I: CRIMES • CHAPTER 12: CIVIL DISORDERS

18 USC § 232. Definitions

> The Gist: The terms used in 18–231, above, are defined.

For purposes of this chapter:

(1) The term "**civil disorder**" means any public disturbance involving acts of violence by assemblages of three or more persons, which causes an immediate danger of or results in damage or injury to the property or person of any other individual.

(2) The term "**commerce**" means commerce (A) between any State or the District of Columbia and any place outside thereof; (B) between points within any State or the District of Columbia, but through any place outside thereof; or (C) wholly within the District of Columbia.

(3) The term "**federally protected function**" means any function, operation, or action carried out, under the laws of the United States, by any department, agency, or instrumentality of the United States or by an officer or employee thereof; and such term shall specifically include, but not be limited to, the collection and distribution of the United States mails.

(4) The term "**firearm**" means any weapon which is designed to or may readily be converted to expel any projectile by the action of an explosive; or the frame or receiver of any such weapon.

(5) The term "**explosive or incendiary device**" means (A) dynamite and all other forms of high explosives, (B) any explosive bomb, grenade, missile, or similar device, and (C) any incendiary bomb or grenade, fire bomb, or similar device, including any device which (i) consists of or includes a breakable container including a flammable liquid or compound, and a wick composed of any material which, when ignited, is capable of igniting such flammable liquid or compound, and (ii) can be carried or thrown by one individual acting alone.

(6) The term "**fireman**" means any member of a fire department (including a volunteer fire department) of any State, any political subdivision of a State, or the District of Columbia.

(7) The term "**law enforcement officer**" means any officer or employee of the United States, any State, any political subdivision of a State, or the District of Columbia, while engaged in the enforcement or prosecution of any of the criminal laws of the United States, a State, any political subdivision of a State, or the District of Columbia; and such term shall specifically include members of the National Guard (as defined in section 101 of title 10), members of the organized militia of any State, or territory of the United States, the Commonwealth of Puerto Rico, or the District of Columbia, not included within the National Guard (as defined in section 101 of title 10), and members of the Armed Forces of the United States, while engaged in suppressing acts of violence or restoring law and order during a civil disorder.

(8) The term "**State**" includes a State of the United States, and any commonwealth, territory, or possession of the United States.

Apr. 11, 1968 (463)
TITLE 18. CRIMES AND CRIMINAL PROCEDURE • PART I: CRIMES • CHAPTER 12: CIVIL DISORDERS

18 USC § 241. Conspiracy against rights

The Gist: If two or more people conspire to injure, oppress, threaten or intimidate any person in the free exercise or enjoyment of any right or privilege secured under the Constitution or laws of the United States, they shall be fined, or imprisoned up to ten years, or both. The same penalty applies if two or more people go, in disguise, on the highway, or on the premises of a person, with similar intent to prevent or hinder such rights or privileges.

If death results from such acts, or if such acts include kidnapping, attempted kidnapping, aggravated sexual assault, attempted aggravated sexual assault, or an attempt to kill, they may be fined, imprisoned for any term of years up to life, or put to death.

Based on the plain language of this statute, it appears that such offenses occur with respect to the right to keep and bear arms, guaranteed by the Second Amendment. See also 18-242, 18-1001 and 42-1983.

If two or more persons conspire to injure, oppress, threaten, or intimidate any person in any State, Territory, Commonwealth, Possession, or District in the free exercise or enjoyment of any right or privilege secured to him by the Constitution or laws of the United States, or because of his having so exercised the same; or

If two or more persons go in disguise on the highway, or on the premises of another, with intent to prevent or hinder his free exercise or enjoyment of any right or privilege so secured—

They shall be fined under this title or imprisoned not more than ten years, or both; and if death results from the acts committed in violation of this section or if such acts include kidnapping or an attempt to kidnap, aggravated sexual abuse or an attempt to commit aggravated sexual abuse, or an attempt to kill, they shall be fined under this title or imprisoned for any term of years or for life, or both, or may be sentenced to death.

June 25, 1948 (171)
TITLE 18. CRIMES AND CRIMINAL PROCEDURE • PART I: CRIMES • CHAPTER 13: CIVIL RIGHTS

18 USC § 242. Deprivation of rights under color of law

The Gist: Anyone who, under color of any law, statute, ordinance, custom or regulation, willfully deprives any person of any rights, privileges, or immunities secured or protected by the Constitution or laws of the United States, shall be fined, or imprisoned for up to one year, or both.

If bodily injury results, or if the violation includes the use or attempted or threatened use of a dangerous weapon, explosive or fire, the prison term rises to up to ten years. If death results, or if such acts include kidnapping, attempted kidnapping, aggravated sexual assault, attempted aggravated sexual assault, or an attempt to kill, the violator may be fined, imprisoned for any term of years up to life, or put to death. This applies also to anyone subjecting a person to different penalties than a citizen would face, because of color, race or being an alien.

Based on the plain language of this statute, it appears that such offenses occur with respect to the right to keep and bear arms, guaranteed by the Second Amendment. See also 18-241, 18-1001 and 42-1983.

Whoever, under color of any law, statute, ordinance, regulation, or custom, willfully subjects any person in any State, Territory, Commonwealth, Possession, or District to the deprivation of any rights, privileges, or immunities secured or protected by the Constitution or laws of the United States, or to different punishments, pains, or penalties, on account of such person being an alien, or by reason of his color, or race, than are prescribed for the punishment of citizens, shall be fined under this title or imprisoned not more than one year, or both; and if bodily injury results from the acts committed in violation of this section or if such acts include the use, attempted use, or threatened use of a dangerous weapon, explosives, or fire, shall be fined under this title or imprisoned not more than ten years, or both; and if death results from the acts committed in violation of this section or if such acts include kidnapping or an attempt to kidnap, aggravated sexual abuse, or an attempt to commit aggravated sexual abuse, or an attempt to kill, shall be fined under this title, or imprisoned for any term of years or for life, or both, or may be sentenced to death.

June 25, 1948 (202)
TITLE 18. CRIMES AND CRIMINAL PROCEDURE • PART I: CRIMES • CHAPTER 13: CIVIL RIGHTS

18 USC § 836. Transportation of fireworks into State prohibiting sale or use

The Gist: It's generally illegal to transport fireworks or deliver fireworks for transport into a state that prohibits them. The definition of fireworks is left up to the individual states. A Statute at Large provides an exception for fireworks used for agricultural purposes (such as are used to scare off animals harmful to crops).

Whoever, otherwise than in the course of continuous interstate transportation through any State, transports fireworks into any State, or delivers them for transportation into any State, or attempts so to do, knowing that such fireworks are to be delivered, possessed, stored, transshipped, distributed, sold, or otherwise dealt with in a manner or for a use prohibited by the laws of such State specifically prohibiting or regulating the use of fireworks, shall be fined under this title or imprisoned not more than one year, or both.

This section shall not apply to a common or contract carrier or to international or domestic water carriers engaged in interstate commerce or to the transportation of fireworks into a State for the use of Federal agencies in the carrying out or the furtherance of their operations.

In the enforcement of this section, the definitions of fireworks contained in the laws of the respective States shall be applied.

As used in this section, the term "State" includes the several States, Territories, and possessions of the United States, and the District of Columbia.

This section shall be effective from and after July 1, 1954.

<Statute at Large:>

This Act (enacting this section) shall not be effective with respect to—

(1) the transportation of fireworks into any State or Territory for use solely for agricultural purposes,

(2) the delivery of fireworks for transportation into any State or Territory for use solely for agricultural purposes, or

(3) any attempt to engage in any such transportation or delivery for use solely for agricultural purposes, until sixty days have elapsed after the commencement of the next regular session of the legislature of such State or Territory which begins after the date of enactment of this Act (June 4, 1954).

June 4, 1954 (289)
TITLE 18. CRIMES AND CRIMINAL PROCEDURE • PART I: CRIMES • CHAPTER 39: EXPLOSIVES AND OTHER DANGEROUS ARTICLES

18 USC § 841. Definitions

> The Gist: Definitions are provided for this chapter (Chapter 40), which deals with explosives.

As used in this chapter—

(a) **"Person"** means any individual, corporation, company, association, firm, partnership, society, or joint stock company.

(b) **"Interstate or foreign commerce"** means commerce between any place in a State and any place outside of that State, or within any possession of the United States (not including the Canal Zone) or the District of Columbia, and commerce between places within the same State but through any place outside of that State. **"State"** includes the District of Columbia, the Commonwealth of Puerto Rico, and the possessions of the United States (not including the Canal Zone).

(c) **"Explosive materials"** means explosives, blasting agents, and detonators.

(d) Except for the purposes of subsections (d), (e), (f), (g), (h), (i), and (j) of section 844 of this title, **"explosives"** means any chemical compound mixture, or device, the primary or common purpose of which is to function by explosion; the term includes, but is not limited to, dynamite and other high explosives, black powder, pellet powder, initiating explosives, detonators, safety fuses, squibs, detonating cord, igniter cord, and igniters. The Attorney General shall publish and revise at least annually in the Federal Register a list of these and any additional explosives which he determines to be within the coverage of this chapter. For the purposes of subsections (d), (e), (f), (g), (h), and (i) of section 844 of this title, the term **"explosive"** is defined in subsection (j) of such section 844.

(e) **"Blasting agent"** means any material or mixture, consisting of fuel and oxidizer, intended for blasting, not otherwise defined as an explosive: Provided, That the finished product, as mixed for use or shipment, cannot be detonated by means of a numbered 8 test blasting cap when unconfined.

(f) **"Detonator"** means any device containing a detonating charge that is used for initiating detonation in an explosive; the term includes, but is not limited to, electric blasting caps of instantaneous and delay types, blasting caps for use with safety fuses and detonating-cord delay connectors.

(g) **"Importer"** means any person engaged in the business of importing or bringing explosive materials into the United States for purposes of sale or distribution.

(h) **"Manufacturer"** means any person engaged in the business of manufacturing explosive materials for purposes of sale or distribution or for his own use.

(i) "Dealer" means any person engaged in the business of distributing explosive materials at wholesale or retail.

(j) "Permittee" means any user of explosives for a lawful purpose, who has obtained either a user permit or a limited permit under the provisions of this chapter.

(k) **"Attorney General"** means the Attorney General of the United States.

(l) **"Crime punishable by imprisonment for a term exceeding one year"** shall not mean

(1) any Federal or State offenses pertaining to antitrust violations, unfair trade practices, restraints of trade, or other similar offenses relating to the regulation of business practices as the Attorney General may by regulation designate, or

(2) any State offense (other than one involving a firearm or explosive) classified by the laws of the State as a misdemeanor and punishable by a term of imprisonment of two years or less.

(m) **"Licensee"** means any importer, manufacturer, or dealer licensed under the provisions of this chapter.

(n) **"Distribute"** means sell, issue, give, transfer, or otherwise dispose of.

(o) **"Convention on the Marking of Plastic Explosives"** means the Convention on the Marking of Plastic Explosives for the Purpose of Detection, Done at Montreal on 1 March 1991.

(p) **"Detection agent"** means any one of the substances specified in this subsection when introduced into a plastic explosive or formulated in such explosive as a part of the manufacturing process in such a manner as to achieve homogeneous distribution in the finished explosive, including—

(1) Ethylene glycol dinitrate (EGDN), C (INFERIOR 2)H (INFERIOR 4)(NO (INFERIOR 3)) (INFERIOR 2), molecular weight 152, when the minimum concentration in the finished explosive is 0.2 percent by mass;

(2) 2,3-Dimethyl-2,3-dinitrobutane (DMNB), C (INFERIOR 6)H (INFERIOR 12)(NO (INFERIOR 2)) (INFERIOR 2), molecular weight 176, when the minimum concentration in the finished explosive is 0.1 percent by mass;

(3) Para-Mononitrotoluene (p-MNT), C (INFERIOR 7)H (INFERIOR 7)NO (INFERIOR 2), molecular weight 137, when the minimum concentration in the finished explosive is 0.5 percent by mass;

(4) Ortho-Mononitrotoluene (o-MNT), C (INFERIOR 7)H (INFERIOR 7)NO (INFERIOR 2), molecular weight 137, when the minimum concentration in the finished explosive is 0.5 percent by mass; and

(5) any other substance in the concentration specified by the Attorney General, after consultation with the Secretary of State and the Secretary of Defense, that has been added to the table in part 2 of the Technical Annex to the Convention on the Marking of Plastic Explosives.

(q) **"Plastic explosive"** means an explosive material in flexible or elastic sheet form formulated with one or more high explosives which in their pure form has a vapor pressure less than 10-Pa at a temperature of 25 (degrees) C., is formulated with a binder material, and is as a mixture malleable or flexible at normal room temperature.

(r) **"Alien"** means any person who is not a citizen or national of the United States.

(s) **"Responsible person"** means an individual who has the power to direct the management and policies of the applicant pertaining to explosive materials.

Oct. 15, 1970 (874)

18 USC § 842. Unlawful acts

The Gist: This section describes federal crimes involving explosives. Among the provisions, it is illegal to: 1–do business in explosives without a license; 2–use deceit to get a license or explosives; 3–transport or receive explosives in interstate commerce without authority; 4–distribute explosives to anyone unlicensed who doesn't live in the state (several exemptions exist for people in adjoining states); 5–distribute explosives to anyone a licensee may believe will transport the explosives to a state where they would be illegal; 6–distribute explosives to the people restricted under subsection (d); 7–handle stolen explosives before or after they are stolen; 8–transport or possess explosives for people identified under subsection (i); 9–in any way handle plastic explosives that do not contain a detection agent (with some exceptions), and more.

Licensees must keep detailed records, which are described. Falsifying records is illegal, and failure to report losses to federal and local authorities within 24 hours is illegal. Explosives must be stored according to regulations established by the Attorney General. The Attorney General took over responsibility for explosives in 2002, from the Treasury Dept., under the Homeland Security Act.

That act also made it illegal to distribute information related to weapons of mass destruction, destructive devices or explosives if: 1–it is intended to teach or demonstrate their use in an activity that is a federal crime of violence, or 2–It is provided to a person who intends to use it in such a manner.

Unlawful acts
(a) It shall be unlawful for any person—
(1) to engage in the business of importing, manufacturing, or dealing in explosive materials without a license issued under this chapter;
(2) knowingly to withhold information or to make any false or fictitious oral or written statement or to furnish or exhibit any false, fictitious, or misrepresented identification, intended or likely to deceive for the purpose of obtaining explosive materials, or a license, permit, exemption, or relief from disability under the provisions of this chapter;
(3) other than a licensee or permittee knowingly—
(A) to transport, ship, cause to be transported, or receive any explosive materials; or
(B) to distribute explosive materials to any person other than a licensee or permittee; or
(4) who is a holder of a limited permit—
(A) to transport, ship, cause to be transported, or receive in interstate or foreign commerce any explosive materials; or
(B) to receive explosive materials from a licensee or permittee, whose premises are located outside the State of residence of the limited permit holder, or on more than 6 separate occasions, during the period of the permit, to receive explosive materials from 1 or more licensees or permittees whose premises are located within the State of residence of the limited permit holder.
(b) It shall be unlawful for any licensee or permittee to knowingly distribute any explosive materials to any person other than—
(1) a licensee;
(2) a holder of a user permit; or
(3) a holder of a limited permit who is a resident of the State where distribution is made and in which the premises of the transferor are located.

(c) It shall be unlawful for any licensee to distribute explosive materials to any person who the licensee has reason to believe intends to transport such explosive materials into a State where the purchase, possession, or use of explosive materials is prohibited or which does not permit its residents to transport or ship explosive materials into it or to receive explosive materials in it.

(d) It shall be unlawful for any person knowingly to distribute explosive materials to any individual who:

(1) is under twenty-one years of age;

(2) has been convicted in any court of a crime punishable by imprisonment for a term exceeding one year;

(3) is under indictment for a crime punishable by imprisonment for a term exceeding one year;

(4) is a fugitive from justice;

(5) is an unlawful user of or addicted to any controlled substance (as defined in section 102 of the Controlled Substances Act (21 U.S.C. 802));

(6) has been adjudicated a mental defective or who has been committed to a mental institution;

(7) is an alien, other than an alien who—

(A) is lawfully admitted for permanent residence (as defined in section 101(a)(20) of the Immigration and Nationality Act); or

(B) is in lawful nonimmigrant status, is a refugee admitted under section 207 of the Immigration and Nationality Act (8 U.S.C. 1157), or is in asylum status under section 208 of the Immigration and Nationality Act (8 U.S.C. 1158), and—

(i) is a foreign law enforcement officer of a friendly foreign government, as determined by the Attorney General in consultation with the Secretary of State, entering the United States on official law enforcement business, and the shipping, transporting, possession, or receipt of explosive materials is in furtherance of this official law enforcement business;

(ii) is a person having the power to direct or cause the direction of the management and policies of a corporation, partnership, or association licensed pursuant to section 843(a), and the shipping, transporting, possession, or receipt of explosive materials is in furtherance of such power;

(iii) is a member of a North Atlantic Treaty Organization (NATO) or other friendly foreign military force, as determined by the Attorney General in consultation with the Secretary of Defense, (whether or not admitted in a nonimmigrant status) who is present in the United States under military orders for training or other military purpose authorized by the United States, and the shipping, transporting, possession, or receipt of explosive materials is in furtherance of the military purpose; or

(iv) is lawfully present in the United States in cooperation with the Director of Central Intelligence, and the shipment, transportation, receipt, or possession of the explosive materials is in furtherance of such cooperation;

(8) has been discharged from the armed forces under dishonorable conditions;

(9) having been a citizen of the United States, has renounced the citizenship of that person.

(e) It shall be unlawful for any licensee knowingly to distribute any explosive materials to any person in any State where the purchase, possession, or use by such person of such explosive materials would be in violation of any State law or any published ordinance applicable at the place of distribution.

(f) It shall be unlawful for any licensee or permittee willfully to manufacture, import, purchase, distribute, or receive explosive materials without making such records as the Attorney General may by regulation require, including, but not limited to, a statement of intended use, the name, date, place of birth, social security number or taxpayer identification number, and place of residence of any natural person to whom explosive materials are distributed. If explosive materials are distributed to a corporation or other business entity, such records shall include the identity and principal and local places of business and the name, date, place of birth, and place of residence of the natural person acting as agent of the corporation or other business entity in arranging the distribution.

(g) It shall be unlawful for any licensee or permittee knowingly to make any false entry in any record which he is required to keep pursuant to this section or regulations promulgated under section 847 of this title.

(h) It shall be unlawful for any person to receive, possess, transport, ship, conceal, store, barter, sell, dispose of, or pledge or accept as security for a loan, any stolen explosive materials which are moving as, which are part of, which constitute, or which have been shipped or transported in, interstate or foreign commerce, either before or after such materials were stolen, knowing or having reasonable cause to believe that the explosive materials were stolen.

(i) It shall be unlawful for any person—

(1) who is under indictment for, or who has been convicted in any court of, a crime punishable by imprisonment for a term exceeding one year;

(2) who is a fugitive from justice;

(3) who is an unlawful user of or addicted to any controlled substance (as defined in section 102 of the Controlled Substances Act (21 U.S.C. 802));

(4) who has been adjudicated as a mental defective or who has been committed to a mental institution;

(5) who is an alien, other than an alien who—

(A) is lawfully admitted for permanent residence (as that term is defined in section 101(a)(20) of the Immigration and Nationality Act); or

(B) is in lawful nonimmigrant status, is a refugee admitted under section 207 of the Immigration and Nationality Act (8 U.S.C. 1157), or is in asylum status under section 208 of the Immigration and Nationality Act (8 U.S.C. 1158), and—

(i) is a foreign law enforcement officer of a friendly foreign government, as determined by the Attorney General in consultation with the Secretary of State, entering the United States on official law enforcement business, and the shipping, transporting, possession, or receipt of explosive materials is in furtherance of this official law enforcement business;

(ii) is a person having the power to direct or cause the direction of the management and policies of a corporation, partnership, or association licensed pursuant to section 843(a), and the shipping, transporting, possession, or receipt of explosive materials is in furtherance of such power;

(iii) is a member of a North Atlantic Treaty Organization (NATO) or other friendly foreign military force, as determined by the Attorney General in consultation with the Secretary of Defense, (whether or not admitted in a nonimmigrant status) who is present in the United States under military orders for training or other military purpose authorized by the United States, and the shipping, transporting, possession, or receipt of explosive materials is in furtherance of the military purpose; or

(iv) is lawfully present in the United States in cooperation with the Director of Central Intelligence, and the shipment, transportation, receipt, or possession of the explosive materials is in furtherance of such cooperation;

(6) who has been discharged from the armed forces under dishonorable conditions;

(7) who, having been a citizen of the United States, has renounced the citizenship of that person;

to ship or transport any explosive in or affecting interstate or foreign commerce or to receive or possess any explosive which has been shipped or transported in or affecting interstate or foreign commerce.

(j) It shall be unlawful for any person to store any explosive material in a manner not in conformity with regulations promulgated by the Attorney General. In promulgating such regulations, the Attorney General shall take into consideration the class, type, and quantity of explosive materials to be stored, as well as the standards of safety and security recognized in the explosives industry.

(k) It shall be unlawful for any person who has knowledge of the theft or loss of any explosive materials from his stock, to fail to report such theft or loss within twenty-four hours of discovery thereof, to the Attorney General and to appropriate local authorities.

(l) It shall be unlawful for any person to manufacture any plastic explosive that does not contain a detection agent.

(m)(1) It shall be unlawful for any person to import or bring into the United States, or export from the United States, any plastic explosive that does not contain a detection agent.

(2) This subsection does not apply to the importation or bringing into the United States, or the exportation from the United States, of any plastic explosive that was imported or brought into, or manufactured in the United States prior to the date of enactment of this subsection by or on behalf of any agency of the United States performing military or police functions (including any military reserve component) or by or on behalf of the National Guard of any State, not later than 15 years after the date of entry into force of the Convention on the Marking of Plastic Explosives, with respect to the United States.

(n)(1) It shall be unlawful for any person to ship, transport, transfer, receive, or possess any plastic explosive that does not contain a detection agent.

(2) This subsection does not apply to—

(A) the shipment, transportation, transfer, receipt, or possession of any plastic explosive that was imported or brought into, or manufactured in the United States prior to the date of enactment of this subsection by any person during the period beginning on that date and ending 3 years after that date of enactment; or

(B) the shipment, transportation, transfer, receipt, or possession of any plastic explosive that was imported or brought into, or manufactured in the United States prior to the date of enactment of this subsection by or on behalf of any agency of the United States performing a military or police function (including any military reserve component) or by or on behalf of the National Guard of any State, not later than 15 years after the date of entry into force of the Convention on the Marking of Plastic Explosives, with respect to the United States.

(o) It shall be unlawful for any person, other than an agency of the United States (including any military reserve component) or the National Guard of any State, possessing any plastic explosive on the date of enactment of this subsection, to fail to report to the Attorney General within 120 days after such date of enactment the quantity of such explosives possessed, the manufacturer or importer, any marks of identification on such explosives, and such other information as the Attorney General may prescribe by regulation.

(p) Distribution of Information Relating to Explosives, Destructive Devices, and Weapons of Mass Destruction.—

(1) Definitions.—In this subsection—

(A) the term "destructive device" has the same meaning as in section 921(a)(4);

(B) the term "explosive" has the same meaning as in section 844(j); and

(C) the term "weapon of mass destruction" has the same meaning as in section 2332a(c)(2).

(2) Prohibition.—It shall be unlawful for any person—

(A) to teach or demonstrate the making or use of an explosive, a destructive device, or a weapon of mass destruction, or to distribute by any means information pertaining to, in whole or in part, the manufacture or use of an explosive, destructive device, or weapon of mass destruction, with the intent that the teaching, demonstration, or information be used for, or in furtherance of, an activity that constitutes a Federal crime of violence; or

(B) to teach or demonstrate to any person the making or use of an explosive, a destructive device, or a weapon of mass destruction, or to distribute to any person, by any means, information pertaining to, in whole or in part, the manufacture or use of an explosive, destructive device, or weapon of mass destruction, knowing that such person intends to use the teaching, demonstration, or information for, or in furtherance of, an activity that constitutes a Federal crime of violence.

Oct. 15, 1970 (2,215)

TITLE 18. CRIMES AND CRIMINAL PROCEDURE • PART I: CRIMES • CHAPTER 40: IMPORTATION, MANUFACTURE, DISTRIBUTION AND STORAGE OF EXPLOSIVE MATERIALS

18 USC § 843. Licenses and user permits

> The Gist: The requirements for applying for an explosives license are
> described. The Attorney General must issue a license to applicants who
> are qualified as described. Administrative and judicial remedies are
> provided for anyone whose license is denied or revoked. The Attorney
> General may inspect explosives and records at any reasonable times.

Licenses and user permits
(a) An application for a user permit or limited permit or a license to import,
manufacture, or deal in explosive materials shall be in such form and contain such
information as the Attorney General shall by regulation prescribe, including the
names of and appropriate identifying information regarding all employees who will
be authorized by the applicant to possess explosive materials, as well as
fingerprints and a photograph of each responsible person. Each applicant for a
license or permit shall pay a fee to be charged as set by the Attorney General, said
fee not to exceed $50 for a limited permit and $200 for any other license or permit.
Each license or user permit shall be valid for not longer than 3 years from the date
of issuance and each limited permit shall be valid for not longer than 1 year from
the date of issuance. Each license or permit shall be renewable upon the same
conditions and subject to the same restrictions as the original license or permit, and
upon payment of a renewal fee not to exceed one-half of the original fee.
(b) Upon the filing of a proper application and payment of the prescribed fee, and
subject to the provisions of this chapter and other applicable laws, the Attorney
General shall issue to such applicant the appropriate license or permit if—
(1) the applicant (or, if the applicant is a corporation, partnership, or association, each
responsible person with respect to the applicant) is not a person described in
section 842(i);
(2) the applicant has not willfully violated any of the provisions of this chapter or
regulations issued hereunder;
(3) the applicant has in a State premises from which he conducts or intends to
conduct business;
(4)(A) the Attorney General verifies by inspection or, if the application is for an original
limited permit or the first or second renewal of such a permit, by such other means
as the Attorney General determines appropriate, that the applicant has a place of
storage for explosive materials which meets such standards of public safety and
security against theft as the Attorney General by regulations shall prescribe; and
(B) subparagraph (A) shall not apply to an applicant for the renewal of a limited permit
if the Attorney General has verified, by inspection within the preceding 3 years, the
matters described in subparagraph (A) with respect to the applicant; and
(5) the applicant has demonstrated and certified in writing that he is familiar with all
published State laws and local ordinances relating to explosive materials for the
location in which he intends to do business;
(6) none of the employees of the applicant who will be authorized by the applicant to
possess explosive materials is any person described in section 842(i); and
(7) in the case of a limited permit, the applicant has certified in writing that the
applicant will not receive explosive materials on more than 6 separate occasions
during the 12-month period for which the limited permit is valid.
(c) The Attorney General shall approve or deny an application within a period of 90
days for licenses and permits, beginning on the date such application is received by
the Attorney General.
(d) The Attorney General may revoke any license or permit issued under this section if
in the opinion of the Attorney General the holder thereof has violated any provision
of this chapter or any rule or regulation prescribed by the Attorney General under
this chapter, or has become ineligible to acquire explosive materials under section
842(d). The Attorney General's action under this subsection may be reviewed only
as provided in subsection (e)(2) of this section.

(e)(1) Any person whose application is denied or whose license or permit is revoked shall receive a written notice from the Attorney General stating the specific grounds upon which such denial or revocation is based. Any notice of a revocation of a license or permit shall be given to the holder of such license or permit prior to or concurrently with the effective date of the revocation.

(2) If the Attorney General denies an application for, or revokes a license, or permit, he shall, upon request by the aggrieved party, promptly hold a hearing to review his denial or revocation. In the case of a revocation, the Attorney General may upon a request of the holder stay the effective date of the revocation. A hearing under this section shall be at a location convenient to the aggrieved party. The Attorney General shall give written notice of his decision to the aggrieved party within a reasonable time after the hearing. The aggrieved party may, within sixty days after receipt of the Attorney General's written decision, file a petition with the United States court of appeals for the district in which he resides or has his principal place of business for a judicial review of such denial or revocation, pursuant to sections 701-706 of title 5, United States Code.

(f) Licensees and holders of user permits shall make available for inspection at all reasonable times their records kept pursuant to this chapter or the regulations issued hereunder, and licensees and permittees shall submit to the Attorney General such reports and information with respect to such records and the contents thereof as he shall by regulations prescribe. The Attorney General may enter during business hours the premises (including places of storage) of any licensee or holder of a user permit, for the purpose of inspecting or examining (1) any records or documents required to be kept by such licensee or permittee, under the provisions of this chapter or regulations issued hereunder, and (2) any explosive materials kept or stored by such licensee or permittee at such premises. Upon the request of any State or any political subdivision thereof, the Attorney General may make available to such State or any political subdivision thereof, any information which he may obtain by reason of the provisions of this chapter with respect to the identification of persons within such State or political subdivision thereof, who have purchased or received explosive materials, together with a description of such explosive materials. The Attorney General may inspect the places of storage for explosive materials of an applicant for a limited permit or, at the time of renewal of such permit, a holder of a limited permit, only as provided in subsection (b)(4).

(g) Licenses and user permits issued under the provisions of subsection (b) of this section shall be kept posted and kept available for inspection on the premises covered by the license and permit.

(h)(1) If the Attorney General receives, from an employer, the name and other identifying information of a responsible person or an employee who will be authorized by the employer to possess explosive materials in the course of employment with the employer, the Attorney General shall determine whether the responsible person or employee is one of the persons described in any paragraph of section 842(i). In making the determination, the Attorney General may take into account a letter or document issued under paragraph (2).

(2)(A) If the Attorney General determines that the responsible person or the employee is not one of the persons described in any paragraph of section 842(i), the Attorney General shall notify the employer in writing or electronically of the determination and issue, to the responsible person or employee, a letter of clearance, which confirms the determination.

(B) If the Attorney General determines that the responsible person or employee is one of the persons described in any paragraph of section 842(i), the Attorney General shall notify the employer in writing or electronically of the determination and issue to the responsible person or the employee, as the case may be, a document that—
(i) confirms the determination;
(ii) explains the grounds for the determination;
(iii) provides information on how the disability may be relieved; and
(iv) explains how the determination may be appealed.

(i) Furnishing of Samples.—

(1) In general.—Licensed manufacturers and licensed importers and persons who manufacture or import explosive materials or ammonium nitrate shall, when required by letter issued by the Attorney General, furnish—

(A) samples of such explosive materials or ammonium nitrate;

(B) information on chemical composition of those products; and

(C) any other information that the Attorney General determines is relevant to the identification of the explosive materials or to identification of the ammonium nitrate.

(2) Reimbursement.—The Attorney General shall, by regulation, authorize reimbursement of the fair market value of samples furnished pursuant to this subsection, as well as the reasonable costs of shipment.

Oct. 15, 1970 (1,426)

TITLE 18. CRIMES AND CRIMINAL PROCEDURE • PART I: CRIMES • CHAPTER 40: IMPORTATION, MANUFACTURE, DISTRIBUTION AND STORAGE OF EXPLOSIVE MATERIALS

18 USC § 844. Penalties

The Gist: Crimes involving explosives are identified, and their corresponding penalties are described. Though firearms are not classified as explosives, some of the components of ammunition can be, and for some of these rules ammunition components are specifically included.

Explosives used illegally are subject to forfeiture and may be destroyed. The owner may seek reimbursement if the illegal use did not involve the owner. Anyone using explosives illegally to kill another person faces life imprisonment and the death penalty; lower penalties are provided for other offenses. Various other illegal acts are described, including using explosives to: make any threats; destroy any federal property, real estate or organization receiving federal funds; interfere with interstate or foreign commerce; conspire to commit an offense; and more. Transferring explosives, knowing or believing they will be used in certain violent or drug-related crimes, is a crime. If a penalty for a felony would be increased if the offender used a firearm, it is increased if the offender uses explosives.

Possession of explosives at an airport is subject to regulations of the Federal Aviation Administration. An exception is provided for properly carried ammunition and certain special research materials. Gunpowder and primers are specifically included in some of the penalties, as outlined in subsection (j).

(a) Any person who—

(1) violates any of subsections (a) through (i) or (l) through (o) of section 842 shall be fined under this title, imprisoned for not more than 10 years, or both; and

(2) violates subsection (p)(2) of section 842, shall be fined under this title, imprisoned not more than 20 years, or both.

(b) Any person who violates any other provision of section 842 of this chapter shall be fined under this title or imprisoned not more than one year, or both.

(c)(1) Any explosive materials involved or used or intended to be used in any violation of the provisions of this chapter or any other rule or regulation promulgated thereunder or any violation of any criminal law of the United States shall be subject to seizure and forfeiture, and all provisions of the Internal Revenue Code of 1986 relating to the seizure, forfeiture, and disposition of firearms, as defined in section 5845(a) of that Code, shall, so far as applicable, extend to seizures and forfeitures under the provisions of this chapter.

(2) Notwithstanding paragraph (1), in the case of the seizure of any explosive materials for any offense for which the materials would be subject to forfeiture in

which it would be impracticable or unsafe to remove the materials to a place of storage or would be unsafe to store them, the seizing officer may destroy the explosive materials forthwith. Any destruction under this paragraph shall be in the presence of at least 1 credible witness. The seizing officer shall make a report of the seizure and take samples as the Attorney General may by regulation prescribe.

(3) Within 60 days after any destruction made pursuant to paragraph (2), the owner of (including any person having an interest in) the property so destroyed may make application to the Attorney General for reimbursement of the value of the property. If the claimant establishes to the satisfaction of the Attorney General that—

(A) the property has not been used or involved in a violation of law; or

(B) any unlawful involvement or use of the property was without the claimant's knowledge, consent, or willful blindness, the Attorney General shall make an allowance to the claimant not exceeding the value of the property destroyed.

(d) Whoever transports or receives, or attempts to transport or receive, in interstate or foreign commerce any explosive with the knowledge or intent that it will be used to kill, injure, or intimidate any individual or unlawfully to damage or destroy any building, vehicle, or other real or personal property, shall be imprisoned for not more than ten years, or fined under this title, or both; and if personal injury results to any person including any public safety officer performing duties as a direct or proximate result of conduct prohibited by this subsection, shall be imprisoned for not more than twenty years or fined under this title, or both; and if death results to any person, including any public safety officer performing duties as a direct or proximate result of conduct prohibited by this subsection, shall be subject to imprisonment for any term of years, or to the death penalty or to life imprisonment.

(e) Whoever, through the use of the mail, telephone, telegraph, or other instrument of interstate or foreign commerce, or in or affecting interstate or foreign commerce, willfully makes any threat, or maliciously conveys false information knowing the same to be false, concerning an attempt or alleged attempt being made, or to be made, to kill, injure, or intimidate any individual or unlawfully to damage or destroy any building, vehicle, or other real or personal property by means of fire or an explosive shall be imprisoned for not more than 10 years or fined under this title, or both.

(f)(1) Whoever maliciously damages or destroys, or attempts to damage or destroy, by means of fire or an explosive, any building, vehicle, or other personal or real property in whole or in part owned or possessed by, or leased to, the United States, or any department or agency thereof, or any institution or organization receiving Federal financial assistance, shall be imprisoned for not less than 5 years and not more than 20 years, fined under this title, or both.

(2) Whoever engages in conduct prohibited by this subsection, and as a result of such conduct, directly or proximately causes personal injury or creates a substantial risk of injury to any person, including any public safety officer performing duties, shall be imprisoned for not less than 7 years and not more than 40 years, fined under this title, or both.

(3) Whoever engages in conduct prohibited by this subsection, and as a result of such conduct directly or proximately causes the death of any person, including any public safety officer performing duties, shall be subject to the death penalty, or imprisoned for not less than 20 years or for life, fined under this title, or both. (g)(1) Except as provided in paragraph (2), whoever possesses an explosive in an airport that is subject to the regulatory authority of the Federal Aviation Administration, or in any building in whole or in part owned, possessed, or used by, or leased to, the United States or any department or agency thereof, except with the written consent of the agency, department, or other person responsible for the management of such building or airport, shall be imprisoned for not more than five years, or fined under this title, or both.

(2) The provisions of this subsection shall not be applicable to—

(A) the possession of ammunition (as that term is defined in regulations issued pursuant to this chapter) in an airport that is subject to the regulatory authority of the Federal Aviation Administration if such ammunition is either in checked baggage or in a closed container; or

(B) the possession of an explosive in an airport if the packaging and transportation of such explosive is exempt from, or subject to and in accordance with, regulations of the Research and Special Projects Administration for the handling of hazardous materials pursuant to chapter 51 of title 49.

(h) Whoever—

(1) uses fire or an explosive to commit any felony which may be prosecuted in a court of the United States, or

(2) carries an explosive during the commission of any felony which may be prosecuted in a court of the United States, including a felony which provides for an enhanced punishment if committed by the use of a deadly or dangerous weapon or device shall, in addition to the punishment provided for such felony, be sentenced to imprisonment for 10 years. In the case of a second or subsequent conviction under this subsection, such person shall be sentenced to imprisonment for 20 years. Notwithstanding any other provision of law, the court shall not place on probation or suspend the sentence of any person convicted of a violation of this subsection, nor shall the term of imprisonment imposed under this subsection run concurrently with any other term of imprisonment including that imposed for the felony in which the explosive was used or carried.

(i) Whoever maliciously damages or destroys, or attempts to damage or destroy, by means of fire or an explosive, any building, vehicle, or other real or personal property used in interstate or foreign commerce or in any activity affecting interstate or foreign commerce shall be imprisoned for not less than 5 years and not more than 20 years, fined under this title or both; and if personal injury results to any person, including any public safety officer performing duties as a direct or proximate result of conduct prohibited by this subsection, shall be imprisoned for not less than 7 years and not more than 40 years, fined under this title or both; and if death results to any person, including any public safety officer performing duties as a direct or proximate result of conduct prohibited by this subsection, shall also be subject to imprisonment for any term of years, or to the death penalty or to life imprisonment.

(j) For the purposes of subsections (d), (e), (f), (g), (h), and (i) of this section and section 842(p), the term "explosive" means gunpowders, powders used for blasting, all forms of high explosives, blasting materials, fuzes (other than electric circuit breakers), detonators, and other detonating agents, smokeless powders, other explosive or incendiary devices within the meaning of paragraph (5) of section 232 of this title, and any chemical compounds, mechanical mixture, or device that contains any oxidizing and combustible units, or other ingredients, in such proportions, quantities, or packing that ignition by fire, by friction, by concussion, by percussion, or by detonation of the compound, mixture, or device or any part thereof may cause an explosion.

(k) A person who steals any explosives materials which are moving as, or are a part of, or which have moved in, interstate or foreign commerce shall be imprisoned for not more than 10 years, fined under this title, or both.

(l) A person who steals any explosive material from a licensed importer, licensed manufacturer, or licensed dealer, or from any permittee shall be fined under this title, imprisoned not more than 10 years, or both.

(m) A person who conspires to commit an offense under subsection (h) shall be imprisoned for any term of years not exceeding 20, fined under this title, or both.

(n) Except as otherwise provided in this section, a person who conspires to commit any offense defined in this chapter shall be subject to the same penalties (other than the penalty of death) as the penalties prescribed for the offense the commission of which was the object of the conspiracy.

(o) Whoever knowingly transfers any explosive materials, knowing or having reasonable cause to believe that such explosive materials will be used to commit a crime of violence (as defined in section 924(c)(3)) or drug trafficking crime (as defined in section 924(c)(2)) shall be subject to the same penalties as may be imposed under subsection (h) for a first conviction for the use or carrying of an explosive material.

(p) Theft Reporting Requirement.—

(1) In general.—A holder of a license or permit who knows that explosive materials have been stolen from that licensee or permittee, shall report the theft to the Attorney General not later than 24 hours after the discovery of the theft.
(2) Penalty.—A holder of a license or permit who does not report a theft in accordance with paragraph (1), shall be fined not more than $10,000, imprisoned not more than 5 years, or both.

Oct. 15, 1970 (1,759)

18 USC § 845. Exceptions; relief from disabilities

The Gist: Exceptions to the laws on explosives misuse are described. For authorized purposes, explosives may be: 1–transported under regulations of the Dept. of Transportation; 2–used in medicines prescribed in the U.S. Pharmacopoeia or National Formulary; 3–delivered to proper government authorities; and 4–made and distributed under military authority. Special exceptions are provided for certain plastic explosives, and those without detection agents, but only as an affirmative defense.

Small arms ammunition and components are exempt. Fifty pounds or less of commercially made black powder and related supplies for sporting, recreational or cultural use in antique firearms and devices is exempt.

A person who loses the ability to be in the explosives business because of a criminal conviction may, under certain circumstances, apply to the Justice Dept. for relief from that restriction.

(a) Except in the case of subsections (l), (m), (n), or (o) of section 842 and subsections (d), (e), (f), (g), (h), and (i) of section 844 of this title, this chapter shall not apply to:
(1) any aspect of the transportation of explosive materials via railroad, water, highway, or air which are regulated by the United States Department of Transportation and agencies thereof, and which pertain to safety;
(2) the use of explosive materials in medicines and medicinal agents in the forms prescribed by the official United States Pharmacopoeia, or the National Formulary;
(3) the transportation, shipment, receipt, or importation of explosive materials for delivery to any agency of the United States or to any State or political subdivision thereof;
(4) small arms ammunition and components thereof;
(5) commercially manufactured black powder in quantities not to exceed fifty pounds, percussion caps, safety and pyrotechnic fuses, quills, quick and slow matches, and friction primers, intended to be used solely for sporting, recreational, or cultural purposes in antique firearms as defined in section 921(a)(16) of title 18 of the United States Code, or in antique devices as exempted from the term "destructive device" in section 921(a)(4) of title 18 of the United States Code; and
(6) the manufacture under the regulation of the military department of the United States of explosive materials for, or their distribution to or storage or possession by the military or naval services or other agencies of the United States; or to arsenals, navy yards, depots, or other establishments owned by, or operated by or on behalf of, the United States.
(b)(1) A person who is prohibited from shipping, transporting, receiving, or possessing any explosive under section 842(i) may apply to the Attorney General for relief from such prohibition.
(2) The Attorney General may grant the relief requested under paragraph (1) if the Attorney General determines that the circumstances regarding the applicability of section 842(i), and the applicant's record and reputation, are such that the applicant

will not be likely to act in a manner dangerous to public safety and that the granting of such relief is not contrary to the public interest.

(3) A licensee or permittee who applies for relief, under this subsection, from the disabilities incurred under this chapter as a result of an indictment for or conviction of a crime punishable by imprisonment for a term exceeding 1 year shall not be barred by such disability from further operations under the license or permit pending final action on an application for relief filed pursuant to this section.

(c) It is an affirmative defense against any proceeding involving subsections (l) through (o) of section 842 if the proponent proves by a preponderance of the evidence that the plastic explosive—

(1) consisted of a small amount of plastic explosive intended for and utilized solely in lawful—

(A) research, development, or testing of new or modified explosive materials;

(B) training in explosives detection or development or testing of explosives detection equipment; or

(C) forensic science purposes; or

(2) was plastic explosive that, within 3 years after the date of enactment of the Antiterrorism and Effective Death Penalty Act of 1996, will be or is incorporated in a military device within the territory of the United States and remains an integral part of such military device, or is intended to be, or is incorporated in, and remains an integral part of a military device that is intended to become, or has become, the property of any agency of the United States performing military or police functions (including any military reserve component) or the National Guard of any State, wherever such device is located.

(3) For purposes of this subsection, the term "military device" includes, but is not restricted to, shells, bombs, projectiles, mines, missiles, rockets, shaped charges, grenades, perforators, and similar devices lawfully manufactured exclusively for military or police purposes.

Oct. 15, 1970 (643)
TITLE 18. CRIMES AND CRIMINAL PROCEDURE • PART I: CRIMES • CHAPTER 40: IMPORTATION, MANUFACTURE, DISTRIBUTION AND STORAGE OF EXPLOSIVE MATERIALS

18 USC § 846. Additional powers of the Attorney General

The Gist: In addition to any other federal investigative authority, the Attorney General may investigate the site of any fire or accident where explosives may have been involved, to take precautions to prevent such incidents if they were caused by accident. The FBI and BATFE may investigate specified violations involving explosives. The AG is authorized to establish a national repository of such incidents, to which federal agencies must report, and to which state and local agencies may report.

(a) The Attorney General is authorized to inspect the site of any accident, or fire, in which there is reason to believe that explosive materials were involved, in order that if any such incident has been brought about by accidental means, precautions may be taken to prevent similar accidents from occurring. In order to carry out the purpose of this subsection, the Attorney General is authorized to enter into or upon any property where explosive materials have been used, are suspected of having been used, or have been found in an otherwise unauthorized location. Nothing in this chapter shall be construed as modifying or otherwise affecting in any way the investigative authority of any other Federal agency. In addition to any other investigatory authority they have with respect to violations of provisions of this chapter, the Federal Bureau of Investigation, together with the Bureau of Alcohol, Tobacco, Firearms, and Explosives, shall have authority to conduct investigations with respect to violations of subsection (d), (e), (f), (g), (h), or (i) of section 844 of this title.

(b) The Attorney General is authorized to establish a national repository of information on incidents involving arson and the suspected criminal misuse of explosives. All

Federal agencies having information concerning such incidents shall report the information to the Attorney General pursuant to such regulations as deemed necessary to carry out the provisions of this subsection. The repository shall also contain information on incidents voluntarily reported to the Attorney General by State and local authorities.

Oct. 15, 1970 (249)

TITLE 18. CRIMES AND CRIMINAL PROCEDURE • PART I: CRIMES • CHAPTER 40: IMPORTATION, MANUFACTURE, DISTRIBUTION AND STORAGE OF EXPLOSIVE MATERIALS

18 USC § 847. Rules and regulations

The Gist: The numerous fine details of carrying out the broad-based laws and controls on explosives are delegated to the Justice Dept. (was the Treasury Dept. prior to 2002), which issues binding regulations. The Dept. is required to hear input from the public in making the regulations.

The administration of this chapter shall be vested in the Attorney General. The Attorney General may prescribe such rules and regulations as he deems reasonably necessary to carry out the provisions of this chapter. The Attorney General shall give reasonable public notice, and afford to interested parties opportunity for hearing, prior to prescribing such rules and regulations.

Oct. 15, 1970 (57)

TITLE 18. CRIMES AND CRIMINAL PROCEDURE • PART I: CRIMES • CHAPTER 40: IMPORTATION, MANUFACTURE, DISTRIBUTION AND STORAGE OF EXPLOSIVE MATERIALS

18 USC § 848. Effect on State law

The Gist: Congress announces that it is not in any way attempting to usurp power from the states, unless state laws conflict with federal laws, in which case federal laws control. Hmmm. Federal laws on explosives take precedence over state laws when the two laws disagree. Federal law supersedes any conflicting state law on explosives.

No provision of this chapter shall be construed as indicating an intent on the part of the Congress to occupy the field in which such provision operates to the exclusion of the law of any State on the same subject matter, unless there is a direct and positive conflict between such provision and the law of the State so that the two cannot be reconciled or consistently stand together.

Oct. 15, 1970 (69)

TITLE 18. CRIMES AND CRIMINAL PROCEDURE • PART I: CRIMES • CHAPTER 40: IMPORTATION, MANUFACTURE, DISTRIBUTION AND STORAGE OF EXPLOSIVE MATERIALS

The Main Federal Gun Laws

If any federal gun laws can be considered the "main" gun laws, here they are—the 920s in Chapter 44 of Title 18 Crimes and Criminal Procedure of the United States Code. These originated with the Gun Control Act of 1968, P.L. 90-618, and new firearms legislation is often placed among these sections. Most of the Brady Law, for example, became subsections (s) and (t) of section 922. Before the GCA was enacted, hardware and department stores carried firearms, guns were bought and sold through the mails, crime was not what it is today, and the country pretty much took firearms in its stride. How things have changed.

Statute at Large

Note: The following is a *Statute at Large;* it received no section number after it was passed by Congress. As such, it does not appear in the regular numbered sections of the U.S. laws. The result is that, although this is law passed by Congress, with the full weight and effect of any other statute, it is not widely known. This is the somewhat troublesome case with so-called *Statutes at Large.* The language here is originally part of the Gun Control Act of 1968.

The language of this statute is surprisingly clear. It describes why Congress felt the need for the Gun Control Act to control crime, and limits government activity with respect to honest citizens.

The Congress hereby declares that the purpose of this title [which amended this chapter] is to provide support to Federal, State, and local law enforcement officials in their fight against crime and violence, and it is not the purpose of this title to place any undue or unnecessary Federal restrictions or burdens on law-abiding citizens with respect to the acquisition, possession, or use of firearms appropriate to the purpose of hunting, trapshooting, targetshooting, personal protection, or any other lawful activity, and that this title is not intended to discourage or eliminate the private ownership or use of firearms by law-abiding citizens for lawful purposes, or provide for the imposition by Federal regulations of any procedures or requirements other than those reasonably necessary to implement and effectuate the provisions of this title.

(a) The Congress hereby finds and declares—

(1) that there is a widespread traffic in firearms moving in or otherwise affecting interstate or foreign commerce, and that the existing Federal controls over such

traffic do not adequately enable the States to control this traffic within their own borders through the exercise of their police power;

(2) that the ease with which any person can acquire firearms other than a rifle or shotgun (including criminals, juveniles without the knowledge or consent of their parents or guardians, narcotics addicts, mental defectives, armed groups who would supplant the functions of duly constituted public authorities, and others whose possession of such weapons is similarly contrary to the public interest) is a significant factor in the prevalence of lawlessness and violent crime in the United States;

(3) that only through adequate Federal control over interstate and foreign commerce in these weapons, and over all persons engaging in the businesses of importing, manufacturing, or dealing in them, can this grave problem be properly dealt with, and effective State and local regulation of this traffic be made possible;

(4) that the acquisition on a mail-order basis of firearms other than a rifle or shotgun by nonlicensed individuals, from a place other than their State of residence, has materially tended to thwart the effectiveness of State laws and regulations, and local ordinances;

(5) that the sale or other disposition of concealable weapons by importers, manufacturers, and dealers holding Federal licenses, to nonresidents of the State in which the licensees' places of business are located, has tended to make ineffective the laws, regulations, and ordinances in the several States and local jurisdictions regarding such firearms;

(6) that there is a causal relationship between the easy availability of firearms other than a rifle or shotgun and juvenile and youthful criminal behavior, and that such firearms have been widely sold by federally licensed importers and dealers to emotionally immature, or thrill-bent juveniles and minors prone to criminal behavior;

(7) that the United States has become the dumping ground of the castoff surplus military weapons of other nations, and that such weapons, and the large volume of relatively inexpensive pistols and revolvers (largely worthless for sporting purposes), imported into the United States in recent years, has contributed greatly to lawlessness and to the Nation's law enforcement problems;

(8) that the lack of adequate Federal control over interstate and foreign commerce in highly destructive weapons (such as bazookas, mortars, anti-tank guns, and so forth, and destructive devices such as explosive or incendiary grenades, bombs, missiles, and so forth) has allowed such weapons and devices to fall into the hands of lawless persons, including armed groups who would supplant lawful authority, thus creating a problem of national concern;

(9) that the existing licensing system under the Federal Firearms Act [former sections 901 to 910 of Title 15] does not provide adequate license fees or proper standards for the granting or denial of licenses, and that this had led to licenses being issued to persons not reasonably entitled thereto, thus distorting the purposes of the licensing system.

(b) The Congress further hereby declares that the purpose of this title [enacting this chapter and repealing sections 901 to 910 of Title 15]; is to cope with the conditions referred to in the foregoing subsection, and that it is not the purpose of this title [enacting this chapter and repealing sections 901 to 910 of Title 15] to place any undue or unnecessary Federal restrictions or burdens on law-abiding citizens with respect to the acquisition, possession, or use of firearms appropriate to the purpose of hunting, trap shooting, target shooting, personal protection, or any other lawful activity, and that this title [enacting this chapter and repealing sections 901 to 910 of Title 15] is not intended to discourage or eliminate the private ownership or use of firearms by law-abiding citizens for lawful purposes, or provide for the imposition by Federal regulations of any procedures or requirements other than those reasonably necessary to implement and effectuate the provisions of this title [enacting this chapter and repealing sections 901 to 910 of Title 15].

Statute at Large

> Note: The following is a *Statute at Large;* it received no section number after it was passed by Congress. As such, it does not appear in the regular numbered sections of the U.S. laws. The result is that, although this is law passed by Congress, with the full weight and effect of any other statute, it is not widely known. This is the somewhat troublesome case with so-called *Statutes at Large.* The language here is originally part of the 1994 Crime Bill.
>
> The statute says the Attorney General must report on the effectiveness of the law within given time frames.

(a) Study.—The Attorney General shall investigate and study the effect of this subtitle [Subtitle A, §§ 110101 to 110106, of Title XI of Pub.L. 103-322, which amended this section and sections 922, 923, and 924 of this title and enacted provisions set out as notes under this section] and the amendments made by this subtitle, and in particular shall determine their impact, if any, on violent and drug trafficking crime. The study shall be conducted over a period of 18 months, commencing 12 months after the date of enactment of this Act [Sept. 13, 1994].

(b) Report.—Not later than 30 months after the date of enactment of this Act [Sept. 13, 1994] the Attorney General shall prepare and submit to the Congress a report setting forth in detail the findings and determinations made in the study under subsection (a).

18 USC § 921. Definitions

> The Gist: Key terms are defined for use in Chapter 44 only. Although definitions of these terms, when used in other parts of the law, may be somewhat different (26–5845 is a powerful example, see its definition for "firearm," and also see 18–232), many commonly used firearm-related terms come directly from these definitions. Examples include firearm, handgun, rifle, shotgun, antique firearm, destructive device, short-barreled rifle or shotgun, armor piercing ammunition, machine gun, silencer, semiautomatic rifle, and more.
>
> In 1998, rifles and shotguns were redefined, by eliminating the "fixed cartridge" portion of their definitions, to include muzzleloaders, which had been exempt from many laws. Antique firearms were redefined to include certain types of muzzleloaders.
>
> The firearms, equipment and characteristics designated as semiautomatic assault weapons under the highly controversial 1994 Public Safety and Recreational Firearms Use Protection Act (also referred to as the Crime Bill) are listed under subsection (a)(30) and (31). They remain listed there for historical purposes, but expired and are no longer effective, as of Sep. 13, 2004.

(a) As used in this chapter—

(1) The term "**person**" and the term "**whoever**" include any individual, corporation, company, association, firm, partnership, society, or joint stock company.

(2) The term "**interstate or foreign commerce**" includes commerce between any place in a State and any place outside of that State, or within any possession of the United States (not including the Canal Zone) or the District of Columbia, but such term does not include commerce between places within the same State but through

any place outside of that State. The term "**State**" includes the District of Columbia, the Commonwealth of Puerto Rico, and the possessions of the United States (not including the Canal Zone).

(3) The term "**firearm**" means

(A) any weapon (including a starter gun) which will or is designed to or may readily be converted to expel a projectile by the action of an explosive;

(B) the frame or receiver of any such weapon;

(C) any firearm muffler or firearm silencer; or

(D) any destructive device. Such term does not include an antique firearm.

(4) The term "**destructive device**" means—

(A) any explosive, incendiary, or poison gas—

(i) bomb,

(ii) grenade,

(iii) rocket having a propellant charge of more than four ounces,

(iv) missile having an explosive or incendiary charge of more than one-quarter ounce,

(v) mine, or

(vi) device similar to any of the devices described in the preceding clauses;

(B) any type of weapon (other than a shotgun or a shotgun shell which the Attorney General finds is generally recognized as particularly suitable for sporting purposes) by whatever name known which will, or which may be readily converted to, expel a projectile by the action of an explosive or other propellant, and which has any barrel with a bore of more than one-half inch in diameter; and

(C) any combination of parts either designed or intended for use in converting any device into any destructive device described in subparagraph (A) or (B) and from which a destructive device may be readily assembled. The term "**destructive device**" shall not include any device which is neither designed nor redesigned for use as a weapon; any device, although originally designed for use as a weapon, which is redesigned for use as a signaling, pyrotechnic, line throwing, safety, or similar device; surplus ordnance sold, loaned, or given by the Secretary of the Army pursuant to the provisions of section 4684(2), 4685, or 4686 of title 10; or any other device which the Attorney General finds is not likely to be used as a weapon, is an antique, or is a rifle which the owner intends to use solely for sporting, recreational or cultural purposes.

(5) The term "**shotgun**" means a weapon designed or redesigned, made or remade, and intended to be fired from the shoulder and designed or redesigned and made or remade to use the energy of an explosive to fire through a smooth bore either a number of ball shot or a single projectile for each single pull of the trigger.

(6) The term "**short-barreled shotgun**" means a shotgun having one or more barrels less than eighteen inches in length and any weapon made from a shotgun (whether by alteration, modification, or otherwise) if such weapon as modified has an overall length of less than twenty-six inches.

(7) The term "**rifle**" means a weapon designed or redesigned, made or remade, and intended to be fired from the shoulder and designed or redesigned and made or remade to use the energy of an explosive to fire only a single projectile through a rifled bore for each single pull of the trigger.

(8) The term "**short-barreled rifle**" means a rifle having one or more barrels less than sixteen inches in length and any weapon made from a rifle (whether by alteration, modification, or otherwise) if such weapon, as modified, has an overall length of less than twenty-six inches.

(9) The term "**importer**" means any person engaged in the business of importing or bringing firearms or ammunition into the United States for purposes of sale or distribution; and the term "**licensed importer**" means any such person licensed under the provisions of this chapter.

(10) The term "**manufacturer**" means any person engaged in the business of manufacturing firearms or ammunition for purposes of sale or distribution; and the term "**licensed manufacturer**" means any such person licensed under the provisions of this chapter.

(11) The term "**dealer**" means

(A) any person engaged in the business of selling firearms at wholesale or retail,

(B) any person engaged in the business of repairing firearms or of making or fitting special barrels, stocks, or trigger mechanisms to firearms, or

(C) any person who is a pawnbroker. The term "**licensed dealer**" means any dealer who is licensed under the provisions of this chapter.

(12) The term "**pawnbroker**" means any person whose business or occupation includes the taking or receiving, by way of pledge or pawn, of any firearm as security for the payment or repayment of money.

(13) The term "**collector**" means any person who acquires, holds, or disposes of firearms as curios or relics, as the Attorney General shall by regulation define, and the term "**licensed collector**" means any such person licensed under the provisions of this chapter.

(14) The term "**indictment**" includes an indictment or information in any court under which a crime punishable by imprisonment for a term exceeding one year may be prosecuted.

(15) The term "**fugitive from justice**" means any person who has fled from any State to avoid prosecution for a crime or to avoid giving testimony in any criminal proceeding.

(16) The term '**antique firearm**' means—

(A) any firearm (including any firearm with a matchlock, flintlock, percussion cap, or similar type of ignition system) manufactured in or before 1898; or

(B) any replica of any firearm described in subparagraph (A) if such replica—

(i) is not designed or redesigned for using rimfire or conventional centerfire fixed ammunition, or

(ii) uses rimfire or conventional centerfire fixed ammunition which is no longer manufactured in the United States and which is not readily available in the ordinary channels of commercial trade; or

(C) any muzzle loading rifle, muzzle loading shotgun, or muzzle loading pistol, which is designed to use black powder, or a black powder substitute, and which cannot use fixed ammunition. For purposes of this subparagraph, the term 'antique firearm' shall not include any weapon which incorporates a firearm frame or receiver, any firearm which is converted into a muzzle loading weapon, or any muzzle loading weapon which can be readily converted to fire fixed ammunition by replacing the barrel, bolt, breechblock, or any combination thereof.

(16) The term "**antique firearm**" means—

(A) any firearm (including any firearm with a matchlock, flintlock, percussion cap, or similar type of ignition system) manufactured in or before 1898; and

(B) any replica of any firearm described in subparagraph (A) if such replica—

(i) is not designed or redesigned for using rimfire or conventional centerfire fixed ammunition, or

(ii) uses rimfire or conventional centerfire fixed ammunition which is no longer manufactured in the United States and which is not readily available in the ordinary channels of commercial trade.

(17)(A) The term "**ammunition**" means ammunition or cartridge cases, primers, bullets, or propellent powder designed for use in any firearm.

(B) The term "**armor piercing ammunition**" means—

(i) a projectile or projectile core which may be used in a handgun and which is constructed entirely (excluding the presence of traces of other substances) from one or a combination of tungsten alloys, steel, iron, brass, bronze, beryllium copper, or depleted uranium; or

(ii) a full jacketed projectile larger than .22 caliber designed and intended for use in a handgun and whose jacket has a weight of more than 25 percent of the total weight of the projectile.

(C) The term "**armor piercing ammunition**" does not include shotgun shot required by Federal or State environmental or game regulations for hunting purposes, a frangible projectile designed for target shooting, a projectile which the Attorney General finds is primarily intended to be used for sporting purposes, or any other projectile or projectile core which the Attorney General finds is intended to be used for industrial purposes, including a charge used in an oil and gas well perforating device.

(18) The term "**Attorney General**" means the Attorney General of the United States.

(19) The term "**published ordinance**" means a published law of any political subdivision of a State which the Attorney General determines to be relevant to the enforcement of this chapter and which is contained on a list compiled by the Attorney General, which list shall be published in the Federal Register, revised annually, and furnished to each licensee under this chapter.

(20) The term "**crime punishable by Imprisonment for a term exceeding one year**" does not include—

(A) any Federal or State offenses pertaining to antitrust violations, unfair trade practices, restraints of trade, or other similar offenses relating to the regulation of business practices, or

(B) any State offense classified by the laws of the State as a misdemeanor and punishable by a term of imprisonment of two years or less. What constitutes a conviction of such a crime shall be determined in accordance with the law of the jurisdiction in which the proceedings were held. Any conviction which has been expunged, or set aside or for which a person has been pardoned or has had civil rights restored shall not be considered a conviction for purposes of this chapter, unless such pardon, expungement, or restoration of civil rights expressly provides that the person may not ship, transport, possess, or receive firearms.

(21) The term "**engaged in the business**" means—

(A) as applied to a manufacturer of firearms, a person who devotes time, attention, and labor to manufacturing firearms as a regular course of trade or business with the principal objective of livelihood and profit through the sale or distribution of the firearms manufactured;

(B) as applied to a manufacturer of ammunition, a person who devotes time, attention, and labor to manufacturing ammunition as a regular course of trade or business with the principal objective of livelihood and profit through the sale or distribution of the ammunition manufactured;

(C) as applied to a dealer in firearms, as defined in section 921(a)(11)(A), a person who devotes time, attention, and labor to dealing in firearms as a regular course of trade or business with the principal objective of livelihood and profit through the repetitive purchase and resale of firearms, but such term shall not include a person who makes occasional sales, exchanges, or purchases of firearms for the enhancement of a personal collection or for a hobby, or who sells all or part of his personal collection of firearms;

(D) as applied to a dealer in firearms, as defined in section 921(a)(11)(B), a person who devotes time, attention, and labor to engaging in such activity as a regular course of trade or business with the principal objective of livelihood and profit, but such term shall not include a person who makes occasional repairs of firearms, or who occasionally fits special barrels, stocks, or trigger mechanisms to firearms;

(E) as applied to an importer of firearms, a person who devotes time, attention, and labor to importing firearms as a regular course of trade or business with the principal objective of livelihood and profit through the sale or distribution of the firearms imported; and

(F) as applied to an importer of ammunition, a person who devotes time, attention, and labor to importing ammunition as a regular course of trade or business with the principal objective of livelihood and profit through the sale or distribution of the ammunition imported.

(22) The term "**with the principal objective of livelihood and profit**" means that the intent underlying the sale or disposition of firearms is predominantly one of obtaining livelihood and pecuniary gain, as opposed to other intents, such as improving or liquidating a personal firearms collection: Provided, That proof of profit shall not be required as to a person who engages in the regular and repetitive purchase and disposition of firearms for criminal purposes or terrorism. For purposes of this paragraph, the term "**terrorism**" means activity, directed against United States persons, which—

(A) is committed by an individual who is not a national or permanent resident alien of the United States;

(B) involves violent acts or acts dangerous to human life which would be a criminal violation if committed within the jurisdiction of the United States; and

(C) is intended—

(i) to intimidate or coerce a civilian population;

(ii) to influence the policy of a government by intimidation or coercion; or

(iii) to affect the conduct of a government by assassination or kidnapping.

(23) The term "**machinegun**" has the meaning given such term in section 5845(b) of the National Firearms Act (26 U.S.C. 5845(b)).

(24) The terms "**firearm silencer**" and "**firearm muffler**" mean any device for silencing, muffling, or diminishing the report of a portable firearm, including any combination of parts, designed or redesigned, and intended for use in assembling or fabricating a firearm silencer or firearm muffler, and any part intended only for use in such assembly or fabrication.

(25) The term "**school zone**" means—

(A) in, or on the grounds of, a public, parochial or private school; or

(B) within a distance of 1,000 feet from the grounds of a public, parochial or private school.

(26) The term "**school**" means a school which provides elementary or secondary education, as determined under State law.

(27) The term "**motor vehicle**" has the meaning given such term in section 10102 of title 49, United States Code.

(28) The term "**semiautomatic rifle**" means any repeating rifle which utilizes a portion of the energy of a firing cartridge to extract the fired cartridge case and chamber the next round, and which requires a separate pull of the trigger to fire each cartridge.

(29) The term "**handgun**" means—

(A) a firearm which has a short stock and is designed to be held and fired by the use of a single hand; and

(B) any combination of parts from which a firearm described in subparagraph (A) can be assembled.

<Section (a)(30) below, expired, here for historical purpose only.>

(30) The term "**semiautomatic assault weapon**" means—

> Note: This is the 1994 Crime Bill list of firearms and parts which were only legal for the public, between the years of 1994 and 2004, if they were made prior to Sep. 13, 1994. When this law expired on Sep. 13, 2004, this list was repealed and all its restrictions ended, but the lists (a)(30) and (a)(31) remain here for historical purposes. They are no longer effective, and aren't included in the word count.

(A) any of the firearms, or copies or duplicates of the firearms in any caliber, known as—

(i) Norinco, Mitchell, and Poly Technologies Avtomat Kalashnikovs (all models);

(ii) Action Arms Israeli Military Industries UZI and Galil;

(iii) Beretta AR70 (SC-70);

(iv) Colt AR-15;

(v) Fabrique National FN/FAL, FN/LAR, and FNC;

(vi) SWD M-10, M-11, M-11/9, and M-12;

(vii) Steyr AUG;

(viii) INTRATEC TEC-9, TEC-DC9 and TEC-22; and

(ix) revolving cylinder shotguns, such as (or similar to) the Street Sweeper and Striker 12;

(B) a semiautomatic rifle that has an ability to accept a detachable magazine and has at least 2 of—

(i) a folding or telescoping stock;

(ii) a pistol grip that protrudes conspicuously beneath the action of the weapon;

(iii) a bayonet mount;

(iv) a flash suppressor or threaded barrel designed to accommodate a flash suppressor; and

(v) a grenade launcher;

(C) a semiautomatic pistol that has an ability to accept a detachable magazine and has at least 2 of—

(i) an ammunition magazine that attaches to the pistol outside of the pistol grip;

(ii) a threaded barrel capable of accepting a barrel extender, flash suppressor, forward handgrip, or silencer;

(iii) a shroud that is attached to, or partially or completely encircles, the barrel and that permits the shooter to hold the firearm with the nontrigger hand without being burned;

(iv) a manufactured weight of 50 ounces or more when the pistol is unloaded; and

(v) a semiautomatic version of an automatic firearm; and

(D) a semiautomatic shotgun that has at least 2 of—

(i) a folding or telescoping stock;

(ii) a pistol grip that protrudes conspicuously beneath the action of the weapon;

(iii) a fixed magazine capacity in excess of 5 rounds; and

(iv) an ability to accept a detachable magazine.

<Note: The above paragraph, (a)(30), expired on Sept. 13, 2004, and remains here for historical purposes.>

<Section (a)(31) below, expired, here for historical purpose only.>

(31) The term "**large capacity ammunition feeding device**"—

(A) means a magazine, belt, drum, feed strip, or similar device manufactured after the date of enactment of the Violent Crime Control and Law Enforcement Act of 1994 that has a capacity of, or that can be readily restored or converted to accept, more than 10 rounds of ammunition; but

(B) does not include an attached tubular device designed to accept, and capable of operating only with, .22 caliber rimfire ammunition.

<Note: The above paragraph, (a)(31), expired on Sept. 13, 2004, and remains here for historical purposes.>

(32) The term "**intimate partner**" means, with respect to a person, the spouse of the person, a former spouse of the person, an individual who is a parent of a child of the person, and an individual who cohabitates or has cohabited with the person.

(b) For the purposes of this chapter, a member of the Armed Forces on active duty is a resident of the State in which his permanent duty station is located.

(33)(A) Except as provided in subparagraph (C), the term "**misdemeanor crime of domestic violence**" means an offense that—

(i) is a misdemeanor under Federal or State law; and

(ii) has, as an element, the use or attempted use of physical force, or the threatened use of a deadly weapon, committed by a current or former spouse, parent, or guardian of the victim, by a person with whom the victim shares a child in common, by a person who is cohabiting with or has cohabited with the victim as a spouse, parent, or guardian, or by a person similarly situated to a spouse, parent, or guardian of the victim.

(B)(i) A person shall not be considered to have been convicted of such an offense for purposes of this chapter, unless—

(I) the person was represented by counsel in the case, or knowingly and intelligently waived the right to counsel in the case; and

(II) in the case of a prosecution for an offense described in this paragraph for which a person was entitled to a jury trial in the jurisdiction in which the case was tried, either

(aa) the case was tried by a jury, or

(bb) the person knowingly and intelligently waived the right to have the case tried by a jury, by guilty plea or otherwise.

(ii) A person shall not be considered to have been convicted of such an offense for purposes of this chapter if the conviction has been expunged or set aside, or is an offense for which the person has been pardoned or has had civil rights restored (if the law of the applicable jurisdiction provides for the loss of civil rights under such an offense) unless the pardon, expungement, or restoration of civil rights expressly provides that the person may not ship, transport, possess, or receive firearms.

(34) The term "**secure gun storage or safety device**" means—

(A) a device that, when installed on a firearm, is designed to prevent the firearm from being operated without first deactivating the device;

(B) a device incorporated into the design of the firearm that is designed to prevent the operation of the firearm by anyone not having access to the device; or

(C) a safe, gun safe, gun case, lock box, or other device that is designed to be or can be used to store a firearm and that is designed to be unlocked only by means of a key, a combination, or other similar means.

(35) The term "**body armor**" means any product sold or offered for sale, in interstate or foreign commerce, as personal protective body covering intended to protect against gunfire, regardless of whether the product is to be worn alone or is sold as a complement to another product or garment.

(b) For the purposes of this chapter, **a member of the Armed Forces** on active duty is a resident of the State in which his permanent duty station is located.

June 19, 1968 (2,918)
TITLE 18. CRIMES AND CRIMINAL PROCEDURE • PART I: CRIMES • CHAPTER 44: FIREARMS

18 USC § 922. Unlawful acts

This is often considered the main federal gun law. It requires licensing and controls on firearms manufacture, distribution and importation, and includes the basic requirements and restrictions for the public and federal firearms-license holders. New legislation has been accumulating here since its inception.

Enacted as the Gun Control Act of 1968, it was largely a response to political assassinations in the early 1960s. It is the second major federal gun law in U.S. history (after the Constitution), although a substantial number of minor laws preceded it. The nation's first major gun law, the National Firearms Act of 1934, was adopted in response to gangster activity of the prohibition era, and can be found in Title 26, the Internal Revenue Service laws. It was placed there because, at the time, the Congress believed it was precluded by the Second Amendment from any legitimate authority to regulate firearms, and so used its ability to levy taxes to get around that restriction, an end run the courts eventually accepted.

From its inception in 1968 this law and related regulations were under the direction of the Treasury Dept., which handled the task through the Bureau of Alcohol, Tobacco and Firearms (BATF). All those rules and controls were transferred to the Attorney General (AG) as part of the overhaul of law enforcement brought about by the Arab muslim terrorist attacks on 9/11/01. The BATF became BATFE, with responsibility for explosives added.

Section 922 brings up an interesting point in many debates—just how many gun laws are there? The popularized statistic puts the number nationally at a bit over 20,000, but, counted how? This single section runs 8,307 words, in 245 paragraphs—more than twice the size of the next largest section (which is the very next section, 18–923, at 3,466 words). Is 18-922 one law? How would you break out and count the separate parts? Is each individual restriction or requirement a separate law? Perhaps you could just count the number of bills (known as "public laws") enacted by Congress that are incorporated (codified) here to arrive at an answer. Although an imperfect solution to this dilemma, Bloomfield Press tracks the size of federal gun law by word count, which at least provides a strict mathematical tally of the body of these laws.

Because the section is so long, *Gists* have been distributed throughout the text for easy reference.

FFL is the commonly used abbreviation for *federal firearms license*. It is used in the notes below as shorthand for the recurring legal phrase (and its variations), "licensed importer, licensed manufacturer, licensed dealer, or licensed collector," and may be thought of as the word, "licensee." Be cautious, however, since all licenses do not convey the same privileges (especially true for collectors).

AG is the abbreviation for Attorney General. The AG is frequently specified in the statutes, but in practice, people designated by the AG carry out the responsibilities.

Shorthand. Where the law uses long strings of terms, the notes below tend to select a single representative term for easier reading. For example, "sell, trade, give, transport, deliver or transfer," might be expressed here as simply, "transfer." This technique, though a great aid to readability that helps convey the gist, requires you to be cautious since it does tend to affect the precision the actual law provides.

18 USC § 922 (a)

(a)(1) It's illegal to import, make or deal in firearms or ammunition without a license. Only an FFL may ship firearms or ammunition in interstate or foreign commerce.

(a)(2) An FFL may only ship firearms in interstate or foreign commerce to another FFL, with two exceptions: a non-FFL may ship a firearm to an FFL and receive it back directly (basically relates to repair and replacement of private firearms), and an FFL can send a firearm through the mails to the proper authorities. This paragraph applies in the U.S., Washington D.C., Puerto Rico, and all U.S. Possessions.

(a)(3) It's illegal to bring a gun you obtain in another state into your home state, unless you're an FFL, with three exceptions: firearms legally obtained through bequest or intestate succession; long guns you obtain as described in (b)(3); and firearms you obtained before the effective date of this chapter (Dec. 16, 1968). Note that this generally prevents family and friends in different states from giving one another firearms, except through an FFL.

(a)(4) Only an FFL may transport destructive devices, machine guns or short-barreled long guns in interstate or foreign commerce. The Attorney General may authorize exceptions.

(a)(5) It's illegal to in any way transfer a firearm to someone you know (or believe) does not live in your state, unless you're an FFL, with two exceptions: firearms legally transferred through bequest or intestate succession, and a temporary loan or rental of a firearm to anyone for lawful sporting purposes. Note that this generally prevents family and friends in different states from giving one another firearms, except through an FFL.

(a)(6) It's illegal to make any false statements or use any false ID to obtain firearms or ammunition from an FFL.

(a)(7) It's illegal to make or import armor piercing ammunition, with three exceptions: for use by the proper authorities, for export, or for testing authorized by the AG.

> (a)(8) It's illegal to sell or deliver armor piercing ammunition, with three exceptions: for use by the proper authorities, for export, or for testing authorized by the AG.
>
> (a)(9) Except for FFLs, it's illegal for any person who doesn't live in any state, to receive firearms except for lawful sporting purposes.

(a) It shall be unlawful—

(1) for any person—

(A) except a licensed importer, licensed manufacturer, or licensed dealer, to engage in the business of importing, manufacturing, or dealing in firearms, or in the course of such business to ship, transport, or receive any firearm in interstate or foreign commerce; or

(B) except a licensed importer or licensed manufacturer, to engage in the business of importing or manufacturing ammunition, or in the course of such business, to ship, transport, or receive any ammunition in interstate or foreign commerce;

(2) for any importer, manufacturer, dealer, or collector licensed under the provisions of this chapter to ship or transport in interstate or foreign commerce any firearm to any person other than a licensed importer, licensed manufacturer, licensed dealer, or licensed collector, except that—

(A) this paragraph and subsection (b)(3) shall not be held to preclude a licensed importer, licensed manufacturer, licensed dealer, or licensed collector from returning a firearm or replacement firearm of the same kind and type to a person from whom it was received; and this paragraph shall not be held to preclude an individual from mailing a firearm owned in compliance with Federal, State, and local law to a licensed importer, licensed manufacturer, licensed dealer, or licensed collector;

(B) this paragraph shall not be held to preclude a licensed importer, licensed manufacturer, or licensed dealer from depositing a firearm for conveyance in the mails to any officer, employee, agent, or watchman who, pursuant to the provisions of section 1715 of this title, is eligible to receive through the mails pistols, revolvers, and other firearms capable of being concealed on the person, for use in connection with his official duty; and

(C) nothing in this paragraph shall be construed as applying in any manner in the District of Columbia, the Commonwealth of Puerto Rico, or any possession of the United States differently than it would apply if the District of Columbia, the Commonwealth of Puerto Rico, or the possession were in fact a State of the United States;

(3) for any person, other than a licensed importer, licensed manufacturer, licensed dealer, or licensed collector to transport into or receive in the State where he resides (or if the person is a corporation or other business entity, the State where it maintains a place of business) any firearm purchased or otherwise obtained by such person outside that State, except that this paragraph

(A) shall not preclude any person who lawfully acquires a firearm by bequest or intestate succession in a State other than his State of residence from transporting the firearm into or receiving it in that State, if it is lawful for such person to purchase or possess such firearm in that State,

(B) shall not apply to the transportation or receipt of a firearm obtained in conformity with subsection (b)(3) of this section, and

(C) shall not apply to the transportation of any firearm acquired in any State prior to the effective date of this chapter;

(4) for any person, other than a licensed importer, licensed manufacturer, licensed dealer, or licensed collector, to transport in interstate or foreign commerce any destructive device, machinegun (as defined in section 5845 of the Internal Revenue Code of 1954), short-barreled shotgun, or short-barreled rifle, except as specifically authorized by the Attorney General consistent with public safety and necessity;

(5) for any person (other than a licensed importer, licensed manufacturer, licensed dealer, or licensed collector) to transfer, sell, trade, give, transport, or deliver any firearm to any person (other than a licensed importer, licensed manufacturer,

licensed dealer, or licensed collector) who the transferor knows or has reasonable cause to believe does not reside in (or if the person is a corporation or other business entity, does not maintain a place of business in) the State in which the transferor resides; except that this paragraph shall not apply to

(A) the transfer, transportation, or delivery of a firearm made to carry out a bequest of a firearm to, or an acquisition by intestate succession of a firearm by, a person who is permitted to acquire or possess a firearm under the laws of the State of his residence, and

(B) the loan or rental of a firearm to any person for temporary use for lawful sporting purposes;

(6) for any person in connection with the acquisition or attempted acquisition of any firearm or ammunition from a licensed importer, licensed manufacturer, licensed dealer, or licensed collector, knowingly to make any false or fictitious oral or written statement or to furnish or exhibit any false, fictitious, or misrepresented identification, intended or likely to deceive such importer, manufacturer, dealer, or collector with respect to any fact material to the lawfulness of the sale or other disposition of such firearm or ammunition under the provisions of this chapter;

(7) for any person to manufacture or import armor piercing ammunition, except that this paragraph shall not apply to—

(A) the manufacture or importation of such ammunition for the use of the United States or any department or agency thereof or any State or any department, agency, or political subdivision thereof;

(B) the manufacture of such ammunition for the purpose of exportation; and

(C) any manufacture or importation for the purposes of testing or experimentation authorized by the Attorney General;

(8) for any manufacturer or importer to sell or deliver armor piercing ammunition, except that this paragraph shall not apply to—

(A) the sale or delivery by a manufacturer or importer of such ammunition for use of the United States or any department or agency thereof or any State or any department, agency, or political subdivision thereof;

(B) the sale or delivery by a manufacturer or importer of such ammunition for the purpose of exportation;

(C) the sale or delivery by a manufacturer or importer of such ammunition for the purposes of testing or experimenting authorized by the Attorney General; and

(9) for any person, other than a licensed importer, licensed manufacturer, licensed dealer, or licensed collector, who does not reside in any State to receive any firearms unless such receipt is for lawful sporting purposes.

18 USC § 922 (b)

(b)(1) It's illegal for an FFL to sell or deliver a rifle or shotgun and matching ammunition to anyone under 18 years old. It's illegal for an FFL to sell or deliver a handgun and matching ammunition to anyone under 21 years old.

(b)(2) It's illegal for an FFL to sell or deliver any firearm in violation of any state law or local ordinance in effect at the place of sale.

(b)(3) It's illegal for an FFL to sell or deliver a firearm to a person who doesn't live in the FFL's state, with two exceptions: the transfer is allowed if the firearm is a rifle or shotgun, the transfer takes place face-to-face, and the transfer would be legal under both states' laws; and a temporary loan or rental of a firearm is allowed to anyone for lawful sporting purposes.

(b)(4) It's illegal for an FFL to sell or deliver a destructive device, machine gun or short-barreled long gun to anyone, except as authorized by the AG.

> (b)(5) An FFL must make an official record of every sale or transfer of all firearms and armor-piercing ammunition. The record must identify the receiving individual or company. The first four paragraphs of this subsection don't apply to FFLs. Research organizations authorized by the AG are exempt from (b)(4).

(b) It shall be unlawful for any licensed importer, licensed manufacturer, licensed dealer, or licensed collector to sell or deliver—

(1) any firearm or ammunition to any individual who the licensee knows or has reasonable cause to believe is less than eighteen years of age, and, if the firearm, or ammunition is other than a shotgun or rifle, or ammunition for a shotgun or rifle, to any individual who the licensee knows or has reasonable cause to believe is less than twenty-one years of age;

(2) any firearm to any person in any State where the purchase or possession by such person of such firearm would be in violation of any State law or any published ordinance applicable at the place of sale, delivery or other disposition, unless the licensee knows or has reasonable cause to believe that the purchase or possession would not be in violation of such State law or such published ordinance;

(3) any firearm to any person who the licensee knows or has reasonable cause to believe does not reside in (or if the person is a corporation or other business entity, does not maintain a place of business in) the State in which the licensee's place of business is located, except that this paragraph

(A) shall not apply to the sale or delivery of any rifle or shotgun to a resident of a State other than a State in which the licensee's place of business is located if the transferee meets in person with the transferor to accomplish the transfer, and the sale, delivery, and receipt fully comply with the legal conditions of sale in both such States (and any licensed manufacturer, importer or dealer shall be presumed, for purposes of this subparagraph, in the absence of evidence to the contrary, to have had actual knowledge of the State laws and published ordinances of both States), and

(B) shall not apply to the loan or rental of a firearm to any person for temporary use for lawful sporting purposes;

(4) to any person any destructive device, machinegun (as defined in section 5845 of the Internal Revenue Code of 1954), short-barreled shotgun, or short-barreled rifle, except as specifically authorized by the Attorney General consistent with public safety and necessity; and

(5) any firearm or armor-piercing ammunition to any person unless the licensee notes in his records, required to be kept pursuant to section 923 of this chapter, the name, age, and place of residence of such person if the person is an individual, or the identity and principal and local places of business of such person if the person is a corporation or other business entity. Paragraphs (1), (2), (3), and (4) of this subsection shall not apply to transactions between licensed importers, licensed manufacturers, licensed dealers, and licensed collectors. Paragraph (4) of this subsection shall not apply to a sale or delivery to any research organization designated by the Attorney General.

18 USC § 922 (c)

> (c) An FFL may sell a firearm to a non-FFL who doesn't personally appear at the FFL's place of business if three conditions are met. First, the purchaser must provide a sworn statement with the language found in (c)(1) and attach any permits or other information that may be required. Next, the FFL must send a copy of the statement and a completed firearm description form by return receipt mail to the chief law enforcement officer where the purchaser lives, and receive back either the postal confirmation-of-delivery or refusal-to-accept-delivery notice from the officer. Finally, the FFL must wait seven days after receiving post office

notice before making delivery. The postal notice must be kept as part of the official records.

(c) In any case not otherwise prohibited by this chapter, a licensed importer, licensed manufacturer, or licensed dealer may sell a firearm to a person who does not appear in person at the licensee's business premises (other than another licensed importer, manufacturer, or dealer) only if—

(1) the transferee submits to the transferor a sworn statement in the following form: "Subject to penalties provided by law, I swear that, in the case of any firearm other than a shotgun or a rifle, I am twenty-one years or more of age, or that, in the case of a shotgun or a rifle, I am eighteen years or more of age; that I am not prohibited by the provisions of chapter 44 of title 18, United States Code, from receiving a firearm in interstate or foreign commerce; and that my receipt of this firearm will not be in violation of any statute of the State and published ordinance applicable to the locality in which I reside. Further, the true title, name, and address of the principal law enforcement officer of the locality to which the firearm will be delivered are ... Signature .... Date ...." and containing blank spaces for the attachment of a true copy of any permit or other information required pursuant to such statute or published ordinance;

(2) the transferor has, prior to the shipment or delivery of the firearm, forwarded by registered or certified mail (return receipt requested) a copy of the sworn statement, together with a description of the firearm, in a form prescribed by the Attorney General, to the chief law enforcement officer of the transferee's place of residence, and has received a return receipt evidencing delivery of the statement or has had the statement returned due to the refusal of the named addressee to accept such letter in accordance with United States Post Office Department regulations; and

(3) the transferor has delayed shipment or delivery for a period of at least seven days following receipt of the notification of the acceptance or refusal of delivery of the statement. A copy of the sworn statement and a copy of the notification to the local law enforcement officer, together with evidence of receipt or rejection of that notification shall be retained by the licensee as a part of the records required to be kept under section 923(g).

18 USC § 922 (d)

(d) It's illegal for anyone to knowingly sell or transfer any firearm or ammunition to anyone who: 1–is charged with or has been convicted of a crime which carries more than a one-year sentence (except for state misdemeanors); 2–is a fugitive from justice; 3–unlawfully uses or is addicted to any illegal drugs; 4–is mentally defective (as determined by a court) or has been committed to a mental institution; 5–is an illegal alien, with narrow exceptions; 6–has been dishonorably discharged from the armed forces; 7–has renounced U.S. citizenship; or 8–is under a specifically described court order restraining harassment, stalking or threatening of an intimate partner or partner's child, or 9–has been convicted of a crime of domestic violence, as described in 18-921(a)(33). Narrow exceptions are provided for FFLs awaiting resolution of an indictment, and anyone who has lost firearms rights and had them officially restored.

(d) It shall be unlawful for any person to sell or otherwise dispose of any firearm or ammunition to any person knowing or having reasonable cause to believe that such person—

(1) is under indictment for, or has been convicted in any court of, a crime punishable by imprisonment for a term exceeding one year;

(2) is a fugitive from justice;

(3) is an unlawful user of or addicted to any controlled substance (as defined in section 102 of the Controlled Substances Act (21 U.S.C. 802));

(4) has been adjudicated as a mental defective or has been committed to any mental institution;

(5) who, being an alien—

(A) is illegally or unlawfully in the United States; or

(B) except as provided in subsection (y)(2), has been admitted to the United States under a nonimmigrant visa (as that term is defined in section 101(a)(26) of the Immigration and Nationality Act (8 U.S.C. 1101(a)(26)));

(6) who has been discharged from the Armed Forces under dishonorable conditions;

(7) who, having been a citizen of the United States, has renounced his citizenship;

(8) is subject to a court order that restrains such person from harassing, stalking, or threatening an intimate partner of such person or child of such intimate partner or person, or engaging in other conduct that would place an intimate partner in reasonable fear of bodily injury to the partner or child, except that this paragraph shall only apply to a court order that—

(A) was issued after a hearing of which such person received actual notice, and at which such person had the opportunity to participate; and

(B)(i) includes a finding that such person represents a credible threat to the physical safety of such intimate partner or child; or

(ii) by its terms explicitly prohibits the use, attempted use, or threatened use of physical force against such intimate partner or child that would reasonably be expected to cause bodily injury; or

(9) has been convicted in any court of a misdemeanor crime of domestic violence.

This subsection shall not apply with respect to the sale or disposition of a firearm or ammunition to a licensed importer, licensed manufacturer, licensed dealer, or licensed collector who pursuant to subsection (b) of section 925 of this chapter is not precluded from dealing in firearms or ammunition, or to a person who has been granted relief from disabilities pursuant to subsection (c) of section 925 of this chapter.

18 USC § 922 (e)

(e) When shipping a firearm or ammunition in interstate or foreign commerce, by a common or contract carrier (for example, a bus line, train, airline, etc.), to anyone who is not an FFL, you must notify the carrier in writing that you are shipping a firearm or ammunition. If you are a passenger transporting a legally owned or possessed firearm in interstate or foreign commerce, by means of a common or contract carrier, you may place the firearm or ammunition in the custody of the pilot, captain, conductor or operator of the carrier for the duration of the trip. The carrier may not in any way tag the outside of your package or luggage to indicate it contains a firearm.

This last provision is a little-known requirement of the Brady Law, designed to stop a common practice that resulted in the frequent theft of transported firearms.

(e) It shall be unlawful for any person knowingly to deliver or cause to be delivered to any common or contract carrier for transportation or shipment in interstate or foreign commerce, to persons other than licensed importers, licensed manufacturers, licensed dealers, or licensed collectors, any package or other container in which there is any firearm or ammunition without written notice to the carrier that such firearm or ammunition is being transported or shipped; except that any passenger who owns or legally possesses a firearm or ammunition being transported aboard any common or contract carrier for movement with the passenger in interstate or foreign commerce may deliver said firearm or ammunition into the custody of the pilot, captain, conductor or operator of such common or contract carrier for the duration of the trip without violating any of the provisions of this chapter. No common or contract carrier shall require or cause any label, tag, or other written notice to be placed on the outside of any package, luggage, or other container that such package, luggage, or other container contains a firearm.

18 USC § 922 (f)

(f)(1) It's illegal for common or contract carriers to transport or deliver a firearm or ammunition, in interstate or foreign commerce, if they believe it would violate any law.

(f)(2) A common or contract carrier must obtain a written acknowledgment of receipt when delivering a firearm in interstate or foreign commerce. (This is another little-known Brady Law requirement.)

(f)(1) It shall be unlawful for any common or contract carrier to transport or deliver in interstate or foreign commerce any firearm or ammunition with knowledge or reasonable cause to believe that the shipment, transportation, or receipt thereof would be in violation of the provisions of this chapter.
(2) It shall be unlawful for any common or contract carrier to deliver in interstate or foreign commerce any firearm without obtaining written acknowledgement of receipt from the recipient of the package or other container in which there is a firearm.

18 USC § 922 (g)   <Prohibited Possessor List>

The list that follows is often called the prohibited possessor list. Under penalty of perjury, a citizen must claim to not be in any of the following categories, when filling out a Form 4473, the form usually required when purchasing a firearm from a licensed dealer.

(g) It's illegal to ship, transport, possess or receive a firearm or ammunition in interstate or foreign commerce, by anyone who: 1–has been convicted of a crime which carries more than a one-year sentence (except for state misdemeanors); 2–is a fugitive from justice; 3–unlawfully uses or is addicted to any illegal drugs; 4–is mentally defective (as determined by a court) or has been committed to a mental institution; 5–is an illegal alien, with narrow exceptions; 6–has been dishonorably discharged from the armed forces; 7–has renounced U.S. citizenship; 8–is under a specifically described court order restraining harassment, stalking or threatening of an intimate partner or partner's child, or 9–has been convicted of a crime of domestic violence, as described in 18-921(a)(33).

Under (g)(9), introduced in 1996 as the "Lautenberg amendment," anyone convicted of a state or federal misdemeanor involving the use or attempted use of physical force, or the threatened use of a deadly weapon, among family members (spouse, parent, guardian, cohabiter, or similar) is added to the list of federal prohibited possessors, and may not ship, transport, possess or receive a firearm or ammunition under federal law.

This marks the first time that a misdemeanor offense serves as grounds for denial of the constitutional right to keep and bear arms. The law is retroactive, affecting an unknown number of people, and no provision is made for the firearms such men and women might already possess. Firearms possession by a prohibited possessor is a five-year federal felony.

A number of narrow conditions may exempt a person from this law, including whether they were represented by an attorney, the type of trial and plea, an expungement or set aside, or a pardon or other restoration of civil rights. The conditions are specified in the definitions in 18-921. Since misdemeanors may be handled by state courts not-of-record, some of these determinations may not be possible.

The current Congressional practice of placing unrelated laws in larger acts, in order to get them passed without debate (or even unnoticed), has raised concerns among many observers. This law is an extreme example of such a practice, and caught both firearms-rights advocates and anti-rights advocates by surprise. The law is drafted broadly, affecting sworn police officers nationwide, the armed forces, and agencies such as the FBI, CIA, Secret Service, Forest Service and others, most of whom are used to being exempted from such laws. So many problems exist with respect to this legislation that is has raised concerns unlike any recent act of Congress. Indeed, some members reportedly were told before voting that this language had been deleted from the final version, and the vote was held before copies of the 2,000-page act were available for review.

Experts close to the issues cite numerous constitutional conflicts (indicated below in parentheses). Among these are: 1–it is *ex post facto*—a law passed after the fact to affect former actions, explicitly prohibited in the Constitution (Art. 1, Sec. 9); 2–it impacts the right to keep and bear arms (2nd Amendment); 3–legally owned items become subject to seizure (4th Amendment); 4–it holds people accountable to a felony without a Grand Jury indictment, represents a second punishment for a single offense creating a double jeopardy, and it requires dispossession of personal property without compensation or due process (5th Amendment); 5–the right to be informed of an accusation, and to counsel and a public jury trial is abrogated by making an existing state misdemeanor the automatic precursor to a federal felony (6th Amendment); 6–using a misdemeanor instead of a felony to deny civil rights may be cruel and unusual punishment (8th Amendment); 7–federal authorities enter an arena historically governed exclusively by the states (10th Amendment); 8–it denies due process, abridges the rights of U.S. citizens by state law and denies equal protection under the law. (14th Amendment).

Domestic violence does not have a single definition at the state level. Divorces for many years included a DV plea as routine expedient for consummating the proceedings. Some states' laws require the arrest of at least one party if the police respond to an apparent domestic-violence report. This raises many issues related to the judicial and plea-bargaining process after an arrest.

An analogy to automobiles crystallizes this law's affects. It is as if a former speeding ticket suddenly became grounds for felony arrest if you own a car or gasoline. When a law is scrutinized for constitutionality it is

> typically held up to a single provision. The eight constitutional issues in this short piece of legislation may set a record.

(g) It shall be unlawful for any person—

(1) who has been convicted in any court of, a crime punishable by imprisonment for a term exceeding one year;

(2) who is a fugitive from justice;

(3) who is an unlawful user of or addicted to any controlled substance (as defined in section 102 of the Controlled Substances Act (21 U.S.C. 802));

(4) who has been adjudicated as a mental defective or who has been committed to a mental institution;

(5) who, being an alien—

(A) is illegally or unlawfully in the United States; or

(B) except as provided in subsection (y)(2), has been admitted to the United States under a nonimmigrant visa (as that term is defined in section 101(a)(26) of the Immigration and Nationality Act (8 U.S.C. 1101(a)(26)));

(6) who has been discharged from the Armed Forces under dishonorable conditions;

(7) who, having been a citizen of the United States, has renounced his citizenship;

(8) who is subject to a court order that—

(A) was issued after a hearing of which such person received actual notice, and at which such person had an opportunity to participate;

(B) restrains such person from harassing, stalking, or threatening an intimate partner of such person or child of such intimate partner or person, or engaging in other conduct that would place an intimate partner in reasonable fear of bodily injury to the partner or child; and

(C)(i) includes a finding that such person represents a credible threat to the physical safety of such intimate partner or child; or

(ii) by its terms explicitly prohibits the use, attempted use, or threatened use of physical force against such intimate partner or child that would reasonably be expected to cause bodily injury; or

(9) who has been convicted in any court of a misdemeanor crime of domestic violence,

to ship or transport in interstate or foreign commerce, or possess in or affecting commerce, any firearm or ammunition; or to receive any firearm or ammunition which has been shipped or transported in interstate or foreign commerce.

18 USC § 922 (h)

> (h) It's illegal for an employee, working for a boss that the employee knows is restricted under subsection (g) above, to receive, have or transport any firearm or ammunition in interstate or foreign commerce, as part of the job.

(h) It shall be unlawful for any individual, who to that individual's knowledge and while being employed for any person described in any paragraph of subsection (g) of this section, in the course of such employment—

(1) to receive, possess, or transport any firearm or ammunition in or affecting interstate or foreign commerce; or

(2) to receive any firearm or ammunition which has been shipped or transported in interstate or foreign commerce.

18 USC § 922 (i)

> (i) It's illegal to ship any firearm or ammunition in interstate or foreign commerce, knowing or believing that it is stolen merchandise.

(i) It shall be unlawful for any person to transport or ship in interstate or foreign commerce, any stolen firearm or stolen ammunition, knowing or having reasonable cause to believe that the firearm or ammunition was stolen.

18 USC § 922 (j)

> (j) It's illegal to in any way handle a firearm or ammunition, if it was ever a part of interstate or foreign commerce, knowing or believing that it is stolen merchandise.

(j) It shall be unlawful for any person to receive, possess, conceal, store, barter, sell, or dispose of any stolen firearm or stolen ammunition, or pledge or accept as security for a loan any stolen firearm or stolen ammunition, which is moving as, which is a part of, which constitutes, or which has been shipped or transported in, interstate or foreign commerce, either before or after it was stolen, knowing or having reasonable cause to believe that the firearm or ammunition was stolen.

18 USC § 922 (k)

> (k) It's illegal to knowingly have, ship or receive a firearm that has its serial number missing or changed, if it was ever a part of interstate or foreign commerce.
>
> Note: You may be wondering why this group of laws repeatedly tie into (or are limited to) "interstate or foreign commerce." This is because the federal government relies upon its Constitutional powers to regulate interstate commerce—matters that involve more than one state (as opposed to intrastate, matters within a single state), for jurisdiction over firearms. This became the vehicle for federal regulation of the firearms business when it occurred in 1968. Congress has been using its power to regulate interstate commerce to get around many of the limitations on its power set out in the Constitution, including in this case the prohibition on infringing on the right of the people to keep and bear arms.

(k) It shall be unlawful for any person knowingly to transport, ship, or receive, in interstate or foreign commerce, any firearm which has had the importer's or manufacturer's serial number removed, obliterated, or altered or to possess or receive any firearm which has had the importer's or manufacturer's serial number removed, obliterated, or altered and has, at any time, been shipped or transported in interstate or foreign commerce.

18 USC § 922 (l)

> (l) It's illegal for a person to bring firearms or ammunition into the country, with limited exceptions described under 18–925 (briefly, for research, training, competition, if it's unserviceable, as a curio or museum piece, if it's for sport, and a person bringing back a firearm that the person took out). It's illegal to knowingly possess illegally imported firearms or ammunition.

(l) Except as provided in section 925(d) of this chapter, it shall be unlawful for any person knowingly to import or bring into the United States or any possession thereof any firearm or ammunition; and it shall be unlawful for any person knowingly to receive any firearm or ammunition which has been imported or brought into the United States or any possession thereof in violation of the provisions of this chapter.

18 USC § 922 (m)

> (m) It's illegal for an FFL to falsify any official records.

(m) It shall be unlawful for any licensed importer, licensed manufacturer, licensed dealer, or licensed collector knowingly to make any false entry in, to fail to make appropriate entry in, or to fail to properly maintain, any record which he is required to keep pursuant to section 923 of this chapter or regulations promulgated thereunder.

18 USC § 922 (n)

> (n) It's illegal for anyone to ship or receive firearms or ammunition in interstate or foreign commerce, if they are under indictment for a crime that carries a term of more than one year.

(n) It shall be unlawful for any person who is under indictment for a crime punishable by imprisonment for a term exceeding one year to ship or transport in interstate or foreign commerce any firearm or ammunition or receive any firearm or ammunition which has been shipped or transported in interstate or foreign commerce.

18 USC § 922 (o)

> (o) It's illegal to have or transfer a machine gun, with two exceptions: the proper authorities are not restricted, and any machine gun transferred or possessed before this law took effect (May 19, 1986) is unaffected.
>
> This is where the national "inventory" of legally owned machine guns comes from. The cut-off date froze the supply in private hands, now numbered at about 190,000.

(o)(1) Except as provided in paragraph (2), it shall be unlawful for any person to transfer or possess a machinegun.
(2) This subsection does not apply with respect to—
(A) a transfer to or by, or possession by or under the authority of, the United States or any department or agency thereof or a State, or a department, agency, or political subdivision thereof; or
(B) any lawful transfer or lawful possession of a machinegun that was lawfully possessed before the date this subsection takes effect.

18 USC § 922 (p)   <Undetectable Handgun Law>

> This subsection comes from the Undetectable Handgun Law of 1988, which was a response to increases in international terrorism and airline hijackings. It was specifically triggered by the introduction of the Austrian-made Glock pistol, with its polymer frame and grips, incorrectly believed at the time to be a totally plastic gun and hence undetectable. When the hysteria subsided it became obvious that the Glock, and similar pistols which followed, were composed largely of metal and were easily detectable, but the law had already been enacted.
>
> (p)(1 &2) It's generally illegal to in any way handle a firearm which is not easily spotted by metal detectors. The AG is required to make an object, called the Security Exemplar (a piece of 17-4 PH stainless steel, shaped like a handgun, with 3.7 ounces of metal), which represents the minimum

detectability allowable. The firearm must be at least as detectable as the Exemplar, even with the stocks, grips and magazines removed. A handgun frame or receiver by itself is exempt. It's illegal to have any major component of a gun which doesn't look like what it actually is under X-rays. The authorities may reduce the size of the Exemplar, making smaller firearms legal, as advances in detector technology allow. As air travelers know, the detectors are now far more sensitive than the Exemplar, capable of picking up pocket change and small belt buckles.

(p)(3) The AG cannot prevent a licensed manufacturer from testing firearms to see if they meet the requirements, and must ensure that any regulations it issues don't impair the manufacture of prototypes or the development of new technology.

(p)(4) The AG cannot prevent a licensed importer or manufacturer from importing a firearm for testing.

(p)(5) This subsection does not apply to any firearm that the proper authorities certify is necessary for military or intelligence operations and is made exclusively for that purpose.

(p)(6) Any firearms made domestically or imported before this law was passed (Nov. 10, 1988) are exempt.

The law became effective Dec. 10, 1988, and was originally set to expire in ten years (1998). Each time it has been about to expire, Congress has increased it, and it is now set to expire in 2013.

(p)(1) It shall be unlawful for any person to manufacture, import, sell, ship, deliver, possess, transfer, or receive any firearm—
(A) that, after removal of grips, stocks, and magazines, is not as detectable as the Security Exemplar, by walk-through metal detectors calibrated and operated to detect the Security Exemplar; or
(B) any major component of which, when subjected to inspection by the types of x-ray machines commonly used at airports, does not generate an image that accurately depicts the shape of the component. Barium sulfate or other compounds may be used in the fabrication of the component.
(2) For purposes of this subsection—
(A) the term "firearm" does not include the frame or receiver of any such weapon;
(B) the term "major component" means, with respect to a firearm, the barrel, the slide or cylinder, or the frame or receiver of the firearm; and
(C) the term "Security Exemplar" means an object, to be fabricated at the direction of the Attorney General, that is—
(i) constructed of, during the 12-month period beginning on the date of the enactment of this subsection, 3.7 ounces of material type 17-4 PH stainless steel in a shape resembling a handgun; and
(ii) suitable for testing and calibrating metal detectors: Provided, however, That at the close of such 12-month period, and at appropriate times thereafter the Attorney General shall promulgate regulations to permit the manufacture, importation, sale, shipment, delivery, possession, transfer, or receipt of firearms previously prohibited under this subparagraph that are as detectable as a "Security Exemplar" which contains 3.7 ounces of material type 17-4 PH stainless steel, in a shape resembling a handgun, or such lesser amount as is detectable in view of advances in state-of-the-art developments in weapons detection technology.
(3) Under such rules and regulations as the Attorney General shall prescribe, this subsection shall not apply to the manufacture, possession, transfer, receipt, shipment, or delivery of a firearm by a licensed manufacturer or any person acting

pursuant to a contract with a licensed manufacturer, for the purpose of examining and testing such firearm to determine whether paragraph (1) applies to such firearm. The Attorney General shall ensure that rules and regulations adopted pursuant to this paragraph do not impair the manufacture of prototype firearms or the development of new technology.

(4) The Attorney General shall permit the conditional importation of a firearm by a licensed importer or licensed manufacturer, for examination and testing to determine whether or not the unconditional importation of such firearm would violate this subsection.

(5) This subsection shall not apply to any firearm which—

(A) has been certified by the Secretary of Defense or the Director of Central Intelligence, after consultation with the Attorney General and the Administrator of the Federal Aviation Administration, as necessary for military or intelligence applications; and

(B) is manufactured for and sold exclusively to military or intelligence agencies of the United States.

(6) This subsection shall not apply with respect to any firearm manufactured in, imported into, or possessed in the United States before the date of the enactment of the Undetectable Firearms Act of 1988.

18 USC § 922 (q)   **<Gun-Free School Zones Law>**

This subsection originated from the Gun-Free School Zones Act amendment of 1991. It is one of the few gun laws presently on the books in which Congress includes a preliminary statement of intent. The statement seeks to justify applying federal authority at a local school level, by stating that interstate and foreign commerce (which Congress has constitutional jurisdiction over) is affected by crime at schools. The declaration, which is paragraph (1), makes interesting reading and is one of the few pieces of statute not written in legalese (although it is numbered in legalese, creating an unusual tempo). The constitutionality of such federal control went to the Supreme Court.

Congress was rebuffed in its attempt to exercise police powers at the state level, when the Court declared this law unconstitutional, in 1995. Congress then simply reenacted it in 1996, to the surprise of many observers, as an unnoticed add-on to a 2,000-page federal spending bill. The new version was essentially identical to the one the Supreme Court overturned, even giving it the same letter, (q). A subtle adjustment to the wording of the interstate commerce phrase was enough, Congress presumed, to bring the law into step with the Constitution, and since another case has not come up to challenge it, it stands.

America had 121,855 public and private schools in 1994. In effect, this law criminalizes the actions of nearly anyone who travels in a populated area with a legally possessed firearm. As with its overturned predecessor, its affect on the very real problem of youth violence is unclear, and of course, any firearm used illegally in America, whether it is near a school or not, is already a serious crime with heavy penalties.

(q) It's illegal to knowingly have a firearm at a place which a person knows, or should reasonably believe, is a school zone. A school zone means in or on the grounds of an elementary or secondary public, private or parochial school, and the area within 1,000 feet from the grounds of the school.

This does not apply to a firearm possessed: 1–on private property that isn't part of school grounds; 2–by a person duly licensed to possess firearms, if the license required the state's law enforcement authorities to verify that the person is qualified under law to receive the license; 3–which is unloaded and in a locked container, or a locked firearms rack which is on a motor vehicle; 4–by a person for use in a program approved by a school in the school zone; 5–by a person in accordance with a contract between a school in the school zone and the person or the person's employer; or 6– which is unloaded and possessed while traversing school premises to gain access to public or private lands open to hunting, if the entry on school premises is authorized by school authorities.

In addition, it's illegal to knowingly or with reckless disregard for another person's safety, fire or attempt to fire a gun in a school zone. This does not apply to firing a gun: on private property that isn't part of school grounds; by a person participating in a program approved by a school in the school zone; or by a person in accordance with a contract between a school in the school zone and the person or the person's employer.

Law enforcement officers acting in an official capacity are exempt.

(q)(1) The Congress finds and declares that—
(A) crime, particularly crime involving drugs and guns, is a pervasive, nationwide problem;
(B) crime at the local level is exacerbated by the interstate movement of drugs, guns, and criminal gangs;
(C) firearms and ammunition move easily in interstate commerce and have been found in increasing numbers in and around schools, as documented in numerous hearings in both the Committee on the Judiciary of the House of Representatives and the Committee on the Judiciary of the Senate;
(D) in fact, even before the sale of a firearm, the gun, its component parts, ammunition, and the raw materials from which they are made have considerably moved in interstate commerce;
(E) while criminals freely move from State to State, ordinary citizens and foreign visitors may fear to travel to or through certain parts of the country due to concern about violent crime and gun violence, and parents may decline to send their children to school for the same reason;
(F) the occurrence of violent crime in school zones has resulted in a decline in the quality of education in our country;
(G) this decline in the quality of education has an adverse impact on interstate commerce and the foreign commerce of the United States;
(H) States, localities, and school systems find it almost impossible to handle gun-related crime by themselves—even States, localities, and school systems that have made strong efforts to prevent, detect, and punish gun-related crime find their efforts unavailing due in part to the failure or inability of other States or localities to take strong measures; and
(I) the Congress has the power, under the interstate commerce clause and other provisions of the Constitution, to enact measures to ensure the integrity and safety of the Nation's schools by enactment of this subsection.
(2)(A) It shall be unlawful for any individual knowingly to possess a firearm that has moved in or that otherwise affects interstate or foreign commerce at a place that the individual knows, or has reasonable cause to believe, is a school zone.
(B) Subparagraph (A) does not apply to the possession of a firearm—
(i) on private property not part of school grounds;
(ii) if the individual possessing the firearm is licensed to do so by the State in which the school zone is located or a political subdivision of the State, and the law of the State or political subdivision requires that, before an individual obtains such a

license, the law enforcement authorities of the State or political subdivision verify that the individual is qualified under law to receive the license;

(iii) that is—

(I) not loaded; and

(II) in a locked container, or a locked firearms rack that is on a motor vehicle;

(iv) by an individual for use in a program approved by a school in the school zone;

(v) by an individual in accordance with a contract entered into between a school in the school zone and the individual or an employer of the individual;

(vi) by a law enforcement officer acting in his or her official capacity; or

(vii) that is unloaded and is possessed by an individual while traversing school premises for the purpose of gaining access to public or private lands open to hunting, if the entry on school premises is authorized by school authorities.

(3)(A) Except as provided in subparagraph (B), it shall be unlawful for any person, knowingly or with reckless disregard for the safety of another, to discharge or attempt to discharge a firearm that has moved in or that otherwise affects interstate or foreign commerce at a place that the person knows is a school zone.

(B) Subparagraph (A) does not apply to the discharge of a firearm—

(i) on private property not part of school grounds;

(ii) as part of a program approved by a school in the school zone, by an individual who is participating in the program;

(iii) by an individual in accordance with a contract entered into between a school in a school zone and the individual or an employer of the individual; or

(iv) by a law enforcement officer acting in his or her official capacity.

(4) Nothing in this subsection shall be construed as preempting or preventing a State or local government from enacting a statute establishing gun free school zones as provided in this subsection.

18 USC § 922 (r)

> (r) It's illegal to assemble a semiautomatic rifle or any shotgun, from imported parts, if the finished firearm is identical to one which may not be imported under 18–925(d)(3). This does not apply to a licensed manufacturer assembling such a firearm for sale or distribution to the proper authorities. The AG may also authorize such assembly for testing.

(r) It shall be unlawful for any person to assemble from imported parts any semiautomatic rifle or any shotgun which is identical to any rifle or shotgun prohibited from importation under section 925(d)(3) of this chapter as not being particularly suitable for or readily adaptable to sporting purposes except that this subsection shall not apply to—

(1) the assembly of any such rifle or shotgun for sale or distribution by a licensed manufacturer to the United States or any department or agency thereof or to any State or any department, agency, or political subdivision thereof; or

(2) the assembly of any such rifle or shotgun for the purposes of testing or experimentation authorized by the Attorney General.

18 USC § 922 (s&t)   <The Brady law>

> The Brady Handgun Violence Prevention Act was signed into law on Nov. 30, 1993. Its provisions for common carriers, reporting multiple handgun sales and license fee increases are among the rules which took effect immediately. The waiting-period provisions took effect on Feb. 28, 1994 and were set to expire on Feb. 27, 1999.
>
> In addition to the regulation of private citizens described below, the Brady law: 1–places special requirements on dealers; 2–sets timetables and budgets for the U.S. Attorney General to implement the law; 3–provides funding; 4–sets basic computer system requirements;

5–mandates criminal-history record sharing among authorities; 6–enhances penalties for gun thieves; 7–prohibits lawsuits against the authorities for allowing a criminal to get a gun or preventing an honest citizen from getting one; and more.

As a sidelight, Brady is one of the few gun laws that goes five layers deep into the legal-outline numbering system, as you can see right at the start with (s)(1)(A)(i)(I), and in other places. Its convoluted language and complex internal cross references make it one of the most, if not the most, difficult gun laws to decipher. In an earlier form before enactment, Brady was a single sentence of 532 words. The main elements of the final version, found here as subsections (s) and (t), comprise 2,279 words. A few provisions are codified elsewhere.

Because the law is so complexly written, it is almost never described accurately. The most notable recurring error is the frequent reference to its supposed five-day waiting period. In fact, Brady required no such thing. As firearms purchasers in many parts of the country discovered, Brady actually required a zero-to-eight day waiting period (or up to nine days during periods when a legal holiday occurs) under its initial five-year term. Sales took place immediately in states that met conditions described below. States also could impose longer delays—Brady was not a guaranteed minimum five days either.

Detecting all this in the law requires a proper reading of ten semicolons, two dashes, three "ands," and the word "or" twice, from (s)(1)(A)(ii)(I) to (s)(1)(F)(ii). Also, rarely mentioned publicly is the allocation of $200 million to the Attorney General, the requirement for a national instant background check system after the five-year start up plan, regulation of common carriers such as airlines and more.

Shorthand: The Brady law refers to a "chief law enforcement officer," defined as the chief of police, the sheriff, an equivalent officer or that person's designee. The description below refers to such persons as "the authorities." Where the law refers to an individual who is unlicensed under 18–923, this description says "private citizen" or "you." Federally licensed dealers, manufacturers and importers are referred to as "dealers." The act of selling, delivering or transferring is called "transferring." The law defines *handgun* as, "a firearm which has a short stock and is designed to be held and fired by the use of a single hand." A combination of parts which can be assembled into a handgun counts as a handgun.

(s&t) Under the first five years of the Brady law (through Nov. 30, 1998), to legally obtain a handgun from a dealer, you had to provide a government-issued picture ID for the dealer to examine, and:

A written statement with only the date the statement was made, notice of your intent to obtain a handgun from the dealer, your name, address, date of birth, the type of ID you used and a statement that you were not: 1–under indictment and hadn't been convicted of a crime that carries a prison term of more than one year, 2–convicted of a misdemeanor crime of domestic violence, 3–a fugitive from justice, 4–an unlawful user of or addicted to any controlled substance, 5–an adjudicated mental defective or a person who has been committed to a mental institution, 6–an illegal alien, with narrow exceptions, 7–dishonorably discharged from the armed forces, or 8–a person who has renounced U.S. citizenship.

Then, before transferring the handgun to you, the dealer had to: 1–Within one day, provide notice of the content and send a copy of the statement to the authorities where you live; 2–Keep a copy of your statement and evidence that it was sent to the authorities; 3–Wait five days during which state offices are open, from the day the dealer gave the authorities notice, and during that time; 4–Receive no information from the authorities that your possession of the handgun would violate federal, state or local laws.

The waiting period ended early if the authorities notified the dealer early that you were eligible. The authorities "shall make a reasonable effort" to check your background in local, state and federal records. Long guns were unaffected by the Brady handgun law until the National Instant Check described below came online, and Brady did not apply to getting your own handgun (or a replacement) back from a dealer you gave it to (e.g., a repair shop, pawnbroker, etc.).

The Brady law excluded you from the waiting period:

1–If you had a written statement from the authorities, valid for 10 days, that you need a handgun because of a threat to your life or a member of your household's life; 2–With a handgun permit, in the state that issued it, if the permit was five years old or less and required a background check (state concealed-weapon permits often met this requirement); 3–In states which had a handgun background check (for example, Arizona's Handgun Clearance Center qualified. Established by state law in response to Brady, and operated by the Dept. of Public Safety, it conducted instant background checks by phone or fax, for handgun purchasers, eliminating the need for Arizona residents to wait for handgun purchases. It has since been abolished.); 4–If the transfer was already regulated by the National Firearms Act of 1934, as with Class III weapons; and 5–If the dealer had been certified as being in an extremely remote location of a sparsely populated state and there was no telecommunications near the dealer's business premises (added for Alaska, though might apply elsewhere).

If a dealer was notified after a transfer that your possession of the handgun was illegal, the dealer had to, within one business day, provide any information they had about you and the gun to the authorities at the dealer's place of business and at your place of residence. The information a dealer received could only be communicated to you, the authorities or by court order. If you were denied a handgun, you could ask the authorities why, and they were required to provide the reason in writing within 20 business days of your request.

Unless the authorities determined that the handgun transferred to you would be illegal, they had to, within 20 days of the date of your statement, destroy all records of the process. The authorities were expressly forbidden to convey or use the information in your statement for anything other than what was needed to carry out the Brady process.

The authorities could not be held liable for damages for either allowing an illegal handgun transfer or preventing a legal one. If you were denied a firearm unjustly, you could sue the political entity responsible and get the information corrected or have the transfer approved, and you could collect reasonable attorney's fees.

National Instant Check: The Brady law required the U.S. Attorney General (AG) to establish a National Instant Criminal Background Check system (NICS) before Nov. 30, 1998. Once this was in effect, the previous waiting process was eliminated. The system was put in place on time. Now, in order to transfer any firearm, not just handguns, with the NICS system in place, a dealer must verify your identity from a government-issued photo-ID card, contact the system (based in Clarksburg, WV, run by the FBI), identify you and either: 1–receive a unique transfer number back from NICS, or 2–wait three days during which state offices are open and the system provides no notice that the transfer would violate relevant laws.

At the outset, 19 states were designated a "Point of Contact" state by the FBI. Dealers in these states contacted a state-run firearms clearance center, which then automatically included a digital check of the federal NICS system. In other states, the dealer contacted the FBI directly, usually by phone, for every sale.

The NICS system is required to issue the transfer number if the transfer would violate no relevant laws, and it is supposed to destroy all records of approved inquiries except for the identifying number and the date it was issued. The FBI, however, had announced they were actually recording the name and address of everyone who bought a gun through the system, in apparent violation of long-standing law (strictly forbidden in both the McClure Volkmer Act, 1986, and the Brady law itself). There is some doubt as to what is exactly taking place currently.

If the transfer is legal, the dealer includes the transfer number in the record of the transaction. The NICS system is bypassed under conditions similar to 2, 4 and 5 listed above (for the five-year startup period) as exceptions to the waiting period (with number 2 broadened to include "firearms" permit).

Whoever violates these requirements is subject to a fine of up to $1,000 and a jail term of up to 1 year.

If you are denied a firearm under NICS, you may request the reason and the system must present you with a written answer within five business days. You may also request the reason from the AG, who must respond immediately. You may provide information to fix any errors in the system, and the AG must immediately consider the information, investigate further, correct any erroneous federal records and notify any federal or state agency that was the source of the errors.

A licensed dealer who violates these requirements is subject to a civil fine of up to $5,000 and suspension or revocation of their license, but only if the system was operating and would have shown that the customer would have been ineligible to make a purchase.

Multiple sales of handguns, (two or more from the same dealer in a five-day period) are already reported to the Bureau of Alcohol, Tobacco, Firearms and Explosives, and must now be reported to local authorities as well. Local authorities may not disclose the information, must destroy the records within 20 days from receipt if the transfer is not illegal and must certify every six months to the AG that they are complying with these provisions. (This Brady provision is codified under 18–923(g)(3)(A).)

Common or contract carriers (airlines, buses, trains, etc.) may not label your luggage or packages to indicate that they contain firearms. Federal law requires you to notify the carrier in writing if you are transporting firearms or ammunition. The long-time labeling practice had been responsible for the frequent theft of luggage containing firearms.

Licensing fees for obtaining a new federal firearms license are increased to $200 for three years. The fee for renewing a currently valid license is $90 for three years.

18 USC § 922 (s) <Brady Law Part 1, now expired, see Part 2, below>

(s)(1) Beginning on the date that is 90 days after the date of enactment of this subsection and ending on the day before the date that is 60 months after such date of enactment, it shall be unlawful for any licensed importer, licensed manufacturer, or licensed dealer to sell, deliver, or transfer a handgun (other than the return of a handgun to the person from whom it was received) to an individual who is not licensed under section 923, unless—

(A) after the most recent proposal of such transfer by the transferee—

(i) the transferor has—

(I) received from the transferee a statement of the transferee containing the information described in paragraph (3);

(II) verified the identity of the transferee by examining the identification document presented;

(III) within 1 day after the transferee furnishes the statement, provided notice of the contents of the statement to the chief law enforcement officer of the place of residence of the transferee; and

(IV) within 1 day after the transferee furnishes the statement, transmitted a copy of the statement to the chief law enforcement officer of the place of residence of the transferee; and

(ii)(I) 5 business days (meaning days on which State offices are open) have elapsed from the date the transferor furnished notice of the contents of the statement to the chief law enforcement officer, during which period the transferor has not received information from the chief law enforcement officer that receipt or possession of the handgun by the transferee would be in violation of Federal, State, or local law; or

(II) the transferor has received notice from the chief law enforcement officer that the officer has no information indicating that receipt or possession of the handgun by the transferee would violate Federal, State, or local law;

(B) the transferee has presented to the transferor a written statement, issued by the chief law enforcement officer of the place of residence of the transferee during the 10-day period ending on the date of the most recent proposal of such transfer by the transferee, stating that the transferee requires access to a handgun because of a threat to the life of the transferee or of any member of the household of the transferee;

(C)(i) the transferee has presented to the transferor a permit that—

(I) allows the transferee to possess or acquire a handgun; and

(II) was issued not more than 5 years earlier by the State in which the transfer is to take place; and

(ii) the law of the State provides that such a permit is to be issued only after an authorized government official has verified that the information available to such official does not indicate that possession of a handgun by the transferee would be in violation of the law;

(D) the law of the State requires that, before any licensed importer, licensed manufacturer, or licensed dealer completes the transfer of a handgun to an individual who is not licensed under section 923, an authorized government official verify that the information available to such official does not indicate that possession of a handgun by the transferee would be in violation of law;

(E) the Attorney General has approved the transfer under section 5812 of the Internal Revenue Code of 1986; or

(F) on application of the transferor, the Attorney General has certified that compliance with subparagraph (A)(i)(III) is impracticable because—

(i) the ratio of the number of law enforcement officers of the State in which the transfer is to occur to the number of square miles of land area of the State does not exceed 0.0025;

(ii) the business premises of the transferor at which the transfer is to occur are extremely remote in relation to the chief law enforcement officer; and

(iii) there is an absence of telecommunications facilities in the geographical area in which the business premises are located.

(2) A chief law enforcement officer to whom a transferor has provided notice pursuant to paragraph (1)(A)(i)(III) shall make a reasonable effort to ascertain within 5 business days whether receipt or possession would be in violation of the law, including research in whatever State and local recordkeeping systems are available and in a national system designated by the Attorney General.

(3) The statement referred to in paragraph (1)(A)(i)(I) shall contain only—

(A) the name, address, and date of birth appearing on a valid identification document (as defined in section 1028(d)(1)) of the transferee containing a photograph of the transferee and a description of the identification used;

(B) a statement that the transferee—

(i) is not under indictment for, and has not been convicted in any court of, a crime punishable by imprisonment for a term exceeding 1 year, and has not been convicted in any court of a misdemeanor crime of domestic violence;

(ii) is not a fugitive from justice;

(iii) is not an unlawful user of or addicted to any controlled substance (as defined in section 102 of the Controlled Substances Act);

(iv) has not been adjudicated as a mental defective or been committed to a mental institution;

(v) is not an alien who—

(I) is illegally or unlawfully in the United States; or

(II) subject to subsection (y)(2), has been admitted to the United States under a nonimmigrant visa (as that term is defined in section 101(a)(26) of the Immigration and Nationality Act (8 U.S.C. 1101(a)(26)));

(vi) has not been discharged from the Armed Forces under dishonorable conditions; and

(vii) is not a person who, having been a citizen of the United States, has renounced such citizenship;

(C) the date the statement is made; and

(D) notice that the transferee intends to obtain a handgun from the transferor.

(4) Any transferor of a handgun who, after such transfer, receives a report from a chief law enforcement officer containing information that receipt or possession of the handgun by the transferee violates Federal, State, or local law shall, within 1 business day after receipt of such request, communicate any information related to the transfer that the transferor has about the transfer and the transferee to—

(A) the chief law enforcement officer of the place of business of the transferor; and

(B) the chief law enforcement officer of the place of residence of the transferee.

(5) Any transferor who receives information, not otherwise available to the public, in a report under this subsection shall not disclose such information except to the transferee, to law enforcement authorities, or pursuant to the direction of a court of law.

(6)(A) Any transferor who sells, delivers, or otherwise transfers a handgun to a transferee shall retain the copy of the statement of the transferee with respect to the handgun transaction, and shall retain evidence that the transferor has complied with subclauses (III) and (IV) of paragraph (1)(A)(i) with respect to the statement.

(B) Unless the chief law enforcement officer to whom a statement is transmitted under paragraph (1)(A)(i)(IV) determines that a transaction would violate Federal, State, or local law—

(i) the officer shall, within 20 business days after the date the transferee made the statement on the basis of which the notice was provided, destroy the statement, any record containing information derived from the statement, and any record created as a result of the notice required by paragraph (1)(A)(i)(III);

(ii) the information contained in the statement shall not be conveyed to any person except a person who has a need to know in order to carry out this subsection; and

(iii) the information contained in the statement shall not be used for any purpose other than to carry out this subsection.

(C) If a chief law enforcement officer determines that an individual is ineligible to receive a handgun and the individual requests the officer to provide the reason for such determination, the officer shall provide such reasons to the individual in writing within 20 business days after receipt of the request.

(7) A chief law enforcement officer or other person responsible for providing criminal history background information pursuant to this subsection shall not be liable in an action at law for damages—

(A) for failure to prevent the sale or transfer of a handgun to a person whose receipt or possession of the handgun is unlawful under this section; or

(B) for preventing such a sale or transfer to a person who may lawfully receive or possess a handgun.

(8) For purposes of this subsection, the term "chief law enforcement officer" means the chief of police, the sheriff, or an equivalent officer or the designee of any such individual.

(9) The Attorney General shall take necessary actions to ensure that the provisions of this subsection are published and disseminated to licensed dealers, law enforcement officials, and the public.

18 USC § 922 (t) <Brady Law Part 2>

(t)(1) Beginning on the date that is 30 days after the Attorney General notifies licensees under section 103(d) of the Brady Handgun Violence Prevention Act that the national instant criminal background check system is established, a licensed importer, licensed manufacturer, or licensed dealer shall not transfer a firearm to any other person who is not licensed under this chapter, unless—

(A) before the completion of the transfer, the licensee contacts the national instant criminal background check system established under section 103 of that Act;

(B)(i) the system provides the licensee with a unique identification number; or

(ii) 3 business days (meaning a day on which State offices are open) have elapsed since the licensee contacted the system, and the system has not notified the licensee that the receipt of a firearm by such other person would violate subsection (g) or (n) of this section; and

(C) the transferor has verified the identity of the transferee by examining a valid identification document (as defined in section 1028(d) of this title) of the transferee containing a photograph of the transferee.

(2) If receipt of a firearm would not violate subsection (g) or (n) or State law, the system shall—

(A) assign a unique identification number to the transfer;

(B) provide the licensee with the number; and

(C) destroy all records of the system with respect to the call (other than the identifying number and the date the number was assigned) and all records of the system relating to the person or the transfer.

(3) Paragraph (1) shall not apply to a firearm transfer between a licensee and another person if—

(A)(i) such other person has presented to the licensee a permit that—

(I) allows such other person to possess or acquire a firearm; and

(II) was issued not more than 5 years earlier by the State in which the transfer is to take place; and

(ii) the law of the State provides that such a permit is to be issued only after an authorized government official has verified that the information available to such official does not indicate that possession of a firearm by such other person would be in violation of law;

(B) the Attorney General has approved the transfer under section 5812 of the Internal Revenue Code of 1986; or

(C) on application of the transferor, the Attorney General has certified that compliance with paragraph (1)(A) is impracticable because—

(i) the ratio of the number of law enforcement officers of the State in which the transfer is to occur to the number of square miles of land area of the State does not exceed 0.0025;

(ii) the business premises of the licensee at which the transfer is to occur are extremely remote in relation to the chief law enforcement officer (as defined in subsection (s)(8)); and

(iii) there is an absence of telecommunications facilities in the geographical area in which the business premises are located.

(4) If the national instant criminal background check system notifies the licensee that the information available to the system does not demonstrate that the receipt of a firearm by such other person would violate subsection (g) or (n) or State law, and the licensee transfers a firearm to such other person, the licensee shall include in the record of the transfer the unique identification number provided by the system with respect to the transfer.

(5) If the licensee knowingly transfers a firearm to such other person and knowingly fails to comply with paragraph (1) of this subsection with respect to the transfer and, at the time such other person most recently proposed the transfer, the national instant criminal background check system was operating and information was available to the system demonstrating that receipt of a firearm by such other person would violate subsection (g) or (n) of this section or State law, the Attorney General may, after notice and opportunity for a hearing, suspend for not more than 6 months or revoke any license issued to the licensee under section 923, and may impose on the licensee a civil fine of not more than $5,000.

(6) Neither a local government nor an employee of the Federal Government or of any State or local government, responsible for providing information to the national instant criminal background check system shall be liable in an action at law for damages—

(A) for failure to prevent the sale or transfer of a firearm to a person whose receipt or possession of the firearm is unlawful under this section; or

(B) for preventing such a sale or transfer to a person who may lawfully receive or possess a firearm.

Statute at Large

Note: The following is a *Statute at Large;* it received no section number after it was passed by Congress. As such, it does not appear in the regular numbered sections of the U.S. laws. The result is that, although this is law passed by Congress, with the full weight and effect of any other statute, it is not widely known. This is the somewhat troublesome case with so-called *Statutes at Large.* The language here is originally part of the Brady

> law. It grants broad protections and redress to people who are mistakenly denied their rights under this law.
>
> See the Brady law *Gist* at 18-922 (s & t) for an explanation.

(a) **Determination of Timetables.** Not later than 6 months after the date of enactment of this Act [Nov. 30, 1993] the Attorney General shall—

(1) determine the type of computer hardware and software that will be used to operate the national instant criminal background check system and the means by which State criminal records systems and the telephone or electronic device of licensees will communicate with the national system;

(2) investigate the criminal records system of each State and determine for each State a timetable by which the State should be able to provide criminal records on an online capacity basis to the national system; and

(3) notify each State of the determinations made pursuant to paragraphs (1) and (2).

(b) **Establishment of System.** Not later than 60 months after the date of the enactment of this Act [Nov. 30, 1993], the Attorney General shall establish a national instant criminal background check system that any licensee may contact, by telephone or by other electronic means in addition to the telephone, for information, to be supplied immediately, on whether receipt of a firearm, by a prospective transferee would violate section 922 of title 18, United States Code [this section], or State law.

(c) **Expedited action by the Attorney General.** The Attorney General shall expedite—

(1) the upgrading and indexing of State criminal history records in the Federal criminal records system maintained by the Federal Bureau of Investigation;

(2) the development of hardware and software systems to link State criminal history check systems into the national instant criminal background check system established by the Attorney General pursuant to this section; and

(3) the current revitalization initiatives by the Federal Bureau of Investigation for technologically advanced fingerprint and criminal records identification.

(d) **Notification of Licensees.** On establishment of the system under this section, the Attorney General shall notify each licensee and the chief law enforcement officer of each State of the existence and purpose of the system and the means to be used to contact the system.

(e) **Administrative Provisions.**

(1) Authority to obtain official information. Notwithstanding any other law, the Attorney General may secure directly from any department or agency of the United States such information on persons for whom receipt of a firearm would violate subsection (g) or (n) of section 922 of title 18, United States Code [subsec. (g) or (n) of this section] or State law, as is necessary to enable the system to operate in accordance with this section. On request of the Attorney General, the head of such department or agency shall furnish such information to the system.

(2) Other authority. The Attorney General shall develop such computer software, design and obtain such telecommunications and computer hardware, and employ such personnel, as are necessary to establish and operate the system in accordance with this section.

(f) **Written Reasons Provided on Request.** If the national instant criminal background check system determines that an individual is ineligible to receive a firearm and the individual requests the system to provide the reasons for the determination, the system shall provide such reasons to the individual, in writing, within 5 business days after the date of the request.

(g) **Correction of Erroneous System Information.** If the system established under this section informs an individual contacting the system that receipt of a firearm by a prospective transferee would violate subsection (g) or (n) of section 922 of title 18, United States Code [subsec. (g) or (n) of this section] or State law, the prospective transferee may request the Attorney General to provide the prospective transferee with the reasons therefor. Upon receipt of such a request, the Attorney General shall immediately comply with the request. The prospective transferee may submit to the Attorney General information to correct, clarify, or supplement records of the system with respect to the prospective transferee. After receipt of such information, the Attorney General shall immediately consider the information, investigate the matter further, and correct all erroneous Federal records relating to the prospective transferee and give notice of the error to any Federal department or agency or any State that was the source of such erroneous records.

(h) **Regulation.** After 90 days' notice to the public and an opportunity for hearing by interested parties, the Attorney General shall prescribe regulations to ensure the privacy and security of the information of the system established under this section.

(i) **Prohibition Relating to Establishment of Registration Systems With Respect to Firearms.** No department, agency, officer, or employee of the United States may—

(1) require that any record or portion thereof generated by the system established under this section be recorded at or transferred to a facility owned, managed, or controlled by the United States or any State or political subdivision thereof; or

(2) use the system established under this section to establish any system for the registration of firearms, firearm owners, or firearm transactions or dispositions, except with respect to persons, prohibited by section 922(g) or (n) of title 18, United States Code [subsec. (g) or (n) of this section] or State law, from receiving a firearm.

(j) **Definitions.** As used in this section:

(1) Licensee. The term 'licensee' means a licensed importer (as defined in section 921(a)(9) of title 18, United States Code [section 921(a)(9) of this title]), a licensed manufacturer (as defined in section 921(a)(10) of that title [section 921(a)(10) of this title]), or a licensed dealer (as defined in section 921(a)(11) of that title [section 921(a)(11) of this title]).

(k) **Authorization of Appropriations.** There are authorized to be appropriated established by section 1115 of Title 31, United States Code [section 1115 of Title 31, Money and Finance] [sic], such sums as are necessary to enable the Attorney General to carry out this section.

Funding for Improvement of Criminal Records
(1) **Grants for the Improvement of Criminal Records.** The Attorney General, through the Bureau of Justice Statistics, shall, subject to appropriations and with preference to States that as of the date of enactment of this Act [Nov. 30, 1993] have the lowest percent currency of case dispositions in computerized criminal history files, make a grant to each State to be used—

(A) for the creation of a computerized criminal history record system or improvement of an existing system;

(B) to improve accessibility to the national instant criminal background system; and

(C) upon establishment of the national system, to assist the State in the transmittal of criminal records to the national system.

Note: The following paragraph covers the Brady Law's $200 million grant to the Attorney General's office, which was used to build the National Instant Check System, the FBI computer capable of instantly checking out any American citizen. The computer went into operation on Nov. 30, 1998.

---

(2) **Authorization of Appropriations.** There are authorized to be appropriated for grants under paragraph (1) established by section 1115 of title 31, United States Code [section 1115 of Title 31, Money and Finance] [sic], a total of $200,000,000 for fiscal year 1994 and all fiscal years thereafter.

(a) **Identification of Felons Ineligible To Purchase Handguns.** The Attorney General shall develop a system for immediate and accurate identification of felons who attempt to purchase 1 or more firearms but are ineligible to purchase firearms by reason of section 922(g)(1) of title 18, United States Code. The system shall be accessible to dealers but only for the purpose of determining whether a potential purchaser is a convicted felon. The Attorney General shall establish a plan (including a cost analysis of the proposed system) for implementation of the system. In developing the system, the Attorney General shall consult with the Secretary of the Treasury, other Federal, State, and local law enforcement officials with expertise in the area, and other experts. The Attorney General shall begin implementation of the system 30 days after the report to the Congress as provided in subsection (b).

(b) **Report To Congress.** Not later than 1 year after the date of the enactment of this Act, the Attorney General shall report to the Congress a description of the system referred to in subsection (a) and a plan (including a cost analysis of the proposed system) for implementation of the system. Such report may include, if appropriate, recommendations for modifications of the system and legislation necessary in order to fully implement such system.

(c) **Additional Study of Other Persons Ineligible To Purchase Firearms.** The Attorney General in consultation with the Secretary of the Treasury shall conduct a study to determine if an effective method for immediate and accurate identification of other persons who attempt to purchase 1 or more firearms but are ineligible to purchase firearms by reason of section 922(g) of title 18, United States Code. In conducting the study, the Attorney General shall consult with the Secretary of the Treasury, other Federal, State, and local law enforcement officials with expertise in the area, and other experts. Such study shall be completed with 18 months after the date of the enactment of this Act and shall be submitted to the Congress and made available to the public. Such study may include, if appropriate, recommendations for legislation.

(d) **Definitions.** As used in this section, the terms 'firearm' and 'dealer' shall have the meanings given such terms in section 921(a) of title 18, United States Code.

18 USC § 922 (u)

> (u) It's illegal to steal firearms that have moved in interstate or foreign commerce from the inventory of an FFL.

(u) It shall be unlawful for a person to steal or unlawfully take or carry away from the person or the premises of a person who is licensed to engage in the business of importing, manufacturing, or dealing in firearms, any firearm in the licensee's business inventory that has been shipped or transported in interstate or foreign commerce.

18 USC § 922 (v&w) EXPIRED

> (v&w) The 1994 Public Safety and Recreational Firearms Use Protection Act (also referred to as the Crime Bill, or the semiautomatic assault-weapons ban), expired Sep. 13, 2004. More at 18-921(30).

18 USC § 922 (x)

> (x) Derived from Arizona law, federal rules generally prohibit people under 18 years old from having handguns or handgun ammunition, or providing such to juveniles, with some additional requirements: While carrying written consent from a parent or guardian (who is not a prohibited possessor), a minor may have a handgun: 1–in the course of employment; 2–in legitimate ranching or farming; 3–for target practice; 4–for hunting, 5–for a class in the safe and lawful use of a handgun; or 6–for transport, unloaded in a locked case, directly to and from such activities. Also excluded is a minor who uses a handgun against an intruder, at home or in another home where the minor is an invited guest. If a handgun or ammo is legally transferred to a minor, who then commits

an offense with the firearm, the firearm must be returned to its lawful owner after legal procedures are concluded. Minors may inherit title (but not possession) of a handgun.

(x)(1) It shall be unlawful for a person to sell, deliver, or otherwise transfer to a person who the transferor knows or has reasonable cause to believe is a juvenile—
(A) a handgun; or
(B) ammunition that is suitable for use only in a handgun.
(2) It shall be unlawful for any person who is a juvenile to knowingly possess—
(A) a handgun; or
(B) ammunition that is suitable for use only in a handgun.
(3) This subsection does not apply to—
(A) a temporary transfer of a handgun or ammunition to a juvenile or to the possession or use of a handgun or ammunition by a juvenile if the handgun and ammunition are possessed and used by the juvenile—
(i) in the course of employment, in the course of ranching or farming related to activities at the residence of the juvenile (or on property used for ranching or farming at which the juvenile, with the permission of the property owner or lessee, is performing activities related to the operation of the farm or ranch), target practice, hunting, or a course of instruction in the safe and lawful use of a handgun;
(ii) with the prior written consent of the juvenile's parent or guardian who is not prohibited by Federal, State, or local law from possessing a firearm, except—
(I) during transportation by the juvenile of an unloaded handgun in a locked container directly from the place of transfer to a place at which an activity described in clause (i) is to take place and transportation by the juvenile of that handgun, unloaded and in a locked container, directly from the place at which such an activity took place to the transferor; or
(II) with respect to ranching or farming activities as described in clause (i), a juvenile may possess and use a handgun or ammunition with the prior written approval of the juvenile's parent or legal guardian and at the direction of an adult who is not prohibited by Federal, State or local law from possessing a firearm;
(iii) the juvenile has the prior written consent in the juvenile's possession at all times when a handgun is in the possession of the juvenile; and
(iv) in accordance with State and local law;
(B) a juvenile who is a member of the Armed Forces of the United States or the National Guard who possesses or is armed with a handgun in the line of duty;
(C) a transfer by inheritance of title (but not possession) of a handgun or ammunition to a juvenile; or
(D) the possession of a handgun or ammunition by a juvenile taken in defense of the juvenile or other persons against an intruder into the residence of the juvenile or a residence in which the juvenile is an invited guest.
(4) A handgun or ammunition, the possession of which is transferred to a juvenile in circumstances in which the transferor is not in violation of this subsection shall not be subject to permanent confiscation by the Government if its possession by the juvenile subsequently becomes unlawful because of the conduct of the juvenile, but shall be returned to the lawful owner when such handgun or ammunition is no longer required by the Government for the purposes of investigation or prosecution.
(5) For purposes of this subsection, the term "juvenile" means a person who is less than 18 years of age.
(6)(A) In a prosecution of a violation of this subsection, the court shall require the presence of a juvenile defendant's parent or legal guardian at all proceedings.
(B) The court may use the contempt power to enforce subparagraph (A).
(C) The court may excuse attendance of a parent or legal guardian of a juvenile defendant at a proceeding in a prosecution of a violation of this subsection for good cause shown.

18 USC § 922 (y)

> (y) Restricts who may keep and bear arms by adding foreigners (aliens with non-immigrant visas), who are here legally, to the prohibited possessor list. Exceptions are provided for foreigners admitted to the U.S. for specified reasons: 1–for lawful sport (a gray area, not defined here or by INS), 2–for lawful hunting, 3–while in possession of a hunting license or permit issued in the U.S., 4–for international proper authorities, 5–for distinguished visitors as determined by the State Dept., and 6–for international law enforcement officers on duty. In addition, the Attorney General can grant waivers to individuals, under narrowly described conditions.

(y) Provisions relating to aliens admitted under non-immigrant visas.—
(1) Definitions.—In this subsection—
(A) the term 'alien' has the same meaning as in section 101(a)(3) of the Immigration and Nationality Act (8 U.S.C. 1101(a)(3)); and
(B) the term 'nonimmigrant visa' has the same meaning as in section 101(a)(26) of the Immigration and Nationality Act (8 U.S.C. 1101(a)(26)).
(2) Exceptions.—Subsections (d)(5)(B), (g)(5)(B), and (s)(3)(B)(v)(II) do not apply to any alien who has been lawfully admitted to the United States under a nonimmigrant visa, if that alien is—
(A) admitted to the United States for lawful hunting or sporting purposes or is in possession of a hunting license or permit lawfully issued in the United States;
(B) an official representative of a foreign government who is—
(i) accredited to the United States Government or the Government's mission to an international organization having its headquarters in the United States; or
(ii) en route to or from another country to which that alien is accredited;
(C) an official of a foreign government or a distinguished foreign visitor who has been so designated by the Department of State; or
(D) a foreign law enforcement officer of a friendly foreign government entering the United States on official law enforcement business.
(3) Waiver.—
(A) Conditions for waiver.—Any individual who has been admitted to the United States under a nonimmigrant visa may receive a waiver from the requirements of subsection (g)(5), if—
(i) the individual submits to the Attorney General a petition that meets the requirements of subparagraph (C); and
(ii) the Attorney General approves the petition.
(B) Petition.—Each petition under subparagraph (B) shall—
(i) demonstrate that the petitioner has resided in the United States for a continuous period of not less than 180 days before the date on which the petition is submitted under this paragraph; and
(ii) include a written statement from the embassy or consulate of the petitioner, authorizing the petitioner to acquire a firearm or ammunition and certifying that the alien would not, absent the application of subsection (g)(5)(B), otherwise be prohibited from such acquisition under subsection (g).
(C) Approval of petition.—The Attorney General shall approve a petition submitted in accordance with this paragraph, if the Attorney General determines that waiving the requirements of subsection (g)(5)(B) with respect to the petitioner—
(i) would be in the interests of justice; and
(ii) would not jeopardize the public safety.
June 19, 1968 (8,084)

18 USC § 923. Licensing

> The Gist: All the main requirements for obtaining firearms licenses are contained in this section. Since many private citizens (as well as larger companies) go into this line of work, this section is of broad relevance and in frequent use. Extensive regulations are issued by the Attorney General (AG) to elaborate on and implement these laws. Prior to 2002, going back to their inception in 1968, the rules were issued by the Treasury Dept. through the former Bureau of Alcohol Tobacco and Firearms. All those rules and controls were transferred to the Attorney General as part of the overhaul of law enforcement brought about by the Arab muslim terrorist attacks on 9/11/01.
>
> Because the section is so long, *Gists* have been distributed throughout the text for easy reference.

18 USC § 923 (a)

> (a) A person must be federally licensed to go into business as a firearms importer, manufacturer or dealer, or as an importer or manufacturer of ammunition. The license application is regulated by the AG, and must include the applicant's photograph, fingerprints, and other information the AG deems necessary. A fee must be paid for each location at which business is done. The amounts and categories of the fees are listed.

(a) No person shall engage in the business of importing, manufacturing, or dealing in firearms, or importing or manufacturing ammunition, until he has filed an application with and received a license to do so from the Attorney General. The application shall be in such form and contain only that information necessary to determine eligibility for licensing as the Attorney General shall by regulation prescribe and shall include a photograph and fingerprints of the applicant. Each applicant shall pay a fee for obtaining such a license, a separate fee being required for each place in which the applicant is to do business, as follows:

(1) If the applicant is a manufacturer—
(A) of destructive devices, ammunition for destructive devices or armor piercing ammunition, a fee of $1,000 per year;
(B) of firearms other than destructive devices, a fee of $50 per year; or
(C) of ammunition for firearms, other than ammunition for destructive devices or armor piercing ammunition, a fee of $10 per year.
(2) If the applicant is an importer—
(A) of destructive devices, ammunition for destructive devices or armor piercing ammunition, a fee of $1,000 per year; or
(B) of firearms other than destructive devices or ammunition for firearms other than destructive devices, or ammunition other than armor piercing ammunition, a fee of $50 per year.
(3) If the applicant is a dealer—
(A) in destructive devices or ammunition for destructive devices, a fee of $1,000 per year; or
(B) who is not a dealer in destructive devices, a fee of $200 for 3 years, except that the fee for renewal of a valid license shall be $90 for 3 years.

18 USC § 923 (b)

> (b) A person may get a license for collecting curios and relic firearms. Eligibility and the application process is determined by the AG.

(b) Any person desiring to be licensed as a collector shall file an application for such license with the Attorney General. The application shall be in such form and contain only that information necessary to determine eligibility as the Attorney General shall by regulation prescribe. The fee for such license shall be $10 per year. Any license granted under this subsection shall only apply to transactions in curios and relics.

18 USC § 923 (c)

(c) The AG must issue a firearms license to anyone who is qualified, if they fill out the application and pay the fee. For a stated period of time, the license entitles the person to conduct interstate or foreign commerce in firearms and ammunition. A person who has a license may deal with a personal collection of firearms (as opposed to the business inventory), the same as any other citizen may, with certain restrictions.

(c) Upon the filing of a proper application and payment of the prescribed fee, the Attorney General shall issue to a qualified applicant the appropriate license which, subject to the provisions of this chapter and other applicable provisions of law, shall entitle the licensee to transport, ship, and receive firearms and ammunition covered by such license in interstate or foreign commerce during the period stated in the license. Nothing in this chapter shall be construed to prohibit a licensed manufacturer, importer, or dealer from maintaining and disposing of a personal collection of firearms, subject only to such restrictions as apply in this chapter to dispositions by a person other than a licensed manufacturer, importer, or dealer. If any firearm is so disposed of by a licensee within one year after its transfer from his business inventory into such licensee's personal collection or if such disposition or any other acquisition is made for the purpose of willfully evading the restrictions placed upon licensees by this chapter, then such firearm shall be deemed part of such licensee's business inventory, except that any licensed manufacturer, importer, or dealer who has maintained a firearm as part of a personal collection for one year and who sells or otherwise disposes of such firearm shall record the description of the firearm in a bound volume, containing the name and place of residence and date of birth of the transferee if the transferee is an individual, or the identity and principal and local places of business of the transferee if the transferee is a corporation or other business entity: Provided, That no other recordkeeping shall be required.

18 USC § 923 (d)

(d) An application for an FFL must be approved if the applicant: 1–is at least 21 years old; 2–isn't prohibited from handling firearms under 18–922 (g) or (n) (briefly, the prohibited possessors list and people under indictment); 3–hasn't willfully violated any provisions of this chapter (Chapter 44); 4–hasn't falsified the application in any way; 5–has or will have a location from which to conduct business or collecting; 6–the applicant certifies that: a) the planned business isn't prohibited by local law; b) within 30 days of approval the business will have complied with any local laws required; c) business won't begin until local requirements have been met; and d) the local chief law enforcement officer has been notified of the application for an FFL; and 7–will make available gun locks, subject to their availability.

Statute at Large. P.L. 105-277, which enacted the gun lock provisions of this section (and of 921(a)(18) and 923(e)), also provided, in an unnumbered statute at large, that:

(1) STATUTORY CONSTRUCTION.—Nothing in the amendments made by this section shall be construed—

(A) as creating a cause of action against any firearms dealer or any other person for any civil liability; or

(B) as establishing any standard of care.

(2) EVIDENCE.—Notwithstanding any other provision of law, evidence regarding compliance or noncompliance with the amendments made by this section shall not be admissible as evidence in any proceeding of any court, agency, board, or other entity.

(d)(1) Any application submitted under subsection (a) or (b) of this section shall be approved if—

(A) the applicant is twenty-one years of age or over;

(B) the applicant (including, in the case of a corporation, partnership, or association, any individual possessing, directly or indirectly, the power to direct or cause the direction of the management and policies of the corporation, partnership, or association) is not prohibited from transporting, shipping, or receiving firearms or ammunition in interstate or foreign commerce under section 922(g) and (n) of this chapter;

(C) the applicant has not willfully violated any of the provisions of this chapter or regulations issued thereunder;

(D) the applicant has not willfully failed to disclose any material information required, or has not made any false statement as to any material fact, in connection with his application;

(E) the applicant has in a State

(i) premises from which he conducts business subject to license under this chapter or from which he intends to conduct such business within a reasonable period of time, or

(ii) in the case of a collector, premises from which he conducts his collecting subject to license under this chapter or from which he intends to conduct such collecting within a reasonable period of time;

(F) the applicant certifies that—

(i) the business to be conducted under the license is not prohibited by State or local law in the place where the licensed premise is located;

(ii)(I) within 30 days after the application is approved the business will comply with the requirements of State and local law applicable to the conduct of the business; and

(II) the business will not be conducted under the license until the requirements of State and local law applicable to the business have been met; and

(iii) that the applicant has sent or delivered a form to be prescribed by the Attorney General, to the chief law enforcement officer of the locality in which the premises are located, which indicates that the applicant intends to apply for a Federal firearms license.

(2) The Attorney General must approve or deny an application for a license within the 60-day period beginning on the date it is received. If the Attorney General fails to act within such period, the applicant may file an action under section 1361 of title 28 to compel the Attorney General to act. If the Attorney General approves an applicant's application, such applicant shall be issued a license upon the payment of the prescribed fee; and

(G) in the case of an application to be licensed as a dealer, the applicant certifies that secure gun storage or safety devices will be available at any place in which firearms are sold under the license to persons who are not licensees (subject to the exception that in any case in which a secure gun storage or safety device is temporarily unavailable because of theft, casualty loss, consumer sales, backorders from a manufacturer, or any other similar reason beyond the control of the licensee, the dealer shall not be considered to be in violation of the requirement under this subparagraph to make available such a device).

18 USC § 923 (e)

> (e) An FFL license may be revoked for willfully violating any law in this chapter (Chapter 44) or any regulation made under this law. A dealer's license may also be revoked for willfully transferring armor piercing ammunition, or for not making gun locks available, subject to availability. However, an FFL must first be notified and have an opportunity for a hearing. If a license is revoked, the only recourse is described in the next subsection, (f).

(e) The Attorney General may, after notice and opportunity for hearing, revoke any license issued under this section if the holder of such license has willfully violated any provision of this chapter or any rule or regulation prescribed by the Attorney General under this chapter or fails to have secure gun storage or safety devices available at any place in which firearms are sold under the license to persons who are not licensees (except that in any case in which a secure gun storage or safety device is temporarily unavailable because of theft, casualty loss, consumer sales, backorders from a manufacturer, or any other similar reason beyond the control of the licensee, the dealer shall not be considered to be in violation of the requirement to make available such a device). The Attorney General may, after notice and opportunity for hearing, revoke the license of a dealer who willfully transfers armor piercing ammunition. The Attorney General's action under this subsection may be reviewed only as provided in subsection (f) of this section.

18 USC § 923 (f)

> (f) If an application for an FFL is denied the AG must give a specific reason, in writing. If a license is revoked, the notice must come before revocation. A person who has been turned down or whose license has been revoked may request a hearing, which the AG must hold promptly, at a location near that person. The AG must delay the revocation date if the person asks for a hearing.
>
> The AG must approve or deny an application within 60 days of receipt. If the AG doesn't act an applicant may attempt to force the issue under 28–1361. If an application is approved, the license must be issued when the fee tax is paid.
>
> If the hearing goes against an applicant, the AG must notify the person. The person then has the option, within 60 days, to go to U.S. District Court to appeal the decision. The court may hear new or old evidence, and must decide the case independent of the AG's decision. If the court decides in the applicant's favor, it must order the AG to comply.
>
> If a person is formally charged with a violation of this chapter (Chapter 44), and is acquitted or the charges are dropped (unless dropped by a government pre-trial motion), the AG is "absolutely barred" from denying or revoking a license on grounds of those charges. If the AG is going to revoke a license based on such an indictment, it must do so within one year.

(f)(1) Any person whose application for a license is denied and any holder of a license which is revoked shall receive a written notice from the Attorney General stating specifically the grounds upon which the application was denied or upon which the license was revoked. Any notice of a revocation of a license shall be given to the holder of such license before the effective date of the revocation.

(2) If the Attorney General denies an application for, or revokes, a license, he shall, upon request by the aggrieved party, promptly hold a hearing to review his denial or revocation. In the case of a revocation of a license, the Attorney General shall upon the request of the holder of the license stay the effective date of the revocation. A hearing held under this paragraph shall be held at a location convenient to the aggrieved party.

(3) If after a hearing held under paragraph (2) the Attorney General decides not to reverse his decision to deny an application or revoke a license, the Attorney General shall give notice of his decision to the aggrieved party. The aggrieved party may at any time within sixty days after the date notice was given under this paragraph file a petition with the United States district court for the district in which he resides or has his principal place of business for a de novo <Latin for "new"> judicial review of such denial or revocation. In a proceeding conducted under this subsection, the court may consider any evidence submitted by the parties to the proceeding whether or not such evidence was considered at the hearing held under paragraph (2). If the court decides that the Attorney General was not authorized to deny the application or to revoke the license, the court shall order the Attorney General to take such action as may be necessary to comply with the judgment of the court.

(4) If criminal proceedings are instituted against a licensee alleging any violation of this chapter or of rules or regulations prescribed under this chapter, and the licensee is acquitted of such charges, or such proceedings are terminated, other than upon motion of the Government before trial upon such charges, the Attorney General shall be absolutely barred from denying or revoking any license granted under this chapter where such denial or revocation is based in whole or in part on the facts which form the basis of such criminal charges. No proceedings for the revocation of a license shall be instituted by the Attorney General more than one year after the filing of the indictment or information.

18 USC § 923 (g)

(g)(1)(A) Licensed dealers, manufacturers and importers must keep firearms records (on importation, production, shipment, receipt, sale or other disposition) at their place of business, in compliance with AG regulations. The only reports the AG may require are defined in this section. If the AG has reasonable grounds to believe that a violation of this chapter (Chapter 44) has occurred and that evidence is at a licensee's site, the AG may get a federal warrant to enter during business hours and examine: 1–any records that must be kept, and 2–any firearms or ammunition on the site.

(g)(1)(B) The AG may inspect a licensed dealer, manufacturer or importer's inventory and records, without a warrant: 1–if it's reasonable as part of a criminal investigation of someone else; 2–not more than once a year to make sure records are being kept properly; 3–at any time if a firearm from a criminal investigation is traced to the licensee; and 4–when required to determine the disposition of a particular firearm as part of a criminal investigation.

(g)(1)(C) The AG may inspect the records of a licensed collector without a warrant, not more than once a year to make sure proper records are being kept, or when it's necessary during a criminal investigation.

(g)(1)(D) Collectors may decide to have their annual inspection take place at the closest appropriate AG office. The AG may not seize any records unless they're material evidence of a violation. If the AG seizes records, the collector must be given copies in a reasonable amount of time.

The AG may give information it obtains under this chapter (Chapter 44) to law enforcement officials if it relates to prohibited possessors who have obtained firearms or ammunition. The AG may provide other information from licensees' records to law enforcement officials on request.

(g)(2) Licensed collectors are required to keep a bound book recording their activity, as defined by the AG The only reports the AG may require are defined in this section.

(g)(3)(A) Licensees must report the sale of more than one handgun to the same person in a five-day period, to the AG and local law enforcement officials. The report must be made before the close of business on the day of the sale.

(g)(3)(B) Except in the case of prohibited possessors or people under indictment, law enforcement agencies: 1–may not give anyone information contained in licensees' forms; 2–must destroy any forms they receive and any records of information from the forms within 20 days of receipt; and 3–certify every six months to the AG that they have told no one and have destroyed all records as required.

(g)(4) When one licensee goes out of business and is followed by another licensee, the records are noted and delivered to the new licensee. When a licensee goes out of business and there is no successor, the records must be sent to the AG within 30 days. If a local law requires such records to go to some other authority, the AG may allow it.

Note that this provision for the deposit of old records from defunct businesses does not authorize anyone to establish a registration system for firearms nationally.

(g)(5) Licensees must comply with the AG's written requests for any records required to be kept under this chapter (Chapter 44). The AG specifies the form the reply must take, but licensees may request an alternate method in writing, and if a good reason exists the AG may agree.

(g)(6) Licensees must report thefts from inventory within 48 hours, to the AG and local law enforcement officials.

(g)(7) Licensees must respond to AG requests for official-records information, related to criminal investigations, within 24 hours. The AG must set up a system so a licensee can positively verify that the person requesting the information is authorized to do so.

(g)(1)(A) Each licensed importer, licensed manufacturer, and licensed dealer shall maintain such records of importation, production, shipment, receipt, sale, or other disposition of firearms at his place of business for such period, and in such form, as the Attorney General may by regulations prescribe. Such importers, manufacturers, and dealers shall not be required to submit to the Attorney General reports and information with respect to such records and the contents thereof, except as expressly required by this section. The Attorney General, when he has reasonable cause to believe a violation of this chapter has occurred and that evidence thereof may be found on such premises, may, upon demonstrating such cause before a Federal magistrate and securing from such magistrate a warrant authorizing entry, enter during business hours the premises (including places of storage) of any licensed firearms importer, licensed manufacturer, licensed dealer, licensed collector, or any licensed importer or manufacturer of ammunition, for the purpose of inspecting or examining—

(i) any records or documents required to be kept by such licensed importer, licensed manufacturer, licensed dealer, or licensed collector under this chapter or rules or regulations under this chapter, and

(ii) any firearms or ammunition kept or stored by such licensed importer, licensed manufacturer, licensed dealer, or licensed collector, at such premises.

(B) The Attorney General may inspect or examine the inventory and records of a licensed importer, licensed manufacturer, or licensed dealer without such reasonable cause or warrant—

(i) in the course of a reasonable inquiry during the course of a criminal investigation of a person or persons other than the licensee;

(ii) for ensuring compliance with the record keeping requirements of this chapter—

(I) not more than once during any 12-month period; or

(II) at any time with respect to records relating to a firearm involved in a criminal investigation that is traced to the licensee; or

(iii) when such inspection or examination may be required for determining the disposition of one or more particular firearms in the course of a bona fide criminal investigation.

(C) The Attorney General may inspect the inventory and records of a licensed collector without such reasonable cause or warrant—

(i) for ensuring compliance with the record keeping requirements of this chapter not more than once during any twelve-month period; or

(ii) when such inspection or examination may be required for determining the disposition of one or more particular firearms in the course of a bona fide criminal investigation.

(D) At the election of a licensed collector, the annual inspection of records and inventory permitted under this paragraph shall be performed at the office of the Attorney General designated for such inspections which is located in closest proximity to the premises where the inventory and records of such licensed collector are maintained. The inspection and examination authorized by this paragraph shall not be construed as authorizing the Attorney General to seize any records or other documents other than those records or documents constituting material evidence of a violation of law. If the Attorney General seizes such records or documents, copies shall be provided the licensee within a reasonable time. The Attorney General may make available to any Federal, State, or local law enforcement agency any information which he may obtain by reason of this chapter with respect to the identification of persons prohibited from purchasing or receiving firearms or ammunition who have purchased or received firearms or ammunition, together with a description of such firearms or ammunition, and he may provide information to the extent such information may be contained in the records required to be maintained by this chapter, when so requested by any Federal, State, or local law enforcement agency.

(2) Each licensed collector shall maintain in a bound volume the nature of which the Attorney General may by regulations prescribe, records of the receipt, sale, or other disposition of firearms. Such records shall include the name and address of any person to whom the collector sells or otherwise disposes of a firearm. Such collector shall not be required to submit to the Attorney General reports and information with respect to such records and the contents thereof, except as expressly required by this section.

(3)(A) Each licensee shall prepare a report of multiple sales or other dispositions whenever the licensee sells or otherwise disposes of, at one time or during any five consecutive business days, two or more pistols, or revolvers, or any combination of pistols and revolvers totalling two or more, to an unlicensed person. The report shall be prepared on a form specified by the Attorney General and forwarded to the office specified thereon and to the department of State police or State law enforcement agency of the State or local law enforcement agency of the local jurisdiction in which the sale or other disposition took place, not later than the close of business on the day that the multiple sale or other disposition occurs.

(B) Except in the case of forms and contents thereof regarding a purchaser who is prohibited by subsection (g) or (n) of section 922 of this title from receipt of a firearm, the department of State police or State law enforcement agency or local law enforcement agency of the local jurisdiction shall not disclose any such form or the contents thereof to any person or entity, and shall destroy each such form and any record of the contents thereof no more than 20 days from the date such form is received. No later than the date that is 6 months after the effective date of this subparagraph, and at the end of each 6-month period thereafter, the department of State police or State law enforcement agency or local law enforcement agency of the local jurisdiction shall certify to the Attorney General of the United States that no disclosure contrary to this subparagraph has been made and that all forms and any record of the contents thereof have been destroyed as provided in this subparagraph.

(4) Where a firearms or ammunition business is discontinued and succeeded by a new licensee, the records required to be kept by this chapter shall appropriately reflect such facts and shall be delivered to the successor. Where discontinuance of the business is absolute, such records shall be delivered within thirty days after the business discontinuance to the Attorney General. However, where State law or local ordinance requires the delivery of records to other responsible authority, the Attorney General may arrange for the delivery of such records to such other responsible authority. <It's important to note that this provision for the deposit of old records from defunct businesses does not authorize anyone to establish a registration system for firearms nationally.>

(5)(A) Each licensee shall, when required by letter issued by the Attorney General, and until notified to the contrary in writing by the Attorney General, submit on a form specified by the Attorney General, for periods and at the times specified in such letter, all record information required to be kept by this chapter or such lesser record information as the Attorney General in such letter may specify.

(B) The Attorney General may authorize such record information to be submitted in a manner other than that prescribed in subparagraph (A) of this paragraph when it is shown by a licensee that an alternate method of reporting is reasonably necessary and will not unduly hinder the effective administration of this chapter. A licensee may use an alternate method of reporting if the licensee describes the proposed alternate method of reporting and the need therefor in a letter application submitted to the Attorney General, and the Attorney General approves such alternate method of reporting.

(6) Each licensee shall report the theft or loss of a firearm from the licensee's inventory or collection, within 48 hours after the theft or loss is discovered, to the Attorney General and to the appropriate local authorities.

(7) Each licensee shall respond immediately to, and in no event later than 24 hours after the receipt of, a request by the Attorney General for information contained in the records required to be kept by this chapter as may be required for determining the disposition of 1 or more firearms in the course of a bona fide criminal investigation. The requested information shall be provided orally or in writing, as the Attorney General may require. The Attorney General shall implement a system whereby the licensee can positively identify and establish that an individual requesting information via telephone is employed by and authorized by the agency to request such information.

18 USC § 923 (h)

(h) FFL licenses issued under these laws must be posted and available for inspection at the licensed site.

(h) Licenses issued under the provisions of subsection (c) of this section shall be kept posted and kept available for inspection on the premises covered by the license.

18 USC § 923 (j)

(j) Licensed dealers, manufacturers and importers may temporarily do business away from their licensed premises, at properly organized gun shows in their state. Records from such shows must indicate the location, and must be stored at the licensed premises. Sales from motorized or towed vehicles are prohibited. A separate fee for the new location is not required. Any inspection of licensee records at a gun show is limited to the records and inventory at the show. This does not authorize the AG to conduct inspections at any site but the licensed site. This subsection does not diminish any right to show or sell firearms or ammunition which was in effect before May 19, 1986.

(j) A licensed importer, licensed manufacturer, or licensed dealer may, under rules or regulations prescribed by the Attorney General, conduct business temporarily at a location other than the location specified on the license if such temporary location is the location for a gun show or event sponsored by any national, State, or local organization, or any affiliate of any such organization devoted to the collection, competitive use, or other sporting use of firearms in the community, and such location is in the State which is specified on the license. Records of receipt and disposition of firearms transactions conducted at such temporary location shall include the location of the sale or other disposition and shall be entered in the permanent records of the licensee and retained on the location specified on the license. Nothing in this subsection shall authorize any licensee to conduct business in or from any motorized or towed vehicle. Notwithstanding the provisions of subsection (a) of this section, a separate fee shall not be required of a licensee with respect to business conducted under this subsection. Any inspection or examination of inventory or records under this chapter by the Attorney General at such temporary location shall be limited to inventory consisting of, or records relating to, firearms held or disposed at such temporary location. Nothing in this subsection shall be construed to authorize the Attorney General to inspect or examine the inventory or records of a licensed importer, licensed manufacturer, or licensed dealer at any location other than the location specified on the license. Nothing in this subsection shall be construed to diminish in any manner any right to display, sell, or otherwise dispose of firearms or ammunition, which is in effect before the date of the enactment of the Firearms Owners' Protection Act, including the right of a licensee to conduct "curios or relics" firearms transfers and business away from their business premises with another licensee without regard as to whether the location of where the business is conducted is located in the State specified on the license of either licensee.

18 USC § 923 (k)

(k) Licensed importers and manufacturers must label armor piercing projectiles and packaging as specified by the AG, who defines what is considered to be armor piercing.

(k) Licensed importers and licensed manufacturers shall mark all armor piercing projectiles and packages containing such projectiles for distribution in the manner prescribed by the Attorney General by regulation. The Attorney General shall furnish information to each dealer licensed under this chapter defining which projectiles are considered armor piercing ammunition as defined in section 921(a)(17)(B).

18 USC § 923 (l)

> (l) The AG must notify local chief law enforcement officers of the names and addresses of anyone who gets an FFL.

(l) The Attorney General shall notify the chief law enforcement officer in the appropriate State and local jurisdictions of the names and addresses of all persons in the State to whom a firearms license is issued.

June 19, 1968 (3,621)
TITLE 18. CRIMES AND CRIMINAL PROCEDURE • PART I: CRIMES • CHAPTER 44: FIREARMS

18 USC § 924. Penalties

> The Gist: Where there's laws there's penalties. The restrictions and requirements described in this chapter (Chapter 44) are referenced below by their citation numbers, and penalties for each are attached. If some of these seem confusing or even illogical it may be that they are; for example, it's less of a crime to commit certain drug offenses with one type of firearm than with another. Aggravating and mitigating circumstances, along with prior offenses, often have an effect on the actual sentence applicable. Federal sentencing guidelines frequently stump the experts—it's possible to reach no consensus on what an actual penalty should be for a given set of circumstances, and people have been sentenced to different penalties for essentially the same violations. The sentencing guidelines for Title 18 fill five books. It is beyond the scope of this book to set all that straight.

(a)(1) Except as otherwise provided in this subsection, subsection (b), or (c) of this section, or in section 929, whoever—
(A) knowingly makes any false statement or representation with respect to the information required by this chapter to be kept in the records of a person licensed under this chapter or in applying for any license or exemption or relief from disability under the provisions of this chapter;
(B) knowingly violates subsection (a)(4), (f), (k) or (r) of section 922;
(C) knowingly imports or brings into the United States or any possession thereof any firearm or ammunition in violation of section 922(l); or
(D) willfully violates any other provision of this chapter, shall be fined under this title, imprisoned not more than five years, or both.
(2) Whoever knowingly violates subsection (a)(6), (d), (g), (h), (i), (j), or (o) of section 922 shall be fined as provided in this title, imprisoned not more than 10 years, or both.
(3) Any licensed dealer, licensed importer, licensed manufacturer, or licensed collector who knowingly—
(A) makes any false statement or representation with respect to the information required by the provisions of this chapter to be kept in the records of a person licensed under this chapter, or
(B) violates subsection (m) of section 922, shall be fined under this title, imprisoned not more than one year, or both.

(4) Whoever violates section 922(q) shall be fined under this title, imprisoned for not more than 5 years, or both. Notwithstanding any other provision of law, the term of imprisonment imposed under this paragraph shall not run concurrently with any other term of imprisonment imposed under any other provision of law. Except for the authorization of a term of imprisonment of not more than 5 years made in this paragraph, for the purpose of any other law a violation of section 922(q) shall be deemed to be a misdemeanor.

(5) Whoever knowingly violates subsection (s) or (t) of section 922 shall be fined under this title, imprisoned for not more than 1 year, or both.

(6)(A)(i) A juvenile who violates section 922(x) shall be fined under this title, imprisoned not more than 1 year, or both, except that a juvenile described in clause (ii) shall be sentenced to probation on appropriate conditions and shall not be incarcerated unless the juvenile fails to comply with a condition of probation.

(ii) A juvenile is described in this clause if—

(I) the offense of which the juvenile is charged is possession of a handgun or ammunition in violation of section 922(x)(2); and

(II) the juvenile has not been convicted in any court of an offense (including an offense under section 922(x) or a similar State law, but not including any other offense consisting of conduct that if engaged in by an adult would not constitute an offense) or adjudicated as a juvenile delinquent for conduct that if engaged in by an adult would constitute an offense.

(B) A person other than a juvenile who knowingly violates section 922(x)—

(i) shall be fined under this title, imprisoned not more than 1 year, or both; and

(ii) if the person sold, delivered, or otherwise transferred a handgun or ammunition to a juvenile knowing or having reasonable cause to know that the juvenile intended to carry or otherwise possess or discharge or otherwise use the handgun or ammunition in the commission of a crime of violence, shall be fined under this title, imprisoned not more than 10 years, or both.

(7) Whoever knowingly violates section 931 shall be fined under this title, imprisoned not more than 3 years, or both.

(b) Whoever, with intent to commit therewith an offense punishable by imprisonment for a term exceeding one year, or with knowledge or reasonable cause to believe that an offense punishable by imprisonment for a term exceeding one year is to be committed therewith, ships, transports, or receives a firearm or any ammunition in interstate or foreign commerce shall be fined under this title, or imprisoned not more than ten years, or both.

(c)(1)(A) Except to the extent that a greater minimum sentence is otherwise provided by this subsection or by any other provision of law, any person who, during and in relation to any crime of violence or drug trafficking crime (including a crime of violence or drug trafficking crime that provides for an enhanced punishment if committed by the use of a deadly or dangerous weapon or device) for which the person may be prosecuted in a court of the United States, uses or carries a firearm, or who, in furtherance of any such crime, possesses a firearm, shall, in addition to the punishment provided for such crime of violence or drug trafficking crime—

(i) be sentenced to a term of imprisonment of not less than 5 years;

(ii) if the firearm is brandished, be sentenced to a term of imprisonment of not less than 7 years; and

(iii) if the firearm is discharged, be sentenced to a term of imprisonment of not less than 10 years.

(B) If the firearm possessed by a person convicted of a violation of this subsection—

(i) is a short-barreled rifle, short-barreled shotgun, or semiautomatic assault weapon, the person shall be sentenced to a term of imprisonment of not less than 10 years; or

(ii) is a machinegun or a destructive device, or is equipped with a firearm silencer or firearm muffler, the person shall be sentenced to a term of imprisonment of not less than 30 years.

(C) In the case of a second or subsequent conviction under this subsection, the person shall—

(i) be sentenced to a term of imprisonment of not less than 25 years; and

(ii) if the firearm involved is a machinegun or a destructive device, or is equipped with a firearm silencer or firearm muffler, be sentenced to imprisonment for life.

(D) Notwithstanding any other provision of law—

(i) a court shall not place on probation any person convicted of a violation of this subsection; and

(ii) no term of imprisonment imposed on a person under this subsection shall run concurrently with any other term of imprisonment imposed on the person, including any term of imprisonment imposed for the crime of violence or drug trafficking crime during which the firearm was used, carried, or possessed.

(2) For purposes of this subsection, the term "drug trafficking crime" means any felony punishable under the Controlled Substances Act (21 U.S.C. 801 et seq.), the Controlled Substances Import and Export Act (21 U.S.C. 951 et seq.), or the Maritime Drug Law Enforcement Act (46 U.S.C. App. 1901 et seq.).

(3) For purposes of this subsection the term "crime of violence" means an offense that is a felony and—

(A) has as an element the use, attempted use, or threatened use of physical force against the person or property of another, or

(B) that by its nature, involves a substantial risk that physical force against the person or property of another may be used in the course of committing the offense.

(4) For purposes of this subsection, the term "brandish" means, with respect to a firearm, to display all or part of the firearm, or otherwise make the presence of the firearm known to another person, in order to intimidate that person, regardless of whether the firearm is directly visible to that person.

(d)(1) Any firearm or ammunition involved in or used in any knowing violation of subsection (a)(4), (a)(6), (f), (g), (h), (i), (j), or (k) of section 922, or knowing importation or bringing into the United States or any possession thereof any firearm or ammunition in violation of section 922(l), or knowing violation of section 924, or willful violation of any other provision of this chapter or any rule or regulation promulgated thereunder, or any violation of any other criminal law of the United States, or any firearm or ammunition intended to be used in any offense referred to in paragraph (3) of this subsection, where such intent is demonstrated by clear and convincing evidence, shall be subject to seizure and forfeiture, and all provisions of the Internal Revenue Code of 1954 relating to the seizure, forfeiture, and disposition of firearms, as defined in section 5845(a) of that Code, shall, so far as applicable, extend to seizures and forfeitures under the provisions of this chapter: Provided, That upon acquittal of the owner or possessor, or dismissal of the charges against him other than upon motion of the Government prior to trial, or lapse of or court termination of the restraining order to which he is subject, the seized or relinquished firearms or ammunition shall be returned forthwith to the owner or possessor or to a person delegated by the owner or possessor unless the return of the firearms or ammunition would place the owner or possessor or his delegate in violation of law. Any action or proceeding for the forfeiture of firearms or ammunition shall be commenced within one hundred and twenty days of such seizure.

(2)(A) In any action or proceeding for the return of firearms or ammunition seized under the provisions of this chapter, the court shall allow the prevailing party, other than the United States, a reasonable attorney's fee, and the United States shall be liable therefor.

(B) In any other action or proceeding under the provisions of this chapter, the court, when it finds that such action was without foundation, or was initiated vexatiously, frivolously, or in bad faith, shall allow the prevailing party, other than the United States, a reasonable attorney's fee, and the United States shall be liable therefor.

(C) Only those firearms or quantities of ammunition particularly named and individually identified as involved in or used in any violation of the provisions of this chapter or any rule or regulation issued thereunder, or any other criminal law of the United States or as intended to be used in any offense referred to in paragraph (3) of this subsection, where such intent is demonstrated by clear and convincing evidence, shall be subject to seizure, forfeiture, and disposition.

(D) The United States shall be liable for attorneys' fees under this paragraph only to the extent provided in advance by appropriation Acts.(3) The offenses referred to in paragraphs (1) and (2)(C) of this subsection are—

(A) any crime of violence, as that term is defined in section 924(c)(3) of this title;

(B) any offense punishable under the Controlled Substances Act (21 U.S.C. 801 et seq.) or the Controlled Substances Import and Export Act (21 U.S.C. 951 et seq.);

(C) any offense described in section 922(a)(1), 922(a)(3), 922(a)(5), or 922(b)(3) of this title, where the firearm or ammunition intended to be used in any such offense is involved in a pattern of activities which includes a violation of any offense described in section 922(a)(1), 922(a)(3), 922(a)(5), or 922(b)(3) of this title;

(D) any offense described in section 922(d) of this title where the firearm or ammunition is intended to be used in such offense by the transferor of such firearm or ammunition;

(E) any offense described in section 922(i), 922(j), 922(l), 922(n), or 924(b) of this title; and

(F) any offense which may be prosecuted in a court of the United States which involves the exportation of firearms or ammunition.

(e)(1) In the case of a person who violates section 922(g) of this title and has three previous convictions by any court referred to in section 922(g)(1) of this title for a violent felony or a serious drug offense, or both, committed on occasions different from one another, such person shall be fined under this title and imprisoned not less than fifteen years, and, notwithstanding any other provision of law, the court shall not suspend the sentence of, or grant a probationary sentence to, such person with respect to the conviction under section 922(g).(2) As used in this subsection—

(A) the term "serious drug offense" means—

(i) an offense under the Controlled Substances Act (21 U.S.C. 801 et seq.), the Controlled Substances Import and Export Act (21 U.S.C. 951 et seq.), or the Maritime Drug Law Enforcement Act (46 U.S.C. App. 1901 et seq.), for which a maximum term of imprisonment of ten years or more is prescribed by law; or

(ii) an offense under State law, involving manufacturing, distributing, or possessing with intent to manufacture or distribute, a controlled substance (as defined in section 102 of the Controlled Substances Act (21 U.S.C. 802)), for which a maximum term of imprisonment of ten years or more is prescribed by law;

(B) the term "violent felony" means any crime punishable by imprisonment for a term exceeding one year, or any act of juvenile delinquency involving the use or carrying of a firearm, knife, or destructive device that would be punishable by imprisonment for such term if committed by an adult, that—

(i) has as an element the use, attempted use, or threatened use of physical force against the person of another; or

(ii) is burglary, arson, or extortion, involves use of explosives, or otherwise involves conduct that presents a serious potential risk of physical injury to another; and

(C) the term "conviction" includes a finding that a person has committed an act of juvenile delinquency involving a violent felony.

(f) Whoever, with the intent to engage in conduct which—

(1) constitutes an offense listed in section 1961(1),

(2) is punishable under the Controlled Substances Act (21 U.S.C. 802 et seq.), the Controlled Substances Import and Export Act (21 U.S.C. 951 et seq.), or the Maritime Drug Law Enforcement Act (46 U.S.C. App. 1901 et seq.),

(3) violates any State law relating to any controlled substance (as defined in section 102(6) of the Controlled Substances Act (21 U.S.C. 802(6))), or

(4) constitutes a crime of violence (as defined in subsection (c)(3)), travels from any State or foreign country into any other State and acquires, transfers, or attempts to acquire or transfer, a firearm in such other State in furtherance of such purpose, shall be imprisoned not more than 10 years, fined in accordance with this title, or both.

(g) Whoever knowingly transfers a firearm, knowing that such firearm will be used to commit a crime of violence (as defined in subsection (c)(3)) or drug trafficking crime (as defined in subsection (c)(2)) shall be imprisoned not more than 10 years, fined in accordance with this title, or both.

(h)(1) A person who knowingly violates section 922(u) shall be fined under this title, imprisoned not more than 10 years, or both.

(2) Nothing contained in this subsection shall be construed as indicating an intent on the part of Congress to occupy the field in which provisions of this subsection operate to the exclusion of State laws on the same subject matter, nor shall any provision of this subsection be construed as invalidating any provision of State law unless such provision is inconsistent with any of the purposes of this subsection.

(i) A person who, in the course of a violation of subsection (c), causes the death of a person through the use of a firearm, shall—

(1) if the killing is a murder (as defined in section 1111), be punished by death or by imprisonment for any term of years or for life; and

(2) if the killing is manslaughter (as defined in section 1112), be punished as provided in that section.

(j) A person who, with intent to engage in or to promote conduct that—

(1) is punishable under the Controlled Substances Act (21 U.S.C. 801 et seq.), the Controlled Substances Import and Export Act (21 U.S.C. 951 et seq.), or the Maritime Drug Law Enforcement Act (46 U.S.C. App. 1901 et seq.);

(2) violates any law of a State relating to any controlled substance (as defined in section 102 of the Controlled Substances Act, 21 U.S.C. 802); or

(3) constitutes a crime of violence (as defined in subsection (c)(3)), smuggles or knowingly brings into the United States a firearm, or attempts to do so, shall be imprisoned not more than 10 years, fined under this title, or both.

(k) A person who steals any firearm which is moving as, or is a part of, or which has moved in, interstate or foreign commerce shall be imprisoned for not more than 10 years, fined under this title, or both.

(l) A person who steals any firearm from a licensed importer, licensed manufacturer, licensed dealer, or licensed collector shall be fined under this title, imprisoned not more than 10 years, or both.

(m) A person who, with the intent to engage in conduct that constitutes a violation of section 922(a)(1)(A), travels from any State or foreign country into any other State and acquires, or attempts to acquire, a firearm in such other State in furtherance of such purpose shall be imprisoned for not more than 10 years.

(n) A person who conspires to commit an offense under subsection (c) shall be imprisoned for not more than 20 years, fined under this title, or both; and if the firearm is a machinegun or destructive device, or is equipped with a firearm silencer or muffler, shall be imprisoned for any term of years or life.

(o) A person who conspires to commit an offense under subsection (c) shall be imprisoned for not more than 20 years, fined under this title, or both; and if the firearm is a machinegun or destructive device, or is equipped with a firearm silencer or muffler, shall be imprisoned for any term of years or life.

June 19, 1968 (2,908)

TITLE 18. CRIMES AND CRIMINAL PROCEDURE • PART I: CRIMES • CHAPTER 44: FIREARMS

18 USC § 925. Exceptions: Relief from disabilities

The Gist: The federal gun laws from this chapter (except for the ban on "undetectable" handguns, and the gun-ban for people with a misdemeanor crime of domestic violence) do not apply to the federal or state government at any level, or to the shipment or receipt of firearms and ammunition as part of the Army Civilian Marksmanship Program (see 10–4308, repealed, 1996). Dealers can ship firearms and ammo to active army personnel outside the country for personal sporting use. The Attorney General (AG) may authorize the importation of personal sporting firearms and war souvenirs to the U.S. residence of a member of the armed forces who is on active duty outside the country. A dealer charged with a violation can continue in business until the charge is settled. A person who is disqualified under federal law from possessing, shipping, transporting or receiving firearms or ammunition may apply to the AG for relief from the disqualification. The AG may grant such relief if they decide that the applicant is unlikely to be a risk to public safety. A person who is turned down may appeal in federal district court.

The AG must allow the importation of firearms and ammunition: 1–for scientific or research purposes; 2–for competition and training under the civilian marksmanship program; 3–if it's unserviceable as a curio or relic (except machine guns); 4–if it's not an NFA weapon (described in 26–5845) and it's generally recognized as suited to sporting purposes; 5–for examination and testing to decide if it will be allowed to be imported; and 6–if it's being brought back to the country by the person who took it out. The AG must allow licensed importers to bring in rifle and shotgun curios and relics, and handgun curios and relics if they are suited to sporting use. Penalties for illegal importation are described.

(a)(1) The provisions of this chapter shall not apply with respect to the transportation, shipment, receipt, possession, or importation of any firearm or ammunition imported for, sold or shipped to, or issued for the use of, the United States or any department or agency thereof or any State or any department, agency, or political subdivision thereof.

(2) The provisions of this chapter shall not apply with respect to

(A) the shipment or receipt of firearms or ammunition when sold or issued by the Secretary of the Army pursuant to section 4308 of title 10 before the repeal of such section by section 1624(a) of the Corporation for the Promotion of Rifle Practice and Firearms safety Act, and

(B) the transportation of any such firearm or ammunition carried out to enable a person, who lawfully received such firearm or ammunition from the Secretary of the Army, to engage in military training or in competitions.

(3) Unless otherwise prohibited by this chapter or any other Federal law, a licensed importer, licensed manufacturer, or licensed dealer may ship to a member of the United States Armed Forces on active duty outside the United States or to clubs, recognized by the Department of Defense, whose entire membership is composed of such members, and such members or clubs may receive a firearm or ammunition determined by the Attorney General to be generally recognized as particularly suitable for sporting purposes and intended for the personal use of such member or club.

(4) When established to the satisfaction of the Attorney General to be consistent with the provisions of this chapter and other applicable Federal and State laws and published ordinances, the Attorney General may authorize the transportation, shipment, receipt, or importation into the United States to the place of residence of any member of the United States Armed Forces who is on active duty outside the United States (or who has been on active duty outside the United States within the sixty day period immediately preceding the transportation, shipment, receipt, or importation), of any firearm or ammunition which is

(A) determined by the Attorney General to be generally recognized as particularly suitable for sporting purposes, or determined by the Department of Defense to be a type of firearm normally classified as a war souvenir, and

(B) intended for the personal use of such member.

(5) For the purpose of paragraphs (3) and (4) of this subsection, the term "United States" means each of the several States and the District of Columbia.

(b) A licensed importer, licensed manufacturer, licensed dealer, or licensed collector who is indicted for a crime punishable by imprisonment for a term exceeding one year, may, notwithstanding any other provision of this chapter, continue operation pursuant to his existing license (if prior to the expiration of the term of the existing license timely application is made for a new license) during the term of such indictment and until any conviction pursuant to the indictment becomes final.

(c) A person who is prohibited from possessing, shipping, transporting, or receiving firearms or ammunition may make application to the Attorney General for relief from the disabilities imposed by Federal laws with respect to the acquisition, receipt, transfer, shipment, transportation, or possession of firearms, and the Attorney General may grant such relief if it is established to his satisfaction that the circumstances regarding the disability, and the applicant's record and reputation, are such that the applicant will not be likely to act in a manner dangerous to public safety and that the granting of the relief would not be contrary to the public interest. Any person whose application for relief from disabilities is denied by the Attorney General may file a petition with the United States district court for the district in which he resides for a judicial review of such denial. The court may in its discretion admit additional evidence where failure to do so would result in a miscarriage of justice. A licensed importer, licensed manufacturer, licensed dealer, or licensed collector conducting operations under this chapter, who makes application for relief from the disabilities incurred under this chapter, shall not be barred by such disability from further operations under his license pending final action on an application for relief filed pursuant to this section. Whenever the Attorney General grants relief to any person pursuant to this section he shall promptly publish in the Federal Register notice of such action, together with the reasons therefor.

(d) The Attorney General shall authorize a firearm or ammunition to be imported or brought into the United States or any possession thereof if the firearm or ammunition—

(1) is being imported or brought in for scientific or research purposes, or is for use in connection with competition or training pursuant to chapter 401 of title 10;

(2) is an unserviceable firearm, other than a machinegun as defined in section 5845(b) of the Internal Revenue Code of 1954 (not readily restorable to firing condition), imported or brought in as a curio or museum piece;

(3) is of a type that does not fall within the definition of a firearm as defined in section 5845(a) of the Internal Revenue Code of 1954 and is generally recognized as particularly suitable for or readily adaptable to sporting purposes, excluding surplus military firearms, except in any case where the Attorney General has not authorized the importation of the firearm pursuant to this paragraph, it shall be unlawful to import any frame, receiver, or barrel of such firearm which would be prohibited if assembled; or

4) was previously taken out of the United States or a possession by the person who is bringing in the firearm or ammunition. The Attorney General shall permit the conditional importation or bringing in of a firearm or ammunition for examination and testing in connection with the making of a determination as to whether the importation or bringing in of such firearm or ammunition will be allowed under this subsection.

(e) Notwithstanding any other provision of this title, the Attorney General shall authorize the importation of, by any licensed importer, the following:

(1) All rifles and shotguns listed as curios or relics by the Attorney General pursuant to section 921(a)(13), and

(2) All handguns, listed as curios or relics by the Attorney General pursuant to section 921(a)(13), provided that such handguns are generally recognized as particularly suitable for or readily adaptable to sporting purposes.

June 19, 1968 (1,080)

TITLE 18. CRIMES AND CRIMINAL PROCEDURE • PART I: CRIMES • CHAPTER 44: FIREARMS

18 USC § 925A. Remedy for erroneous denial of firearm

The Gist: Anyone denied a firearm due to inaccurate information found during a background check required by the Brady law, may file a lawsuit against the government to get the information corrected or the firearm transfer approved. The courts may allow the winner in such a suit to collect reasonable attorney's fees.

Any person denied a firearm pursuant to subsection (s) or (t) of section 922—
(1) due to the provision of erroneous information relating to the person by any State or political subdivision thereof, or by the national instant criminal background check system established under section 103 of the Brady Handgun Violence Prevention Act; or
(2) who was not prohibited from receipt of a firearm pursuant to subsection (g) or (n) of section 922, may bring an action against the State or political subdivision responsible for providing the erroneous information, or responsible for denying the transfer, or against the United States, as the case may be, for an order directing that the erroneous information be corrected or that the transfer be approved, as the case may be. In any action under this section, the court, in its discretion, may allow the prevailing party a reasonable attorney's fee as part of the costs.

Nov. 30, 1993 (151)
TITLE 18. CRIMES AND CRIMINAL PROCEDURE • PART I: CRIMES • CHAPTER 44: FIREARMS

18 USC § 926. Rules and regulations

The Gist: The Attorney General may make only the rules needed to implement this chapter of law, including; 1–requiring licensees to show official copies of their licenses; 2–making license copies available at a reasonable cost; 3–requiring the government to securely store seized firearms; and 4–guarantee that no federal or other governmental entity registers private firearms. All proposed regulations must be issued in draft form for 90 days to allow review by interested parties. Black powder for private use in antique firearms is exempt.

Note that the fourth numbered item above (which comes from (a)(3) in the statute below) expressly forbids using collected records from defunct dealers, or any other method, to establish national firearms registration.

(a) The Attorney General may prescribe only such rules and regulations as are necessary to carry out the provisions of this chapter, including—
(1) regulations providing that a person licensed under this chapter, when dealing with another person so licensed, shall provide such other licensed person a certified copy of this license;
(2) regulations providing for the issuance, at a reasonable cost, to a person licensed under this chapter, of certified copies of his license for use as provided under regulations issued under paragraph (1) of this subsection; and
(3) regulations providing for effective receipt and secure storage of firearms relinquished by or seized from persons described in subsection (d)(8) or (g)(8) of section 922. No such rule or regulation prescribed after the date of the enactment of the Firearms Owners' Protection Act may require that records required to be maintained under this chapter or any portion of the contents of such records, be recorded at or transferred to a facility owned, managed, or controlled by the United States or any State or any political subdivision thereof, nor that any system of registration of firearms, firearms owners, or firearms transactions or dispositions be established. Nothing in this section expands or restricts the Attorney General's authority to inquire into the disposition of any firearm in the course of a criminal investigation.
(b) The Attorney General shall give not less than ninety days public notice, and shall afford interested parties opportunity for hearing, before prescribing such rules and regulations.
(c) The Attorney General shall not prescribe rules or regulations that require purchasers of black powder under the exemption provided in section 845(a)(5) of this title to complete affidavits or forms attesting to that exemption.

June 19, 1968 (282)
TITLE 18. CRIMES AND CRIMINAL PROCEDURE • PART I: CRIMES • CHAPTER 44: FIREARMS

18 USC § 926A. Interstate transportation of firearms

The Gist: This is **the federal firearms transportation guarantee**. It was included as part of the 1986 Firearm Owners' Protection Act, to help curb abuses that had become common. Federal law guarantees that a person may legally transport a firearm from one place where its possession is legal to another place where possession is legal, provided it is unloaded and the firearm and any ammunition are not readily accessible from the passenger compartment of the vehicle. The law doesn't say it in so many words, but the trunk is the only non-accessible spot in the average passenger car. If a vehicle has no separate compartment for this purpose, the firearm and ammunition may be in a locked container other than the glove compartment or console.

Note that there are cases of local authorities who have not complied with this law, creating a degree of risk for people otherwise legally transporting firearms. It is probably also accurate to say that many local authorities neither know nor care about this rule, and may act outside the protections it intends for the public.

Transporting a firearm is not the same as carrying a firearm. As many people have discovered, differing state laws make it nearly impossible to legally travel interstate with a firearm available for protection. See the notes on state laws and travel in the front Overview section.

Those readers who purchased this book or other books (notably, *The Traveler's Guide to the Firearm Laws of the 50 States*), hoping it would somehow enable or empower them to travel interstate with a loaded personal firearm, must contact their representatives and begin to ask about the lost National Right to Carry. That right has a name, the Second Amendment, and it has essentially evaporated for interstate travelers.

Notwithstanding any other provision of any law or any rule or regulation of a State or any political subdivision thereof, any person who is not otherwise prohibited by this chapter from transporting, shipping, or receiving a firearm shall be entitled to transport a firearm for any lawful purpose from any place where he may lawfully possess and carry such firearm to any other place where he may lawfully possess and carry such firearm if, during such transportation the firearm is unloaded, and neither the firearm nor any ammunition being transported is readily accessible or is directly accessible from the passenger compartment of such transporting vehicle: Provided, That in the case of a vehicle without a compartment separate from the driver's compartment the firearm or ammunition shall be contained in a locked container other than the glove compartment or console.

July 8, 1986 (139)
TITLE 18. CRIMES AND CRIMINAL PROCEDURE • PART I: CRIMES • CHAPTER 44: FIREARMS

18 USC § 926B. Carrying of concealed firearms by qualified law enforcement officers

The Law Enforcement Officers Safety Act of 2004. This bill, quietly signed into law by President Bush on July 22, 2004, and generally ignored by the news media, frees specified current and former law-enforcement officers to carry concealed firearms, in states with bans on carrying concealed handguns. It took 12 years of intensive lobbying by the Virginia-based police group, the Law Enforcement Alliance of America, to get Congress to accept a national concealed-carry provision, even for these off-duty and former police.

The bill is highly controversial to gun-rights activists, who view it as an elitist provision to arm the "proper authorities," giving those people, and excluding the public, from constitutionally guaranteed rights. The LEAA's claim that "America's men and women in blue deserved the right to protect themselves and their families from threats that didn't go away at the state line," advocates say, applies constitutionally to people who aren't "in blue."

On the other hand, the law does arm nearly two million civilians, forced Congress to move in a direction of recognizing and requiring the right to keep and bear arms, and plans are in place to continue the momentum toward some form of public national right to carry. And it is certainly true, as LEAA points out, that people "in blue" do face "criminal grudges that didn't end at the officer's retirement party." The level of resistance to restoring lost gun-carry rights is revealed in the fact that it took more than a decade to get such a provision in place for such a select group as the police.

Parallel efforts for national carry rights for the public, currently underway, tend to focus on reciprocity or recognition for permit holders only, and is also highly contentious, since only about 1% of the public has signed up for state "rights permits," which include taxes, testing, fingerprinting, expiration dates, and onerous federal and state watch lists. Most estimates suggest that more than 50% of all Americans own firearms, leaving almost all of us out of such plans.

For contrast, see the proposed American Historical Rights Protection Act, posted at gunlaws.com, which would simply eliminate any bans on the non-criminal possession of firearms for all Americans. It states that possession of private property, namely firearms, absent some overtly criminal behavior, is not in and of itself a criminal act, and should not be subject to sanctions of any kind.

The Gist: No state law may prevent a qualified law enforcement officer (QLEO, described below), who is carrying proper ID, from carrying a concealed firearm, if the firearm has been shipped or transported in interstate or foreign commerce. (The phrase about commerce is used to help establish congressional authority to do this—overruling state laws—using the commerce clause authority in the Constitution.)

The overruling of state law does not include any state law about private people banning or restricting firearms on their property, or state governments banning or restricting firearms on state or local government property.

Under this law a QLEO is: 1–a government agency employee who has specified legal authority to enforce the law and statutory powers of arrest; 2–is authorized by the agency to carry a firearm; 3–is not the subject of any disciplinary action; 4–meets the standards, if any, to regularly qualify in using a firearm; 5–is not under the influence of drugs or alcohol; and 6–is not banned under federal law from receiving a firearm.

Proper identification is a photo ID issued by the government agency where the person is employed as a law enforcement officer.

A concealed firearm does not include a machinegun, a silencer, or any destructive device, as those items are defined by federal law.

The background and history of HR 218, the original bill, can be reviewed at leaa.org. Regulations needed to implement the new law nationwide are in development, and reportedly tied up in inter-agency bickering and bureaucratic delays.

(a) Notwithstanding any other provision of the law of any State or any political subdivision thereof, an individual who is a qualified law enforcement officer and who is carrying the identification required by subsection (d) may carry a concealed firearm that has been shipped or transported in interstate or foreign commerce, subject to subsection (b).

(b) This section shall not be construed to supersede or limit the laws of any State that—

(1) permit private persons or entities to prohibit or restrict the possession of concealed firearms on their property; or

(2) prohibit or restrict the possession of firearms on any State or local government property, installation, building, base, or park.

(c) As used in this section, the term qualified law enforcement officer' means an employee of a governmental agency who—

(1) is authorized by law to engage in or supervise the prevention, detection, investigation, or prosecution of, or the incarceration of any person for, any violation of law, and has statutory powers of arrest;

(2) is authorized by the agency to carry a firearm;

(3) is not the subject of any disciplinary action by the agency;

(4) meets standards, if any, established by the agency which require the employee to regularly qualify in the use of a firearm;

(5) is not under the influence of alcohol or another intoxicating or hallucinatory drug or substance; and

(6) is not prohibited by Federal law from receiving a firearm.

(d) The identification required by this subsection is the photographic identification issued by the governmental agency for which the individual is employed as a law enforcement officer.

(e) As used in this section, the term firearm' does not include—

(1) any machinegun (as defined in section 5845 of the National Firearms Act);

(2) any firearm silencer (as defined in section 921 of this title); and

(3) any destructive device (as defined in section 921 of this title).

July 22, 2004 (314)

18 USC § 926C. Carrying of concealed firearms by qualified retired law enforcement officers

The Gist: All the conditions of 18-926B, above, also apply to a qualified retired law enforcement officer (QRLEO). A QRLEO is a person who: 1–retired in good standing as a law enforcement officer (except for reasons of mental instability); 2–before retiring had specified legal authority to enforce the law and statutory powers of arrest; 3–was regularly employed as a LEO for an aggregate of at least 15 years before retiring (with special consideration for a probationary period due to a service-connected disability); 4–has a non-forfeitable right to retirement-plan benefits from the agency; 5–has in the last 12 months, at the person's own expense, met the state standards for active LEOs to carry firearms; 6–is not under the influence of drugs or alcohol; and 7–and is not banned under federal law from receiving a firearm. The law appears to require QRLEOs to requalify, under item 5 above, at their own expense, every 12 months.

Proper identification for a QRLEO is a photo ID from the agency that formerly employed the person as an LEO, indicating that the person has qualified or otherwise meets the standards within the last year to carry a firearm of the same type the person is carrying concealed. A separate state certification of firearm qualification, in addition to photo ID from the agency, is also acceptable.

Machineguns, silencers and destructive devices are banned for concealed carry by QRLEOs.

(a) Notwithstanding any other provision of the law of any State or any political subdivision thereof, an individual who is a qualified retired law enforcement officer and who is carrying the identification required by subsection (d) may carry a concealed firearm that has been shipped or transported in interstate or foreign commerce, subject to subsection (b).

(b) This section shall not be construed to supersede or limit the laws of any State that—

(1) permit private persons or entities to prohibit or restrict the possession of concealed firearms on their property; or

(2) prohibit or restrict the possession of firearms on any State or local government property, installation, building, base, or park.

(c) As used in this section, the term qualified retired law enforcement officer' means an individual who—

(1) retired in good standing from service with a public agency as a law enforcement officer, other than for reasons of mental instability;

(2) before such retirement, was authorized by law to engage in or supervise the prevention, detection, investigation, or prosecution of, or the incarceration of any person for, any violation of law, and had statutory powers of arrest;

(3)(A) before such retirement, was regularly employed as a law enforcement officer for an aggregate of 15 years or more; or

(B) retired from service with such agency, after completing any applicable probationary period of such service, due to a service-connected disability, as determined by such agency;

(4) has a nonforfeitable right to benefits under the retirement plan of the agency;

(5) during the most recent 12-month period, has met, at the expense of the individual, the State's standards for training and qualification for active law enforcement officers to carry firearms;

(6) is not under the influence of alcohol or another intoxicating or hallucinatory drug or substance; and

(7) is not prohibited by Federal law from receiving a firearm.

(d) The identification required by this subsection is—

(1) a photographic identification issued by the agency from which the individual retired from service as a law enforcement officer that indicates that the individual has, not less recently than one year before the date the individual is carrying the concealed firearm, been tested or otherwise found by the agency to meet the standards established by the agency for training and qualification for active law enforcement officers to carry a firearm of the same type as the concealed firearm; or

(2)(A) a photographic identification issued by the agency from which the individual retired from service as a law enforcement officer; and

(B) a certification issued by the State in which the individual resides that indicates that the individual has, not less recently than one year before the date the individual is carrying the concealed firearm, been tested or otherwise found by the State to meet the standards established by the State for training and qualification for active law enforcement officers to carry a firearm of the same type as the concealed firearm.

(e) As used in this section, the term firearm' does not include—

(1) any machinegun (as defined in section 5845 of the National Firearms Act);

(2) any firearm silencer (as defined in section 921 of this title); and

(3) a destructive device (as defined in section 921 of this title).

July 22, 2004 (538)

TITLE 18. CRIMES AND CRIMINAL PROCEDURE • PART I: CRIMES • CHAPTER 44: FIREARMS

18 USC § 927. Effect on State law

> The Gist: Congress expresses its intent to not conflict with similar state laws, unless the state laws disagree with Congress, in which case Congress rules. Say what?

No provision of this chapter shall be construed as indicating an intent on the part of the Congress to occupy the field in which such provision operates to the exclusion of the law of any State on the same subject matter, unless there is a direct and positive conflict between such provision and the law of the State so that the two cannot be reconciled or consistently stand together.

June 19, 1968 (69)

TITLE 18. CRIMES AND CRIMINAL PROCEDURE • PART I: CRIMES • CHAPTER 44: FIREARMS

18 USC § 928. Separability clause

> The Gist: Just because one part of Title 18 Chapter 44 may not be valid doesn't mean that any other part is invalid.

If any provision of this chapter or the application thereof to any person or circumstances is held invalid, the remainder of the chapter and the application of such provision to other persons not similarly situated or to other circumstances shall not be affected thereby.

June 19, 1968 (44)

TITLE 18. CRIMES AND CRIMINAL PROCEDURE • PART I: CRIMES • CHAPTER 44: FIREARMS

18 USC § 929. Use of restricted ammunition

> The Gist: Committing a violent crime or a drug trafficking crime with a firearm, while in possession of armor piercing ammunition which fits the firearm, increases the sentence and eliminates the possibility of parole.

(a)(1) Whoever, during and in relation to the commission of a crime of violence or drug trafficking crime (including a crime of violence or drug trafficking crime which provides for an enhanced punishment if committed by the use of a deadly or dangerous weapon or device) for which he may be prosecuted in a court of the United States, uses or carries a firearm and is in possession of armor piercing ammunition capable of being fired in that firearm, shall, in addition to the punishment provided for the commission of such crime of violence or drug trafficking crime be sentenced to a term of imprisonment for not less than five years.

(2) For purposes of this subsection, the term "drug trafficking crime" means any felony punishable under the Controlled Substances Act (21 U.S.C. 801 et seq.), the Controlled Substances Import and Export Act (21 U.S.C. 951 et seq.), or the Maritime Drug Law Enforcement Act (46 U.S.C. App. 1901 et seq.).

(b) Notwithstanding any other provision of law, the court shall not suspend the sentence of any person convicted of a violation of this section, nor place the person on probation, nor shall the terms of imprisonment run concurrently with any other terms of imprisonment, including that imposed for the crime in which the armor piercing ammunition was used or possessed.

Oct. 12, 1984 (221)
TITLE 18. CRIMES AND CRIMINAL PROCEDURE • PART I: CRIMES • CHAPTER 44: FIREARMS

18 USC § 930. Possession of firearms and dangerous weapons in Federal facilities

> The Gist: It's a crime to bring a firearm into a federal facility, except for hunting or other lawful purposes. It's a greater crime to bring a firearm into a federal court. It's an even greater crime to bring a firearm into a federal facility for use in a crime. This applies to any dangerous weapon except for a pocket knife with a blade less than 2.5 inches in length. The various penalties are described or cross referenced, and proper authorities are exempted. A person cannot be convicted of bringing a gun into a federal facility (other than a court, and without other criminal wrongdoing) unless the facilities are clearly labeled or the person had other notice of the requirement. A U.S. court may prohibit weapons in its buildings and grounds, and punish violators.

(a) Except as provided in subsection (d), whoever knowingly possesses or causes to be present a firearm or other dangerous weapon in a Federal facility (other than a Federal court facility), or attempts to do so, shall be fined under this title or imprisoned not more than 1 year, or both.

(b) Whoever, with intent that a firearm or other dangerous weapon be used in the commission of a crime, knowingly possesses or causes to be present such firearm or dangerous weapon in a Federal facility, or attempts to do so, shall be fined under this title or imprisoned not more than 5 years, or both.

(c) A person who kills any person in the course of a violation of subsection (a) or (b), or in the course of an attack on a Federal facility involving the use of a firearm or other dangerous weapon, or attempts or conspires to do such an act, shall be punished as provided in sections 1111, 1112, 1113, and 1117.

(d) Subsection (a) shall not apply to—

(1) the lawful performance of official duties by an officer, agent, or employee of the United States, a State, or a political subdivision thereof, who is authorized by law to engage in or supervise the prevention, detection, investigation, or prosecution of any violation of law;

(2) the possession of a firearm or other dangerous weapon by a Federal official or a member of the Armed Forces if such possession is authorized by law; or

(3) the lawful carrying of firearms or other dangerous weapons in a Federal facility incident to hunting or other lawful purposes.

(e)(1) Except as provided in paragraph (2), whoever knowingly possesses or causes to be present a firearm in a Federal court facility, or attempts to do so, shall be fined under this title, imprisoned not more than 2 years, or both.

(2) Paragraph (1) shall not apply to conduct which is described in paragraph (1) or (2) of subsection (d).

(f) Nothing in this section limits the power of a court of the United States to punish for contempt or to promulgate rules or orders regulating, restricting, or prohibiting the possession of weapons within any building housing such court or any of its proceedings, or upon any grounds appurtenant to such building.

(g) As used in this section:

(1) The term "Federal facility" means a building or part thereof owned or leased by the Federal Government, where Federal employees are regularly present for the purpose of performing their official duties.

(2) The term "dangerous weapon" means a weapon, device, instrument, material, or substance, animate or inanimate, that is used for, or is readily capable of, causing death or serious bodily injury, except that such term does not include a pocket knife with a blade of less than 2 1/2 inches in length.

(3) The term "Federal court facility" means the courtroom, judges' chambers, witness rooms, jury deliberation rooms, attorney conference rooms, prisoner holding cells, offices of the court clerks, the United States attorney, and the United States marshal, probation and parole offices, and adjoining corridors of any court of the United States.

(h) Notice of the provisions of subsections (a) and (b) shall be posted conspicuously at each public entrance to each Federal facility, and notice of subsection (e) shall be posted conspicuously at each public entrance to each Federal court facility, and no person shall be convicted of an offense under subsection (a) or (e) with respect to a Federal facility if such notice is not so posted at such facility, unless such person had actual notice of subsection (a) or (e), as the case may be.

Nov. 18, 1988 (606)

TITLE 18. CRIMES AND CRIMINAL PROCEDURE • PART I: CRIMES • CHAPTER 44: FIREARMS

18 USC § 931. Prohibition on purchase, ownership, or possession of body armor by violent felons

> The Gist: It is illegal for violent felons to buy, own or have body armor. An exception is provided for use in lawful business activity, as defined.

(a) In General.—Except as provided in subsection (b), it shall be unlawful for a person to purchase, own, or possess body armor, if that person has been convicted of a felony that is—

(1) a crime of violence (as defined in section 16); or

(2) an offense under State law that would constitute a crime of violence under paragraph (1) if it occurred within the special maritime and territorial jurisdiction of the United States.

(b) Affirmative Defense.—

(1) In general.—It shall be an affirmative defense under this section that—

(A) the defendant obtained prior written certification from his or her employer that the defendant's purchase, use, or possession of body armor was necessary for the safe performance of lawful business activity; and

(B) the use and possession by the defendant were limited to the course of such performance.

(2) Employer.—In this subsection, the term "employer" means any other individual employed by the defendant's business that supervises defendant's activity. If that defendant has no supervisor, prior written certification is acceptable from any other employee of the business.

Nov. 2, 2002 (179)

TITLE 18. CRIMES AND CRIMINAL PROCEDURE • PART I: CRIMES • CHAPTER 44: FIREARMS

18 USC § 961. Strengthening armed vessel of foreign nation

> The Gist: It's illegal for anyone within the U.S. to fortify or arm a ship of a foreign power that is at war with another foreign power, if the other foreign power is at peace with the United States.

Whoever, within the United States, increases or augments the force of any ship of war, cruiser, or other armed vessel which, at the time of her arrival within the United States, was a ship of war, or cruiser, or armed vessel, in the service of any foreign prince or state, or of any colony, district, or people, or belonging to the subjects or citizens of any such prince or state, colony, district, or people, the same being at war with any foreign prince or state, or of any colony, district, or people, with whom the United States is at peace, by adding to the number of the guns of such vessel, or by changing those on board of her for guns of a larger caliber, or by adding thereto any equipment solely applicable to war, shall be fined under this title or imprisoned not more than one year, or both.

June 25, 1948 (150)
TITLE 18. CRIMES AND CRIMINAL PROCEDURE • PART I: CRIMES • CHAPTER 45: FOREIGN RELATIONS

18 USC § 962. Arming vessel against friendly nation

> The Gist: It's illegal for anyone within the U.S. to provide or arm any ship, with the intent that the ship will be used by a foreign power against any friendly nation of the United States. Commissioning a vessel for this purpose is illegal. Any such vessel, including its arms and ammunition are forfeited, one half to the United States and one half to the informer.

Whoever, within the United States, furnishes, fits out, arms, or attempts to furnish, fit out or arm, any vessel, with intent that such vessel shall be employed in the service of any foreign prince, or state, or of any colony, district, or people, to cruise, or commit hostilities against the subjects, citizens, or property of any foreign prince or state, or of any colony, district, or people with whom the United States is at peace; or

Whoever issues or delivers a commission within the United States for any vessel, to the intent that she may be so employed—

Shall be fined under this title or imprisoned not more than three years, or both.

Every such vessel, her tackle, apparel, and furniture, together with all materials, arms, ammunition, and stores which may have been procured for the building and equipment thereof, shall be forfeited, one half to the use of the informer and the other half to the use of the United States.

June 25, 1948 (162)
TITLE 18. CRIMES AND CRIMINAL PROCEDURE • PART I: CRIMES • CHAPTER 45: FOREIGN RELATIONS

18 USC § 963. Detention of armed vessel

> The Gist: Any armed ship can be stopped by federal authorities until the owner provides satisfactory proof that the ship won't be used in hostilities against a nation at peace with the United States. Such a ship is subject to forfeiture.

(a) During a war in which the United States is a neutral nation, the President, or any person authorized by him, may detain any armed vessel owned wholly or in part by citizens of the United States, or any vessel, domestic or foreign (other than one which has entered the ports of the United States as a public vessel), which is manifestly built for warlike purposes or has been converted or adapted from a private vessel to one suitable for warlike use, until the owner or master, or person having charge of such vessel, shall furnish proof satisfactory to the President, or to the person duly authorized by him, that the vessel will not be employed to cruise against or commit or attempt to commit hostilities upon the subjects, citizens, or property of any foreign prince or state, or of any colony, district, or people with which the United States is at peace, and that the said vessel will not be sold or delivered to any belligerent nation, or to an agent, officer, or citizen of such nation, by them or any of them, within the jurisdiction of the United States, or upon the high seas.

(b) Whoever, in violation of this section takes, or attempts to take, or authorizes the taking of any such vessel, out of port or from the United States, shall be fined under this title or imprisoned not more than ten years, or both.

In addition, such vessel, her tackle, apparel, furniture, equipment, and her cargo shall be forfeited to the United States.

June 25, 1948 (258)
TITLE 18. CRIMES AND CRIMINAL PROCEDURE • PART I: CRIMES • CHAPTER 45: FOREIGN RELATIONS

18 USC § 964. Delivering armed vessel to belligerent nation

> The Gist: It's illegal to provide an armed ship to a nation at war when the U.S. is neutral in that war.

(a) During a war in which the United States is a neutral nation, it shall be unlawful to send out of the United States any vessel built, armed, or equipped as a vessel of war, or converted from a private vessel into a vessel of war, with any intent or under any agreement or contract that such vessel will be delivered to a belligerent nation, or to an agent, officer, or citizen of such nation, or with reasonable cause to believe that the said vessel will be employed in the service of any such belligerent nation after its departure from the jurisdiction of the United States.

(b) Whoever, in violation of this section, takes or attempts to take, or authorizes the taking of any such vessel, out of port or from the United States, shall be fined under this title or imprisoned not more than ten years, or both.

In addition, such vessel, her tackle, apparel, furniture, equipment, and her cargo shall be forfeited to the United States.

June 25, 1948 (168)
TITLE 18. CRIMES AND CRIMINAL PROCEDURE • PART I: CRIMES • CHAPTER 45: FOREIGN RELATIONS

18 USC § 1001. Statements or entries generally

> The Gist: A person who knowingly and willfully makes any false, fictitious, or fraudulent statements, in any matter within the jurisdiction of the executive, legislative or judicial branches of the federal government, shall be fined, or imprisoned for up to five years, or both. The offense includes falsifying, concealing or covering up by any trick, scheme or device, a material fact, or making or using any false writing or document. The degree to which this applies to denial of the right to keep and bear arms, under false or misleading pretense by law enforcement or other officials, is unclear. Limited exceptions to this statute exist for certain judicial proceedings, legislative activity and investigations by Congress. This law has roots that trace back to March 4, 1909. See also 18-241, 18-242 and 42-1983.

(a) Except as otherwise provided in this section, whoever, in any matter within the jurisdiction of the executive, legislative, or judicial branch of the Government of the United States, knowingly and willfully—

(1) falsifies, conceals, or covers up by any trick, scheme, or device a material fact;
(2) makes any materially false, fictitious, or fraudulent statement or representation; or
(3) makes or uses any false writing or document knowing the same to contain any materially false, fictitious, or fraudulent statement or entry;
shall be fined under this title or imprisoned not more than 5 years, or both.
(b) Subsection (a) does not apply to a party to a judicial proceeding, or that party's counsel, for statements, representations, writings or documents submitted by such party or counsel to a judge or magistrate in that proceeding.
(c) With respect to any matter within the jurisdiction of the legislative branch, subsection (a) shall apply only to—
(1) administrative matters, including a claim for payment, a matter related to the procurement of property or services, personnel or employment practices, or support services, or a document required by law, rule, or regulation to be submitted to the Congress or any office or officer within the legislative branch; or
(2) any investigation or review, conducted pursuant to the authority of any committee, subcommittee, commission or office of the Congress, consistent with applicable rules of the House or Senate.

June 25, 1948 (232)
TITLE 18. CRIMES AND CRIMINAL PROCEDURE • PART I: CRIMES • CHAPTER 47: FRAUD AND FALSE STATEMENTS

18 USC § 1114. Protection of officers and employees of the United States

The Gist: Using or attempting to use deadly force against anyone in the federal government or the military, if the attack is because of the person's government role, is a federal crime. All former personnel are included. Federal penalties for an attack on anyone in this protected class are defined. In the case of such an assault, a gun is considered a gun, even if it jams due to a defective part.

Historical note: The federal government's effort to place itself in a specially protected class in this manner began in 1948. By the time it was amended in 1996 to read as described above, it had become a 721-word single-sentence, amended at least 32 times to add new special people to the list. That list included:

Whoever kills or attempts to kill any judge of the United States, any United States Attorney, any Assistant United States Attorney, or any United States marshal or deputy marshal or person employed to assist such marshal or deputy marshal, any officer or employee of the Federal Bureau of Investigation of the Department of Justice, any officer or employee of the Postal Service, any officer or employee of the Secret Service or of the Drug Enforcement Administration, any officer or member of the United States Capitol Police, any member of the Coast Guard, any employee of the Coast Guard assigned to perform investigative, inspection or law enforcement functions, any officer or employee of the Federal Railroad Administration assigned to perform investigative, inspection, or law enforcement functions, any officer or employee of any United States penal or correctional institution, any officer, employee or agent of the customs or of the internal revenue or any person assisting him in the execution of his duties, any immigration officer, any officer or employee of the Department of Agriculture or of the Department of the Interior designated by the Secretary of Agriculture or the Secretary of the

Interior to enforce any Act of Congress for the protection, preservation, or restoration of game and other wild birds and animals, any employee of the Department of Agriculture designated by the Secretary of Agriculture to carry out any law or regulation, or to perform any function in connection with any Federal or State program or any program of Puerto Rico, Guam, the Virgin Islands or any other commonwealth, territory, or possession of the United States, or the District of Columbia, for the control of eradication or prevention of the introduction or dissemination of animal diseases, any officer or employee of the National Park Service, any civilian official or employee of the Army Corps of Engineers assigned to perform investigations, inspections, law or regulatory enforcement functions, or field-level real estate functions, any officer or employee of, or assigned to duty in, the field service of the Bureau of Land Management, or any officer or employee of the Indian field service of the United States, or any officer or employee of the National Aeronautics and Space Administration directed to guard and protect property of the United States under the administration and control of the National Aeronautics and Space Administration, any security officer of the Department of State or the Foreign Service, or any officer or employee of the Department of Education, the Department of Health and Human Services, the Consumer Product Safety Commission, Interstate Commerce Commission, the Department of Commerce, or of the Department of Labor or of the Department of the Interior, or of the Department of Agriculture assigned to perform investigative, inspection, or law enforcement functions, or any officer or employee of the Federal Communications Commission performing investigative, inspection, or law enforcement functions, or any officer or employee of the Department of Veterans Affairs assigned to perform investigative or law enforcement functions, or any United States probation or pretrial services officer, or any United States magistrate, or any officer or employee of any department or agency within the Intelligence Community (as defined in section 3.4(f) of Executive Order 12333, December 8, 1981, or successor orders) not already covered under the terms of this section, any attorney, liquidator, examiner, claim agent, or other employee of the Federal Deposit Insurance Corporation, the Comptroller of the Currency, the Office of Thrift Supervision, the Federal Housing Finance Board, the Resolution Trust Corporation, the Board of Governors of the Federal Reserve System, any Federal Reserve bank, or the National Credit Union Administration, or any other officer or employee of the United States or any agency thereof designated for coverage under this section in regulations issued by the Attorney General engaged in or on account of the performance of his official duties, or any officer or employee of the United States or any agency thereof designated to collect or compromise a Federal claim in accordance with sections 3711 and 3716-3718 of title 31 or other statutory authority shall be punished, in the case of murder, as provided under section 1111, or, in the case of manslaughter, as provided under section 1112, except that any such person who is found guilty of attempted murder shall be imprisoned for not more than twenty years.

Whoever kills or attempts to kill any officer or employee of the United States or of any agency in any branch of the United States Government (including any member of the uniformed services) while such officer or employee is engaged in or on account

of the performance of official duties, or any person assisting such an officer or employee in the performance of such duties or on account of that assistance, shall be punished—
(1) in the case of murder, as provided under section 1111;
(2) in the case of manslaughter, as provided under section 1112; or
(3) in the case of attempted murder or manslaughter, as provided in section 1113.

June 25, 1948 (111)
TITLE 18. CRIMES AND CRIMINAL PROCEDURE • PART I: CRIMES • CHAPTER 51: HOMICIDE

18 USC § 1385. Use of Army and Air Force as posse comitatus

The Gist: From the Latin phrase *posse comitatus* comes the word we all know so well from Western movies, the posse. This is not a gun law in the narrow sense, but has recently caused a great deal of confusion in the gun debate and so has been included. The statute's history dates back to June 18, 1878.

"In a proper case the sheriff may summon to his assistance any person to assist him in making an arrest for a felony. A person so summoned is neither an officer nor a mere private person but occupies the legal position of a posse comitatus and, while acting under the sheriff's orders, is just as much clothed with the protection of the law as the sheriff himself. It is not essential for a posse comitatus to be and remain in the actual physical presence of the sheriff..." (from 449 South Western Reporter, second series, 656, 661)

The posse comitatus concept is a valuable one, and obviously can lead directly to activities involving firearms. The idea of using military forces in this role, that is, to use an army to subject the public to the law, runs against the fundamental underpinnings of American society.

Although posse status is ruled out, the military *is* specifically allowed to work closely with law enforcement officials under Acts of Congress, such as 10-372 and 10-373 (involving supplies, training, bases, research and more). Under the exceptions of 10-331 and 10-333 the militia, national guard and armed forces can be used to quell insurrection and other breaches in the fabric of society.

In an unusual use of structure, the law does not say, as would be more typical, "it is illegal to use the armed forces as a posse," it says "whoever does so shall be jailed and fined." This aberration from tradition places blame squarely on the shoulders of whoever is giving orders, which speaks, perhaps, to the seriousness with which the posse comitatus limitation is taken.

This law was amended in 1994, removing a $10,000 fine limitation.

Whoever, except in cases and under circumstances expressly authorized by the Constitution or Act of Congress, willfully uses any part of the Army or the Air Force as a posse comitatus or otherwise to execute the laws shall be fined under this title or imprisoned not more than two years, or both.

Aug. 10, 1956 (52)
TITLE 18. CRIMES AND CRIMINAL PROCEDURE • PART I: CRIMES • CHAPTER 67: MILITARY AND NAVY

18 USC § 1715. Firearms as nonmailable; regulations

> **The Gist:** Concealable firearms may not be mailed by citizens, but may be mailed by the proper authorities, who are described.

Pistols, revolvers, and other firearms capable of being concealed on the person are nonmailable and shall not be deposited in or carried by the mails or delivered by any officer or employee of the Postal Service. Such articles may be conveyed in the mails, under such regulations as the Postal Service shall prescribe, for use in connection with their official duty, to officers of the Army, Navy, Air Force, Coast Guard, Marine Corps, or Organized Reserve Corps; to officers of the National Guard or Militia of a State, Territory, Commonwealth, Possession, or District; to officers of the United States or of a State, Territory, Commonwealth, Possession, or District whose official duty is to serve warrants of arrest or commitments; to employees of the Postal Service; to officers and employees of enforcement agencies of the United States; and to watchmen engaged in guarding the property of the United States, a State, Territory, Commonwealth, Possession, or District. Such articles also may be conveyed in the mails to manufacturers of firearms or bona fide dealers therein in customary trade shipments, including such articles for repairs or replacement of parts, from one to the other, under such regulations as the Postal Service shall prescribe.

Whoever knowingly deposits for mailing or delivery, or knowingly causes to be delivered by mail according to the direction thereon, or at any place to which it is directed to be delivered by the person to whom it is addressed, any pistol, revolver, or firearm declared nonmailable by this section, shall be fined under this title or imprisoned not more than two years, or both.

Feb. 8, 1927 (265)
TITLE 18. CRIMES AND CRIMINAL PROCEDURE • PART I: CRIMES • CHAPTER 83: POSTAL SERVICE

18 USC § 1791. Providing or possessing contraband in prison

> **The Gist:** It's a crime to provide or attempt to provide a firearm or ammunition to a prison inmate. It's a crime for a prison inmate to have, make, or attempt to obtain a firearm or ammunition.

(a) Offense.—Whoever—
(1) in violation of a statute or a rule or order issued under a statute, provides to an inmate of a prison a prohibited object, or attempts to do so; or
(2) being an inmate of a prison, makes, possesses, or obtains, or attempts to make or obtain, a prohibited object;
shall be punished as provided in subsection (b) of this section.
(b) Punishment.—The punishment for an offense under this section is a fine under this title or—
(2) imprisonment for not more than 10 years, or both, if the object is specified in subsection (d)(1)(A) of this section;
(3) imprisonment for not more than 5 years, or both, if the object is specified in subsection (d)(1)(B) of this section;
(5) imprisonment for not more than 6 months, or both, if the object is specified in subsection (d)(1)(F) of this section.
(c) Any punishment imposed under subsection (b) for a violation of this section involving a controlled substance shall be consecutive to any other sentence imposed by any court for an offense involving such a controlled substance. Any punishment imposed under subsection (b) for a violation of this section by an inmate of a prison shall be consecutive to the sentence being served by such inmate at the time the inmate commits such violation.
(d) Definitions.—As used in this section—
(1) the term "prohibited object" means—

(A) a firearm or destructive device or a controlled substance in schedule I or II, other than marijuana or a controlled substance referred to in subparagraph (C) of this subsection;

(B) marijuana or a controlled substance in schedule III, other than a controlled substance referred to in subparagraph (C) of this subsection, ammunition, a weapon (other than a firearm or destructive device), or an object that is designed or intended to be used as a weapon or to facilitate escape from a prison;

(F) any other object that threatens the order, discipline, or security of a prison, or the life, health, or safety of an individual;

(2) the terms "ammunition", "firearm", and "destructive device" have, respectively, the meanings given those terms in section 921 of this title;

(4) the term "prison" means a Federal correctional, detention, or penal facility.

June 25, 1948 (376)
TITLE 18: CRIMES AND CRIMINAL PROCEDURE • PART I: CRIMES • CHAPTER 87: PRISONS

18 USC § 1864. Hazardous or injurious devices on Federal lands

The Gist: Setting booby traps on federal land to interfere with timber harvest, to run drugs, or with reckless disregard for the danger involved, is a crime. Booby traps include firearms or ammunition rigged with trip wires or similar triggering mechanisms. A person injured in this manner may pursue relief in a civil action and collect court and related costs.

(a) Whoever—
(1) with the intent to violate the Controlled Substances Act,
(2) with the intent to obstruct or harass the harvesting of timber, or
(3) with reckless disregard to the risk that another person will be placed in danger of death or bodily injury and under circumstances manifesting extreme indifference to such risk, uses a hazardous or injurious device on Federal land, on an Indian reservation, or on an Indian allotment while the title to such allotment is held in trust by the United States or while such allotment remains inalienable by the allottee without the consent of the United States shall be punished under subsection (b).

(b) An individual who violates subsection (a) shall—
(1) if death of an individual results, be fined under this title or imprisoned for any term of years or for life, or both:
(2) if serious bodily injury to any individual results, be fined under this title or imprisoned for not more than 40 years, or both:
(3) if bodily injury to any individual results, be fined under this title or imprisoned for not more than 20 years, or both:
(4) if damage to the property of any individual results or if avoidance costs have been incurred exceeding $10,000, in the aggregate, be fined under this title or imprisoned for not more than 20 years, or both; and
(5) in any other case, be fined under this title or imprisoned for not more than one year.

(c) Any individual who is punished under subsection (b)(5) after one or more prior convictions under any such subsection shall be fined under this title or imprisoned for not more than 20 years, or both.

(d) As used in this section—
(1) the term "serious bodily injury" means bodily injury which involves:
(A) a substantial risk of death:
(B) extreme physical pain:
(C) protracted and obvious disfigurement; and
(D) protracted loss or impairment of the function of bodily member, organ, or mental faculty:
(2) the term "bodily injury" means—
(A) a cut, abrasion, bruise, burn, or disfigurement:
(B) physical pain:
(C) illness:

(D) impairment of the function of a bodily member, organ, or mental faculty; or
(E) any other injury to the body, no matter how temporary; and
(3) the term "hazardous or injurious device" means a device, which when assembled or placed, is capable of causing bodily injury, or damage to property, by the action of any person making contact with such device subsequent to the assembly or placement. Such term includes guns attached to trip wires or other triggering mechanisms, ammunition attached to trip wires or other triggering mechanisms, or explosive devices attached to trip wires or other triggering mechanisms, sharpened stakes, lines or wires, lines or wires with hooks attached, nails placed so that the sharpened ends are positioned in an upright manner, or tree spiking devices including spikes, nails, or other objects hammered, driven, fastened, or otherwise placed into or on any timber, whether or not severed from the stump.
(4) the term "avoidance costs" means costs incurred by any individual for the purpose of—
(A) detecting a hazardous or injurious device; or
(B) preventing death, serious bodily injury, bodily injury, or property damage likely to result from the use of a hazardous or injurious device in violation of subsection (a).
(e) Any person injured as the result of a violation of subsection (a) may commence a civil action on his own behalf against any person who is alleged to be in violation of subsection (a). The district courts shall have jurisdiction, without regard to the amount in controversy or the citizenship of the parties, in such civil actions. The court may award, in addition to monetary damages for any injury resulting from an alleged violation of subsection (a), costs of litigation, including reasonable attorney and expert witness fees, to any prevailing or substantially prevailing party, whenever the court determines such award is appropriate.

Nov. 18, 1988 (651)
TITLE 18. CRIMES AND CRIMINAL PROCEDURE • PART I: CRIMES • CHAPTER 91: PUBLIC LANDS

18 USC § 1956. Laundering of monetary instruments

The Gist: The lengthy list of crimes related to a money laundering statute was increased in 2000 to include smuggling of anything controlled by the United States Munitions List, unlawful import or trafficking in firearms, and certain gun-related terrorist activity.

(c) As used in this section—
(7) the term "specified unlawful activity" means—
(B) with respect to a financial transaction occurring in whole or in part in the United States, an offense against a foreign nation involving—
(v) smuggling or export control violations involving—
(I) an item controlled on the United States Munitions List established under section 38 of the Arms Export Control Act (22 U.S.C. 2778);
(D) an offense under ... section 922(l) (relating to the unlawful importation of firearms), section 924(n) (relating to firearms trafficking) ... section 2332b (relating to international terrorist acts transcending national boundaries), or section 2339A or 2339B (relating to providing material support to terrorists) of this title ... section 38(c) (relating to criminal violations) of the Arms Export Control Act

Oct. 30, 2000 (126)
TITLE 18. CRIMES AND CRIMINAL PROCEDURE • PART I: CRIMES • CHAPTER 95: RACKETEERING

18 USC § 2114. Mail, money, or other property of United States

The Gist: The jail term for assault with intent to rob anyone carrying the U.S. Mail, or money or property owned by the United States, increases if a dangerous weapon (which includes a firearm) is used.

(a) Assault.—A person who assaults any person having lawful charge, control, or custody of any mail matter or of any money or other property of the United States, with intent to rob, steal, or purloin such mail matter, money, or other property of the United States, or robs or attempts to rob any such person of mail matter, or of any money, or other property of the United States, shall, for the first offense, be imprisoned not more than ten years; and if in effecting or attempting to effect such robbery he wounds the person having custody of such mail, money, or other property of the United States, or puts his life in jeopardy by the use of a dangerous weapon, or for a subsequent offense, shall be imprisoned not more than twenty-five years.

(b) Receipt, possession, concealment, or disposal of property.—A person who receives, possesses, conceals, or disposes of any money or other property that has been obtained in violation of this section, knowing the same to have been unlawfully obtained, shall be imprisoned not more than 10 years, fined under this title, or both.

June 25, 1948 (189)
TITLE 18. CRIMES AND CRIMINAL PROCEDURE • PART I: CRIMES • CHAPTER 103: ROBBERY AND BURGLARY

18 USC § 2118. Robberies and burglaries involving controlled substances

> The Gist: The penalty for stealing controlled substances ("illegal drugs") from a person registered with the Drug Enforcement Administration is increased if a dangerous weapon is used. The penalty for entering the place of a person registered with the DEA, with intent to steal controlled substances, is increased if a firearm is used.

(a) Whoever takes or attempts to take from the person or presence of another by force or violence or by intimidation any material or compound containing any quantity of a controlled substance belonging to or in the care, custody, control, or possession of a person registered with the Drug Enforcement Administration under section 302 of the Controlled Substances Act (21 U.S.C. 822) shall, except as provided in subsection (c), be fined under this title or imprisoned not more than twenty years, or both, if (1) the replacement cost of the material or compound to the registrant was not less than $500, (2) the person who engaged in such taking or attempted such taking traveled in interstate or foreign commerce or used any facility in interstate or foreign commerce to facilitate such taking or attempt, or (3) another person was killed or suffered significant bodily injury as a result of such taking or attempt.

(b) Whoever, without authority, enters or attempts to enter, or remains in, the business premises or property of a person registered with the Drug Enforcement Administration under section 302 of the Controlled Substances Act (21 U.S.C. 822) with the intent to steal any material or compound containing any quantity of a controlled substance shall, except as provided in subsection (c), be fined under this title or imprisoned not more than twenty years, or both, if (1) the replacement cost of the controlled substance to the registrant was not less than $500, (2) the person who engaged in such entry or attempted such entry or who remained in such premises or property traveled in interstate or foreign commerce or used any facility in interstate or foreign commerce to facilitate such entry or attempt or to facilitate remaining in such premises or property, or (3) another person was killed or suffered significant bodily injury as a result of such entry or attempt.

(c)(1) Whoever in committing any offense under subsection (a) or (b) assaults any person, or puts in jeopardy the life of any person, by the use of a dangerous weapon or device shall be fined under this title and imprisoned for not more than twenty-five years.

(2) Whoever in committing any offense under subsection (a) or (b) kills any person shall be fined under this title or imprisoned for any term of years or life, or both.

(d) If two or more persons conspire to violate subsection (a) or (b) of this section and one or more of such persons do any overt act to effect the object of the conspiracy, each shall be fined under this title or imprisoned not more than ten years or both.

(e) For purposes of this section—

(1) the term "controlled substance" has the meaning prescribed for that term by section 102 of the Controlled Substances Act:

(2) the term "business premises or property" includes conveyances and storage facilities; and

(3) the term "significant bodily injury" means bodily injury which involves a risk of death, significant physical pain, protracted and obvious disfigurement, or a protracted loss or impairment of the function of a bodily member, organ, or mental or sensory faculty.

May 31, 1984 (526)

TITLE 18. CRIMES AND CRIMINAL PROCEDURE • PART I: CRIMES • CHAPTER 103: ROBBERY AND BURGLARY

18 USC § 2231. Assault or resistance

> The Gist: The penalty for forcibly resisting a person who is authorized to serve a search warrant or to conduct searches and seizures is increased if a dangerous weapon is used.

(a) Whoever forcibly assaults, resists, opposes, prevents, impedes, intimidates, or interferes with any person authorized to serve or execute search warrants or to make searches and seizures while engaged in the performance of his duties with regard thereto or on account of the performance of such duties, shall be fined under this title or imprisoned not more than three years, or both; and—

(b) Whoever, in committing any act in violation of this section, uses any deadly or dangerous weapon, shall be fined under this title or imprisoned not more than ten years, or both.

June 25, 1948 (101)

TITLE 18. CRIMES AND CRIMINAL PROCEDURE • PART I: CRIMES • CHAPTER 109: SEARCHES AND SEIZURES

18 USC § 2277. Explosives or dangerous weapons aboard vessels

> The Gist: It's illegal to have a firearm aboard any U.S. ship without the owner's or master's prior permission. It's illegal to have a firearm aboard any ship which has been seized by the United States, without prior permission from the captain of the port where the ship is docked. The proper authorities are exempt from these requirements.

(a) Whoever brings, carries, or possesses any dangerous weapon, instrument, or device, or any dynamite, nitroglycerin, or other explosive article or compound on board of any vessel registered, enrolled, or licensed under the laws of the United States, or any vessel purchased, requisitioned, chartered, or taken over by the United States pursuant to the provisions of Act June 6, 1941, ch. 174, 55 Stat. 242, as amended, without previously obtaining the permission of the owner or the master of such vessel; or

Whoever brings, carries, or possesses any such weapon or explosive on board of any vessel in the possession and under the control of the United States or which has been seized and forfeited by the United States or upon which a guard has been placed by the United States pursuant to the provisions of section 191 of Title 50, without previously obtaining the permission of the captain of the port in which such vessel is located, shall be fined under this title or imprisoned not more than one year, or both.

(b) This section shall not apply to the personnel of the Armed Forces of the United States or to officers or employees of the United States or of a State or of a political subdivision thereof, while acting in the performance of their duties, who are authorized by law or by rules or regulations to own or possess any such weapon or explosive.

June 25, 1948 (236)
TITLE 18. CRIMES AND CRIMINAL PROCEDURE • PART I: CRIMES • CHAPTER 111: SHIPPING

18 USC § 2278. Explosives on vessels carrying steerage passengers

The Gist: It's generally illegal for the master of a steamship that carries steerage passengers to have onboard any explosives, acids or gunpowder, except for the ship's use, or any other articles, which may endanger the passengers' lives or health or the ship's safety.

Whoever, being the master of a steamship or other vessel referred to in section 151 of Title 46, except as otherwise expressly provided by law, takes, carries, or has on board of any such vessel any nitroglycerin, dynamite, or any other explosive article or compound, or any vitriol or like acids, or gunpowder, except for the ship's use, or any article or number of articles, whether as a cargo or ballast, which, by reason of the nature or quantity or mode of storage thereof, shall, either singly or collectively, be likely to endanger the health or lives of the passengers or the safety of the vessel, shall be fined under this title or imprisoned not more than one year, or both.

June 25, 1948 (121)
TITLE 18. CRIMES AND CRIMINAL PROCEDURE • PART I: CRIMES • CHAPTER 111: SHIPPING

18 USC § 2332b. Acts of terrorism transcending national boundaries.

The Gist: Using a gun in an assault on any person in the U.S. is a federal crime if: 1–the assault uses "conduct transcending national boundaries" (as described) and 2–if any of these exist: a) any perpetrator uses mail or interstate or foreign commerce; b) the offense affects interstate or foreign commerce; c) the victim is in the federal government or military; d) any federal government structure or property is damaged, or e) the offense occurs in special U.S. territorial jurisdictions.

Violations carry jail terms up to life in prison, and the death penalty if a death occurs due to conduct prohibited by this section. The maximum penalty in a non-lethal assault with a firearm is 30 years.

Threatening, attempting conspiring or being an accessory to commit the above acts is a crime, and various penalties are defined.

The phrase "conduct transcending national boundaries" means "conduct occurring outside of the United States in addition to the conduct occurring in the United States." It is not clear what this might include.

The Attorney General is in charge of investigating "federal crimes of terrorism." Such crimes occur when any of a long list of felonies is committed to influence the government by intimidation or coercion, or to retaliate against government actions. An assault involving conduct transcending national boundaries, described in the first part of this law, is one of the felonies.

(a) Prohibited acts.—
(1) Offenses.—Whoever, involving conduct transcending national boundaries and in a circumstance described in subsection (b)—
(A) kills, kidnaps, maims, commits an assault resulting in serious bodily injury, or assaults with a dangerous weapon any person within the United States; or
(B) creates a substantial risk of serious bodily injury to any other person by destroying or damaging any structure, conveyance, or other real or personal property within the United States or by attempting or conspiring to destroy or damage any structure, conveyance, or other real or personal property within the United States; in violation of the laws of any State, or the United States, shall be punished as prescribed in subsection (c).
(2) Treatment of threats, attempts and conspiracies.—Whoever threatens to commit an offense under paragraph (1), or attempts or conspires to do so, shall be punished under subsection (c).
(b) Jurisdictional bases.—
(1) Circumstances.—The circumstances referred to in subsection (a) are—
(A) any of the offenders uses the mail or any facility of interstate or foreign commerce in furtherance of the offense;
(B) the offense obstructs, delays, or affects interstate or foreign commerce, or would have so obstructed, delayed, or affected interstate or foreign commerce if the offense had been consummated;
(C) the victim, or intended victim, is the United States Government, a member of the uniformed services, or any official, officer, employee, or agent of the legislative, executive, or judicial branches, or of any department or agency, of the United States;
(D) the structure, conveyance, or other real or personal property is, in whole or in part, owned, possessed, or leased to the United States, or any department or agency of the United States;
(E) the offense is committed in the territorial sea (including the airspace above and the seabed and subsoil below, and artificial islands and fixed structures erected thereon) of the United States; or
(F) the offense is committed within the special maritime and territorial jurisdiction of the United States.
(2) Co-conspirators and accessories after the fact—
Jurisdiction shall exist over all principals and co-conspirators of an offense under this section, and accessories after the fact to any offense under this section, if at least one of the circumstances described in subparagraphs (A) through (F) of paragraph (1) is applicable to at least one offender.
(c) Penalties—
(1) Penalties—Whoever violates this section shall be punished—
(A) for a killing, or if death results to any person from any other conduct prohibited by this section, by death, or by imprisonment for any term of years or for life;
(B) for kidnapping, by imprisonment for any term of years or for life;
(C) for maiming, by imprisonment for not more than 35 years;
(D) for assault with a dangerous weapon or assault resulting in serious bodily injury, by imprisonment for not more than 30 years;
(E) for destroying or damaging any structure, conveyance, or other real or personal property, by imprisonment for not more than 25 years;
(F) for attempting or conspiring to commit an offense, for any term of years up to the maximum punishment that would have applied had the offense been completed; and
(G) for threatening to commit an offense under this section, by imprisonment for not more than 10 years.
(2) Consecutive sentence—Notwithstanding any other provision of law, the court shall not place on probation any person convicted of a violation of this section; nor shall the term of imprisonment imposed under this section run concurrently with any other term of imprisonment.
(d) Proof requirements—The following shall apply to prosecutions under this section:
(1) Knowledge—The prosecution is not required to prove knowledge by any defendant of a jurisdictional base alleged in the indictment.

(2) State law—In a prosecution under this section that is based upon the adoption of State law, only the elements of the offense under State law, and not any provisions pertaining to criminal procedure or evidence, are adopted.

(e) Extraterritorial jurisdiction—There is extraterritorial Federal jurisdiction-

(1) over any offense under subsection (a), including any threat, attempt, or conspiracy to commit such offense; and

(2) over conduct which, under section 3, renders any person an accessory after the fact to an offense under subsection (a).

(f) Investigative authority—In addition to any other investigative authority with respect to violations of this title, the Attorney General shall have primary investigative responsibility for all Federal crimes of terrorism, and any violation of section 351(e), 844(e), 844(f)(1), 956(b), 1361, 1366(b), 1366(c), 1751(e), 2152, or 2156 of this title, and the Secretary of the Treasury shall assist the Attorney General at the request of the Attorney General. Nothing in this section shall be construed to interfere with the authority of the United States Secret Service under section 3056.

(g) Definitions—As used in this section—

(1) the term "conduct transcending national boundaries" means conduct occurring outside of the United States in addition to the conduct occurring in the United States;

(2) the term "facility of interstate or foreign commerce" has the meaning given that term in section 1958(b)(2);

(3) the term "serious bodily injury" has the meaning given that term in section 1365(g)(3);

(4) the term "territorial sea of the United States" means all waters extending seaward to 12 nautical miles from the baselines of the United States, determined in accordance with international law; and

(5) the term "Federal crime of terrorism" means an offense that—

(A) is calculated to influence or affect the conduct of government by intimidation or coercion, or to retaliate against government conduct; and

(B) is a violation of—

(i) section 32 (relating to destruction of aircraft or aircraft facilities), 37 (relating to violence at international airports), 81 (relating to arson within special maritime and territorial jurisdiction), 175 or 175b (relating to biological weapons), 229 (relating to chemical weapons), subsection (a), (b), (c), or (d) of section 351 (relating to congressional, cabinet, and Supreme Court assassination, kidnapping, and assault), 831 (relating to nuclear materials), 842 (m) or (n) (relating to plastic explosives), 844(f)(2) or (3) (relating to arson and bombing of Government property risking or causing death), 844(i) (relating to arson and bombing of property used in interstate commerce), 930(c) (relating to killing or attempted killing during an attack on a Federal facility with a dangerous weapon), 956(a)(1) (relating to conspiracy to murder, kidnap, or maim persons abroad), 1030(a)(1) (relating to protection of computers), 1030(a)(5)(A)(i) resulting in damage as defined in 1030(a)(5)(B)(ii) through (v) (relating to protection of computers), 1114 (relating to killing or attempted killing of officers and employees of the United States), 1116 (relating to murder or manslaughter of foreign officials, official guests, or internationally protected persons), 1203 (relating to hostage taking), 1361 (relating to injury of Government property or contracts), 1362 (relating to destruction of communication lines, stations, or systems), 1363 (relating to injury to buildings or property within special maritime and territorial jurisdiction of the United States), 1366(a) (relating to destruction of an energy facility), 1751(a), (b), (c), or (d) (relating to Presidential and Presidential staff assassination and kidnaping), 1992 (relating to wrecking trains), 1993 (relating to terrorist attacks and other acts of violence against mass transportation systems), 2155 (relating to destruction of national defense materials, premises, or utilities), 2156 (relating to production of defective national defense materials, premises, or utilities), 2280 (relating to violence against maritime navigation), 2281 (relating to violence against maritime fixed platforms), 2332 (relating to certain homicides and other violence against United States nationals occurring outside of the United States), 2332a (relating to use of weapons of mass destruction), 2332b (relating to acts of terrorism transcending national boundaries), 2332f (relating to bombing of public places and facilities), 2339 (relating to

harboring terrorists), 2339A (relating to providing material support to terrorists), 2339B (relating to providing material support to terrorist organizations), 2339C (relating to financing of terrorism), or 2340A (relating to torture) of this title;
(ii) section 236 (relating to sabotage of nuclear facilities or fuel) of the Atomic Energy Act of 1954 (42 U.S.C. 2284); or
(iii) section 46502 (relating to aircraft piracy), the second sentence of section 46504 (relating to assault on a flight crew with a dangerous weapon), section 46505(b)(3) or (c) (relating to explosive or incendiary devices, or endangerment of human life by means of weapons, on aircraft), section 46506 if homicide or attempted homicide is involved (relating to application of certain criminal laws to acts on aircraft), or section 60123(b) (relating to destruction of interstate gas or hazardous liquid pipeline facility) of title 49.

April 24, 1996 (1,415)
TITLE 18. CRIMES AND CRIMINAL PROCEDURE • PART I: CRIMES • CHAPTER 113B

18 USC § 2339A. Providing material support to terrorists

> The Gist: Providing firearms, or hiding firearms, knowing or intending that they be used for any of a long list of serious crimes, is a crime.

Sec. 2339A. Providing material support to terrorists
(a) Offense—Whoever, within the United States, provides material support or resources or conceals or disguises the nature, location, source, or ownership of material support or resources, knowing or intending that they are to be used in preparation for, or in carrying out, a violation of section 32, 37, 81, 175, 351, 831, 842 (m) or (n), 844 (f) or (i), 956, 1114, 1116, 1203, 1361, 1362, 1363, 1366, 1751, 2155, 2156, 2280, 2281, 2332, 2332a, 2332b, or 2340A of this title or section 46502 of title 49, or in preparation for, or in carrying out, the concealment from the commission of any such violation, shall be fined under this title, imprisoned not more than 10 years, or both.
(b) Definition—In this section, the term "material support or resources" means currency or other financial securities, financial services, lodging, training, safehouses, false documentation or identification, communications equipment, facilities, weapons, lethal substances, explosives, personnel, transportation, and other physical assets, except medicine or religious materials.

April 24, 1996 (170)
TITLE 18. CRIMES AND CRIMINAL PROCEDURE • PART I: CRIMES • CHAPTER 113B

18 USC § 2339B. Providing material support or resources to designated foreign terrorist organizations

> The Gist: Giving, or attempting or conspiring to give firearms to a foreign terrorist organization is illegal. The phrase "material support or resources," which includes firearms, is described above in 18-2339A.

(a) Prohibited activities-
(1) Unlawful conduct.—Whoever, within the United States or subject to the jurisdiction of the United States, knowingly provides material support or resources to a foreign terrorist organization, or attempts or conspires to do so, shall be fined under this title or imprisoned not more than 15 years, or both, and, if the death of any person results, shall be imprisoned for any term of years or for life.

April 24, 1996 (53)
TITLE 18. CRIMES AND CRIMINAL PROCEDURE • PART I: CRIMES • CHAPTER 113B:

18 USC § 2344. Penalties

> The Gist: The laws that apply to the seizure and forfeiture of NFA weapons defined in 26–5845(a), apply to this chapter (Chapter 114) relating to trafficking in contraband cigarettes.

(c) Any contraband cigarettes involved in any violation of the provisions of this chapter shall be subject to seizure and forfeiture, and all provisions of the Internal Revenue Code of 1954 relating to the seizure, forfeiture, and disposition of firearms, as defined in section 5845(a) of such Code, shall, so far as applicable, extend to seizures and forfeitures under the provisions of this chapter.

Nov. 2, 1978 (65)
TITLE 18. CRIMES AND CRIMINAL PROCEDURE • PART I: CRIMES • CHAPTER 114: TRAFFICKING IN CONTRABAND CIGARETTES

18 USC § 2386. Registration of certain organizations

> The Gist: Three types of organizations must be registered with the U.S. Attorney General and, among many other requirements, provide a description, including serial numbers, of any firearms or other weapons they own. Included are all organizations that: 1–are under foreign control and engage in political activity; 2–engage in civilian military activity and political activity; and 3–are under foreign control and engage in civilian military activity. For the purposes of this law, special definitions apply. *Civilian military activity* means: 1–instruction in the use of firearms or in military or naval science; 2– engaging in military or naval maneuvers; and 3–military or naval drills or parades, with or without arms. *Political activity* means the overthrow or control by force of national or local governmental authority. *Subject to foreign control* means having anything to do with a foreign government or its agencies, or foreign political organizations. The proper authorities and other listed groups are exempt. Note that the numbering system for the paragraphs of this law are not consistent with the rest of federal gun laws.

(A) For the purposes of this section:
"Attorney General" means the Attorney General of the United States;
"Organization" means any group, club, league, society, committee, association, political party, or combination of individuals, whether incorporated or otherwise, but such term shall not include any corporation, association, community chest, fund, or foundation, organized and operated exclusively for religious, charitable, scientific, literary, or educational purposes;
"Political activity" means any activity the purpose or aim of which, or one of the purposes or aims of which, is the control by force or overthrow of the Government of the United States or a political subdivision thereof, or any State or political subdivision thereof;
An organization is engaged in "civilian military activity" if:
(1) it gives instruction to, or prescribes instruction for, its members in the use of firearms or other weapons or any substitute therefor, or military or naval science; or
(2) it receives from any other organization or from any individual instruction in military or naval science; or
(3) it engages in any military or naval maneuvers or activities; or

(4) it engages, either with or without arms, in drills or parades of a military or naval character; or

(5) it engages in any other form of organized activity which in the opinion of the Attorney General constitutes preparation for military action;

An organization is "subject to foreign control" if:

(a) it solicits or accepts financial contributions, loans, or support of any kind, directly or indirectly, from, or is affiliated directly or indirectly with, a foreign government or a political subdivision thereof, or an agent, agency, or instrumentality of a foreign government or political subdivision thereof, or a political party in a foreign country, or an international political organization; or

(b) its policies, or any of them, are determined by or at the suggestion of, or in collaboration with, a foreign government or political subdivision thereof, or an agent, agency, or instrumentality of a foreign government of a political subdivision thereof, or a political party in a foreign country, or an international political organization.

(B) (1) The following organizations shall be required to register with the Attorney General: Every organization subject to foreign control which engages in political activity; Every organization which engages both in civilian military activity and in political activity; Every organization subject to foreign control which engages in civilian military activity; and

(2) This section shall not require registration or the filing of any statement with the Attorney General by:

(a) The armed forces of the United States; or

(b) The organized militia or National Guard of any State, Territory, District, or possession of the United States; or

(c) Any law-enforcement agency of the United States or of any Territory, District or possession thereof, or of any State or political subdivision of a State, or of any agency or instrumentality of one or more States; or

(d) Any duly established diplomatic mission or consular office of a foreign government which is so recognized by the Department of State; or

(e) Any nationally recognized organization of persons who are veterans of the armed forces of the United States, or affiliates of such organizations.

(k) A description of all firearms or other weapons owned by the organization, or by any chapter, branch, or affiliate of the organization, identified by the manufacturer's number thereon

June 25, 1948 (551)

TITLE 18. CRIMES AND CRIMINAL PROCEDURE • PART I: CRIMES • CHAPTER 115: TREASON, SEDITION AND SUBVERSIVE ACTIVITIES

18 USC § 2516. Authorization for interception of wire or oral communication

The Gist: This section describes the conditions under which the FBI may be authorized to eavesdrop on private communications. Among the many crimes that justify such surveillance are firearms violations related to arms export, firearm felonies, and IRS requirements, described in subsections (k), (m), and (n) respectively. The conditions under which other authorities may conduct eavesdropping are also described.

(1) The Attorney General, Deputy Attorney General, Associate Attorney General, or any Assistant Attorney General, any acting Assistant Attorney General, or any Deputy Assistant Attorney General or acting Deputy Assistant Attorney General in the Criminal Division specially designated by the Attorney General, may authorize an application to a Federal judge of competent jurisdiction for, and such judge may grant in conformity with section 2518 of this chapter an order authorizing or approving the interception of wire or oral communications by the Federal Bureau of Investigation, or a Federal agency having responsibility for the investigation of the offense as to which the application is made, when such interception may provide or has provided evidence of—

(a) any offense punishable by death or by imprisonment for more than one year under sections 2274 through 2277 of title 42 of the United States Code (relating to the enforcement of the Atomic Energy Act of 1954), section 2284 of title 42 of the United States Code (relating to sabotage of nuclear facilities or fuel), or under the following chapters of this title: chapter 37 (relating to espionage), chapter 90 (relating to prosecution of trade secrets), chapter 105 (relating to sabotage), chapter 115 (relating to treason), chapter 102 (relating to riots) chapter 65 (relating to malicious mischief), chapter 111 (relating to destruction of vessels), or chapter 81 (relating to piracy);

(b) a violation of section 186 or section 501(c) of title 29, United States Code (dealing with restrictions on payments and loans to labor organizations), or any offense which involves murder, kidnapping, robbery, or extortion, and which is punishable under this title;

(c) any offense which is punishable under the following sections of this title: section 201 (bribery of public officials and witnesses), section 215 (relating to bribery of bank officials), section 224 (bribery in sporting contests), subsection (d), (e), (f), (g), (h), or (i) of section 844 (unlawful use of explosives), section 1032 (relating to concealment of assets), section 1084 (transmission of wagering information), section 751 (relating to escape), section 1014 (relating to loans and credit applications generally; renewals and discounts), sections 1503, 1512, and 1513 (influencing or injuring an officer, juror, or witness generally), section 1510 (obstruction of criminal investigations), section 1511 (obstruction of State or local law enforcement), section 1751 (Presidential and Presidential staff assassination, kidnapping, and assault), section 1951 (interference with commerce by threats or violence), section 1952 (interstate and foreign travel or transportation in aid of racketeering enterprises), section 1958 (relating to use of interstate commerce facilities in the commission of murder for hire), section 1959 (relating to violent crimes in aid of racketeering activity), section 1954 (offer, acceptance, or solicitation to influence operations of employee benefit plan), section 1955 (prohibition of business enterprises of gambling), section 1956 (laundering of monetary instruments), section 1957 (relating to engaging in monetary transactions in property derived from specified unlawful activity), section 659 (theft from interstate shipment), section 664 (embezzlement from pension and welfare funds), section 1343 (fraud by wire, radio, or television), section 1344 (relating to bank fraud), sections 2251 and 2252 (sexual exploitation of children), sections 2312, 2313, 2314, and 2315 (interstate transportation of stolen property), section 2321 (relating to trafficking in certain motor vehicles or motor vehicle parts), section 1203 (relating to hostage taking), section 1029 (relating to fraud and related activity in connection with access devices), section 3146 (relating to penalty for failure to appear), section 3521(b)(3) (relating to witness relocation and assistance), section 32 (relating to destruction of aircraft or aircraft facilities), section 38 (relating to aircraft parts fraud), section 1963 (violations with respect to racketeer influenced and corrupt organizations), section 115 (relating to threatening or retaliating against a Federal official), and section 1341 (relating to mail fraud), a felony violation of section 1030 (relating to computer fraud and abuse), section 351 (violations) with respect to congressional, Cabinet, or Supreme Court assassinations, kidnapping, and assault), section 831 (relating to prohibited transactions involving nuclear materials), section 33 (relating to destruction of motor vehicles or motor vehicle facilities), section 175 (relating to biological weapons), section 1992 (relating to wrecking trains), a felony violation of section 1028 (relating to production of false identification documentation), section 1425 (relating to the procurement of citizenship or nationalization unlawfully), section 1426 (relating to the reproduction of naturalization or citizenship papers), section 1427 (relating to the sale of naturalization or citizenship papers), section 1541 (relating to passport issuance without authority), section 1542 (relating to false statements in passport applications), section 1543 (relating to forgery or false use of passports), section 1544 (relating to misuse of passports), or section 1546 (relating to fraud and misuse of visas, permits, and other documents);

(d) any offense involving counterfeiting punishable under section 471, 472, or 473 of this title;

(e) any offense involving fraud connected with a case under title 11 or the manufacture, importation, receiving, concealment, buying, selling, or otherwise dealing in narcotic drugs, marihuana, or other dangerous drugs, punishable under any law of the United States;

(f) any offense including extortionate credit transactions under sections 892, 893, or 894 of this title;

(g) a violation of section 5322 of title 31, United States Code (dealing with the reporting of currency transactions);

(h) any felony violation of sections 2511 and 2512 (relating to interception and disclosure of certain communications and to certain intercepting devices) of this title;

(i) any felony violation of chapter 71 (relating to obscenity) of this title;

(j) any violation of section 60123(b) (relating to destruction of a natural gas pipeline) or 46502 (relating to aircraft piracy) of title 49;

(k) any criminal violation of section 2778 of title 22 (relating to the Arms Export Control Act);

(l) the location of any fugitive from justice from an offense described in this section;

(m) a violation of section 274, 277, or 278 of the Immigration and Nationality Act (8 U.S.C. 1324, 1327, or 1328) (relating to the smuggling of aliens);

(n) any felony violation of sections 922 and 924 of title 18, United States Code (relating to firearms);

(o) any violation of section 5861 of the Internal Revenue Code of 1986 (relating to firearms);

(p) a felony violation of section 1028 (relating to production of false identification documents), section 1542 (relating to false statements in passport applications), section 1546 (relating to fraud and misuse of visas, permits, and other documents) of this title or a violation of section 274, 277, or 278 of the Immigration and Nationality Act (relating to the smuggling of aliens); or

(q) any criminal violation of section 229 (relating to chemical weapons); or sections 2332, 2332a, 2332b, 2332d, 2332f, 2339A, 2339B, or 2339C of this title (relating to terrorism); or

(r) any conspiracy to commit any offense described in any subparagraph of this paragraph.

(2) The principal prosecuting attorney of any State, or the principal prosecuting attorney of any political subdivision thereof, if such attorney is authorized by a statute of that State to make application to a State court judge of competent jurisdiction for an order authorizing or approving the interception of wire, oral, or electronic communications, may apply to such judge for, and such judge may grant in conformity with section 2518 of this chapter and with the applicable State statute an order authorizing, or approving the interception of wire, oral, or electronic communications by investigative or law enforcement officers having responsibility for the investigation of the offense as to which the application is made, when such interception may provide or has provided evidence of the commission of the offense of murder, kidnapping, gambling, robbery, bribery, extortion, or dealing in narcotic drugs, marihuana or other dangerous drugs, or other crime dangerous to life, limb, or property, and punishable by imprisonment for more than one year, designated in any applicable State statute authorizing such interception, or any conspiracy to commit any of the foregoing offenses.

(3) Any attorney for the Government (as such term is defined for the purposes of the Federal Rules of Criminal Procedure) may authorize an application to a Federal judge of competent jurisdiction for, and such judge may grant, in conformity with section 2518 of this title, or order authorizing or approving the interception of electronic communications by an investigative or law enforcement officer having responsibility for the investigation of the offense as to which the application is made, when such interception may provide or has provided evidence of any Federal felony.

Oct. 15, 1970 (1,393)

18 USC § 3050. Bureau of Prisons employees' powers

> The Gist: Officers and employees of the Bureau of Prisons may be authorized to carry firearms.

An officer or employee of the Bureau of Prisons may—
(1) make arrests on or off of Bureau of Prisons property without warrant for violations of the following provisions regardless of where the violation may occur: sections 111 (assaulting officers), 751 (escape), and 752 (assisting escape) of title 18, United States Code, and section 1826(c) (escape) of title 28, United States Code:
(2) make arrests on Bureau of Prisons premises or reservation land of a penal, detention, or correctional facility without warrant for violations occurring thereon of the following provisions: sections 661 (theft), 1361 (depredation of property), 1363 (destruction of property), 1791 (contraband), 1792 (mutiny and riot), and 1793 (trespass) of title 18, United States Code; and
(3) arrest without warrant for any other offense described in title 18 or 21 of the United States Code, if committed on the premises or reservation of a penal or correctional facility of the Bureau of Prisons if necessary to safeguard security, good order, or government property; if such officer or employee has reasonable grounds to believe that the arrested person is guilty of such offense, and if there is likelihood of such person's escaping before an arrest warrant can be obtained. If the arrested person is a fugitive from custody, such prisoner shall be returned to custody. Officers and employees of the said Bureau of Prisons may carry firearms under such rules and regulations as the Attorney General may prescribe.

June 25, 1948 (239)
TITLE 18. CRIMES AND CRIMINAL PROCEDURE • PART II: CRIMINAL PROCEDURE • CHAPTER 203: ARREST AND COMMITMENT

18 USC § 3051. Powers of agents of the Bureau of Alcohol, Tobacco, Firearms, and Explosives

> The Gist: Agents of the changed Bureau of Alcohol, Tobacco, Firearms and Explosives (2002) are authorized to carry firearms and perform law enforcement work. Any firearms forfeited for violation of a law of the U.S. are to be governed by a specified section of the Internal Revenue Code.

(a) Special agents of the Bureau of Alcohol, Tobacco, Firearms, and Explosives, as well as any other investigator or officer charged by the Attorney General with the duty of enforcing any of the criminal, seizure, or forfeiture provisions of the laws of the United States, may carry firearms, serve warrants and subpoenas issued under the authority of the United States and make arrests without warrant for any offense against the United States committed in their presence, or for any felony cognizable under the laws of the United States if they have reasonable grounds to believe that the person to be arrested has committed or is committing such felony.
(c)(3) Notwithstanding any other provision of law, the disposition of firearms forfeited by reason of a violation of any law of the United States shall be governed by the provisions of section 5872(b) of the Internal Revenue Code of 1986.

Nov. 25, 2002 (148)
TITLE 18. CRIMES AND CRIMINAL PROCEDURE • PART II: CRIMINAL PROCEDURE • CHAPTER 203: ARREST AND COMMITMENT

18 USC § 3052. Powers of Federal Bureau of Investigation

> The Gist: The leaders, inspectors and agents of the FBI may carry firearms.

The Director, Associate Director, Assistant to the Director, Assistant Directors, inspectors, and agents of the Federal Bureau of Investigation of the Department of Justice may carry firearms, serve warrants and subpoenas issued under the authority of the United States and make arrests without warrant for any offense against the United States committed in their presence, or for any felony cognizable under the laws of the United States if they have reasonable grounds to believe that the person to be arrested has committed or is committing such felony.

June 25, 1948 (87)

TITLE 18. CRIMES AND CRIMINAL PROCEDURE • PART II: CRIMINAL PROCEDURE • CHAPTER 203: ARREST AND COMMITMENT

18 USC § 3053. Powers of marshals and deputies

> The Gist: United States marshals and their deputies may carry firearms.

United States marshals and their deputies may carry firearms and may make arrests without warrant for any offense against the United States committed in their presence, or for any felony cognizable under the laws of the United States if they have reasonable grounds to believe that the person to be arrested has committed or is committing such felony.

June 25, 1948 (58)

TITLE 18. CRIMES AND CRIMINAL PROCEDURE • PART II: CRIMINAL PROCEDURE • CHAPTER 203: ARREST AND COMMITMENT

18 USC § 3056. Powers, authorities, and duties of United States Secret Service

> The Gist: Officers and agents of the Secret Service may carry firearms.

(c)(1) Under the direction of the Secretary of Homeland Security, officers and agents of the Secret Service are authorized to—
(B) carry firearms:

June 25, 1948 (23)

TITLE 18. CRIMES AND CRIMINAL PROCEDURE • PART II: CRIMINAL PROCEDURE • CHAPTER 203: ARREST AND COMMITMENT

18 USC § 3061. Investigative powers of Postal Service personnel

> The Gist: Postal inspectors and certain other USPS staff may be authorized to carry firearms.

(a) Subject to subsection (b) of this section, Postal Inspectors and other agents of the United States Postal Service designated by the Board of Governors to investigate criminal matters related to the Postal Service and the mails may—
(4) carry firearms
(b) The powers granted by subsection (a) of this section shall be exercised only—
(1) in the enforcement of laws regarding property in the custody of the Postal Service, property of the Postal Service, the use of the mails, and other postal offenses; and
(2) to the extent authorized by the Attorney General pursuant to agreement between the Attorney General and the Postal Service, in the enforcement of other laws of the United States, if the Attorney General determines that violations of such laws have a detrimental effect upon the operations of the Postal Service.

Oct. 12, 1968 (136)

TITLE 18. CRIMES AND CRIMINAL PROCEDURE • PART II: CRIMINAL PROCEDURE • CHAPTER 203: ARREST AND COMMITMENT

18 USC § 3063. Powers of Environmental Protection Agency

> The Gist: Certain law enforcement officers of the Environmental
> Protection Agency may carry firearms.

(a) Upon designation by the Administrator of the Environmental Protection Agency,
any law enforcement officer of the Environmental Protection Agency with
responsibility for the investigation of criminal violations of a law administered by the
Environmental Protection Agency, may—
(1) carry firearms

Nov. 1, 1988 (41)
TITLE 18. CRIMES AND CRIMINAL PROCEDURE • PART II: CRIMINAL PROCEDURE • CHAPTER 203: ARREST
AND COMMITMENT

18 USC § 3142. Release or detention of a defendant pending trial

> The Gist: A person awaiting trial may be released from custody before
> the trial, under a combination of conditions, following the guidelines
> provided here. One of the conditions a court may require for release on
> personal recognizance or unsecured bond is a prohibition from firearm
> possession.
>
> No pre-trial release is available to a person who is believed to have
> committed a drug trafficking crime involving firearms, defined under
> 18–924(c).

(a) In general.—Upon the appearance before a judicial officer of a person charged
with an offense, the judicial officer shall issue an order that, pending trial, the
person be—
(1) released on personal recognizance or upon execution of an unsecured
appearance bond, under subsection (b) of this section:
(2) released on a condition or combination of conditions under subsection (c) of this
section:
(3) temporarily detained to permit revocation of conditional release, deportation, or
exclusion under subsection (d) of this section; or
(4) detained under subsection (e) of this section.
(b) Release on personal recognizance or unsecured appearance bond.—The judicial
officer shall order the pretrial release of the person on personal recognizance, or
upon execution of an unsecured appearance bond in an amount specified by the
court, subject to the condition that the person not commit a Federal, State, or local
crime during the period of release, unless the judicial officer determines that such
release will not reasonably assure the appearance of the person as required or will
endanger the safety of any other person or the community.
(c) Release on conditions.—
(1) If the judicial officer determines that the release described in subsection (b) of this
section will not reasonably assure the appearance of the person as required or will
endanger the safety of any other person or the community, such judicial officer shall
order the pretrial release of the person—
(A) subject to the condition that the person not commit a Federal, State, or local crime
during the period of release; and
(B) subject to the least restrictive further condition, or combination of conditions, that
such judicial officer determines will reasonably assure the appearance of the
person as required and the safety of any other person and the community, which
may include the condition that the person—
(viii) refrain from possessing a firearm, destructive device, or other dangerous weapon
(e) Detention.—If, after a hearing pursuant to the provisions of subsection (f) of this
section, the judicial officer finds that no condition or combination of conditions will

reasonably assure the appearance of the person as required and the safety of any other person and the community, such judicial officer shall order the detention of the person before trial. In a case described in subsection (f)(1) of this section, a rebuttable presumption arises that no condition or combination of conditions will reasonably assure the safety of any other person and the community if such judicial officer finds that—

(3) a period of not more than five years has elapsed since the date of conviction, or the release of the person from imprisonment, for the offense described in paragraph (1) of this subsection, whichever is later.

Subject to rebuttal by the person, it shall be presumed that no condition or combination of conditions will reasonably assure the appearance of the person as required and the safety of the community if the judicial officer finds that there is probable cause to believe that the person committed an offense for which a maximum term of imprisonment of ten years or more is prescribed in the Controlled Substances Act (21 U.S.C. 801 et seq.), the Controlled Substances Import and Export Act (21 U.S.C. 951 et seq.), the Maritime Drug Law Enforcement Act (46 U.S.C. App. 1901 et seq.), or an offense under section 924(c), 956(a), or 2332b of title 18 of the United States Code.

Oct. 12, 1984 (564)

TITLE 18. CRIMES AND CRIMINAL PROCEDURE • PART II: CRIMINAL PROCEDURE • CHAPTER 207: RELEASE AND DETENTION PENDING JUDICIAL PROCEEDINGS

18 USC § 3559. Sentencing classification of offenses

The Gist: In terms of imprisoning violent felons, "firearms use" refers to use in connection with violent or drug trafficking crimes.

(c) Imprisonment of Certain Violent Felons.—

(2) Definitions.—For purposes of this subsection—

(D) the term "firearms use" means an offense that has as its elements those described in section 924(c) or 929(a), if the firearm was brandished, discharged, or otherwise used as a weapon and the crime of violence or drug trafficking crime during and relation to which the firearm was used was subject to prosecution in a court of the United States or a court of a State, or both;

(F) the term "serious violent felony" means—

(i) a Federal or State offense, by whatever designation and wherever committed, consisting of murder (as described in section 1111); manslaughter other than involuntary manslaughter (as described in section 1112); assault with intent to commit murder (as described in section 113(a)); assault with intent to commit rape; aggravated sexual abuse and sexual abuse (as described in sections 2241 and 2242); abusive sexual contact (as described in sections 2244(a)(1) and (a)(2)); kidnapping; aircraft piracy (as described in section 46502 of Title 49); robbery (as described in section 2111, 2113, or 2118); carjacking (as described in section 2119); extortion; arson; firearms use; firearms possession (as described in section 924(c)); or attempt, conspiracy, or solicitation to commit any of the above offenses;

Oct. 12, 1984 (82)

TITLE 18. CRIMES AND CRIMINAL PROCEDURE • CHAPTER 227: SENTENCES • SUBCHAPTER A: GENERAL PROVISIONS

18 USC § 3563. Conditions of probation

The Gist: Among the many conditions a court can impose on a person on probation is a prohibition against possessing a firearm.

(b) Discretionary conditions.—The court may provide, as further conditions of a sentence of probation, to the extent that such conditions are reasonably related to the factors set forth in section 3553(a)(1) and (a)(2) and to the extent that such

conditions involve only such deprivations of liberty or property as are reasonably necessary for the purposes indicated in section 3553(a)(2), that the defendant—
(8) refrain from possessing a firearm, destructive device, or other dangerous weapon

Oct. 12, 1984 (80)
TITLE 18. CRIMES AND CRIMINAL PROCEDURE • PART II: CRIMINAL PROCEDURE • CHAPTER 227: SENTENCES • SUBCHAPTER B: PROBATION

18 USC § 3565. Revocation of probation

> The Gist: A person on probation must be sentenced to imprisonment for breaking a federal firearms law while on probation, or for possessing a firearm if that's prohibited under the probation.

(b) Mandatory revocation for possession of controlled substance or firearm or refusal to comply with drug testing.—If the defendant—
(2) possesses a firearm, as such term is defined in section 921 of this title, in violation of Federal law, or otherwise violates a condition of probation prohibiting the defendant from possessing a firearm
the court shall revoke the sentence of probation and resentence the defendant under subchapter A to a sentence that includes a term of imprisonment.

June 25, 1948 (78)
TITLE 18. CRIMES AND CRIMINAL PROCEDURE • CHAPTER 227: SENTENCE, JUDGMENT, AND EXECUTION

18 USC § 3592. Mitigating and aggravating factors to be considered in determining whether a sentence of death is justified

> The Gist: When the death penalty is considered in a homicide case, a prior conviction for a serious firearms offense must be taken into consideration. When the death penalty is considered for a drug offense, the use of a firearm in the crime, or encouraging someone else to use a firearm, must be taken into consideration.

(c) Aggravating factors for homicide.—In determining whether a sentence of death is justified for an offense described in section 3591(a)(2), the jury, or if there is no jury, the court, shall consider each of the following aggravating factors for which notice has been given and determine which, if any, exists:
(2) Previous conviction of violent felony involving firearm.—For any offense, other than an offense for which a sentence of death is sought on the basis of section 924(c), the defendant has previously been convicted of a Federal or State offense punishable by a term of imprisonment of more than 1 year, involving the use or attempted or threatened use of a firearm (as defined in section 921) against another person.
(d) Aggravating factors for drug offense death penalty.—In determining whether a sentence of death is justified for an offense described in section 3591(b), the jury, or if there is no jury, the court, shall consider each of the following aggravating factors for which notice has been given and determine which, if any, exist:
(4) Use of firearm.—In committing the offense, or in furtherance of a continuing criminal enterprise of which the offense was a part, the defendant used a firearm or knowingly directed, advised, authorized, or assisted another to use a firearm to threaten, intimidate, assault, or injure a person.

Sept. 13, 1994 (228)
TITLE 18. CRIMES AND CRIMINAL PROCEDURE • CHAPTER 228: DEATH SENTENCE

18 USC § 3665. Firearms possessed by convicted felons

> The Gist: Firearms found on a person at the time of arrest for either a violent felony, a felony committed with a firearm, or for interstate motor-vehicle theft, may be confiscated, and forfeited if the person is convicted. The court may give the firearms to the agency which caught the criminal, and the agency may decide what to do with the firearm.

A judgment of conviction for transporting a stolen motor vehicle in interstate or foreign commerce or for committing or attempting to commit a felony in violation of any law of the United States involving the use of threats, force, or violence or perpetrated in whole or in part by the use of firearms, may, in addition to the penalty provided by law for such offense, order the confiscation and disposal of firearms and ammunition found in the possession or under the immediate control of the defendant at the time of his arrest.

The court may direct the delivery of such firearms or ammunition to the law-enforcement agency which apprehended such person, for its use or for any other disposition in its discretion.

Oct. 12, 1984 (123)

TITLE 18. CRIMES AND CRIMINAL PROCEDURE • PART II: CRIMINAL PROCEDURE • CHAPTER 232: MISCELLANEOUS SENTENCING PROVISIONS

Title 19 • Customs Duties

19 USC § 1491. Unclaimed merchandise

> The Gist: Imported merchandise which has not had all its duties and
> taxes paid must remain warehoused and not released. After six months,
> the merchandise is considered abandoned and is appraised and sold at
> public auction by the Customs Dept., or disposed of in other ways. In the
> case of gunpowder, explosives or other merchandise that may lose
> enough of its value by waiting that they won't cover the taxes and other
> charges involved, the sale may take place immediately, under regulations
> set up by the Treasury Dept. A person may, under certain circumstances,
> request possession of or compensation for merchandise affected by this
> law.

(a) Sale at public auction
Any entered or unentered merchandise (except merchandise entered under section
1557 of this title, but including merchandise entered for transportation in bond or for
exportation) which shall remain in a bonded warehouse pursuant to section 1490 of
this title for 6 months from the date of importation thereof, without all estimated
duties, taxes, fees, interest, storage, or other charges thereon having been paid,
shall be considered unclaimed and abandoned to the Government and shall be
appraised and sold by the Customs Service at public auction under such
regulations as the Secretary of the Treasury shall prescribe. All gunpowder and
other explosive substances and merchandise liable to depreciation in value by
damage, leakage, or other cause to such extent that the proceeds of sale thereof
may be insufficient to pay the duties, taxes, fees, interest, storage, and other
charges, if permitted to remain in pursuant to section 1490 of this title in a bonded
warehouse for 6 months, may be sold forthwith, under such regulations as the
Secretary of the Treasury may prescribe. Merchandise subject to sale hereunder or
under section 1559 of this title may be entered or withdrawn for consumption at any
time prior to such sale upon payment of all duties, taxes, fees, interest, storage,
and other charges, and expenses that may have accrued thereon, but such
merchandise after becoming subject to sale may not be exported prior to sale
without the payment of such duties, taxes, fees, interest, charges, and expenses
nor may it be entered for warehouse. The computation of duties, taxes, interest,
and fees for the purposes of this section and sections 1493 and 1559 of this title
shall be at the rate or rates applicable at the time the merchandise becomes
subject to sale.
(b) Notice of title vesting in the United States
At the end of the 6-month period referred to in subsection (a) of this section, the
Customs Service may, in lieu of sale of the merchandise, provide notice to all
known interested parties that the title to such merchandise shall be considered to
vest in the United States free and clear of any liens or encumbrances, on the 30th
day after the date of the notice unless, before such 30th day—

(1) the subject merchandise is entered or withdrawn for consumption; and

(2) payment is made of all duties, taxes, fees, transfer and storage charges, and other expenses that may have accrued thereon.

(c) Retention, transfer, destruction, or other disposition

If title to any merchandise vests in the United States by operation of subsection (b) of this section, such merchandise may be retained by the Customs Service for official use, transferred to any other Federal agency or to any State or local agency, destroyed, or otherwise disposed of in accordance with such regulations as the Secretary shall prescribe. All transfer and storage charges or expenses accruing on retained or transferred merchandise shall be paid by the receiving agency.

(d) Petition

Whenever any party, having lost a substantial interest in merchandise by virtue of title vesting in the United States under subsection (b) of this section, can establish such title or interest to the satisfaction of the Secretary within 30 days after the day on which title vests in the United States under subsection (b) of this section, or can establish to the satisfaction of the Secretary that the party did not receive notice under subsection (b) of this section, the Secretary may, upon receipt of a timely and proper petition and upon finding that the facts and circumstances warrant, pay such party out of the Treasury of the United States the amount the Secretary believes the party would have received under section 1493 of this title had the merchandise been sold and a proper claim filed. The decision of the Secretary with respect to any such petition is final and conclusive on all parties.

June 17, 1930 (648)

TITLE 19. CUSTOMS DUTIES • CHAPTER 4: TARIFF ACT OF 1930 • SUBTITLE III: ADMINISTRATIVE PROVISIONS • PART III: ASCERTAINMENT, COLLECTION, AND RECOVERY OF DUTIES

19 USC § 2072. Officers and employees

> The Gist: Customs agents may be armed at the discretion of the Secretary of the Treasury. See 31-321.

(c) Duties of personnel

The personnel of the United States Customs Service shall perform such duties as the Secretary of the Treasury may prescribe.

July 31, 1950 (24)

TITLE 19. CUSTOMS DUTIES • CHAPTER 10: CUSTOMS SERVICE

1791 to 1893

New Sections of Law	0
Words Added	0
% of Total (Then)	0
% of Total (Now)	0

1894 to 1909

New Sections of Law	1
Words Added	547
% of Total (Then)	—
% of Total (Now)	0.6%

The 1910s

New Sections of Law	7
Words Added	1,481
% of Total (Then)	271%
% of Total (Now)	1.7%

The 1920s

New Sections of Law	8
Words Added	1,543
% of Total (Then)	43.2%
% of Total (Now)	1.7%

The 1930s

New Sections of Law	9
Words Added	1,736
% of Total (Then)	32.7%
% of Total (Now)	2.0%

The 1940s

New Sections of Law	37
Words Added	7,498
% of Total (Then)	58.6%
% of Total (Now)	8.5%

The 1950s

New Sections of Law	41
Words Added	7,102
% of Total (Then)	35.7%
% of Total (Now)	8.0%

The 1960s

New Sections of Law	51
Words Added	27,908
% of Total (Then)	58.4%
% of Total (Now)	31.5%

The 1970s

New Sections of Law	26
Words Added	11,407
% of Total (Then)	19.3%
% of Total (Now)	12.9%

The 1980s

New Sections of Law	28
Words Added	6,777
% of Total (Then)	10.3%
% of Total (Now)	7.7%

1990 to 1998

New Sections of Law	Not all codified
Words Added	22,585
% of Total (Then)	34.2%
% of Total (Now)	25.5%

For complete statistics see the chart
Growth in Federal Gun Laws
in the introduction

"% of Total (Now)" is through 1995.

Title 20 • Education

20 USC § 60. Army articles furnished to National Museum

The Gist: The Army may give arms and ammunition to the Smithsonian Institution for display, if the museum asks.

The Secretary of the Army is authorized to furnish to the National Museum, for exhibition, upon request therefor by the administrative head thereof, such articles of arms, materiel, equipment, or clothing as have been issued from time to time to the United States Army, or which have been or may hereafter be produced for the United States Army, and which are objects of general interest or of foreign or curious research, provided that such articles can be spared.

Mar. 4, 1921 (78)
TITLE 20. EDUCATION • CHAPTER 3: SMITHSONIAN INSTITUTION, NATIONAL MUSEUMS AND ART GALLERIES • SUBCHAPTER I: CHARTER PROVISIONS

20 USC § 3351. Gun-free requirements <Historical Note>

The Gist: This law has been "omitted" from the United States Code, effective Oct. 20, 1994.

Part of the highly publicized Educational Goals 2000, this statute prevented the federal government from giving money to schools, if the school did not have an expulsion requirement for any student who, without authorization, brought a gun to school. Local school systems, if they were to continue receiving federal funds, had to provide assurance that they would expel (or at least review) students who brought guns to school. Also required were reports on the number of expulsions and types of weapons involved. Exceptions to the expulsion rule could be granted on a case-by-case basis by the head of the school system.

Enacted on March 31, 1994, this forced schools nationwide to quickly implement expulsion requirements, casting a decidedly negative pallor on the classic right to bear arms. Until the 1960s, many schools had firing ranges on campus, and guns could be brought to school for numerous reasons, such as hunting on the way home after class, ROTC training, varsity competition, and even show-and-tell.

Later the same year (Oct. 20, 1994), after schools had scrambled to put the expulsion policies in place, the law was quietly "omitted" from a general amendment of the Elementary and Secondary Education Act of 1965, of which this was a part, thus eliminating this restriction on federal spending. In other words, the federal government can give funds to schools, and maintain the influence that implies, even if the school has no expulsion requirement. Left in place though are all the expulsion requirements schools had already implemented. Detecting and deciphering this omission in federal law was arguably the most challenging research in this tenth anniversary edition of *Gun Laws of America*.

Related portions of Goals 2000, which appeared in prior editions, namely 20-5821, 20-5822 and 20-5823, were repealed on Jan. 8, 2002.

20 USC § 5811. Purpose

The Gist: The laws that follow establish national goals for the education system.

The purpose of this subchapter is to establish National Education Goals.
Mar. 31, 1994 (11)
TITLE 20. EDUCATION • CHAPTER 68: NATIONAL EDUCATION REFORMS • SUBCHAPTER 1: NATIONAL EDUCATION GOALS

20 USC § 5812. National Education Goals

The Gist: The National Education Goals include that schools must develop programs to eliminate unauthorized firearms. Rules for monitoring and encouraging compliance with these goals are set up in the laws that follow.

The Congress declares that the National Education Goals are the following:
(7) Safe, disciplined, and alcohol and drug free schools
(A) By the year 2000, every school in the United States will be free of drugs, violence, and the unauthorized presence of firearms and alcohol and will offer a disciplined environment conducive to learning.
(B) The objectives for this goal are that—
(ii) parents, businesses, governmental and community organizations will work together to ensure the rights of students to study in a safe and secure environment that is free of drugs and crime, and that schools provide a healthy environment and are a safe haven for all children;
(iii) every local educational agency will develop and implement a policy to ensure that all schools are free of violence and the unauthorized presence of weapons;
(vi) community-based teams should be organized to provide students and teachers with needed support;
Mar. 31, 1994 (148)
TITLE 20. EDUCATION • CHAPTER 68: NATIONAL EDUCATION REFORMS • SUBCHAPTER 1: NATIONAL EDUCATION GOALS

Title 21 • Food and Drugs

21 USC § 372. Examinations and investigations—Authority to conduct

The Gist: Designated officials of the Health and Human Services Dept. may be authorized to carry firearms.

(e) Powers of enforcement personnel
Any officer or employee of the Department designated by the Secretary to conduct examinations, investigations, or inspections under this chapter relating to counterfeit drugs may, when so authorized by the Secretary—
(1) carry firearms

June 25, 1938 (39)
TITLE 21. FOOD AND DRUGS • CHAPTER 9: FEDERAL FOOD, DRUG, AND COSMETIC ACT • SUBCHAPTER VII: GENERAL AUTHORITY • PART A: GENERAL ADMINISTRATIVE PROVISIONS

21 USC § 461. Offenses and punishment

The Gist: It is illegal to forcibly interfere with federal poultry inspectors or related staff. Using a firearm to interfere increases the penalty.

(c) Assaulting, resisting, or impeding certain persons; murder; punishments
Any person who forcibly assaults, resists, opposes, impedes, intimidates, or interferes with any person while engaged in or on account of the performance of his official duties under this chapter shall be fined not more than $5,000 or imprisoned not more than three years, or both. Whoever, in the commission of any such acts, uses a deadly or dangerous weapon, shall be fined not more than $10,000 or imprisoned not more than ten years, or both. Whoever kills any person while engaged in or on account of the performance of his official duties under this chapter shall be punished as provided under sections 1111 and 1114 of Title 18.

Aug. 28, 1957 (120)
TITLE 21. FOOD AND DRUGS • CHAPTER 10: POULTRY AND POULTRY PRODUCTS INSPECTION

21 USC § 878. Powers of enforcement personnel

The Gist: Officers and employees of the Drug Enforcement Administration, and any local law enforcement officers, may be designated to carry firearms by the Attorney General.

(a) Officers or employees of Drug Enforcement Administration or any State or local law enforcement officer

Any officer or employee of the Drug Enforcement Administration or any State or local law enforcement officer designated by the Attorney General may—

(1) carry firearms;

Oct. 27, 1970 (42)

TITLE 21. FOOD AND DRUGS • CHAPTER 13: DRUG ABUSE PREVENTION AND CONTROL • SUBCHAPTER I: CONTROL AND ENFORCEMENT • PART E: ADMINISTRATIVE AND ENFORCEMENT PROVISIONS

21 USC § 1041. Enforcement provisions

> The Gist: It is illegal to forcibly interfere with federal egg inspectors or related staff. Using a firearm in such interference increases the penalty.

(b) Persons preventing enforcement of chapter; term of imprisonment and fine

Any person who forcibly assaults, resists, opposes, impedes, intimidates, or interferes with any person while engaged in or on account of the performance of his official duties under this chapter shall be fined not more than $5,000 or imprisoned not more than three years, or both. Whoever, in the commission of any such act, uses a deadly or dangerous weapon, shall be fined not more than $10,000 or imprisoned not more than ten years, or both. Whoever kills any person while engaged in or on account of the performance of his official duties under this chapter shall be punished as provided under sections 1111 and 1112 of Title 18.

Dec. 29, 1970 (120)

TITLE 21. FOOD AND DRUGS • CHAPTER 15: EGG PRODUCTS INSPECTION

Title 22 • Foreign Relations and Intercourse

22 USC § 277d-3. Authorization for appropriations; activities for which available; contracts for excess amounts

> The Gist: Money allocated to the International Boundary and Water Commission, for carrying out treaty provisions with Mexico that involve the United States Section of that Commission, may be used to buy firearms and ammunition for guards.

There are authorized to be appropriated to the Department of State for the use of the Commission, out of any money in the Treasury not otherwise appropriated, such sums as may be necessary to carry out the provisions of the Treaty of February 3, 1944, and other treaties and conventions between the United States of America and the United Mexican States, under which the United States Section operates, and to discharge the statutory functions and duties of the United States Section. Such sums shall be available for
purchase of firearms and ammunition for guard purposes

Sept. 13, 1950 (95)
TITLE 22. FOREIGN RELATIONS AND INTERCOURSE • CHAPTER 7: INTERNATIONAL BUREAUS, CONGRESSES, ETC. • SUBCHAPTER IV: INTERNATIONAL BOUNDARY AND WATER COMMISSION

22 USC § 401. Illegal exportation of war materials

> The Gist: The proper authorities may seize any arms or war munitions which are being smuggled out of the country. Any ships, vehicles or aircraft used may also be seized. Anything seized under this law is forfeited. Other laws on seizure and forfeiture of property may also apply, as long as they don't conflict with this law. Such property is disposed of as the Secretary of Defense decides, or as customs law requires. Under this law, an informant may only be paid from funds specifically designated for such payments (limiting an informant's participation in "the take.")

(a) Seizure and forfeiture of materials and carriers
Whenever an attempt is made to export or ship from or take out of the United States any arms or munitions of war or other articles in violation of law, or whenever it is known or there shall be probable cause to believe that any arms or munitions of war or other articles are intended to be or are being or have been exported or removed from the United States in violation of law, the Secretary of the Treasury, or any person duly authorized for the purpose by the President, may seize and detain such arms or munitions of war or other articles and may seize and detain any vessel, vehicle, or aircraft containing the same or which has been or is being used

in exporting or attempting to export such arms or munitions of war or other articles. The Secretary of Commerce may seize and detain any commodity (other than arms or munitions of war) or technology which is intended to be or is being exported in violation of laws governing such exports and may seize and detain any vessel, vehicle, or aircraft containing the same or which has been used or is being used in exporting or attempting to export such articles. All arms or munitions of war and other articles, vessels, vehicles, and aircraft seized pursuant to this subsection shall be forfeited.

(b) Applicability of laws relating to seizure, forfeiture, and condemnation

All provisions of law relating to seizure, summary and judicial forfeiture and condemnation for violation of the customs laws, the disposition of the property forfeited or condemned or the proceeds from the sale thereof; the remission or mitigation of such forfeitures; and the compromise of claims and the award of compensation to informers in respect of such forfeitures shall apply to seizures and forfeitures incurred, or alleged to have been incurred, under the provisions of this section, insofar as applicable and not inconsistent with the provisions hereof. However, with respect to seizures and forfeitures of property under this section by the Secretary of Commerce, such duties as are imposed upon the customs officer or any other person with respect to the seizure and forfeiture of property under the customs law may be performed by such officers as are designated by the Secretary of Commerce or, upon the request of the Secretary of Commerce, by any other agency that has authority to manage and dispose of seized property. Awards of compensation to informers under this section may be paid only out of funds specifically appropriated therefor.

(c) Disposition of forfeited materials

Arms and munitions of war forfeited under subsection (b) of this section shall be delivered to the Secretary of Defense for such use or disposition as he may deem in the public interest, or, in the event that the Secretary of Defense refuses to accept such arms and munitions of war, they shall be sold or otherwise disposed of as prescribed under existing law in the case of forfeitures for violation of the customs laws.

June 15, 1917 (508)

TITLE 22. FOREIGN RELATIONS AND INTERCOURSE • CHAPTER 9: FOREIGN WARS, WAR MATERIALS, AND NEUTRALITY • SUBCHAPTER I: WAR MATERIALS

22 USC § 406. Interference with foreign trade

The Gist: The law prohibiting smuggling arms and war munitions does not apply to legal trade permitted under specified laws and treaties.

Except in those cases in which the exportation of arms and munitions of war or other articles is forbidden by proclamation or otherwise by the President, as provided in section 401 of this title, nothing herein contained shall be construed to extend to, or interfere with any trade in such commodities, conducted with any foreign port or place whersoever, or with any other trade which might have been lawfully carried on before June 15, 1917, under the law of nations, or under the treaties or conventions entered into by the United States, or under the laws thereof.

June 15, 1917 (97)

TITLE 22. FOREIGN RELATIONS AND INTERCOURSE • CHAPTER 9: FOREIGN WARS, WAR MATERIALS, AND NEUTRALITY • SUBCHAPTER I: WAR MATERIALS

22 USC § 2291a. Authorization of appropriations

The Gist: Money appropriated to combat illegal drugs in foreign countries may not be used to buy firearms or ammunition, except to defensively arm aircraft used for narcotic-related purposes, and to

defensively arm employees and contractors of the Dept. of State in similar
activities, with prior notice to Congress.

(b) Procurement of weapons and ammunition
(1) Prohibition
Except as provided in paragraph (2), funds made available to carry out this part shall
not be made available for the procurement of weapons or ammunition.
(2) Exceptions
Paragraph (1) shall not apply with respect to funds for the procurement of—
(A) weapons or ammunition provided only for the defensive arming of aircraft used for
narcotics-related purposes, or
(B) firearms and related ammunition provided only for defensive purposes to
employees or contract personnel of the Department of State engaged in activities
under this part, if, at least 15 days before obligating those funds, the President
notifies the appropriate congressional committees in accordance with the
procedures applicable to reprogramming notifications under section 2394-1 of this
title.

July 13, 1972 (123)
TITLE 22. FOREIGN RELATIONS AND INTERCOURSE • CHAPTER 32: FOREIGN ASSISTANCE • SUBCHAPTER I:
INTERNATIONAL DEVELOPMENT

Arms Control and Disarmament

"An ultimate goal of the United States is a world which is free from the scourge of war and the dangers and burdens of armaments..." So begins a set of laws which are found under Title 22, Foreign Relations and Intercourse. Not gun laws in the ordinary sense, they are remnants of the Cold War era, written in response to nuclear-conflict fears with the Cold War enemy socialists and communists. Summarizing these policy statements is quite different from clarifying legalese, and yields a different result. The opinions expressed in the first *Gist* that follows reflect the philosophies built into the statutes and not editorial comment.

Shorthand: For ease of reading, the term *disarmament* is used in the *Gists* to mean *arms control, nonproliferation and disarmament.*

22 USC § 2551. Congressional statement of purpose

The Gist: The United States stands for a world without war, strife or weapons. A world where force would not be used instead of law, and where the whole world would be in agreement. The laws of this chapter are designed to help create the world peace envisioned. An "agency of peace"* is created to work toward total world disarmament.

The Secretary of State (now replacing The United States Arms Control and Disarmament Agency) must be capable of performing detailed valid research on everything about disarmament, to use in setting policy. The Secretary reports to the President, and is authorized to: 1–Handle U.S. involvement in international disarmament negotiations and implementation; 2–As the President directs, handle U.S. involvement in international nonproliferation negotiations and implementation; 3–Do research for disarmament policy; 4–Handle U.S. participation in disarmament control systems if the U.S. becomes involved in that; and 5–Give information to the public about what's happening regarding disarmament.

Historical note: The United States Arms Control and Disarmament Agency, established in 1961 (22-2561), was abolished, with its functions, staff and stuff transferred to the State Dept., in 1998.

*The *agency of peace* phrase was removed in 1998, when the Arms Control Agency was rolled into the State Dept.

An ultimate goal of the United States is a world which is free from the scourge of war and the dangers and burdens of armaments; in which the use of force has been subordinated to the rule of law; and in which international adjustments to a changing world are achieved peacefully. It is the purpose of this chapter to provide impetus toward this goal by addressing the problem of reduction and control of armaments looking toward ultimate world disarmament.

The Secretary of State must have the capacity to provide the essential scientific, economic, political, military, psychological, and technological information upon which realistic arms control, nonproliferation, and disarmament policy must be based. The Secretary of State shall have the authority, under the direction of the President, to carry out the following primary functions:

(1) The preparation for and management of United States participation in international negotiations and implementation for a <plural of forum> in the arms control, nonproliferation, and disarmament field.

(2) The conduct, support, and coordination of research for arms control, nonproliferation, and disarmament policy formulation.

(3) The preparation for, operation of, or direction of, United States participation in such control systems as may become part of United States arms control, nonproliferation, and disarmament activities.

(4) The dissemination and coordination of public information concerning arms control, nonproliferation, and disarmament.

Sept. 26, 1961 (218)
TITLE 22. FOREIGN RELATIONS AND INTERCOURSE • CHAPTER 35: ARMS CONTROL AND DISARMAMENT • SUBCHAPTER I: GENERAL PROVISIONS

22 USC § 2552. Definitions

The Gist: When used in this chapter (Chapter 35) *arms control* and *disarmament* mean finding, controlling and eliminating armed forces and armaments of all kinds, under international agreement. It includes taking necessary steps to ensure international control, or to create and strengthen international peace organizations. *Government agency* means anything under the executive branch of government.

As used in this chapter—

(a) The terms "**arms control**" and "**disarmament**" mean the identification, verification, inspection, limitation, control, reduction, or elimination, of armed forces and armaments of all kinds under international agreement including the necessary steps taken under such an agreement to establish an effective system of international control, or to create and strengthen international organizations for the maintenance of peace.

(b) The term "**Government agency**" means any executive department, commission, agency, independent establishment, corporation wholly or partly owned by the United States which is an instrumentality of the United States, or any board, bureau, division, service, office, officer, authority, administration, or other establishment in the executive branch of Government.

Sept. 26, 1961 (111)
TITLE 22. FOREIGN RELATIONS AND INTERCOURSE • CHAPTER 35: ARMS CONTROL AND DISARMAMENT • SUBCHAPTER I: GENERAL PROVISIONS

22 USC § 2567. Presidential Special Representatives

The Gist: The President may appoint Special Representatives for disarmament, with the rank of ambassador, subject to confirmation by the Senate. The Special Representatives act under the direction of the

President and Secretary of State, and the Secretary provides administrative support.

The President may appoint, by and with the advice and consent of the Senate, Special Representatives of the President for arms control, nonproliferation, and disarmament matters. Each Presidential Special Representative shall hold the rank of ambassador. Presidential Special Representatives appointed under this section shall perform their duties and exercise their powers under the direction of the President and the Secretary of State. The Department of State shall be the Government agency responsible for providing administrative support, including funding, staff, and office space, to all Presidential Special Representatives.

Aug. 17, 1977 (87)
TITLE 22. FOREIGN RELATIONS AND INTERCOURSE • CHAPTER 35: ARMS CONTROL AND DISARMAMENT • SUBCHAPTER II: SPECIAL REPRESENTATIVES AND VISITING SCHOLARS

22 USC § 2568. Program for visiting scholars

The Gist: The State Dept. runs programs to acquire assistance from disarmament experts. The Dept. chooses the experts, who serve for a period of one to two years.

A program for visiting scholars in the fields of arms control, nonproliferation, and disarmament shall be established by the Secretary of State in order to obtain the services of scholars from the faculties of recognized institutions of higher learning. The purpose of the program will be to give specialists in the physical sciences and other disciplines relevant to the Department of State's activities an opportunity for active participation in the arms control, nonproliferation, and disarmament activities of the Department of State and to gain for the Department of State the perspective and expertise such persons can offer. Each fellow in the program shall be appointed for a term of one year, except that such term may be extended for a 1-year period.

Dec. 2, 1983 (122)
TITLE 22. FOREIGN RELATIONS AND INTERCOURSE • CHAPTER 35: ARMS CONTROL AND DISARMAMENT • SUBCHAPTER II: SPECIAL REPRESENTATIVES AND VISITING SCHOLARS

22 USC § 2571. Research, development and other studies

The Gist: The Secretary of State, under direction from the President, is charged with obtaining theoretical and practical knowledge on disarmament, nonproliferation and arms control. The Secretary may conduct the work or use outside resources and people. The research, development and other studies are limited to: 1–the control, reduction and elimination of armed forces and armaments, 2–development of weapon detection systems, 3–control of armaments in space, under water and below the planet's surface, 4–training people to operate control systems, 5–study of foreign budgets and industry to determine spending on armaments, 6–reducing the danger of war from accident, miscalculation or surprise attack, 7–studying the political, economic and policy issues associated with arms control, 8–national security and foreign policy implications, 9–ways to have peace and security during disarmament, 10–anything else the Secretary feels is warranted, and more.

The Secretary of State is authorized and directed to exercise his powers in this subchapter in this title in such manner as to ensure the acquisition of a fund of theoretical and practical knowledge concerning disarmament and nonproliferation. To this end, the Director is authorized and directed, under the direction of the President,

(1) to ensure the conduct of research, development, and other studies in the fields of arms control, nonproliferation, and disarmament;

(2) to make arrangements (including contracts, agreements, and grants) for the conduct of research, development, and other studies in the fields of arms control, nonproliferation, and disarmament by private or public institutions or persons; and

(3) to coordinate the research, development, and other studies conducted in the fields of arms control, nonproliferation, and disarmament by or for other Government agencies. In carrying out his responsibilities under this chapter, the Secretary of State shall, to the maximum extent feasible, make full use of available facilities, Government and private. The authority of the Secretary under this Act with respect to research, development, and other studies concerning arms control, nonproliferation, and disarmament shall be limited to participation in the following:

(a) Control, reduction and elimination of armed forces and armaments

the detection, identification, inspection, monitoring, limitation, reduction, control, and elimination of armed forces and armaments, including thermonuclear, nuclear, missile, conventional, bacteriological, chemical, and radiological weapons:

(b) Weapon detection and identification tests

the techniques and systems of detecting, identifying, inspecting, and monitoring of tests of nuclear, thermonuclear, and other weapons:

(c) Analysis of national budgets and economic indicators

the analysis of national budgets, levels of industrial production, and economic indicators to determine the amounts spent by various countries for armaments and of all aspects of antisatellite activities:

(d) Space, earth's surface and underwater regions

the control, reduction, and elimination of armed forces and armaments in space, in areas on and beneath the earth's surface, and in underwater regions:

(e) Structure and operation of international control

the structure and operation of international control and other organizations useful for arms control, nonproliferation, and disarmament:

(f) Training of control system personnel

the training of scientists, technicians, and other personnel for manning the control systems which may be created by international arms control, nonproliferation, and disarmament agreements:

(g) Danger of war from accident, miscalculation, or surprise attack

the reduction and elimination of the danger of war resulting from accident, miscalculation, or possible surprise attack, including (but not limited to) improvements in the methods of communications between nations:

(h) Economic and political consequences of disarmament

the economic and political consequences of arms control, nonproliferation, and disarmament, including the problems of readjustment arising in industry and the reallocation of national resources:

(i) Disarmament implications of foreign and national security policies of United States

the arms control, nonproliferation, and disarmament implications of foreign and national security policies of the United States with a view to a better understanding of the significance of such policies for the achievement of arms control, nonproliferation, and disarmament:

(j) National security and foreign policy implications of disarmament

the national security and foreign policy implications of arms control, nonproliferation, and disarmament proposals with a view to a better understanding of the effect of such proposals upon national security and foreign policy:

(k) Methods for maintenance of peace and security during stages of disarmament

methods for the maintenance of peace and security during different stages of arms control, nonproliferation, and disarmament:

(l) War prevention factors

the scientific, economic, political, legal, social, psychological, military, and technological factors related to the prevention of war with a view to a better understanding of how the basic structure of a lasting peace may be established: and

(m) Other related problems

such related problems as the Secretary of State may determine to be in need of research, development, or study in order to carry out the provisions of this chapter.

Sept. 26, 1961 (648)

TITLE 22. FOREIGN RELATIONS AND INTERCOURSE • CHAPTER 35: ARMS CONTROL AND DISARMAMENT • SUBCHAPTER III: FUNCTIONS

22 USC § 2572. Patents; availability to general public; protection of background rights

> The Gist: All research paid for by the government and related to this chapter of law (Arms Control and Disarmament) is open to the public, unless the Secretary decides otherwise. An exemption is made so that this section doesn't make patent holders lose their patents.

All research within the United States contracted for, sponsored, cosponsored, or authorized under authority of this chapter, shall be provided for in such manner that all information as to uses, products, processes, patents, and other developments resulting from such research developed by Government expenditure will (with such exceptions and limitations, if any, as the Secretary of State may find to be necessary in the public interest) be available to the general public. This section shall not be so construed as to deprive the owner of any background patent relating thereto of such rights as he may have thereunder.

Sept. 26, 1961 (98)

TITLE 22. FOREIGN RELATIONS AND INTERCOURSE • CHAPTER 35: ARMS CONTROL AND DISARMAMENT • SUBCHAPTER III: FUNCTIONS

22 USC § 2573. Policy formulation

> The Gist: The Secretary of State has the responsibility of preparing advice and recommendations on arms control for the President and government leaders. Anything that would require the United States to significantly reduce its armed forces or armaments is prohibited, except under the Constitutional treaty-making powers of the President, or by act of Congress.
>
> Fearing that these laws might eventually be used to attempt to deprive American citizens of keeping and bearing arms, the original act included a specific restriction on any such action by the former Arms Control and Disarmament Agency. Although the State Dept. should, under traditional procedure continue to operate under this (and all other) restrictions after it absorbed the former Agency's responsibilities in 1998, Congress decided to reinforce that concept by reenacting the restrictive language separately. See paragraph (c).
>
> Under this law, no agencies of government are authorized to do anything, "which would interfere with, restrict, or prohibit the acquisition, possession, or use of firearms by an individual for the lawful purpose of personal defense, sport, recreation, education, or training." This had an immediate protective effect, since the State Dept., upon taking over the

Agency, issued a proposed rule rescinding all former Agency regulations, without suggesting a replacement set.

(a) Formulation
The Secretary of State shall prepare for the President, and the heads of such other Government agencies as the President may determine, recommendations and advice concerning United States arms control, nonproliferation, and disarmament policy.
(b) Prohibition
No action shall be taken pursuant to this chapter or any other Act that would obligate the United States to reduce or limit the Armed Forces or armaments of the United States in a militarily significant manner, except pursuant to the treaty-making power of the President set forth in Article II, Section 2, Clause 2 of the Constitution or unless authorized by the enactment of further affirmative legislation by the Congress of the United States.
(c) Statutory construction.—Nothing contained in this chapter shall be construed to authorize any policy or action by any Government agency which would interfere with, restrict, or prohibit the acquisition, possession, or use of firearms by an individual for the lawful purpose of personal defense, sport, recreation, education, or training.

Sept. 26, 1961 (113)
TITLE 22. FOREIGN RELATIONS AND INTERCOURSE • CHAPTER 35: ARMS CONTROL AND DISARMAMENT • SUBCHAPTER III: FUNCTIONS

22 USC § 2574. Negotiation management

The Gist: The Secretary of State, under direction of the President, has primary responsibility for participating in international disarmament proceedings. The President's Special Representatives serve as representatives to international organizations and related activities.

The Secretary is authorized to make plans and preparations for disarmament inspection and control systems, and to implement such systems.

(a) Responsibilities
The Secretary of State, under the direction of the President, shall have primary responsibility for the preparation, conduct, and management of United States participation in all international negotiations and implementation fora <plural of forum> in the field of arms control, non-proliferation, and disarmament. In furtherance of these responsibilities, Special Representatives of the President appointed pursuant to section 2567 of this title, shall, as directed by the President, serve as United States Government representatives to international organizations, conferences, and activities relating to the field of nonproliferation, such as the preparations for and conduct of the review relating to the Treaty on the Non-Proliferation of Nuclear Weapons.
(b) Authority
The Secretary of State is authorized—
(1) to formulate plans and make preparations for the establishment, operation, and funding of inspections and control systems which may become part of the United States arms control, nonproliferation, and disarmament activities; and
(2) as authorized by law, to put into effect, direct, or otherwise assume United States responsibility for such systems.

Sept. 26, 1961 (167)
TITLE 22. FOREIGN RELATIONS AND INTERCOURSE • CHAPTER 35: ARMS CONTROL AND DISARMAMENT • SUBCHAPTER III: FUNCTIONS

22 USC § 2577. Verification of compliance

The Gist: The Secretary of State must report to Congress on how well the arms control agreements we have entered into can be verified, and any degradation in our ability to adequately verify agreements. The report must include the amount of money and number of people involved in such work. The Secretary must presume that efforts are deliberately made to impede verification. Sensitive information may be withheld.

(a) In general

In order to ensure that arms control, nonproliferation, and disarmament agreements can be adequately verified, the Secretary of State shall report to Congress, on a timely basis, or upon request by an appropriate committee of the Congress—

(1) in the case of any arms control, nonproliferation, or disarmament agreement that has been concluded by the United States, the determination of the Secretary of State as to the degree to which the components of such agreement can be verified;

(2) in the case of any arms control, nonproliferation, or disarmament agreement that has entered into force, any significant degradation or alteration in the capacity of the United States to verify compliance of the components of such agreement;

(3) the amount and percentage of research funds expended by the Department of State for the purpose of analyzing issues relating to arms control, nonproliferation, and disarmament verification; and

(4) the number of professional personnel assigned to arms control verification on a full-time basis by each Government agency.

(b) Assessments upon request

Upon the request of the chairman or ranking minority member of the Committee on Foreign Relations of the Senate or the Committee on International Relations of the House of Representatives, in case of an arms control, nonproliferation, or disarmament proposal presented to a foreign country by the United States or presented to the United States by a foreign country, the Secretary of State shall submit a report to the Committee on the degree to which elements of the proposal are capable of being verified.

(c) Standard for verification of compliance

In making determinations under paragraphs (1) and (2) of subsection (a) of this section, the Secretary of State shall assume that all measures of concealment not expressly prohibited could be employed and that standard practices could be altered so as to impede verification.

(d) Rule of construction

Except as otherwise provided for by law, nothing in this section may be construed as requiring the disclosure of sensitive information relating to intelligence sources or methods or persons employed in the verification of compliance with arms control, nonproliferation, and disarmament agreements.

Aug. 17, 1977 (350)

TITLE 22. FOREIGN RELATIONS AND INTERCOURSE • CHAPTER 35: ARMS CONTROL AND DISARMAMENT • SUBCHAPTER III: FUNCTIONS

22 USC § 2651. Establishment of Department

The Gist: This section, with an enormously long history, authorizes the U.S. State Dept., which in 1998 incorporated the abolished Arms Control and Disarmament Agency.

There shall be at the seat of government an executive department to be known as the "Department of State", and a Secretary of State, who shall be the head thereof.

July 27, 1789 (30)

TITLE 22. FOREIGN RELATIONS AND INTERCOURSE • CHAPTER 38 DEPARTMENT OF STATE

22 USC § 2709. Special agents

> The Gist: Special qualified agents of the Dept. of State or of the Foreign Service may be authorized to carry firearms. Regulations for carrying and using such firearms are controlled by the Attorney General.

(a) General authority
Under such regulations as the Secretary of State may prescribe, special agents of the Department of State and the Foreign Service may—
(4) if designated by the Secretary and qualified, under regulations approved by the Attorney General, for the use of firearms, carry firearms for the purpose of performing the duties authorized by this section; and
(b) Agreement with Attorney General and firearms regulations
(1) Agreement with Attorney General
The authority conferred by paragraphs (1), (2), (4), and (5) of subsection (a) of this section shall be exercised subject to an agreement with the Attorney General and shall not be construed to affect the investigative authority of any other Federal law enforcement agency.
(2) Firearms regulations
The Secretary of State shall prescribe regulations, which shall be approved by the Attorney General, with respect to the carrying and use of firearms by special agents under this section.
(c) Secret Service not affected
Nothing in subsection (a)(3) of this section shall be construed to preclude or limit in any way the authority of the United States Secret Service to provide protective services pursuant to section 202 of Title 3 or section 3056 of Title 18 at a level commensurate with protective requirements as determined by the United States Secret Service. The Secretary of State, the Attorney General, and the Secretary of the Treasury shall enter into an interagency agreement with respect to their law enforcement functions.

Aug. 1, 1956 (237)
TITLE 22. FOREIGN RELATIONS AND INTERCOURSE • CHAPTER 38: DEPARTMENT OF STATE

22 USC § 2778. Control of arms and exports

> The Gist: The President is authorized to name selected goods and services as items important to defense, and to authorize the import and export of such items (Arms Export Control Act of 1976). These items make up the United States Munitions List.
>
> Any non-government person involved in making, exporting, importing or brokering items on the U.S. Munitions List must be registered with the government and pay a fee. The items themselves must be licensed for import or export, with exceptions for the proper authorities, and detailed reporting requirements apply. Nations with a proper signed agreement with the United States for controlling such munitions, which is described, may be exempted from the licensing requirements.
>
> Military firearms or ammunition provided to a foreign government may be returned to the U.S. for sale to the armed forces, or to state or local law enforcement agencies, but not to citizens. Such arms (and components, parts, accessories, attachments and ammo) may be sold to the public if they qualify as curios and relics owned by a foreign government, or if they have been completely reworked into items of foreign manufacture.

An unexpected consequence of this provision was to embargo large numbers of collectible WWII-vintage .30 caliber M-1 rifles returning from overseas.

An export license for items on the Munitions List must consider if the items would affect an arms race, international terrorism, an outbreak or increase in conflict, development of mass destruction weapons, prejudice arms control plans and more. People who may be restricted from participating in U.S. Munitions List matters are identified or cross referenced to other parts of the law. A private foreign citizen cannot be licensed to receive such exports. Violations are subject to fines up to $1 million and up to ten years in prison.

The President must periodically review the U.S. Munitions List for any items that no longer warrant controls and should be removed. Controls and requirements on presidential action are described.

The President's decisions about which items are on the list are not subject to judicial review.

(a) Presidential control of exports and imports of defense articles and services, guidance of policy, etc.; designation of United States Munitions List; issuance of export licenses; condition for export; negotiations information

(1) In furtherance of world peace and the security and foreign policy of the United States, the President is authorized to control the import and the export of defense articles and defense services and to provide foreign policy guidance to persons of the United States involved in the export and import of such articles and services. The President is authorized to designate those items which shall be considered as defense articles and defense services for the purposes of this section and to promulgate regulations for the import and export of such articles and services. The items so designated shall constitute the United States Munitions List.

(2) Decisions on issuing export licenses under this section shall take into account whether the export of an article would contribute to an arms race, aid in the development of weapons of mass destruction, support international terrorism, increase the possibility of outbreak or escalation of conflict, or prejudice the development of bilateral or multilateral arms control or nonproliferation agreements or other arrangements.

(3) In exercising the authorities conferred by this section, the President may require that any defense article or defense service be sold under this chapter as a condition of its eligibility for export, and may require that persons engaged in the negotiation for the export of defense articles and services keep the President fully and currently informed of the progress and future prospects of such negotiations.

(b) Registration and licensing requirements for manufacturers, exporters, or importers of designated defense articles and defense services

(1)(A)(i) As prescribed in regulations issued under this section, every person (other than an officer or employee of the United States Government acting in an official capacity) who engages in the business of manufacturing, exporting, or importing any defense articles or defense services designated by the President under subsection (a)(1) of this section shall register with the United States Government agency charged with the administration of this section, and shall pay a registration fee which shall be prescribed by such regulations. Such regulations shall prohibit the return to the United States for sale in the United States (other than for the Armed Forces of the United States and its allies or for any State or local law enforcement agency) of any military firearms or ammunition of United States manufacture furnished to foreign governments by the United States under this chapter or any other foreign assistance or sales program of the United States, whether or not enhanced in value or improved in condition in a foreign country. This prohibition shall not extend to similar firearms that have been so substantially transformed as to become, in effect, articles of foreign manufacture.

(ii)(I) As prescribed in regulations issued under this section, every person (other than an officer or employee of the United States Government acting in official capacity) who engages in the business of brokering activities with respect to the manufacture, export, import, or transfer of any defense article or defense service designated by the President under subsection (a)(1) of this section, or in the business of brokering activities with respect to the manufacture, export, import, or transfer of any foreign defense article or defense service (as defined in subclause (IV)), shall register with the United States Government agency charged with the administration of this section, and shall pay a registration fee which shall be prescribed by such regulations.

(II) Such brokering activities shall include the financing, transportation, freight forwarding, or taking of any other action that facilitates the manufacture, export, or import of a defense article or defense service.

(III) No person may engage in the business of brokering activities described in subclause (I) without a license, issued in accordance with this chapter, except that no license shall be required for such activities undertaken by or for an agency of the United States Government—

(aa) for use by an agency of the United States Government; or

(bb) for carrying out any foreign assistance or sales program authorized by law and subject to the control of the President by other means.

(IV) For purposes of this clause, the term "foreign defense article or defense service" includes any non-United States defense article or defense service of a nature described on the United States Munitions List regardless of whether such article or service is of United States origin or whether such article or service contains United States origin components.

(B) The prohibition under such regulations required by the second sentence of subparagraph (A) shall not extend to any military firearms (or ammunition, components, parts, accessories, and attachments for such firearms) of United States manufacture furnished to any foreign government by the United States under this chapter or any other foreign assistance or sales program of the United States if—

(i) such firearms are among those firearms that the Secretary of the Treasury is, or was at any time, required to authorize the importation of by reason of the provisions of section 925(e) of Title 18 (including the requirement for the listing of such firearms as curios or relics under section 921(a)(13) of that title); and

(ii) such foreign government certifies to the United States Government that such firearms are owned by such foreign government.

(B) <Note: two subparagraphs B were enacted> A copy of each registration made under this paragraph shall be transmitted to the Secretary of the Treasury for review regarding law enforcement concerns. The Secretary shall report to the President regarding such concerns as necessary.

(2) Except as otherwise specifically provided in regulations issued under subsection (a)(1) of this section, no defense articles or defense services designated by the President under subsection (a)(1) of this section may be exported or imported without a license for such export or import, issued in accordance with this chapter and regulations issued under this chapter, except that no license shall be required for exports or imports made by or for an agency of the United States Government

(A) for official use by a department or agency of the United States Government, or

(B) for carrying out any foreign assistance or sales program authorized by law and subject to the control of the President by other means.

(3)(A) For each of the fiscal years 1988 and 1989, $250,000 of registration fees collected pursuant to paragraph (1) shall be credited to a Department of State account, to be available without fiscal year limitation. Fees credited to that account shall be available only for the payment of expenses incurred for—

(i) contract personnel to assist in the evaluation of munitions control license applications, reduce processing time for license applications, and improve monitoring of compliance with the terms of licenses; and

(ii) the automation of munitions control functions and the processing of munitions control license applications, including the development, procurement, and utilization of computer equipment and related software.

(B) The authority of this paragraph may be exercised only to such extent or in such amounts as are provided in advance in appropriation Acts.

(c) Criminal violations; punishment

Any person who willfully violates any provision of this section or section 2779 of this title, or any rule or regulation issued under either section, or who willfully, in a registration or license application or required report, makes any untrue statement of a material fact or omits to state a material fact required to be stated therein or necessary to make the statements therein not misleading, shall upon conviction be fined for each violation not more than $1,000,000 or imprisoned not more than ten years, or both.

(d) Repealed. Pub. L. 96-70, Title III, s 3303(a)(4), Sept. 27, 1979, 93 Stat. 499

(e) Enforcement powers of President

In carrying out functions under this section with respect to the export of defense articles and defense services, the President is authorized to exercise the same powers concerning violations and enforcement which are conferred upon departments, agencies and officials by subsections (c), (d), (e), and (g) of section 11 of the Export Administration Act of 1979 <50 App. USC § 2410(c), (d), (e), and (g)>, and by subsections (a) and (c) of section 12 of such Act <50 App. USC § 2411(a) and (c)>, subject to the same terms and conditions as are applicable to such powers under such Act <50 App. USC § 2401 et seq.>, except that section 11(c)(2)(B) of such Act shall not apply, and instead, as prescribed in regulations issued under this section, the Secretary of State may assess civil penalties for violations of this chapter and regulations prescribed thereunder and further may commence a civil action to recover such civil penalties, and except further that the names of the countries and the types and quantities of defense articles for which licenses are issued under this section shall not be withheld from public disclosure unless the President determines that the release of such information would be contrary to the national interest. Nothing in this subsection shall be construed as authorizing the withholding of information from the Congress. Notwithstanding section 11(c) of the Export Administration Act of 1979 <50 App. USC § 2410(c)>, the civil penalty for each violation involving controls imposed on the export of defense articles and defense services under this section may not exceed $500,000.

(f) Periodic review of items on Munitions List

(1)The President shall periodically review the items on the United States Munitions List to determine what items, if any, no longer warrant export controls under this section. The results of such reviews shall be reported to the Speaker of the House of Representatives and to the Committee on Foreign Relations and the Committee on Banking, Housing, and Urban Affairs of the Senate. Such a report shall be submitted at least 30 days before any item is removed from the Munitions List and shall describe the nature of any controls to be imposed on that item under the Export Administration Act of 1979 <50 App. USC § 2401 et seq.>

(2) The President may not authorize an exemption for a foreign country from the licensing requirements of this chapter for the export of defense items under subsection (j) of this section or any other provision of this chapter until 30 days after the date on which the President has transmitted to the Committee on International Relations of the House of Representatives and the Committee on Foreign Relations of the Senate a notification that includes—

(A) a description of the scope of the exemption, including a detailed summary of the defense articles, defense services, and related technical data covered by the exemption; and (B) a determination by the Attorney General that the bilateral agreement concluded under subsection (j) of this section requires the compilation and maintenance of sufficient documentation relating to the export of United States defense articles, defense services, and related technical data to facilitate law enforcement efforts to detect, prevent, and prosecute criminal violations of any provision of this chapter, including the efforts on the part of countries and factions engaged in international terrorism to illicitly acquire sophisticated United States defense items.

(3) Paragraph (2) shall not apply with respect to an exemption for Canada from the licensing requirements of this chapter for the export of defense items.

(g) Identification of persons convicted or subject to indictment for violations of certain provisions

(1) The President shall develop appropriate mechanisms to identify, in connection with the export licensing process under this section—

(A) persons who are the subject of an indictment for, or have been convicted of, a violation under—

(i) this section,

(ii) section 11 of the Export Administration Act of 1979 (50 U.S.C. App. 2410),

(iii) section 793, 794, or 798 of Title 18 (relating to espionage involving defense or classified information) or section 2339A of such title (relating to providing material support to terrorists),

(iv) section 16 of the Trading with the Enemy Act (50 U.S.C. App. 16),

(v) section 206 of the International Emergency Economic Powers Act (relating to foreign assets controls; 50 U.S.C. App. 1705),

(vi) section 30A of the Securities Exchange Act of 1934 (15 U.S.C. 78dd-1) or section 104 of the Foreign Corrupt Practices Act (15 U.S.C. 78dd-2),

(vii) chapter 105 of Title 18 (relating to sabotage),

(viii) section 4(b) of the Internal Security Act of 1950 (relating to communication of classified information; 50 U.S.C. 783(b)),

(ix) section 57, 92, 101, 104, 222, 224, 225, or 226 of the Atomic Energy Act of 1954 (42 U.S.C. 2077, 2122, 2131, 2134, 2272, 2274, 2275, and 2276),

(x) section 601 of the National Security Act of 1947 (relating to intelligence identities protection; 50 U.S.C. 421), or

(xi) section 603(b) or (c) of the Comprehensive Anti-Apartheid Act of 1986 (22 U.S.C. 5113(b) and (c));

(B) persons who are the subject of an indictment or have been convicted under section 371 of Title 18 for conspiracy to violate any of the statutes cited in subparagraph (A); and

(C) persons who are ineligible—

(i) to contract with,

(ii) to receive a license or other form of authorization to export from, or

(iii) to receive a license or other form of authorization to import defense articles or defense services from, any agency of the United States Government.

(2) The President shall require that each applicant for a license to export an item on the United States Munitions List identify in the application all consignees and freight forwarders involved in the proposed export.

(3) If the President determines—

(A) that an applicant for a license to export under this section is the subject of an indictment for a violation of any of the statutes cited in paragraph (1),

(B) that there is reasonable cause to believe that an applicant for a license to export under this section has violated any of the statutes cited in paragraph (1), or

(C) that an applicant for a license to export under this section is ineligible to contract with, or to receive a license or other form of authorization to import defense articles or defense services from, any agency of the United States Government, the President may disapprove the application. The President shall consider requests by the Secretary of the Treasury to disapprove any export license application based on these criteria.

(4) A license to export an item on the United States Munitions List may not be issued to a person—

(A) if that person, or any party to the export, has been convicted of violating a statute cited in paragraph (1), or

(B) if that person, or any party to the export, is at the time of the license review ineligible to receive export licenses (or other forms of authorization to export) from any agency of the United States Government, except as may be determined on a case-by-case basis by the President, after consultation with the Secretary of the Treasury, after a thorough review of the circumstances surrounding the conviction or ineligibility to export and a finding by the President that appropriate steps have been taken to mitigate any law enforcement concerns.

(5) A license to export an item on the United States Munitions List may not be issued to a foreign person (other than a foreign government).

(6) The President may require a license (or other form of authorization) before any item on the United States Munitions List is sold or otherwise transferred to the control or possession of a foreign person or a person acting on behalf of a foreign person.

(7) The President shall, in coordination with law enforcement and national security agencies, develop standards for identifying high-risk exports for regular end-use verification. These standards shall be published in the Federal Register and the initial standards shall be published not later than October 1, 1988.

(8) Upon request of the Secretary of State, the Secretary of Defense and the Secretary of the Treasury shall detail to the office primarily responsible for export licensing functions under this section, on a nonreimbursable basis, personnel with appropriate expertise to assist in the initial screening of applications for export licenses under this section in order to determine the need for further review of those applications for foreign policy, national security, and law enforcement concerns.

(9) For purposes of this subsection—

(A) the term "foreign corporation" means a corporation that is not incorporated in the United States;

(B) the term "foreign government" includes any agency or subdivision of a foreign government, including an official mission of a foreign government;

(C) the term "foreign person" means any person who is not a citizen or national of the United States or lawfully admitted to the United States for permanent residence under the Immigration and Nationality Act <8 USC § 1101 et seq.>, and includes foreign corporations, international organizations, and foreign governments;

(D) the term "party to the export" means—

(i) the president, the chief executive officer, and other senior officers of the license applicant;

(ii) the freight forwarders or designated exporting agent of the license application; and

(iii) any consignee or end user of any item to be exported; and

(E) the term "person" means a natural person as well as a corporation, business association, partnership, society, trust, or any other entity, organization, or group, including governmental entities.

(h) Judicial review of designation of items as defense articles or services

The designation by the President (or by an official to whom the President's functions under subsection (a) of this section have been duly delegated), in regulations issued under this section, of items as defense articles or defense services for purposes of this section shall not be subject to judicial review.

(i) Report to Department of State

As prescribed in regulations issued under this section, a United States person to whom a license has been granted to export an item on the United States Munitions List shall, not later than 15 days after the item is exported, submit to the Department of State a report containing all shipment information, including a description of the item and the quantity, value, port of exit, and end-user and country of destination of the item.

(j) Requirements relating to country exemptions for licensing of defense items for export to foreign countries

(1) Requirement for bilateral agreement

(A) In general

The President may utilize the regulatory or other authority pursuant to this chapter to exempt a foreign country from the licensing requirements of this chapter with respect to exports of defense items only if the United States Government has concluded a binding bilateral agreement with the foreign country. Such agreement shall—

(i) meet the requirements set forth in paragraph (2); and

(ii) be implemented by the United States and the foreign country in a manner that is legally-binding under their domestic laws.

(B) Exception

The requirement to conclude a bilateral agreement in accordance with subparagraph (A) shall not apply with respect to an exemption for Canada from the licensing requirements of this chapter for the export of defense items.

(2) Requirements of bilateral agreement

A bilateral agreement referred to in paragraph (1)—

(A) shall, at a minimum, require the foreign country, as necessary, to revise its policies and practices, and promulgate or enact necessary modifications to its laws and regulations to establish an export control regime that is at least comparable to United States law, regulation, and policy requiring—

(i) conditions on the handling of all United States-origin defense items exported to the foreign country, including prior written United States Government approval for any reexports to third countries;

(ii) end-use and retransfer control commitments, including securing binding end-use and retransfer control commitments from all end-users, including such documentation as is needed in order to ensure compliance and enforcement, with respect to such United States-origin defense items;

(iii) establishment of a procedure comparable to a "watchlist" (if such a watchlist does not exist) and full cooperation with United States Government law enforcement agencies to allow for sharing of export and import documentation and background information on foreign businesses and individuals employed by or otherwise connected to those businesses; and

(iv) establishment of a list of controlled defense items to ensure coverage of those items to be exported under the exemption; and

(B) should, at a minimum, require the foreign country, as necessary, to revise its policies and practices, and promulgate or enact necessary modifications to its laws and regulations to establish an export control regime that is at least comparable to United States law, regulation, and policy regarding—

(i) controls on the export of tangible or intangible technology, including via fax, phone, and electronic media;

(ii) appropriate controls on unclassified information relating to defense items exported to foreign nationals;

(iii) controls on international arms trafficking and brokering;

(iv) cooperation with United States Government agencies, including intelligence agencies, to combat efforts by third countries to acquire defense items, the export of which to such countries would not be authorized pursuant to the export control regimes of the foreign country and the United States; and

(v) violations of export control laws, and penalties for such violations.

(3) Advance certification

Not less than 30 days before authorizing an exemption for a foreign country from the licensing requirements of this chapter for the export of defense items, the President shall transmit to the Committee on International Relations of the House of Representatives and the Committee on Foreign Relations of the Senate a certification that—

(A) the United States has entered into a bilateral agreement with that foreign country satisfying all requirements set forth in paragraph (2);

(B) the foreign country has promulgated or enacted all necessary modifications to its laws and regulations to comply with its obligations under the bilateral agreement with the United States; and

(C) the appropriate congressional committees will continue to receive notifications pursuant to the authorities, procedures, and practices of section 2776 of this title for defense exports to a foreign country to which that section would apply and without regard to any form of defense export licensing exemption otherwise available for that country.

(4) Definitions.—In this section:

(A) Defense items

The term "defense items" means defense articles, defense services, and related technical data.

(B) Appropriate congressional committees

The term "appropriate congressional committees" means—

(i) the Committee on International Relations and the Committee on Appropriations of the House of Representatives; and
(ii) the Committee on Foreign Relations and the Committee on Appropriations of the Senate.

June 30, 1976 (3,724)
TITLE 22. FOREIGN RELATIONS AND INTERCOURSE • CHAPTER 39: ARMS EXPORT CONTROL • SUBCHAPTER III: MILITARY EXPORT CONTROLS

22 USC § 5512. Antiterrorism measures

> The Gist: Congress encourages the Transportation Dept. to use and train other government agencies, which have duties related to international airports, in detecting firearms that could threaten international air travel.

(d) Sense of Congress
It is the sense of Congress that the Secretary of Transportation should take appropriate measures to utilize and train properly the officers and employees of other United States Government agencies who have functions at international airports in the United States and abroad in the detection of explosives and firearms which could be a threat to international civil aviation.

Nov. 16, 1990 (62)
TITLE 22. FOREIGN RELATIONS AND INTERCOURSE • CHAPTER 64: UNITED STATES RESPONSE TO TERRORISM AFFECTING AMERICANS ABROAD

Title 25 • Indians

25 USC § 1771c. Conditions precedent to Federal purchase of settlement lands

> **The Gist:** As part of a land settlement with the Wampanoag Indians, Massachusetts must grant authority to the Wampanoag Tribal Council of Gay Head, Inc., to regulate hunting by Indians on settlement lands, by means other than firearms and crossbow.

(a) Initial determination of State and local action

No action shall be taken by the Secretary under section 1771d of this title before the Secretary publishes notice in the Federal Register of the determination by the Secretary that—

(1) the Commonwealth of Massachusetts has enacted legislation which provides that—

(A) the town of Gay Head, Massachusetts, is authorized to convey to the Secretary to be held in trust for the Wampanoag Tribal Council of Gay Head, Inc. the public settlement lands and the Cook lands subject to the conditions and limitations set forth in the Settlement Agreement; and

(B) the Wampanoag Tribal Council of Gay Head, Inc. shall have the authority, after consultation with appropriate State and local officials, to regulate any hunting by Indians on the settlement lands that is conducted by means other than firearms or crossbow to the extent provided in, and subject to the conditions and limitations set forth in, the Settlement Agreement;

(2) the Wampanoag Tribal Council of Gay Head, Inc., has submitted to the Secretary an executed waiver or waivers of the claims covered by the Settlement Agreement all claims extinguished by this subchapter, and all claims arising because of the approval of transfers and extinguishment of titles and claims under this subchapter, and

(3) the town of Gay Head, Massachusetts, has authorized the conveyance of the public settlement lands and the Cook Lands to the Secretary in trust for the Wampanoag Tribal Council of Gay Head, Inc.

(b) Reliance upon the Attorney General of Massachusetts

In making the findings required in subsection (a) of this section, the Secretary may rely upon the opinion of the Attorney General of the Commonwealth of Massachusetts.

Aug. 18, 1987 (279)

TITLE 25. INDIANS • CHAPTER 19: INDIAN LAND CLAIMS SETTLEMENTS • SUBCHAPTER V: MASSACHUSETTS INDIAN LAND CLAIMS SETTLEMENT

25 USC § 2803. Law enforcement authority

> The Gist: Employees of the Bureau of Indian Affairs of the Dept. of the Interior may be authorized to carry firearms.

The Secretary may charge employees of the Bureau with law enforcement responsibilities and may authorize those employees to—
(1) carry firearms

Aug. 18, 1990 (21)
TITLE 25. INDIANS • CHAPTER 30: INDIAN LAW ENFORCEMENT REFORM

Title 26 • Internal Revenue Code

26 USC § 4181. Imposition of tax

> The Gist: The sale of all firearms and ammunition, by the manufacturer or importer, is taxed.

Imposition of tax
There is hereby imposed upon the sale by the manufacturer, producer, or importer of the following articles a tax equivalent to the specified percent of the price for which so sold:
Articles taxable at 10 percent—
Pistols.
Revolvers.
Articles taxable at 11 percent—
Firearms (other than pistols and revolvers).
Shells, and cartridges.

Aug. 16, 1954 (55)
TITLE 26. INTERNAL REVENUE CODE • SUBTITLE D: MISCELLANEOUS EXCISE TAXES • CHAPTER 32: MANUFACTURERS EXCISE TAX • SUBCHAPTER D: RECREATIONAL EQUIPMENT • PART III: FIREARMS

26 USC § 4182. Exemptions

> The Gist: The tax established in 26–4181 doesn't apply to firearms taxed under 26–5811. Firearms purchased by the military are not taxed. With certain exceptions, federally licensed firearms dealers can't be required to collect names and other information about people buying long gun ammunition or ammunition parts.

(a) Machine guns and short barrelled firearms.
The tax imposed by section 4181 shall not apply to any firearm on which the tax provided by section 5811 has been paid.
(b) Sales to Defense Department.
No firearms, pistols, revolvers, shells, and cartridges purchased with funds appropriated for the military department shall be subject to any tax imposed on the sale or transfer of such articles.
(c) Records.
Notwithstanding the provisions of sections 922(b)(5) and 923(g) of title 18, United States Code, no person holding a Federal license under chapter 44 of title 18, United States Code, shall be required to record the name, address, or other information about the purchaser of shotgun ammunition, ammunition suitable for use only in rifles generally available in commerce, or component parts for the aforesaid types of ammunition.

Aug. 16, 1954 (136)
TITLE 26. INTERNAL REVENUE CODE • SUBTITLE D: MISCELLANEOUS EXCISE TAXES • CHAPTER 32: MANUFACTURERS EXCISE TAX • SUBCHAPTER D: RECREATIONAL EQUIPMENT • PART III: FIREARMS

26 USC § 5685. Penalty and forfeiture relating to possession of devices for emitting gas, smoke, etc., explosives and firearms, when violating liquor laws

> The Gist: Special penalties are defined for possession of firearms while committing crimes involving alcohol bootlegging. Increased penalties are provided if the firearm is a machinegun, a sawed-off rifle or a sawed-off shotgun. Firearms so used are forfeited.

(a) Penalty for possession of devices for emitting gas, smoke, etc.—Whoever, when violating any law of the United States, or of any possession of the United States, or of the District of Columbia, in regard to the manufacture, taxation, or transportation of or traffic in distilled spirits, wines, or beer, or when aiding in any such violation, has in his possession or in his control any device capable of causing emission of gas, smoke, or fumes, and which may be used for the purpose of hindering, delaying, or preventing pursuit or capture, any explosive, or any firearm (as defined in section 5845), except a machine gun, or a shotgun having a barrel or barrels less than 18 inches in length, or a rifle having a barrel or barrels less than 16 inches in length, shall be fined not more than $5,000, or imprisoned not more than 10 years, or both, and all persons engaged in any such violation or in aiding in any such violation shall be held to be in possession or control of such device, firearm, or explosive.

(b) Penalty for possession of machine gun, etc.—Whoever, when violating any such law, has in his possession or in his control a machine gun, or any shotgun having a barrel or barrels less than 18 inches in length, or a rifle having a barrel or barrels less than 16 inches in length, shall be imprisoned not more than 20 years; and all persons engaged in any such violation or in aiding in any such violation shall be held to be in possession and control of such machine gun, shotgun, or rifle.

(c) Forfeiture of firearms, devices, etc.—Every such firearm or device for emitting gas, smoke, or fumes, and every such explosive, machine gun, shotgun, or rifle, in the possession or control of any person when violating any such law, shall be seized and shall be forfeited and disposed of in the manner provided by section 5872.

(d) Definition of machine gun.—As used in this section, the term "machine gun" means a machinegun as defined in section 5845(b).

Sept. 2, 1958 (353)

TITLE 26. INTERNAL REVENUE CODE • SUBTITLE E: ALCOHOL, TOBACCO, AND CERTAIN OTHER EXCISE TAXES • CHAPTER 51: DISTILLED SPIRITS, WINES, AND BEER • SUBCHAPTER J: PENALTIES, SEIZURES, AND FORFEITURES RELATING TO LIQUORS • PART IV: PENALTY, SEIZURE, AND FORFEITURE PROVISIONS COMMON TO LIQUORS

Introduction to the laws of the National Firearms Act

The laws that follow, from 26–5801 through 26–5872, apply to a special category of firearms often called National Firearms Act (NFA) weapons. The situation for NFA weapons is substantially different from that of other firearms, and the two should not be confused. In these sections, the word *firearm* means machine gun, silencer, short-barreled shotgun or rifle, and other specific weapons defined in 26–5845(a). The NFA, originally passed in 1934, was a response to gangster violence during the prohibition era, and sought to control certain types of weapons through tax regulation. It was substantially amended in 1968 to include explosives and incorporate other statutes. For clarity, the *Gist* information uses the phrase *NFA weapon* instead of firearm, and the term *licensee* refers to federally licensed firearms manufacturers, importers or dealers.

26 USC § 5801. Imposition of tax

> The Gist: NFA-weapon licensees must pay an annual tax. Smaller licensees pay a reduced tax.

(a) General rule.—On 1st engaging in business and thereafter on or before July 1 of each year, every importer, manufacturer, and dealer in firearms shall pay a special (occupational) tax for each place of business at the following rates:
(1) Importers and manufacturers: $1,000 a year or fraction thereof.
(2) Dealers: $500 a year or fraction thereof.
(b) Reduced rates of tax for small importers and manufacturers.—
(1) In general.—Paragraph (1) of subsection (a) shall be applied by substituting "$500" for "$1,000" with respect to any taxpayer the gross receipts of which (for the most recent taxable year ending before the 1st day of the taxable period to which the tax imposed by subsection (a) relates) are less than $500,000.
(2) Controlled group rules.—All persons treated as 1 taxpayer under section 5061(e)(3) shall be treated as 1 taxpayer for purposes of paragraph (1).
(3) Certain rules to apply.—For purposes of paragraph (1), rules similar to the rules of subparagraphs (B) and (C) of section 448(c)(3) shall apply.

Oct. 22, 1968 (178)

TITLE 26. INTERNAL REVENUE CODE • SUBTITLE E: ALCOHOL, TOBACCO, AND CERTAIN OTHER EXCISE TAXES • CHAPTER 53: MACHINE GUNS, DESTRUCTIVE DEVICES, AND CERTAIN OTHER FIREARMS • SUBCHAPTER A: TAXES • PART I: SPECIAL (OCCUPATIONAL) TAXES

26 USC § 5802. Registration of importers, manufacturers, and dealers

> The Gist: Anyone dealing, manufacturing or importing NFA weapons must first register with the Treasury Dept.

On first engaging in business and thereafter on or before the first day of July of each year, each importer, manufacturer, and dealer in firearms shall register with the Secretary in each internal revenue district in which such business is to be carried on, his name, including any trade name, and the address of each location in the district where he will conduct such business. An individual required to register under this section shall include a photograph and fingerprints of the individual with the initial application. Where there is a change during the taxable year in the location of, or the trade name used in, such business, the importer, manufacturer, or dealer shall file an application with the Secretary to amend his registration. Firearms operations of an importer, manufacturer, or dealer may not be commenced at the new location or under a new trade name prior to approval by the Secretary of the application.

Oct. 22, 1968 (154)
TITLE 26. INTERNAL REVENUE CODE • SUBTITLE E: ALCOHOL, TOBACCO, AND CERTAIN OTHER EXCISE TAXES • CHAPTER 53: MACHINE GUNS, DESTRUCTIVE DEVICES, AND CERTAIN OTHER FIREARMS • SUBCHAPTER A: TAXES • PART I: SPECIAL (OCCUPATIONAL) TAXES

26 USC § 5811. Transfer tax

> The Gist: The person transferring an NFA weapon or other weapon specified in 26–5845(e) must pay a tax.

(a) Rate.—There shall be levied, collected, and paid on firearms transferred a tax at the rate of $200 for each firearm transferred, except, the transfer tax on any firearm classified as any other weapon under section 5845(e) shall be at the rate of $5 for each such firearm transferred.
(b) By whom paid.—The tax imposed by subsection (a) of this section shall be paid by the transferor.
(c) Payment.—The tax imposed by subsection (a) of this section shall be payable by the appropriate stamps prescribed for payment by the Secretary.

Oct. 22, 1968 (94)
TITLE 26. INTERNAL REVENUE CODE • SUBTITLE E: ALCOHOL, TOBACCO, AND CERTAIN OTHER EXCISE TAXES • CHAPTER 53: MACHINE GUNS, DESTRUCTIVE DEVICES, AND CERTAIN OTHER FIREARMS • SUBCHAPTER A: TAXES • PART II: TAX ON TRANSFERRING FIREARMS

26 USC § 5812. Transfers

> The Gist: An NFA weapon may not be transferred unless: 1–the person making the transfer applies in writing on forms approved by the Treasury Dept.; 2–the proper tax stamp is affixed to the form; 3–the person receiving the NFA weapon is identified, along with fingerprints and photograph; 4–the NFA weapon is identified as required by the Treasury Dept.; and 5–the Treasury Dept. approves the transfer. The transfer may not legally take place without Treasury Dept. approval, and the transfer may not take place if the person receiving the NFA weapon would be breaking the law by receiving it.

(a) Application.—A firearm shall not be transferred unless

(1) the transferor of the firearm has filed with the Secretary a written application, in duplicate, for the transfer and registration of the firearm to the transferee on the application form prescribed by the Secretary;

(2) any tax payable on the transfer is paid as evidenced by the proper stamp affixed to the original application form;

(3) the transferee is identified in the application form in such manner as the Secretary may by regulations prescribe, except that, if such person is an individual, the identification must include his fingerprints and his photograph;

(4) the transferor of the firearm is identified in the application form in such manner as the Secretary may by regulations prescribe;

(5) the firearm is identified in the application form in such manner as the Secretary may by regulations prescribe; and

(6) the application form shows that the Secretary has approved the transfer and the registration of the firearm to the transferee. Applications shall be denied if the transfer, receipt, or possession of the firearm would place the transferee in violation of law.

(b) Transfer of possession.—The transferee of a firearm shall not take possession of the firearm unless the Secretary has approved the transfer and registration of the firearm to the transferee as required by subsection (a) of this section.

Oct. 22, 1968 (224)

TITLE 26. INTERNAL REVENUE CODE • SUBTITLE E: ALCOHOL, TOBACCO, AND CERTAIN OTHER EXCISE TAXES • CHAPTER 53: MACHINE GUNS, DESTRUCTIVE DEVICES, AND CERTAIN OTHER FIREARMS • SUBCHAPTER A: TAXES • PART II: TAX ON TRANSFERRING FIREARMS

26 USC § 5821. Making tax

The Gist: A person making an NFA weapon must pay a $200 tax for every one made.

(a) Rate.—There shall be levied, collected, and paid upon the making of a firearm a tax at the rate of $200 for each firearm made.

(b) By whom paid.—The tax imposed by subsection (a) of this section shall be paid by the person making the firearm.

(c) Payment.—The tax imposed by subsection (a) of this section shall be payable by the stamp prescribed for payment by the Secretary.

Oct. 22, 1968 (71)

TITLE 26. INTERNAL REVENUE CODE • SUBTITLE E: ALCOHOL, TOBACCO, AND CERTAIN OTHER EXCISE TAXES • CHAPTER 53: MACHINE GUNS, DESTRUCTIVE DEVICES, AND CERTAIN OTHER FIREARMS • SUBCHAPTER A: TAXES • PART III: TAX ON MAKING FIREARMS

26 USC § 5822. Making <this is the full section name >

The Gist: A person cannot legally make an NFA weapon without first registering with the Treasury Dept., paying any required tax, identifying themselves and the weapon, and obtaining approval from the Treasury Dept. before proceeding. An application must be denied if possession of the weapon by the applicant would be illegal.

No person shall make a firearm unless he has

(a) filed with the Secretary a written application, in duplicate, to make and register the firearm on the form prescribed by the Secretary;

(b) paid any tax payable on the making and such payment is evidenced by the proper stamp affixed to the original application form;

(c) identified the firearm to be made in the application form in such manner as the Secretary may by regulations prescribe;

(d) identified himself in the application form in such manner as the Secretary may by regulations prescribe, except that, if such person is an individual, the identification must include his fingerprints and his photograph; and

(e) obtained the approval of the Secretary to make and register the firearm and the application form shows such approval. Applications shall be denied if the making or possession of the firearm would place the person making the firearm in violation of law.

Oct. 22, 1968 (154)
TITLE 26. INTERNAL REVENUE CODE • SUBTITLE E: ALCOHOL, TOBACCO, AND CERTAIN OTHER EXCISE TAXES • CHAPTER 53: MACHINE GUNS, DESTRUCTIVE DEVICES, AND CERTAIN OTHER FIREARMS • SUBCHAPTER A: TAXES • PART III: TAX ON MAKING FIREARMS

26 USC § 5841. Registration of firearms

> The Gist: This section establishes the National Firearms Registration and Transfer Record, maintained by the Treasury Dept. The NFRTR tracks every NFA weapon and its owner, and is updated every time an NFA weapon is transferred. The Treasury Dept. must approve every transfer of a weapon on the NFRTR. Weapons legally owned on the effective date of this act were deemed to be registered automatically. Owners must keep proof that an NFA weapon is registered to them (the registration papers serve this purpose).

(a) Central registry.—The Secretary shall maintain a central registry of all firearms in the United States which are not in the possession or under the control of the United States. This registry shall be known as the National Firearms Registration and Transfer Record. The registry shall include—

(1) identification of the firearm;

(2) date of registration; and

(3) identification and address of person entitled to possession of the firearm.

(b) By whom registered.—Each manufacturer, importer, and maker shall register each firearm he manufactures, imports, or makes. Each firearm transferred shall be registered to the transferee by the transferor.

(c) How registered.—Each manufacturer shall notify the Secretary of the manufacture of a firearm in such manner as may by regulations be prescribed and such notification shall effect the registration of the firearm required by this section. Each importer, maker, and transferor of a firearm shall, prior to importing, making, or transferring a firearm, obtain authorization in such manner as required by this chapter or regulations issued thereunder to import, make, or transfer the firearm, and such authorization shall effect the registration of the firearm required by this section.

(d) Firearms registered on effective date of this act.—A person shown as possessing a firearm by the records maintained by the Secretary pursuant to the National Firearms Act in force on the day immediately prior to the effective date of the National Firearms Act of 1968 shall be considered to have registered under this section the firearms in his possession which are disclosed by that record as being in his possession.

(e) Proof of registration.—A person possessing a firearm registered as required by this section shall retain proof of registration which shall be made available to the Secretary upon request.

Oct. 22, 1968 (292)
TITLE 26. INTERNAL REVENUE CODE • SUBTITLE E: ALCOHOL, TOBACCO, AND CERTAIN OTHER EXCISE TAXES • CHAPTER 53: MACHINE GUNS, DESTRUCTIVE DEVICES, AND CERTAIN OTHER FIREARMS • SUBCHAPTER B: GENERAL PROVISIONS AND EXEMPTIONS • PART I: GENERAL PROVISIONS

26 USC § 5842. Identification of firearms

> **The Gist:** All NFA weapons or destructive devices made or imported must have identifying markings. A person who has a firearm with no ID number must obtain an ID number for the firearm from the Treasury Dept. The Treasury Dept. decides how destructive devices must be labeled.

(a) Identification of firearms other than destructive devices.—Each manufacturer and importer and anyone making a firearm shall identify each firearm, other than a destructive device, manufactured, imported, or made by a serial number which may not be readily removed, obliterated, or altered, the name of the manufacturer, importer, or maker, and such other identification as the Secretary may by regulations prescribe.

(b) Firearms without serial number.—Any person who possesses a firearm, other than a destructive device, which does not bear the serial number and other information required by subsection (a) of this section shall identify the firearm with a serial number assigned by the Secretary and any other information the Secretary may by regulations prescribe.

(c) Identification of destructive device.—Any firearm classified as a destructive device shall be identified in such manner as the Secretary may by regulations prescribe.

Oct. 22, 1968 (142)

TITLE 26. INTERNAL REVENUE CODE • SUBTITLE E: ALCOHOL, TOBACCO, AND CERTAIN OTHER EXCISE TAXES • CHAPTER 53: MACHINE GUNS, DESTRUCTIVE DEVICES, AND CERTAIN OTHER FIREARMS • SUBCHAPTER B: GENERAL PROVISIONS AND EXEMPTIONS • PART I: GENERAL PROVISIONS

26 USC § 5843. Records and returns

> **The Gist:** Licensees must keep records and make reports, as determined by the Treasury Dept., of all NFA weapons made, imported or sold.

Importers, manufacturers, and dealers shall keep such records of, and render such returns in relation to, the importation, manufacture, making, receipt, and sale, or other disposition, of firearms as the Secretary may by regulations prescribe.

Oct. 22, 1968 (35)

TITLE 26. INTERNAL REVENUE CODE • SUBTITLE E: ALCOHOL, TOBACCO, AND CERTAIN OTHER EXCISE TAXES • CHAPTER 53: MACHINE GUNS, DESTRUCTIVE DEVICES, AND CERTAIN OTHER FIREARMS • SUBCHAPTER B: GENERAL PROVISIONS AND EXEMPTIONS • PART I: GENERAL PROVISIONS

26 USC § 5844. Importation

> **The Gist:** No NFA weapon may be imported into the United States unless it is specifically for the proper authorities, for science or research, for testing, or for use as a sample.

No firearm shall be imported or brought into the United States or any territory under its control or jurisdiction unless the importer establishes, under regulations as may be prescribed by the Secretary, that the firearm to be imported or brought in is—

(1) being imported or brought in for the use of the United States or any department, independent establishment, or agency thereof or any State or possession or any political subdivision thereof; or

(2) being imported or brought in for scientific or research purposes; or

(3) being imported or brought in solely for testing or use as a model by a registered manufacturer or solely for use as a sample by a registered importer or registered

dealer; except that, the Secretary may permit the conditional importation or bringing in of a firearm for examination and testing in connection with classifying the firearm.

Oct. 22, 1968 (143)
TITLE 26. INTERNAL REVENUE CODE • SUBTITLE E: ALCOHOL, TOBACCO, AND CERTAIN OTHER EXCISE TAXES • CHAPTER 53: MACHINE GUNS, DESTRUCTIVE DEVICES, AND CERTAIN OTHER FIREARMS • SUBCHAPTER B: GENERAL PROVISIONS AND EXEMPTIONS • PART I: GENERAL PROVISIONS

26 USC § 5845. Definitions

The Gist: Definitions are provided for this chapter (Chapter 53) only. It is important to remember that definitions, when provided, only relate to the specific portions of the law that are noted. It is possible to find examples of words which have different legal meanings, depending on where they are used, and this chapter is a perfect example. In this chapter, the word *firearm* only refers to so-called NFA weapons—machine guns, short-barreled rifles or shotguns, silencers and other strictly controlled weapons. In most other uses, *firearm* refers to any weapon designed to expel a projectile by means of an explosive, and includes most regular handguns and long guns.

For the purpose of this chapter—
(a) **Firearm**.—The term "firearm" means
(1) a shotgun having a barrel or barrels of less than 18 inches in length;
(2) a weapon made from a shotgun if such weapon as modified has an overall length of less than 26 inches or a barrel or barrels of less than 18 inches in length;
(3) a rifle having a barrel or barrels of less than 16 inches in length;
(4) a weapon made from a rifle if such weapon as modified has an overall length of less than 26 inches or a barrel or barrels of less than 16 inches in length;
(5) any other weapon, as defined in subsection (e);
(6) a machinegun;
(7) any silencer (as defined in section 921 of title 18, United States Code); and
(8) a destructive device. The term **"firearm"** shall not include an antique firearm or any device (other than a machinegun or destructive device) which, although designed as a weapon, the Secretary finds by reason of the date of its manufacture, value, design, and other characteristics is primarily a collector's item and is not likely to be used as a weapon.
(b) **Machinegun**.—The term "machinegun" means any weapon which shoots, is designed to shoot, or can be readily restored to shoot, automatically more than one shot, without manual reloading, by a single function of the trigger. The term shall also include the frame or receiver of any such weapon, any part designed and intended solely and exclusively, or combination of parts designed and intended, for use in converting a weapon into a machinegun, and any combination of parts from which a machinegun can be assembled if such parts are in the possession or under the control of a person.
(c) **Rifle**.—The term "rifle" means a weapon designed or redesigned, made or remade, and intended to be fired from the shoulder and designed or redesigned and made or remade to use the energy of the explosive in a fixed cartridge to fire only a single projectile through a rifled bore for each single pull of the trigger, and shall include any such weapon which may be readily restored to fire a fixed cartridge.
(d) **Shotgun**.—The term "shotgun" means a weapon designed or redesigned, made or remade, and intended to be fired from the shoulder and designed or redesigned and made or remade to use the energy of the explosive in a fixed shotgun shell to fire through a smooth bore either a number of projectiles (ball shot) or a single projectile for each pull of the trigger, and shall include any such weapon which may be readily restored to fire a fixed shotgun shell.

(e) **Any other weapon.**—The term "any other weapon" means any weapon or device capable of being concealed on the person from which a shot can be discharged through the energy of an explosive, a pistol or revolver having a barrel with a smooth bore designed or redesigned to fire a fixed shotgun shell, weapons with combination shotgun and rifle barrels 12 inches or more, less than 18 inches in length, from which only a single discharge can be made from either barrel without manual reloading, and shall include any such weapon which may be readily restored to fire. Such term shall not include a pistol or a revolver having a rifled bore, or rifled bores, or weapons designed, made, or intended to be fired from the shoulder and not capable of firing fixed ammunition.

(f) **Destructive device.**—The term "destructive device" means

(1) any explosive, incendiary, or poison gas

(A) bomb,

(B) grenade,

(C) rocket having a propellent charge of more than four ounces,

(D) missile having an explosive or incendiary charge of more than one-quarter ounce,

(E) mine, or

(F) similar device;

(2) any type of weapon by whatever name known which will, or which may be readily converted to, expel a projectile by the action of an explosive or other propellant, the barrel or barrels of which have a bore of more than one- half inch in diameter, except a shotgun or shotgun shell which the Secretary finds is generally recognized as particularly suitable for sporting purposes; and

(3) any combination of parts either designed or intended for use in converting any device into a destructive device as defined in subparagraphs (1) and (2) and from which a destructive device may be readily assembled. The term "**destructive device**" shall not include any device which is neither designed nor redesigned for use as a weapon; any device, although originally designed for use as a weapon, which is redesigned for use as a signaling, pyrotechnic, line throwing, safety, or similar device; surplus ordnance sold, loaned, or given by the Secretary of the Army pursuant to the provisions of section 4684(2), 4685, or 4686 of title 10 of the United States Code; or any other device which the Secretary finds is not likely to be used as a weapon, or is an antique or is a rifle which the owner intends to use solely for sporting purposes.

(g) **Antique firearm.**—The term "antique firearm" means any firearm not designed or redesigned for using rim fire or conventional center fire ignition with fixed ammunition and manufactured in or before 1898 (including any matchlock, flintlock, percussion cap, or similar type of ignition system or replica thereof, whether actually manufactured before or after the year 1898) and also any firearm using fixed ammunition manufactured in or before 1898, for which ammunition is no longer manufactured in the United States and is not readily available in the ordinary channels of commercial trade.

(h) **Unserviceable firearm.**—The term "unserviceable firearm" means a firearm which is incapable of discharging a shot by means of an explosive and incapable of being readily restored to a firing condition.

(i) **Make.**—The term "make", and the various derivatives of such word, shall include manufacturing (other than by one qualified to engage in such business under this chapter), putting together, altering, any combination of these, or otherwise producing a firearm.

(j) **Transfer.**—The term "transfer" and the various derivatives of such word, shall include selling, assigning, pledging, leasing, loaning, giving away, or otherwise disposing of.

(k) **Dealer.**—The term "dealer" means any person, not a manufacturer or importer, engaged in the business of selling, renting, leasing, or loaning firearms and shall include pawnbrokers who accept firearms as collateral for loans.

(l) **Importer.**—The term "importer" means any person who is engaged in the business of importing or bringing firearms into the United States.

(m) **Manufacturer.**—The term "manufacturer" means any person who is engaged in the business of manufacturing firearms.

Oct. 22, 1968 (1,112)
TITLE 26. INTERNAL REVENUE CODE • SUBTITLE E: ALCOHOL, TOBACCO, AND CERTAIN OTHER EXCISE TAXES • CHAPTER 53: MACHINE GUNS, DESTRUCTIVE DEVICES, AND CERTAIN OTHER FIREARMS • SUBCHAPTER B: GENERAL PROVISIONS AND EXEMPTIONS • PART I: GENERAL PROVISIONS

26 USC § 5846. Other laws applicable

The Gist: The special taxes imposed by Chapter 51 (on alcoholic beverages) that are inconsistent with this chapter (Chapter 53) do not apply to NFA weapons.

All provisions of law relating to special taxes imposed by chapter 51 and to engraving, issuance, sale, accountability, cancellation, and distribution of stamps for tax payment shall, insofar as not inconsistent with the provisions of this chapter, be applicable with respect to the taxes imposed by sections 5801, 5811, and 5821.

Oct. 22, 1968 (51)
TITLE 26. INTERNAL REVENUE CODE • SUBTITLE E: ALCOHOL, TOBACCO, AND CERTAIN OTHER EXCISE TAXES • CHAPTER 53: MACHINE GUNS, DESTRUCTIVE DEVICES, AND CERTAIN OTHER FIREARMS • SUBCHAPTER B: GENERAL PROVISIONS AND EXEMPTIONS • PART I: GENERAL PROVISIONS

26 USC § 5847. Effect on other laws

The Gist: The laws of this chapter (Chapter 53) do not affect the rules about importing and exporting goods and services on the United States Munitions List, as described in 22-2778.

Nothing in this chapter shall be construed as modifying or affecting the requirements of section 414 of the Mutual Security Act of 1954, as amended, <now, 22 USC § 2778> with respect to the manufacture, exportation, and importation of arms, ammunition, and implements of war.

Oct. 22, 1968 (44)
TITLE 26. INTERNAL REVENUE CODE • SUBTITLE E: ALCOHOL, TOBACCO, AND CERTAIN OTHER EXCISE TAXES • CHAPTER 53: MACHINE GUNS, DESTRUCTIVE DEVICES, AND CERTAIN OTHER FIREARMS • SUBCHAPTER B: GENERAL PROVISIONS AND EXEMPTIONS • PART I: GENERAL PROVISIONS

26 USC § 5848. Restrictive use of information

The Gist: The information a person is required to provide under this chapter (Chapter 53) may not be used to violate the 5th Amendment Constitutional right against self-incrimination. However, providing false information remains a crime.

(a) General rule.—No information or evidence obtained from an application, registration, or records required to be submitted or retained by a natural person in order to comply with any provision of this chapter or regulations issued thereunder, shall, except as provided in subsection (b) of this section, be used, directly or indirectly, as evidence against that person in a criminal proceeding with respect to a violation of law occurring prior to or concurrently with the filing of the application or registration, or the compiling of the records containing the information or evidence.
(b) Furnishing false information.—Subsection (a) of this section shall not preclude the use of any such information or evidence in a prosecution or other action under any applicable provision of law with respect to the furnishing of false information.

Oct. 22, 1968 (133)
TITLE 26. INTERNAL REVENUE CODE • SUBTITLE E: ALCOHOL, TOBACCO, AND CERTAIN OTHER EXCISE TAXES • CHAPTER 53: MACHINE GUNS, DESTRUCTIVE DEVICES, AND CERTAIN OTHER FIREARMS • SUBCHAPTER B: GENERAL PROVISIONS AND EXEMPTIONS • PART I: GENERAL PROVISIONS

26 USC § 5849. Citation of chapter

The Gist: This chapter (Chapter 53) is officially designated The National Firearms Act.

This chapter may be cited as the "National Firearms Act" and any reference in any other provision of law to the "National Firearms Act" shall be held to refer to the provisions of this chapter.
Oct. 22, 1968 (35)

TITLE 26. INTERNAL REVENUE CODE • SUBTITLE E: ALCOHOL, TOBACCO, AND CERTAIN OTHER EXCISE TAXES • CHAPTER 53: MACHINE GUNS, DESTRUCTIVE DEVICES, AND CERTAIN OTHER FIREARMS • SUBCHAPTER B: GENERAL PROVISIONS AND EXEMPTIONS • PART I: GENERAL PROVISIONS

26 USC § 5851. Special (occupational) tax exemption

The Gist: The Treasury Dept. may exclude a person from certain taxes related to firearms, or from any provisions of this chapter, if they determine that all the person's business is conducted with the proper authorities. Application for such an exemption is made on forms provided by the Treasury Dept., and must be renewed annually.

(a) Business with United States.—Any person required to pay special (occupational) tax under section 5801 shall be relieved from payment of that tax if he establishes to the satisfaction of the Secretary that his business is conducted exclusively with, or on behalf of, the United States or any department, independent establishment, or agency thereof. The Secretary may relieve any person manufacturing firearms for, or on behalf of, the United States from compliance with any provision of this chapter in the conduct of such business.

(b) Application.—The exemption provided for in subsection (a) of this section may be obtained by filing with the Secretary an application on such form and containing such information as may by regulations be prescribed. The exemptions must thereafter be renewed on or before July 1 of each year. Approval of the application by the Secretary shall entitle the applicant to the exemptions stated on the approved application.
Oct. 22, 1968 (153)

TITLE 26. INTERNAL REVENUE CODE • SUBTITLE E: ALCOHOL, TOBACCO, AND CERTAIN OTHER EXCISE TAXES • CHAPTER 53: MACHINE GUNS, DESTRUCTIVE DEVICES, AND CERTAIN OTHER FIREARMS • SUBCHAPTER B: GENERAL PROVISIONS AND EXEMPTIONS • PART II: EXEMPTIONS

26 USC § 5852. General transfer and making tax exemption

The Gist: Transfer and manufacturing taxes are waived for NFA weapons made for the Army or proper authorities. Transfer taxes do not apply to NFA weapons transferred between licensees. An NFA weapon which is unserviceable may be transferred without tax. The Treasury Department must approve all such transactions.

(a) Transfer.—Any firearm may be transferred to the United States or any department, independent establishment, or agency thereof, without payment of the transfer tax imposed by section 5811.

(b) Making by a person other than a qualified manufacturer.—Any firearm may be made by, or on behalf of, the United States, or any department, independent establishment, or agency thereof, without payment of the making tax imposed by section 5821.

(c) Making by a qualified manufacturer.—A manufacturer qualified under this chapter to engage in such business may make the type of firearm which he is qualified to manufacture without payment of the making tax imposed by section 5821.

(d) Transfers between special (occupational) taxpayers.—A firearm registered to a person qualified under this chapter to engage in business as an importer, manufacturer, or dealer may be transferred by that person without payment of the transfer tax imposed by section 5811 to any other person qualified under this chapter to manufacture, import, or deal in that type of firearm.

(e) Unserviceable firearm.—An unserviceable firearm may be transferred as a curio or ornament without payment of the transfer tax imposed by section 5811, under such requirements as the Secretary may by regulations prescribe.

(f) Right to exemption.—No firearm may be transferred or made exempt from tax under the provisions of this section unless the transfer or making is performed pursuant to an application in such form and manner as the Secretary may by regulations prescribe.

Oct. 22, 1968 (246)
TITLE 26. INTERNAL REVENUE CODE • SUBTITLE E: ALCOHOL, TOBACCO, AND CERTAIN OTHER EXCISE TAXES • CHAPTER 53: MACHINE GUNS, DESTRUCTIVE DEVICES, AND CERTAIN OTHER FIREARMS • SUBCHAPTER B: GENERAL PROVISIONS AND EXEMPTIONS • PART II: EXEMPTIONS

26 USC § 5853. Transfer and making tax exemption available to certain governmental entities

> The Gist: Transfer taxes are waived for NFA weapons transferred to the proper authorities. An NFA weapon may be made for the proper authorities without paying the manufacturing tax. The Treasury Dept. must approve all such transactions.

(a) Transfer.—A firearm may be transferred without the payment of the transfer tax imposed by section 5811 to any State, possession of the United States, any political subdivision thereof, or any official police organization of such a government entity engaged in criminal investigations.

(b) Making.—A firearm may be made without payment of the making tax imposed by section 5821 by, or on behalf of, any State, or possession of the United States, any political subdivision thereof, or any official police organization of such a government entity engaged in criminal investigations.

(c) Right to exemption.—No firearm may be transferred or made exempt from tax under this section unless the transfer or making is performed pursuant to an application in such form and manner as the Secretary may by regulations prescribe.

Oct. 22, 1968 (132)
TITLE 26. INTERNAL REVENUE CODE • SUBTITLE E: ALCOHOL, TOBACCO, AND CERTAIN OTHER EXCISE TAXES • CHAPTER 53: MACHINE GUNS, DESTRUCTIVE DEVICES, AND CERTAIN OTHER FIREARMS • SUBCHAPTER B: GENERAL PROVISIONS AND EXEMPTIONS • PART II: EXEMPTIONS

26 USC § 5854. Exportation of firearms exempt from transfer tax

> The Gist: Transfer taxes are waived for exported NFA weapons. The Treasury Dept. must approve all such transactions.

A firearm may be exported without payment of the transfer tax imposed under section 5811 provided that proof of the exportation is furnished in such form and manner as the Secretary may by regulations prescribe.

Oct. 22, 1968 (35)
TITLE 26. INTERNAL REVENUE CODE • SUBTITLE E: ALCOHOL, TOBACCO, AND CERTAIN OTHER EXCISE TAXES • CHAPTER 53: MACHINE GUNS, DESTRUCTIVE DEVICES, AND CERTAIN OTHER FIREARMS • SUBCHAPTER B: GENERAL PROVISIONS AND EXEMPTIONS • PART II: EXEMPTIONS

26 USC § 5861. Prohibited acts

> **The Gist:** Violating the provisions of this chapter (53), which are listed below, is illegal. In general terms, NFA weapons (those listed in 26–5845) must be registered.

It shall be unlawful for any person—
(a) to engage in business as a manufacturer or importer of, or dealer in, firearms without having paid the special (occupational) tax required by section 5801 for his business or having registered as required by section 5802; or(b) to receive or possess a firearm transferred to him in violation of the provisions of this chapter; or
(c) to receive or possess a firearm made in violation of the provisions of this chapter; or
(d) to receive or possess a firearm which is not registered to him in the National Firearms Registration and Transfer Record; or
(e) to transfer a firearm in violation of the provisions of this chapter; or
(f) to make a firearm in violation of the provisions of this chapter; or
(g) to obliterate, remove, change, or alter the serial number or other identification of a firearm required by this chapter; or
(h) to receive or possess a firearm having the serial number or other identification required by this chapter obliterated, removed, changed, or altered; or
(i) to receive or possess a firearm which is not identified by a serial number as required by this chapter; or
(j) to transport, deliver, or receive any firearm in interstate commerce which has not been registered as required by this chapter; or
(k) to receive or possess a firearm which has been imported or brought into the United States in violation of section 5844; or
(l) to make, or cause the making of, a false entry on any application, return, or record required by this chapter, knowing such entry to be false.

Oct. 22, 1968 (269)

TITLE 26. INTERNAL REVENUE CODE • SUBTITLE E: ALCOHOL, TOBACCO, AND CERTAIN OTHER EXCISE TAXES • CHAPTER 53: MACHINE GUNS, DESTRUCTIVE DEVICES, AND CERTAIN OTHER FIREARMS • SUBCHAPTER C: PROHIBITED ACTS

26 USC § 5872. Forfeitures

> **The Gist:** Any NFA weapon used in violation of the laws of this chapter is subject to seizure and forfeiture. Note that because IRS forfeiture laws apply, the burden of proof is on the NFA weapon owner to prove that this chapter has not been violated. Forfeited arms may not be sold to the public, but may be sold or given to the proper authorities, or destroyed.

(a) Laws applicable.—Any firearm involved in any violation of the provisions of this chapter shall be subject to seizure and forfeiture, and (except as provided in subsection (b)) all the provisions of internal revenue laws relating to searches, seizures, and forfeitures of unstamped articles are extended to and made to apply to the articles taxed under this chapter, and the persons to whom this chapter applies.
(b) Disposal.—In the case of the forfeiture of any firearm by reason of a violation of this chapter, no notice of public sale shall be required; no such firearm shall be sold at public sale; if such firearm is forfeited for a violation of this chapter and there is no remission or mitigation of forfeiture thereof, it shall be delivered by the Secretary to the Administrator of General Services, General Services Administration, who may order such firearm destroyed or may sell it to any State, or possession, or political subdivision thereof, or at the request of the Secretary, may authorize its retention for official use of the Treasury Department, or may transfer it without

charge to any executive department or independent establishment of the
Government for use by it.

Oct. 22, 1968 (197)
TITLE 26. INTERNAL REVENUE CODE • SUBTITLE E: ALCOHOL, TOBACCO, AND CERTAIN OTHER EXCISE
TAXES • CHAPTER 53: MACHINE GUNS, DESTRUCTIVE DEVICES, AND CERTAIN OTHER FIREARMS •
SUBCHAPTER D: PENALTIES AND FORFEITURES

26 USC § 6334. Property exempt from levy

The Gist: Certain personal property is exempt from forfeiture when the
government seizes property to pay back taxes. Included are firearms for
the personal use of the head of a family, as long as the value of the
firearms, combined with the value of exempt fuel, provisions, furniture,
personal effects, livestock and poultry, does not exceed $6,250. A means
for appraising the value is described.

(a) Enumeration.—There shall be exempt from levy—
(2) Fuel, provisions, furniture, and personal effects
So much of the fuel, provisions, furniture, and personal effects in the taxpayer's
    household, and of the arms for personal use, livestock, and poultry of the taxpayer,
    as does not exceed $6,250 in value;
(b) Appraisal.—The officer seizing property of the type described in subsection (a)
    shall appraise and set aside to the owner the amount of such property declared to
    be exempt. If the taxpayer objects at the time of the seizure to the valuation fixed by
    the officer making the seizure, the Secretary shall summon three disinterested
    individuals who shall make the valuation.
(c) No other property exempt.—Notwithstanding any other law of the United States
    (including section 207 of the Social Security Act), no property or rights to property
    shall be exempt from levy other than the property specifically made exempt by
    subsection (a).

Aug. 16, 1954 (153)
TITLE 26. INTERNAL REVENUE CODE • SUBTITLE F: PROCEDURE AND ADMINISTRATION • CHAPTER 64:
COLLECTION • SUBCHAPTER D: SEIZURE OF PROPERTY FOR COLLECTION OF TAXES

26 USC § 6651. Failure to file tax return or to pay tax

The Gist: Deliberately failing to pay appropriate taxes on an NFA
weapon in a timely way, creates an additional tax surcharge. Fraudulently
failing to pay the required taxes increases the tax penalty. Methods for
calculating the penalties, and increased penalties for willful or prolonged
failure to pay are described.

(a) Addition to the tax.—In case of failure—
(1) to file any return required under authority of subchapter A of chapter 61 (other than
    part III thereof), subchapter A of chapter 51 (relating to distilled spirits, wines, and
    beer), or of subchapter A of chapter 52 (relating to tobacco, cigars, cigarettes, and
    cigarette papers and tubes), or of subchapter A of chapter 53 (relating to machine
    guns and certain other firearms), on the date prescribed therefor (determined with
    regard to any extension of time for filing), unless it is shown that such failure is due
    to reasonable cause and not due to willful neglect, there shall be added to the
    amount required to be shown as tax on such return 5 percent of the amount of such
    tax if the failure is for not more than 1 month, with an additional 5 percent for each
    additional month or fraction thereof during which such failure continues, not
    exceeding 25 percent in the aggregate:
(2) to pay the amount shown as tax on any return specified in paragraph (1) on or
    before the date prescribed for payment of such tax (determined with regard to any

extension of time for payment), unless it is shown that such failure is due to reasonable cause and not due to willful neglect, there shall be added to the amount shown as tax on such return 0.5 percent of the amount of such tax if the failure is for not more than 1 month, with an additional 0.5 percent for each additional month or fraction thereof during which such failure continues, not exceeding 25 percent in the aggregate; or

(3) to pay any amount in respect of any tax required to be shown on a return specified in paragraph (1) which is not so shown (including an assessment made pursuant to section 6213(b)) within 21 calendar days from the date of notice and demand therefor (10 business days if the amount for which such notice and demand is made equals or exceeds $100,000), unless it is shown that such failure is due to reasonable cause and not due to willful neglect, there shall be added to the amount of tax stated in such notice and demand 0.5 percent of the amount of such tax if the failure is for not more than 1 month, with an additional 0.5 percent for each additional month or fraction thereof during which such failure continues, not exceeding 25 percent in the aggregate.

In the case of a failure to file a return of tax imposed by chapter 1 within 60 days of the date prescribed for filing of such return (determined with regard to any extensions of time for filing), unless it is shown that such failure is due to reasonable cause and not due to willful neglect, the addition to tax under paragraph (1) shall not be less than the lesser of $100 or 100 percent of the amount required to be shown as tax on such return.

(b) Penalty imposed on net amount due.—For purposes of—

(1) subsection (a)(1), the amount of tax required to be shown on the return shall be reduced by the amount of any part of the tax which is paid on or before the date prescribed for payment of the tax and by the amount of any credit against the tax which may be claimed on the return,

(2) subsection (a)(2), the amount of tax shown on the return shall, for purposes of computing the addition for any month, be reduced by the amount of any part of the tax which is paid on or before the beginning of such month and by the amount of any credit against the tax which may be claimed on the return, and

(3) subsection (a)(3), the amount of tax stated in the notice and demand shall, for the purpose of computing the addition for any month, be reduced by the amount of any part of the tax which is paid before the beginning of such month.

(c) Limitations and special rule.—

(1) Additions under more than one paragraph.—With respect to any return, the amount of the addition under paragraph (1) of subsection (a) shall be reduced by the amount of the addition under paragraph (2) of subsection (a) for any month (or fraction thereof) to which an addition to tax applies under both paragraphs (1) and (2). In any case described in the last sentence of subsection (a), the amount of the addition under paragraph (1) of subsection (a) shall not be reduced under the preceding sentence below the amount provided in such last sentence.

(2) Amount of tax shown more than amount required to be shown.—If the amount required to be shown as tax on a return is less than the amount shown as tax on such return, subsections (a)(2) and (b)(2) shall be applied by substituting such lower amount.

(d) Increase in penalty for failure to pay tax in certain cases.—

(1) In general.—In the case of each month (or fraction thereof) beginning after the day described in paragraph (2) of this subsection, paragraphs (2) and (3) of subsection (a) shall be applied by substituting "1 percent" for "0.5 percent" each place it appears.

(2) Description.—For purposes of paragraph (1), the day described in this paragraph is the earlier of—

(A) the day 10 days after the date on which notice is given under section 6331(d), or

(B) the day on which notice and demand for immediate payment is given under the last sentence of section 6331(a)

(e) Exception for estimated tax.—This section shall not apply to any failure to pay any estimated tax required to be paid by section 6654 or 6655.

(f) Increase in penalty for fraudulent failure to file.—If any failure to file any return is fraudulent, paragraph (1) of subsection (a) shall be applied—

(1) by substituting "15 percent" for "5 percent" each place it appears, and
(2) by substituting "75 percent" for "25 percent".
(g) Treatment of returns prepared by Secretary under section 6020(b)
In the case of any return made by the Secretary under section 6020(b)—
(1) such return shall be disregarded for purposes of determining the amount of the addition under paragraph (1) of subsection (a), but
(2) such return shall be treated as the return filed by the taxpayer for purposes of determining the amount of the addition under paragraphs (2) and (3) of subsection (a).
(h) Limitation on penalty on individual's failure to pay for months during period of installment agreement
In the case of an individual who files a return of tax on or before the due date for the return (including extensions), paragraphs (2) and (3) of subsection (a) shall each be applied by substituting "0.25" for "0.5" each place it appears for purposes of determining the addition to tax for any month during which an installment agreement under section 6159 is in effect for the payment of such tax.

Aug. 16, 1954 (1,164)
TITLE 26. INTERNAL REVENUE CODE • SUBTITLE F: PROCEDURE AND ADMINISTRATION • CHAPTER 68: ADDITIONS TO THE TAX, ADDITIONAL AMOUNTS, AND ASSESSABLE PENALTIES • SUBCHAPTER A: ADDITIONS TO THE TAX AND ADDITIONAL AMOUNTS • PART I: GENERAL PROVISIONS

26 USC § 6658. Coordination with title 11

The Gist: Penalties imposed on late tax payments for NFA weapons may not be increased for payments that are delayed by certain court proceedings.

(a) Certain failures to pay tax.—No addition to the tax shall be made under section 6651, 6654, or 6655 for failure to make timely payment of tax with respect to a period during which a case is pending under title 11 of the United States Code—
(1) if such tax was incurred by the estate and the failure occurred pursuant to an order of the court finding probable insufficiency of funds of the estate to pay administrative expenses, or
(2) if—
(A) such tax was incurred by the debtor before the earlier of the order for relief or (in the involuntary case) the appointment of a trustee, and
(B)(i) the petition was filed before the due date prescribed by law (including extensions) for filing a return of such tax, or
(ii) the date for making the addition to the tax occurs on or after the day on which the petition was filed.
(b) Exception for collected taxes.—Subsection (a) shall not apply to any liability for an addition to the tax which arises from the failure to pay or deposit a tax withheld or collected from others and required to be paid to the United States.

Dec. 24, 1980 (198)
TITLE 26. INTERNAL REVENUE CODE • SUBTITLE F: PROCEDURE AND ADMINISTRATION • CHAPTER 68: ADDITIONS TO THE TAX, ADDITIONAL AMOUNTS, AND ASSESSABLE PENALTIES • SUBCHAPTER A: ADDITIONS TO THE TAX AND ADDITIONAL AMOUNTS • PART I: GENERAL PROVISIONS

26 USC § 7608. Authority of internal revenue enforcement officers

The Gist: Designated IRS agents may carry firearms.

(a) Enforcement of subtitle E and other laws pertaining to liquor, tobacco, and firearms.—Any investigator, agent, or other internal revenue officer by whatever term designated, whom the Secretary charges with the duty of enforcing any of the criminal, seizure, or forfeiture provisions of subtitle E or of any other law of the

United States pertaining to the commodities subject to tax under such subtitle for the enforcement of which the Secretary is responsible, may—

(1) carry firearms

Sept. 2, 1958 (78)
TITLE 26. INTERNAL REVENUE CODE • SUBTITLE F: PROCEDURE AND ADMINISTRATION • CHAPTER 78: DISCOVERY OF LIABILITY AND ENFORCEMENT OF TITLE • SUBCHAPTER A: EXAMINATION AND INSPECTION

Title 28 • Judiciary and Judicial Procedure

28 USC § 566. Powers and duties

> The Gist: United States marshals and any other officials of the U.S.
> Marshals Service may be authorized to carry firearms.

(d) Each United States marshal, deputy marshal, and any other official of the Service
as may be designated by the Director may carry firearms and make arrests without
warrant for any offense against the United States committed in his or her presence,
or for any felony cognizable under the laws of the United States if he or she has
reasonable grounds to believe that the person to be arrested has committed or is
committing such felony.

Nov. 18, 1988 (76)
TITLE 28. JUDICIARY AND JUDICIAL PROCEDURE • PART II: DEPT. OF JUSTICE • CHAPTER 37: UNITED
STATES MARSHALS SERVICE

Title 31 • Money and Finance

31 USC § 321. General authority of the Secretary

> The Gist: The Treasury Dept. may buy arms and ammunition for their employees who need them to perform their duties.

(b) The Secretary may—
(6) buy arms and ammunition required by officers and employees of the Department in carrying out their duties and powers

Sept. 13, 1982 (24)

TITLE 31. MONEY AND FINANCE • CHAPTER 3. DEPARTMENT OF TREASURY • SUBCHAPTER II. ADMINISTRATION

Title 32 • National Guard

The laws that follow, for the most part, do not specifically mention firearms. However, a current topic and frequently confused element of federal gun law, at least recently, concerns the role of the National Guard. The "Militia" is mentioned in relation to the security of a free State, in the Second Amendment of the Bill of Rights. Is the Militia the National Guard?

Part of the answer can be derived from the discussions of the nation's founders, which may be studied in their original form in surviving papers from those times. For an exhaustive review of those papers (with 1,300 attribution notes!) read Stephen P. Halbrook's scholarly text, *That Every Man Be Armed*, available from Bloomfield Press.

Another part of the answer may be obtained from the federal statutes that describe the organized and unorganized Militia, found in 10–311 et seq. Still another part of the answer comes from the laws related to the National Guard, which as seen below, is a federally funded entity, affiliated with the Army and Air Force, with its members and officers drawn from part of the states' organized militias.

32 USC § 101. Definitions

The Gist: Definitions that apply to all of Title 10 Armed Forces appear in this section. The term *National Guard* includes the Army National Guard and the Air National Guard. These are assembled from a part of each state's and territory's organized militia; they must be trained and have officers selected by the individual states, as required by Article I of the Constitution; and they must be organized, armed and equipped, at least partially, by the federal government. The National Guard has active and reserve members.

In addition to the definitions in sections 1-5 of title 1, the following definitions apply in this title:

(1) "**Territory**" means any Territory organized after this title is enacted, so long as it remains a Territory. However, for purposes of this title and other laws relating to the militia, the National Guard, the Army National Guard of the United States, and the Air National Guard of the United States, "Territory" includes Guam and the Virgin Islands.

(2) "**Armed forces**" means the Army, Navy, Air Force, Marine Corps, and Coast Guard.

(3) "**National Guard**" means the Army National Guard and the Air National Guard.

(4) "**Army National Guard**" means that part of the organized militia of the several States and Territories, Puerto Rico, and the District of Columbia, active and inactive, that—

(A) is a land force;

(B) is trained, and has its officers appointed, under the sixteenth clause of section 8, article I, of the Constitution;

(C) is organized, armed, and equipped wholly or partly at Federal expense; and

(D) is federally recognized.

(5) "**Army National Guard of the United States**" means the reserve component of the Army all of whose members are members of the Army National Guard.

(6) "**Air National Guard**" means that part of the organized militia of the several States and Territories, Puerto Rico, and the District of Columbia, active and inactive, that—

(A) is an air force;

(B) is trained, and has its officers appointed, under the sixteenth clause of section 8, article I, of the Constitution;

(C) is organized, armed, and equipped wholly or partly at Federal expense; and

(D) is federally recognized.

(7) "**Air National Guard of the United States**" means the reserve component of the Air Force all of whose members are members of the Air National Guard.

(8) "**Officer**" means commissioned or warrant officer.

(9) "**Enlisted member**" means a person enlisted in, or inducted, called, or conscripted into, an armed force in an enlisted grade.

(10) "**Grade**" means a step or degree, in a graduated scale of office or military rank, that is established and designated as a grade by law or regulation.

(11) "**Rank**" means the order of precedence among members of the armed forces.

(12) "**Active duty**" means full-time duty in the active military service of the United States. It includes such Federal duty as full-time training duty, annual training duty, and attendance, while in the active military service, at a school designated as a service school by law or by the Secretary of the military department concerned. It does not include full-time National Guard duty.

(13) "**Supplies**" includes material, equipment, and stores of all kinds.

(14) "**Shall**" is used in an imperative sense.

(15) "**May**" is used in a permissive sense. The words "no person may ..." mean that no person is required, authorized, or permitted to do the act prescribed.

(16) "**Includes**" means "includes but is not limited to".

(17) "**Pay**" includes basic pay, special pay, incentive pay, retired pay, and equivalent pay, but does not include allowances.

(18) "**Spouse**" means husband or wife, as the case may be.

(19) "**Full-time National Guard duty**" means training or other duty, other than inactive duty, performed by a member of the Army National Guard of the United States or the Air National Guard of the United States in the member's status as a member of the National Guard of a State or territory, the Commonwealth of Puerto Rico, or the District of Columbia under section 316, 502, 503, 504, or 505 of this

title for which the member is entitled to pay from the United States or for which the member has waived pay from the United States.

Aug. 10, 1956 (613)
TITLE 32. NATIONAL GUARD • CHAPTER 1: ORGANIZATION

32 USC § 102. General policy

> The Gist: The National Guard is part of the first line of defense of the United States and must be maintained at all times. Congress may call the National Guard into federal service for as long as needed, whenever it decides that the regular ground and air forces of the country are not sufficient for national security.

In accordance with the traditional military policy of the United States, it is essential that the strength and organization of the Army National Guard and the Air National Guard as an integral part of the first line defenses of the United States be maintained and assured at all times. Whenever Congress determines that more units and organizations are needed for the national security than are in the regular components of the ground and air forces, the Army National Guard of the United States and the Air National Guard of the United States, or such parts of them as are needed, together with such units of other reserve components as are necessary for a balanced force, shall be ordered to active Federal duty and retained as long as so needed.

Aug. 10, 1956 (129)
TITLE 32. NATIONAL GUARD • CHAPTER 1: ORGANIZATION

32 USC § 501. Training generally

> The Gist: The Army National Guard is trained and disciplined by the Army. The Air National Guard is trained and disciplined by the Air Force.

(a) The discipline, including training, of the Army National Guard shall conform to that of the Army. The discipline, including training, of the Air National Guard shall conform to that of the Air Force.
(b) The training of the National Guard shall be conducted by the several States and Territories, Puerto Rico, and the District of Columbia in conformity with this title.

Aug. 10, 1956 (62)
TITLE 32. NATIONAL GUARD • CHAPTER 5: TRAINING

32 USC § 502. Required drills and field exercises

> The Gist: The Army and Air Force issue regulations for their respective branches of the National Guard that must include at least, 1–Drills, instruction and indoor target practice at least 48 times a year; and 2–Outdoor camping, maneuvers and target practice for at least 15 days. Requirements are set up for who must participate and how the exercises may be timed, so that compliance may be measured. Indoor target practice and other drills and instruction must be for at least 90 minutes at a time to count. National Guard members may be ordered to train or be at duty for longer than the times described.

(a) Under regulations to be prescribed by the Secretary of the Army or the Secretary of the Air Force, as the case may be, each company, battery, squadron, and

detachment of the National Guard, unless excused by the Secretary concerned, shall—
(1) assemble for drill and instruction, including indoor target practice, at least 48 times each year; and
(2) participate in training at encampments, maneuvers, outdoor target practice, or other exercises, at least 15 days each year.

However, no member of such unit who has served on active duty for one year or longer shall be required to participate in such training if the first day of such training period falls during the last one hundred and twenty days of his required membership in the National Guard.

(b) An assembly for drill and instruction may consist of a single ordered formation of a company, battery, squadron, or detachment, or, when authorized by the Secretary concerned, a series of ordered formations of parts of those organizations. However, to have a series of formations credited as an assembly for drill and instruction, all parts of the unit must be included in the series within 90 consecutive days.

(c) The total attendance at the series of formations constituting an assembly shall be counted as the attendance at that assembly for the required period. No member may be counted more than once or receive credit for more than one required period of attendance, regardless of the number of formations that he attends during the series constituting the assembly for the required period.

(d) No organization may receive credit for an assembly for drill or indoor target practice unless—
(1) the number of members present equals or exceeds the minimum number prescribed by the President;
(2) the period of military duty or instruction for which a member is credited is at least one and one-half hours; and
(3) the training is of the type prescribed by the Secretary concerned.

(e) An appropriately rated member of the National Guard who performs an aerial flight under competent orders may receive credit for attending drill for the purposes of this section, if the flight prevented him from attending a regularly scheduled drill.

(f) Under regulations to be prescribed by the Secretary of the Army or Secretary of the Air Force, as the case may be, a member of the National Guard may—
(1) without his consent, but with the pay and allowances provided by law; or
(2) with his consent, either with or without pay and allowances;
be ordered to perform training or other duty in addition to that prescribed under subsection (a). Duty without pay shall be considered for all purposes as if it were duty with pay.

Aug. 10, 1956 (452)
TITLE 32. NATIONAL GUARD • CHAPTER 5: TRAINING

32 USC § 503. Participation in field exercises

The Gist: The Army and Air Force may include the National Guard in their camp outs, maneuvers, outdoor target practice or other exercises for field or coast defense. They may also provide such training independent of their own activities. Money is authorized to cover the costs of these exercises and to pay the National Guard members.

(a) Under such regulations as the President may prescribe, the Secretary of the Army and the Secretary of the Air Force, as the case may be, may provide for the participation of the National Guard in encampments, maneuvers, outdoor target practice, or other exercises for field or coast-defense instruction, independently of or in conjunction with the Army or the Air Force, or both.

(b) Amounts necessary for the pay, subsistence, transportation, and other proper expenses of any part of the National Guard of a State or Territory, Puerto Rico, or the District of Columbia participating in an exercise under subsection (a) may be set aside from funds allocated to it from appropriations for field or coast-defense instruction.

(c) Members of the National Guard participating in an exercise under subsection (a) may, after being mustered, be paid for the period beginning with the date of leaving home and ending with the date of return, as determined in advance. If otherwise correct, such a payment passes to the credit of the disbursing officer.

Aug. 10, 1956 (173)
TITLE 32. NATIONAL GUARD • CHAPTER 5: TRAINING

32 USC § 504. National Guard schools and small arms competitions

The Gist: The National Guard may attend schools conducted by the Army or the Air Force, conduct or attend its own schools, and take part in small arms competitions. The location of these activities is not restricted.

(a) Under regulations to be prescribed by the Secretary of the Army or Secretary of the Air Force, as the case may be, members of the National Guard may—
(1) attend schools conducted by the Army or the Air Force, as appropriate:
(2) conduct or attend schools conducted by the National Guard; or
(3) participate in small arms competitions.
(b) Activities authorized under subsection (a) for members of the National Guard of a State or territory, Puerto Rico, or the District of Columbia may be held inside or outside its boundaries.

Aug. 10, 1956 (91)
TITLE 32. NATIONAL GUARD • CHAPTER 5: TRAINING

32 USC § 507. Instruction in firing; supply of ammunition

The Gist: Training ammunition for the National Guard may be provided by the Army and Air Force. Firearms instruction must be under the direction of a commissioned officer.

Ammunition for instruction in firing and for target practice may be furnished, in such amounts as may be prescribed by the Secretary of the Army or the Secretary of the Air Force, as the case may be, to units of the National Guard encamped at a post, camp, or air base. The instruction shall be under the direction of a commissioned officer selected for that purpose by the proper military commander.

Aug. 10, 1956 (71)
TITLE 32. NATIONAL GUARD • CHAPTER 5: TRAINING

32 USC § 701. Uniforms, arms, and equipment to be same as Army or Air Force

The Gist: National Guard uniforms, arms and equipment match those of the Army and Air Force.

So far as practicable, the same types of uniforms, arms, and equipment as are issued to the Army shall be issued to the Army National Guard, and the same types of uniforms, arms, and equipment as are issued to the Air Force shall be issued to the Air National Guard.

Aug. 10, 1956 (50)
TITLE 32. NATIONAL GUARD • CHAPTER 7: SERVICE, SUPPLY, AND PROCUREMENT

32 USC § 702. Issue of supplies

> The Gist: The Army and Air Force may make or buy uniforms, arms and equipment for the National Guard, and issue these supplies on request from a state's or territory's Governor (or the commanding general of the District of Columbia National Guard). When a state's National Guard is properly organized, armed and equipped for field duty, its share of federal National Guard funds may be used to buy any items issued by the Army or Air Force.

(a) Under such regulations as the President may prescribe, the Secretary of the Army and the Secretary of the Air Force may buy or manufacture and, upon requisition of the governor of any State or Territory or Puerto Rico or the commanding general of the National Guard of the District of Columbia, issue to its Army National Guard and Air National Guard, respectively, the supplies necessary to uniform, arm, and equip that Army National Guard or Air National Guard for field duty.

(b) Whenever the Secretary concerned is satisfied that the Army National Guard or the Air National Guard, as the case may be, of any State or Territory, Puerto Rico, or the District of Columbia is properly organized, armed, and equipped for field duty, funds allotted to that jurisdiction for its Army National Guard or Air National Guard may be used to buy any article issued by the Army or the Air Force, as the case may be.

(c) Under such regulations as the President may prescribe, the issue of new types of equipment, small arms, or field guns to the National Guard of any State or Territory, Puerto Rico, or the District of Columbia shall be without charge against appropriations for the National Guard.

(d) No property may be issued to the National Guard of a State or Territory, Puerto Rico, or the District of Columbia, unless that jurisdiction makes provision, satisfactory to the Secretary concerned, for its protection and care.

Aug. 10, 1956 (243)

TITLE 32. NATIONAL GUARD • CHAPTER 7: SERVICE, SUPPLY, AND PROCUREMENT

32 USC § 706. Return of arms and equipment upon relief from Federal service

> The Gist: When National Guard units and members are relieved from federal service, the arms and equipment they need for peacetime service, as determined by the Army and Air Force, stay with them.

So far as practicable, whenever units, organizations, or members of the National Guard are returned to their National Guard status under section 325(b) of this title, arms and equipment that the Secretary concerned determines are sufficient to accomplish their peacetime mission shall be returned with them.

Aug. 10, 1956 (47)

TITLE 32. NATIONAL GUARD • CHAPTER 7: SERVICE, SUPPLY, AND PROCUREMENT

Title 33 • Navigation and Navigable Waters

33 USC § 3. Regulations to prevent injuries from target practice

> **The Gist:** The Army is authorized to regulate any navigable waters of the United States which may be endangered by artillery fire or other weapons testing. Such regulations must be posted in an obvious way, and it is illegal to willfully violate the regulations.
>
> This law, identified because it contains the phrase *target practice*, really doesn't relate to bearing arms, and serves as another example of how the lines had to be drawn when excerpting the federal laws for this book.

Authority to adopt regulations. In the interest of the national defense, and for the better protection of life and property on the navigable waters of the United States, the Secretary of the Army is authorized and empowered to prescribe such regulations as he may deem best for the use and navigation of any portion or area of the navigable waters of the United States or waters under the jurisdiction of the United States endangered or likely to be endangered by Artillery fire in target practice or otherwise, or by the proving operations of the Government ordnance proving grounds at Sandy Hook, New Jersey, or at any Government ordnance proving ground that may be established elsewhere on or near such waters, and of any portion or area of said waters occupied by submarine mines, mine fields, submarine cables, or other material and accessories pertaining to seacoast fortifications, or by any plant or facility engaged in the execution of any public project of river and harbor improvement; and the said Secretary shall have like power to regulate the transportation of explosives upon any of said waters: Provided, That the authority conferred shall be so exercised as not unreasonably to interfere with or restrict the food fishing industry, and the regulations prescribed in pursuance hereof shall provide for the use of such waters by food fishermen operating under permits granted by the Department of the Army.

Detail of vessels to enforce regulations. To enforce the regulations prescribed pursuant to this section, the Secretary of the Army may detail any public vessel in the service of the Department of the Army, or, upon the request of the Secretary of the Army, the head of any other department may enforce, and the head of any such department is authorized to enforce, such regulations by means of any public vessel of such department.

Posting and violation of regulations. The regulations made by the Secretary of the Army pursuant to this section shall be posted in conspicuous and appropriate places, designated by him, for the information of the public; and every person who and every corporation which shall willfully violate any regulations made by the said Secretary pursuant to this section shall be deemed guilty of a misdemeanor, and upon conviction thereof in any court of competent jurisdiction shall be punished by a fine not exceeding $500, or by imprisonment (in the case of a natural person) not exceeding six months, in the discretion of the court.

July 9, 1918 (410)
TITLE 33. NAVIGATION AND NAVIGABLE WATERS • CHAPTER 1: NAVIGABLE WATERS GENERALLY • SUBCHAPTER I: GENERAL PROVISIONS

Title 36 • Patriotic and National Observances, Ceremonies, and Organizations

36 USC § 40701. Organization

The Civilian Marksmanship Program, run by the U.S. Army, has served as the federal government's official firearms training, supply and competitions program for U.S. citizens, since 1956. See related background at 10-4309. Its history traces back to the late 1800s, when programs were first established to help ensure that the populace could shoot straight, in the event an army had to be raised to defend the country. The program was privatized in 1996 (P.L. 104-106), remaining in Title 10, moving to Title 36 in 1998 (P.L. 105-225).

The federal government transfers the responsibility and facilities for training civilians in the use of small arms to a new non-profit corporation. All law-abiding citizens are eligible to participate, and priority is given to reaching and training youth in the safe, lawful and accurate use of firearms.

Functions formerly performed for this program by the Army are now the responsibility of this new corporation. The Army is required to provide direct support to make the program work in its privatized form.

The Gist: The Corporation for the Promotion of Rifle Practice and Firearms Safety is a private corporation, chartered by the federal government.

(a) Federal Charter.—Corporation for the Promotion of Rifle Practice and Firearms Safety (in this chapter, the "corporation") is a federally chartered corporation.
(b) Non-Governmental Status.—The corporation is a private corporation, not a department, agency, or instrumentality of the United States Government. An officer or employee of the corporation is not an officer or employee of the Government.

Aug. 10, 1956, Aug. 12, 1990 (59)

36 USC § 40702. Governing body

> The Gist: A board of directors runs the Civilian Marksmanship Program (CMP). It has at least nine directors, serving renewable two-year terms, and a Director of Civilian Marksmanship (DCM) who runs the operations.

(a) Board of Directors.—
(1) The board of directors is the governing body of the corporation. The board of directors may adopt bylaws, policies, and procedures for the corporation and may take any other action that it considers necessary for the management and operation of the corporation.
(2) The board shall have at least 9 directors.
(3) The term of office of a director is 2 years. A director may be reappointed.
(4) A vacancy on the board of directors shall be filled by a majority vote of the remaining directors.
(b) Director of Civilian Marksmanship.
(1) The board of directors shall appoint the Director of Civilian Marksmanship.
(2) The Director is responsible for—
(A) the daily operation of the corporation; and
(B) the duties of the corporation under subchapter II of this chapter.

Aug. 10, 1956, Aug. 12, 1998 (134)
TITLE 36: PATRIOTIC AND NATIONAL OBSERVANCES, CEREMONIES, AND ORGANIZATIONS. • SUBTITLE II: PATRIOTIC AND NATIONAL ORGANIZATIONS • PART B: ORGANIZATIONS • SUBCHAPTER I: CORPORATION

36 USC § 40703. Powers

> The Gist: The Corporation for the Promotion of Rifle Practice and Firearms Safety may do the routine things it needs to, in carrying out its business. It is authorized to charge fees to cover its costs.

The corporation may—
(1) adopt, use, and alter a corporate seal, which shall be judicially noticed;
(2) make contracts;
(3) acquire, own, lease, encumber, and transfer property as necessary or convenient to carry out the activities of the corporation;
(4) incur and pay obligations;
(5) charge fees to cover the corporation's costs in carrying out the Civilian Marksmanship Program; and
(6) do any other act necessary and proper to carry out the activities of the corporation.

Aug. 10, 1956, Aug. 12, 1998 (76)
TITLE 36: PATRIOTIC AND NATIONAL OBSERVANCES, CEREMONIES, AND ORGANIZATIONS. • SUBTITLE II: PATRIOTIC AND NATIONAL ORGANIZATIONS • PART B: ORGANIZATIONS • SUBCHAPTER I: CORPORATION

36 USC § 40704. Restrictions

> The Gist: The Corporation may not operate for profit. All funds must go to support the Civilian Marksmanship Program.

(a) Profit.—The corporation may not operate for profit.
(b) Use of Amounts Collected.—Amounts collected under section 40703(3) and (5) of this title, including proceeds from the sale of firearms, ammunition, repair parts, and other supplies, may be used only to support the Civilian Marksmanship Program.

Aug. 10, 1956, Aug. 12, 1998 (47)
TITLE 36: PATRIOTIC AND NATIONAL OBSERVANCES, CEREMONIES, AND ORGANIZATIONS. • SUBTITLE II: PATRIOTIC AND NATIONAL ORGANIZATIONS • PART B: ORGANIZATIONS • SUBCHAPTER I: CORPORATION

36 USC § 40705. Duty to maintain tax-exempt status

The Gist: The Corporation is a "501(c)(3)" not-for-profit firm.

The corporation shall be operated in a manner and for purposes that qualify the corporation for exemption from taxation under section 501(a) of the Internal Revenue Code of 1986 (26 U.S.C. 501(a)) as an organization described in section 501(c)(3) of that Code (26 U.S.C. 501(c)(3)).

Aug. 10, 1956, Aug. 12, 1998 (45)

TITLE 36: PATRIOTIC AND NATIONAL OBSERVANCES, CEREMONIES, AND ORGANIZATIONS. • SUBTITLE II: PATRIOTIC AND NATIONAL ORGANIZATIONS • PART B: ORGANIZATIONS • SUBCHAPTER I: CORPORATION

36 USC § 40706. Distribution of assets on dissolution

The Gist: If the Corporation is dissolved, the Army gets the guns stored at the Anniston, Alabama armory, all CMP M-16 rifles, and certain trophies. Other assets may be distributed to organizations (not individuals) that do similar work to the CMP. Any other assets are to be sold.

(a) Secretary of the Army.—On dissolution of the corporation, title to the following items, and the right to possess the items, vest in the Secretary of the Army—
(1) firearms stored at Defense Distribution Depot, Anniston, Anniston, Alabama on the date of dissolution.
(2) M-16 rifles under control of the corporation.
(3) trophies received from the National Board for the Promotion of Rifle Practice through the date of dissolution.
(b) Tax-Exempt Organizations.—
(1) On dissolution of the corporation, an asset not described in subsection (a) of this section may be distributed to an organization that—
(A) is exempt from taxation under section 501(a) of the Internal Revenue Code of 1986 (26 U.S.C. 501(a)) as an organization described in section 501(c)(3) of that Code (26 U.S.C. 501(c)(3)); and
(B) performs functions similar to the functions described in section 40722 of this title.
(2) An asset distributed under this subsection may not be distributed to an individual.
(c) Treasury.—On dissolution of the corporation, any asset not distributed under subsection (a) or (b) of this section shall be sold and the proceeds shall be deposited in the Treasury.

Aug. 10, 1956, Aug. 12, 1998 (187)

TITLE 36: PATRIOTIC AND NATIONAL OBSERVANCES, CEREMONIES, AND ORGANIZATIONS. • SUBTITLE II: PATRIOTIC AND NATIONAL ORGANIZATIONS • PART B: ORGANIZATIONS • SUBCHAPTER I: CORPORATION

36 USC § 40707. Nonapplication of audit requirements

The Gist: Certain audit requirements do not apply to the firm.

The audit requirements of section 10101 of this title do not apply to the corporation.

Aug. 10, 1956, Aug. 12, 1998 (15)

TITLE 36: PATRIOTIC AND NATIONAL OBSERVANCES, CEREMONIES, AND ORGANIZATIONS. • SUBTITLE II: PATRIOTIC AND NATIONAL ORGANIZATIONS • PART B: ORGANIZATIONS • SUBCHAPTER I: CORPORATION

36 USC § 40721. Responsibility of corporation

The Gist: The Corporation oversees the Civilian Marksmanship Program.

The corporation shall supervise and control the Civilian Marksmanship Program.
Aug. 10, 1956, Aug. 12, 1998 (10)
TITLE 36: PATRIOTIC AND NATIONAL OBSERVANCES, CEREMONIES, AND ORGANIZATIONS. • SUBTITLE II: PATRIOTIC AND NATIONAL ORGANIZATIONS • PART B: ORGANIZATIONS • SUBCHAPTER II: CIVILIAN MARKSMANSHIP PROGRAM

36 USC § 40722. Functions

The Gist: The Civilian Marksmanship Program:

1–Instructs citizens of the United States in marksmanship;

2–Promotes practice and safety in the use of firearms;

3–Conducts firearms competitions and awards trophies, prizes, badges and other insignia to competitors;

4–Controls the firearms, ammunition, and other equipment of the program;

5–Issues, loans, or sells firearms, ammunition, repair parts, and other supplies under sections 40731 and 40732 of this program; and

6–Obtains the supplies and services needed to run the program.

The functions of the Civilian Marksmanship Program are—
(1) to instruct citizens of the United States in marksmanship;
(2) to promote practice and safety in the use of firearms;
(3) to conduct competitions in the use of firearms and to award trophies, prizes, badges, and other insignia to competitors;
(4) to secure and account for firearms, ammunition, and other equipment for which the corporation is responsible;
(5) to issue, loan, or sell firearms, ammunition, repair parts, and other supplies under sections 40731 and 40732 of this title; and
(6) to procure necessary supplies and services to carry out the Program.
Aug. 10, 1956, Aug. 12, 1998 (100)
TITLE 36: PATRIOTIC AND NATIONAL OBSERVANCES, CEREMONIES, AND ORGANIZATIONS. • SUBTITLE II: PATRIOTIC AND NATIONAL ORGANIZATIONS • PART B: ORGANIZATIONS • SUBCHAPTER II: CIVILIAN MARKSMANSHIP PROGRAM

36 USC § 40723. Eligibility for participation

The Gist: Participants must certify in writing that they are not felons, have not violated the main federal gun laws and do not advocate violent overthrow of the government. They can be required to get law enforcement certification of a clean record. A felony or a conviction under the main federal gun laws makes a person ineligible. The Director can limit participation to ensure safety, security of the arms and supplies, and the quality of instruction.

(a) Certification.—
(1) An individual shall certify by affidavit, before participating in an activity sponsored or supported by the corporation, that the individual—
(A) has not been convicted of a felony;

(B) has not been convicted of a violation of section 922 of title 18; and
(C) is not a member of an organization that advocates the violent overthrow of the United States Government.
(2) The Director of Civilian Marksmanship may require an individual to provide certification from law enforcement agencies to verify that the individual has not been convicted of a felony or a violation of section 922 of title 18.
(b) Ineligibility.—An individual may not participate in an activity sponsored or supported by the corporation if the individual—
(1) has been convicted of a felony; or
(2) has been convicted of a violation of section 922 of title 18.
(c) Limiting Participation.—The Director may limit participation in the program as necessary to ensure—
(1) the safety of participants;
(2) the security of firearms, ammunition, and equipment; and
(3) the quality of instruction in the use of firearms.

Aug. 10, 1956, Aug. 12, 1998 (181)
TITLE 36: PATRIOTIC AND NATIONAL OBSERVANCES, CEREMONIES, AND ORGANIZATIONS. • SUBTITLE II: PATRIOTIC AND NATIONAL ORGANIZATIONS • PART B: ORGANIZATIONS • SUBCHAPTER II: CIVILIAN MARKSMANSHIP PROGRAM

36 USC § 40724. Priority of youth participation

> The Gist: Activities that benefit youth and that reach as many youth participants as possible have priority.

In carrying out the Civilian Marksmanship Program, the corporation shall give priority to activities that benefit firearms safety, training, and competition for youth and that reach as many youth participants as possible.

Aug. 10, 1956, Aug. 12, 1998 (32)
TITLE 36: PATRIOTIC AND NATIONAL OBSERVANCES, CEREMONIES, AND ORGANIZATIONS. • SUBTITLE II: PATRIOTIC AND NATIONAL ORGANIZATIONS • PART B: ORGANIZATIONS • SUBCHAPTER II: CIVILIAN MARKSMANSHIP PROGRAM

36 USC § 40725. National Matches and small-arms firing school

> The Gist: National rifle and pistol matches shall be held, to be run by the Army. Various government agencies, citizen-soldier groups, rifle clubs and civilians are eligible to compete. A small-arms school is held in conjunction with the National Matches. The National Rifle Association also holds competitions in connection with the matches.

(a) Annual Competition.—An annual competition called the "National Matches" and consisting of rifle and pistol matches for a national trophy, medals, and other prizes shall be held as prescribed by the Secretary of the Army.
(b) Eligible Participants.—The National Matches are open to members of the Armed Forces, National Guard, Reserve Officers' Training Corps, Air Force Reserve Officers' Training Corps, Citizens' Military Training Camps, Citizens' Air Training Camps, and rifle clubs, and to civilians.
(c) Small-Arms Firing School.—A small-arms firing school shall be held in connection with the National Matches.
(d) Other Competitions.—Competitions for which trophies and medals are provided by the National Rifle Association of America shall be held in connection with the National Matches.

Aug. 10, 1956, Aug. 12, 1998 (120)
TITLE 36: PATRIOTIC AND NATIONAL OBSERVANCES, CEREMONIES, AND ORGANIZATIONS. • SUBTITLE II: PATRIOTIC AND NATIONAL ORGANIZATIONS • PART B: ORGANIZATIONS • SUBCHAPTER II: CIVILIAN MARKSMANSHIP PROGRAM

36 USC § 40726. Allowances for junior competitors

> The Gist: A special category of "Junior Competitor" at the National Match consists of those under 18 years of age, and college and university gun-club members. An allowance to juniors for travel and expenses may be paid by the Army, and the allowance for return travel may be paid in advance.

(a) Definition.—In this section, a "junior competitor" is a competitor at the National Matches, a small-arms firing school, a competition in connection with the National Matches, or a special clinic under section 40725 of this title who is—
(1) less than 18 years of age; or
(2) a member of a gun club organized for the students of a college or university.
(b) Subsistence Allowance.—A junior competitor may be paid a subsistence allowance in an amount prescribed by the Secretary of the Army.
(c) Travel Allowance.—A junior competitor may be paid a travel allowance in an amount prescribed by the Secretary instead of travel expenses and subsistence while traveling. The travel allowance for the return trip may be paid in advance.

Aug. 10, 1956, Aug. 12, 1998 (124)
TITLE 36: PATRIOTIC AND NATIONAL OBSERVANCES, CEREMONIES, AND ORGANIZATIONS. • SUBTITLE II: PATRIOTIC AND NATIONAL ORGANIZATIONS • PART B: ORGANIZATIONS • SUBCHAPTER II: CIVILIAN MARKSMANSHIP PROGRAM

36 USC § 40727. Army support

> The Gist: The Army provides logistical support to the Civilian Marksmanship Program for competitions and other activities, and is paid for its direct costs by the Corporation. The Army provides personnel to support the National Matches without cost. The matches may be held where they were held before 2/10/96.

(a) Logistical Support.—The Secretary of the Army shall provide logistical support to the Civilian Marksmanship Program for competitions and other activities. The corporation shall reimburse the Secretary for incremental direct costs incurred in providing logistical support. The reimbursements shall be credited to the appropriations account of the Department of the Army that is charged to provide the logistical support.
(b) National Matches.—
(1) The National Matches may be held at Department of Defense facilities where the National Matches were held before February 10, 1996.
(2) The Secretary shall provide, without cost to the corporation, members of the National Guard and Army Reserve to support the National Matches as part of the annual training under title 10 and title 32.
(c) Regulations.—The Secretary shall prescribe regulations to carry out this section.

Aug. 10, 1956, Aug. 12, 1998 (132)
TITLE 36: PATRIOTIC AND NATIONAL OBSERVANCES, CEREMONIES, AND ORGANIZATIONS. • SUBTITLE II: PATRIOTIC AND NATIONAL ORGANIZATIONS • PART B: ORGANIZATIONS • SUBCHAPTER II: CIVILIAN MARKSMANSHIP PROGRAM

36 USC § 40728. Transfer of firearms, ammunition, and parts

> The Gist: The materials controlled under the former Civilian Marksmanship Program are transferred to the Corporation. The transfers are to take place in a timely way. The Corporation gains title to the transferred goods when issued to an eligible recipient. The program's

> arms are stored by the Army at no cost to the Corporation, until they are issued by or transferred to the Corporation. Parts for rifles designated to be demilitarized may be transferred to the Corporation by the Army. The Army may not demilitarize a serviceable M-1 rifle in its inventory. Army transfers to the Corporation are made without cost, but the Corporation picks up the cost for preparing and transporting arms and ammunition under the program.

(a) Required Transfers.—In accordance with subsection (b) of this section, the Secretary of the Army shall transfer to the corporation all firearms and ammunition that, on February 9, 1996, were under the control of the director of civilian marksmanship (as that position existed under section 4307 of title 10 on February 9, 1996), including—
(1) all firearms on loan to affiliated clubs and State associations;
(2) all firearms in the possession of the Civilian Marksmanship Support Detachment; and
(3) all M-1 Garand and caliber .22 rimfire rifles stored at Defense Distribution Depot, Anniston, Anniston, Alabama.
(b) Time for Transfers.—The Secretary shall transfer firearms and ammunition under subsection (a) of this section as and when necessary to enable the corporation—
(1) to issue or loan firearms or ammunition under section 40731 of this title; or
(2) to sell firearms or ammunition under section 40732 of this title.
(c) Vesting of Title in Transferred Items.—Title to an item transferred to the corporation under this section shall vest in the corporation—
(1) on the issuance of the item to an eligible recipient under section 40731 of this title; or
(2) immediately before the corporation delivers the item to a purchaser in accordance with a contract for sale of the item that is authorized under section 40732 of this title.
(d) Storage of Firearms.—Firearms stored at Defense Distribution Depot, Anniston, Anniston, Alabama, before February 10, 1996, and used for the Civilian Marksmanship Program (as that program existed under section 4308(e) of title 10 before February 10, 1996), shall remain at that facility or another storage facility designated by the Secretary, without cost to the corporation, until the firearms are issued, loaned, or sold by the corporation, or otherwise transferred to the corporation.
(e) Discretionary Transfer of Parts.—The Secretary may transfer from the inventory of the Department of the Army to the corporation any part from a rifle designated to be demilitarized.
(f) Limitation on Demilitarization of M-1 Rifles.—After February 10, 1996, the Secretary may not demilitarize an M-1 Garand rifle in the inventory of the Army unless the Defense Logistics Agency decides the rifle is unserviceable.
(g) Cost of Transfers.—A transfer of firearms, ammunition, or parts to the corporation under this section shall be made without cost to the corporation, except that the corporation shall assume the cost of preparation and transportation of firearms and ammunition transferred under this section.

Aug. 10, 1956, Aug. 12, 1998 (403)
TITLE 36: PATRIOTIC AND NATIONAL OBSERVANCES, CEREMONIES, AND ORGANIZATIONS. • SUBTITLE II: PATRIOTIC AND NATIONAL ORGANIZATIONS • PART B: ORGANIZATIONS • SUBCHAPTER II: CIVILIAN MARKSMANSHIP PROGRAM

36 USC § 40729. Reservation of firearms, ammunition, and parts

> The Gist: The Army shall reserve rifles and ammunition for the program, for transfer to the Corporation, and certain M-16 rifles used in the small-arms school, and parts and supplies for surplus .30 caliber and .22-caliber rimfire rifles.

(a) Reservation.—The Secretary of the Army shall reserve for the corporation—
(1) firearms described in section 40728(a) of this title;
(2) ammunition for firearms described in 40728(a) of this title;
(3) M-16 rifles held by the Department of the Army on February 10, 1996, and used to support the small-arms firing school; and
(4) parts from, and other supplies for, surplus caliber .30 and caliber .22 rimfire rifles.
(b) Exception.—This section does not supersede the authority provided in section 1208 of the National Defense Authorization Act for Fiscal Years 1990 and 1991 (Public Law 101-189; 10 U.S.C. 372 note).

Aug. 10, 1956, Aug. 12, 1998 (101)
TITLE 36: PATRIOTIC AND NATIONAL OBSERVANCES, CEREMONIES, AND ORGANIZATIONS. • SUBTITLE II: PATRIOTIC AND NATIONAL ORGANIZATIONS • PART B: ORGANIZATIONS • SUBCHAPTER II: CIVILIAN MARKSMANSHIP PROGRAM

36 USC § 40730. Surplus property

> The Gist: The Corporation may also obtain certain other surplus government property for use in the program, without cost.

The corporation may obtain surplus property from the Defense Reutilization Marketing Service to carry out the Civilian Marksmanship Program. A transfer of property to the corporation under this section shall be made without cost to the corporation.

Aug. 10, 1956, Aug. 12, 1998 (37)
TITLE 36: PATRIOTIC AND NATIONAL OBSERVANCES, CEREMONIES, AND ORGANIZATIONS. • SUBTITLE II: PATRIOTIC AND NATIONAL ORGANIZATIONS • PART B: ORGANIZATIONS • SUBCHAPTER II: CIVILIAN MARKSMANSHIP PROGRAM

36 USC § 40731. Issuance or loan of firearms and supplies

> The Gist: To conduct training and competition, the Corporation may issue or loan, with or without charges to recover administrative costs, .22-caliber rimfire and .30 caliber surplus rifles, matching ammunition, air rifles, repair parts and other supplies necessary for activities related to the Civilian Marksmanship Program. The goods may go to organizations affiliated with the Corporation that provide firearms training to youth, the Boy Scouts, 4-H Clubs, Future Farmers, and other youth organizations. The Corporation is responsible for overseeing the security of the firearms issued or loaned.

(a) Issuance or Loan.—For purposes of training and competition, the corporation may issue or loan, with or without charges to recover administrative costs, caliber .22 rimfire and caliber .30 surplus rifles, air rifles, caliber .22 and .30 ammunition, repair parts, and other supplies necessary for activities related to the Civilian Marksmanship Program to—
(1) organizations affiliated with the corporation that provide firearms training to youth;
(2) the Boy Scouts of America;
(3) 4-H Clubs;
(4) the Future Farmers of America; and
(5) other youth oriented organizations.
(b) Security of Firearms.—The corporation shall ensure adequate oversight and accountability for firearms issued or loaned under this section. The corporation shall prescribe procedures for the security of issued or loaned firearms in accordance with United States, State, and local laws.

Aug. 10, 1956, Aug. 12, 1998 (129)
TITLE 36: PATRIOTIC AND NATIONAL OBSERVANCES, CEREMONIES, AND ORGANIZATIONS. • SUBTITLE II: PATRIOTIC AND NATIONAL ORGANIZATIONS • PART B: ORGANIZATIONS • SUBCHAPTER II: CIVILIAN MARKSMANSHIP PROGRAM

36 USC § 40732. Sale of firearms and supplies

The Gist: The Corporation may sell, at fair market value, .22-caliber rimfire and .30 caliber surplus rifles, matching ammunition, air rifles, repair parts and other supplies to organizations affiliated with the Corporation that provide training in the use of firearms. The Corporation may similarly sell goods necessary for target practice to a citizen of the United States who is over 18 years of age and who is a member of a gun club affiliated with the Corporation. Such sales must conform with all applicable law, and must include a background check. Parts for conversion to full-auto fire may not be sold. No items may be sold to felons or people with violations of the main federal gun laws.

(a) Affiliated Organizations.—The corporation may sell, at fair market value, caliber .22 rimfire and caliber .30 surplus rifles, air rifles, caliber .22 and .30 ammunition, repair parts, and other supplies to organizations affiliated with the corporation that provide training in the use of firearms.

(b) Gun Club Members.—

(1) The corporation may sell, at fair market value, caliber .22 rimfire and caliber .30 surplus rifles, ammunition, repair parts and other supplies necessary for target practice to a citizen of the United States who is over 18 years of age and who is a member of a gun club affiliated with the corporation.

(2) Except as provided in section 40733 of this title, sales under this subsection are subject to applicable United States, State, and local law. In addition to any other requirement, the corporation shall establish procedures to obtain a criminal records check of the individual with United States Government and State law enforcement agencies.

(c) Limitation on Sales.—

(1) The corporation may not sell a repair part designed to convert a firearm to fire in a fully automatic mode.

(2) The corporation may not sell any item to an individual who has been convicted of—

(A) a felony; or

(B) a violation of section 922 of title 18.

Aug. 10, 1956, Aug. 12, 1998 (210)

TITLE 36: PATRIOTIC AND NATIONAL OBSERVANCES, CEREMONIES, AND ORGANIZATIONS. • SUBTITLE II: PATRIOTIC AND NATIONAL ORGANIZATIONS • PART B: ORGANIZATIONS • SUBCHAPTER II: CIVILIAN MARKSMANSHIP PROGRAM

36 USC § 40733. Applicability of other law

The Gist: The Corporation is exempt from the laws that would require a federal firearms license to conduct its business.

Section 922(a)(1)-(3) and (5) of title 18 does not apply to the shipment, transportation, receipt, transfer, sale, issuance, loan, or delivery by the corporation, of an item that the corporation is authorized to issue, loan, sell, or receive under this chapter.

Aug. 10, 1956, Aug. 12, 1998 (41)

TITLE 36: PATRIOTIC AND NATIONAL OBSERVANCES, CEREMONIES, AND ORGANIZATIONS. • SUBTITLE II: PATRIOTIC AND NATIONAL ORGANIZATIONS • PART B: ORGANIZATIONS • SUBCHAPTER II: CIVILIAN MARKSMANSHIP PROGRAM

Title 38 • Veterans' Benefits

38 USC § 902. Enforcement and arrest authority of Department police officers

> The Gist: Police officers of the Dept. of Veterans Affairs may be authorized to carry firearms and other weapons.

(b) The Secretary shall prescribe regulations with respect to Department police officers. Such regulations shall include—
(3) rules limiting the carrying and use of weapons by Department police officers.

Aug. 6, 1991 (29)
TITLE 38. VETERANS' BENEFITS • PART I: GENERAL PROVISIONS • CHAPTER 9: SECURITY AND LAW
ENFORCEMENT ON PROPERTY UNDER THE JURISDICTION OF THE DEPARTMENT

38 USC § 904. Equipment and weapons

> The Gist: The Dept. of Veterans Affairs provides firearms and related equipment to its police officers.

The Secretary shall furnish Department police officers with such weapons and related equipment as the Secretary determines to be necessary and appropriate.

Aug. 6, 1991 (22)
TITLE 38. VETERANS' BENEFITS • PART I: GENERAL PROVISIONS • CHAPTER 9: SECURITY AND LAW
ENFORCEMENT ON PROPERTY UNDER THE JURISDICTION OF THE DEPARTMENT

Title 39 • Postal Service

39 USC § 3001. Nonmailable matter

> The Gist: It's illegal for a citizen to mail a concealable firearm, though the proper authorities may, as described in 18–1715. This statute takes the award for the worst English grammar in all the federal gun laws.

(a) Matter the deposit of which in the mails is punishable under section 1302, 1341, 1342, 1461, 1463, 1715, 1716, 1717, or 1738 of title 18, or section 26 of the Animal Welfare Act is nonmailable.

Aug. 12, 1970 (36)
TITLE 39. POSTAL SERVICES • PART IV: MAIL MATTER • CHAPTER 30: NONMAILABLE MATTER

Title 40 • Public Buildings, Property and Works

40 USC § 13j. Firearms or fireworks; speeches; objectionable language; Supreme Court Building and grounds

> The Gist: You must act in a safe and civilized manner at the Supreme Court, and firing guns is illegal.

It shall be unlawful to discharge any firearm, firework or explosive, set fire to any combustible, make any harangue or oration, or utter loud, threatening, or abusive language in the Supreme Court Building or grounds.

Aug. 18, 1949 (35)
TITLE 40. PUBLIC BUILDINGS, PROPERTY, AND WORKS • CHAPTER 1: PUBLIC BUILDINGS, GROUNDS, PARKS, AND WHARVES IN DISTRICT OF COLUMBIA

40 USC § 13n. Policing authority

> The Gist: The Marshal of the Supreme Court and the Supreme Court Police may be authorized to carry firearms as part of their official duties.

(a) Authority of Marshal of the Supreme Court and Supreme Court Police
The Marshal of the Supreme Court and the Supreme Court Police shall have authority, in accordance with regulations prescribed by the Marshal and approved by the Chief Justice of the United States—
(5) to carry firearms as may be required for the performance of duties under sections 13f to 13p of this title.

Aug. 18, 1949 (65)
TITLE 40. PUBLIC BUILDINGS, PROPERTY, AND WORKS • CHAPTER 1: PUBLIC BUILDINGS, GROUNDS, PARKS, AND WHARVES IN DISTRICT OF COLUMBIA

40 USC § 193f. Capitol Grounds and Buildings security

> The Gist: It's illegal to have or discharge firearms or other devices on the U.S. Capitol grounds or in U.S. Capitol buildings. The Capitol Police Board may allow exceptions.

(a) Firearms, dangerous weapons, explosives, or incendiary devices
It shall be unlawful for any person or group of persons—

(1) Except as authorized by regulations which shall be promulgated by the Capitol Police Board:
(A) to carry on or have readily accessible to the person of any individual upon the United States Capitol Grounds or within any of the Capitol Buildings any firearm, dangerous weapon, explosive, or incendiary device; or
(B) to discharge any firearm or explosive, to use any dangerous weapon, or to ignite any incendiary device, upon the United States Capitol Grounds or within any of the Capitol Buildings; or
(C) to transport by any means upon the United States Capitol Grounds or within any of the Capitol Buildings any explosive or incendiary device

July 31, 1946 (126)
TITLE 40. PUBLIC BUILDINGS, PROPERTY, AND WORKS • CHAPTER 2: CAPITOL BUILDING AND GROUNDS

40 USC § 193h. Prosecution and punishment of offenses

> **The Gist:** The penalty for firearm offenses on Capitol grounds is a felony, with up to five years in prison and a $5,000 fine.

(a) Firearms, dangerous weapons, explosives, or incendiary device offenses
Any violation of section 193f(a) of this title, and any attempt to commit any such violation, shall be a felony punishable by a fine not exceeding $5,000, or imprisonment not exceeding five years, or both.

July 31, 1946 (46)
TITLE 40. PUBLIC BUILDINGS, PROPERTY AND WORKS • CHAPTER 2: CAPITOL BUILDING AND GROUNDS

40 USC § 193m. Definitions

> **The Gist:** Certain words are defined for law number 40–193f, above. The definition of a dangerous weapon excludes knives with a blade of three inches or less.

As used in sections 193a to 193m, 212a, 212a-2, and 212b of this title—
(1) The term "**Capitol Buildings**" means the United States Capitol, the Senate and House Office Buildings and garages, the Capitol Power Plant, all subways and enclosed passages connecting two or more of such structures, and the real property underlying and enclosed by any such structure.
(2) The term "**firearm**" shall have the same meaning as when used in section 901(3) of Title 15 <repealed>.
(3) The term "**dangerous weapon**" includes all articles enumerated in section 14(a) of the Act of July 8, 1932 (47 Stat. 654, as amended; D.C. Code, sec. 22-3214(a)) and also any device designed to expel or hurl a projectile capable of causing injury to persons or property, daggers, dirks, stilettoes, and knives having blades over three inches in length.
(4) The term "**explosive**" shall have the same meaning as when used in section 121(1) of Title 50.
(5) The term "**act of physical violence**" means any act involving (1) an assault or any other infliction or threat of infliction of death or bodily harm upon any individual, or (2) damage to or destruction of any real property or personal property.

July 31, 1946 (204)
TITLE 40. PUBLIC BUILDINGS, PROPERTY, AND WORKS • CHAPTER 2: CAPITOL BUILDING AND GROUNDS

40 USC § 193t. Police power; Smithsonian grounds

> **The Gist:** Smithsonian Institution police may carry revolvers. Revolvers and ammunition are provided to them at no charge.

The special police provided for in section 193n of this title shall have the power, within the specified buildings and grounds, to enforce and make arrests for violations of any provision of sections 193o to 193q of this title, of any regulation prescribed under section 193r of this title, or of any law of the United States or of any State or any regulation promulgated pursuant thereto, and they may be furnished, without charge, with uniforms and such other equipment as may be necessary for the proper performance of their duties, including badges, revolvers, and ammunition.

Oct. 24, 1951 (96)
TITLE 40. PUBLIC BUILDINGS, PROPERTY, AND WORKS • CHAPTER 2: CAPITOL BUILDING AND GROUNDS

40 USC § 210. Uniform, belts and arms; Capitol Police

> The Gist: The Capitol Police may carry firearms. Firearms are paid for from the contingent fund of the Senate and House of Representatives.

The Sergeant at Arms of the Senate and the Sergeant at Arms of the House of Representatives shall select and regulate the pattern for a uniform for the Capitol police and watchmen, and furnish each member of the force with the necessary belts and arms, payable out of the contingent fund of the Senate and House of Representatives upon the certificate of the officers above named. Such arms so furnished shall be carried by each officer and member of the Capitol Police, while in the Capitol Buildings (as defined in section 193m(a)(1) of this title), and while within or outside of the boundaries of the United States Capitol Grounds (as defined in section 193a of this title), in such manner and at such times as the Sergeant at Arms of the Senate and the Sergeant at Arms of the House of Representatives may, by regulations, prescribe.

Oct. 31, 1972 (148)
TITLE 40. PUBLIC BUILDINGS, PROPERTY, AND WORKS • CHAPTER 2: CAPITOL BUILDING AND GROUNDS

40 USC § 304m. Effect on other laws; abandoned or forfeited property excluded from allocation

> The Gist: NFA weapons and military arms are not subject to certain laws in Title 40 related to property abandoned, forfeited, or pending forfeiture.

Nothing contained in sections 304f to 304m of this title shall be construed as repealing any other laws relating to the disposition of forfeited or abandoned property, except such provisions of such laws as are directly in conflict with any provisions of said sections.
The following classes of property shall not be subject to allocation under sections 304g to 304i of this title, but shall be disposed of in the manner otherwise provided by law:
(1) arms or munitions of war included in section 404 of Title 22 <repealed>:
(2) narcotic drugs, as defined in the Controlled Substances Act <21 USC § 801 et seq.>.
(3) firearms, as defined in section 5845 of Title 26; and
(4) such other classes or kinds of property as the Administrator, with the approval of the Secretary of the Treasury, may deem in the public interest, and may by rules and regulations provide.

Aug. 27, 1935 (151)
TITLE 40. PUBLIC BUILDINGS, PROPERTY, AND WORKS • CHAPTER 4: THE PUBLIC PROPERTY

40 USC § 314. Sale of war supplies, lands, and buildings

> The Gist: The President may authorize the sale of war supplies and war-supply factories to governments at war with a country which the U.S. is

also at war with. The President may authorize the sale of arms and ammunition to the National Rifle Association and similar organizations in the United States to encourage target practice.

Note: This World War I law is part of the historical cooperation between the NRA and the government to train citizens in the use of small arms. It is a direct outgrowth, as are most gun laws, of the Constitutional presumption that the American population is armed. See also the Civilian Marksmanship Program laws starting at 10-4307.

The President is authorized, through the head of any executive department, to sell, upon such terms as the head of such department shall deem expedient, to any person, partnership, association, corporation, or any other department of the Government, or to any foreign State or Government, engaged in war against any Government with which the United States is at war, any war supplies, material and equipment, and any by-products thereof, and any building, plant or factory, acquired since April sixth, nineteen hundred and seventeen, including the lands upon which the plant or factory may be situated, for the production of such war supplies, materials, and equipment which, during the emergency existing July 9, 1918, may have been purchased, acquired, or manufactured by the United States: Provided further, That sales of guns and ammunition made under the authority contained in this section or any other Act shall be limited to sales to other departments of the Government and to foreign States or Governments engaged in war against any Government with which the United States is at war, and to members of the National Rifle Association and of other recognized associations organized in the United States for the encouragement of small-arms target practice.
July 9, 1918 (202)
TITLE 40. PUBLIC BUILDINGS, PROPERTY, AND WORKS • CHAPTER 4: THE PUBLIC PROPERTY

40 USC § 318d. Nonuniformed special policemen; powers; arrests without warrant

The Gist: Certain officers and employees of the General Services Administration may carry firearms.

Officials or employees of the General Services Administration who have been duly authorized to perform investigative functions may be empowered by the Administrator of General Services, or officials of General Services Administration duly authorized by him, to act as nonuniformed special policemen in order to protect property under the charge and control of the General Services Administration and to carry firearms, whether on Federal property or in travel status. Such officials or employees who are empowered to act as nonuniformed special policemen shall have, while on real property under the charge and control of the General Services Administration, the power to enforce Federal laws for the protection of persons and property and the power to enforce rules and regulations made and published for such purposes by the Administrator or duly authorized officials of the General Services Administration. Any such special policeman may make arrests without warrant for any offense committed upon such property if he has reasonable ground to believe (1) the offense constitutes a felony under the laws of the United States, and (2) that the person to be arrested is guilty of that offense.
June 1, 1948 (186)
TITLE 40. PUBLIC BUILDINGS, PROPERTY, AND WORKS • CHAPTER 4: THE PUBLIC PROPERTY

40 USC § 490. Operation of buildings and related activities by Administrator

> **The Gist:** The General Services Administration protection force may carry firearms, which are provided for them along with ammunition.

(a) General duties
Whenever and to the extent that the Administrator has been or hereafter may be authorized by any provision of law other than this subsection to maintain, operate, and protect any building, property, or grounds situated in or outside the District of Columbia, including the construction, repair, preservation, demolition, furnishing, and equipment thereof, he is authorized in the discharge of the duties so conferred upon him—
(2) to furnish arms and ammunition for the protection force maintained by the General Services Administration

June 30, 1949 (84)
TITLE 40. PUBLIC BUILDINGS, PROPERTY, AND WORKS • CHAPTER 10. MANAGEMENT AND DISPOSAL OF GOVERNMENT PROPERTY • SUBCHAPTER II: PROPERTY MANAGEMENT

40 USC § 1315. Law enforcement authority of Secretary of Homeland Security for protection of public property

> **The Gist:** A new federal police force is authorized within the Dept. of Homeland Security to carry firearms and perform specified law enforcement work, subject to approval by both the Secretary of Homeland Security and the Attorney General. Blurring the lines between local police power and federal authority, paragraph (e) authorizes the Secretary of Homeland Security to enter into agreements with federal, state and local agencies, to enforce federal, state and local laws, concurrently with each other.

(b) Officers And Agents—
(1) Designation—The Secretary may designate employees of the Department of Homeland Security, including employees transferred to the Department from the Office of the Federal Protective Service of the General Services Administration pursuant to the Homeland Security Act of 2002, as officers and agents for duty in connection with the protection of property owned or occupied by the Federal Government and persons on the property, including duty in areas outside the property to the extent necessary to protect the property and persons on the property.
(2) Powers—While engaged in the performance of official duties, an officer or agent designated under this subsection may—
(B) carry firearms;
(e) Authority Outside Federal Property—For the protection of property owned or occupied by the Federal Government and persons on the property, the Secretary may enter into agreements with Federal agencies and with State and local governments to obtain authority for officers and agents designated under this section to enforce Federal laws and State and local laws concurrently with other Federal law enforcement officers and with State and local law enforcement officers.
(f) Secretary And Attorney General Approval—The powers granted to officers and agents designated under this section shall be exercised in accordance with guidelines approved by the Secretary and the Attorney General.

Nov. 25, 2002 (215)
TITLE 40. PUBLIC BUILDINGS, PROPERTY, AND WORKS

Title 42 • The Public Health and Welfare

42 USC § 1711. Definitions

> The Gist: Definitions of firearms and related materials, in the context of war-risk hazards, are provided for use in this chapter (Chapter 12). This is related to a World War II law under which the U.S. can provide compensation for injury, death or capture of a U.S. civilian working outside the country under contract for the government.

When used in this chapter—

(a) The term "**Secretary**" means the Secretary of Labor.

(b) The term "**war-risk hazard**" means any hazard arising during a war in which the United States is engaged; during an armed conflict in which the United States is engaged, whether or not war has been declared; or during a war or armed conflict between military forces of any origin, occurring within any country in which a person covered by this chapter is serving; from—

(1) the discharge of any missile (including liquids and gas) or the use of any weapon, explosive, or other noxious thing by a hostile force or person or in combating an attack or an imagined attack by a hostile force or person; or

(2) action of a hostile force or person, including rebellion or insurrection against the United States or any of its Allies; or

(3) the discharge or explosion of munitions intended for use in connection with a war or armed conflict with a hostile force or person as defined herein (except with respect to employees of a manufacturer, processor, or transporter of munitions during the manufacture, processing, or transporting thereof, or while stored on the premises of the manufacturer, processor, or transporter); or

(4) the collision of vessels in convoy or the operation of vessels or aircraft without running lights or without other customary peacetime aids to navigation; or

(5) the operation of vessels or aircraft in a zone of hostilities or engaged in war activities.

(c) The term "**hostile force or person**" means any nation, any subject of a foreign nation, or any other person serving a foreign nation (1) engaged in a war against the United States or any of its allies, (2) engaged in armed conflict, whether or not war has been declared, against the United States or any of its allies, or (3) engaged in a war or armed conflict between military forces of any origin in any country in which a person covered by this chapter is serving.

(d) The term "**allies**" means any nation with which the United States is engaged in a common military effort or with which the United States has entered into a common defensive military alliance.

(e) The term "**war activities**" includes activities directly relating to military operations.

(f) The term "continental United States" means the States and the District of Columbia.

Dec. 2, 1942 (400)

TITLE 42. THE PUBLIC HEALTH AND WELFARE • CHAPTER 12—COMPENSATION FOR INJURY, DEATH, OR DETENTION OF EMPLOYEES OF CONTRACTORS WITH THE UNITED STATES OUTSIDE UNITED STATES • SUBCHAPTER II—MISCELLANEOUS PROVISIONS

42 USC § 1983. Civil action for deprivation of rights

The Gist: Every person who, under color of law or other presumption of authority, deprives a person of any right, privilege or immunity secured by the Constitution or by law, is liable to that person for damages in a lawsuit or other proper form of redress. Limited exceptions exist for judicial officers acting in their official capacity. The roots of this law stretch back to the post-Civil War era, in the Civil Rights Act of Apr. 20, 1871. The tangential but obvious connection of this law to gun law is part of a reexamination of the guarantee of the Second Amendment right to keep and bear arms as a basic civil right. See also 18-241, 18-242 and 18-1001.

Every person who, under color of any statute, ordinance, regulation, custom, or usage, of any State or Territory or the District of Columbia, subjects, or causes to be subjected, any citizen of the United States or other person within the jurisdiction thereof to the deprivation of any rights, privileges, or immunities secured by the Constitution and laws, shall be liable to the party injured in an action at law, suit in equity, or other proper proceeding for redress, except that in any action brought against a judicial officer for an act or omission taken in such officer's judicial capacity, injunctive relief shall not be granted unless a declaratory decree was violated or declaratory relief was unavailable. For the purposes of this section, any Act of Congress applicable exclusively to the District of Columbia shall be considered to be a statute of the District of Columbia.

Dec. 29, 1979 (145)
TITLE 42. THE PUBLIC HEALTH AND WELFARE • CHAPTER 21: CIVIL RIGHTS • SUBCHAPTER I: GENERALLY

42 USC § 2201. General duties of Commission

The Gist: Members, officers and employees of the Atomic Energy Commission may be authorized to carry firearms. Certain contractors and subcontractors of the Commission may be authorized to carry firearms.

In the performance of its functions the Commission is authorized to—
(k) Carrying of firearms; authority to make arrests without warrant
authorize such of its members, officers, and employees as it deems necessary in the interest of the common defense and security to carry firearms while in the discharge of their official duties. The Commission may also authorize such of those employees of its contractors and subcontractors (at any tier) engaged in the protection of property under the jurisdiction of the United States located at facilities owned by or contracted to the United States or being transported to or from such facilities as it deems necessary in the interests of the common defense and security to carry firearms while in the discharge of their official duties. A person authorized to carry firearms under this subsection may, while in the performance of, and in connection with, official duties, make arrests without warrant for any offense against the United States committed in that person's presence or for any felony cognizable under the laws of the United States if that person has reasonable grounds to believe that the individual to be arrested has committed or is committing such felony. An employee of a contractor or subcontractor authorized to carry firearms under this subsection may make such arrests only when the individual to be arrested is within, or in direct flight from, the area of such offense. A person granted authority to make arrests by this subsection may exercise that authority only in the enforcement of
(1) laws regarding the property of the United States in the custody of the Department of Energy, the Nuclear Regulatory Commission, or a contractor of the Department of Energy or Nuclear Regulatory Commission, or

(2) any provision of this chapter that may subject an offender to a fine, imprisonment, or both. The arrest authority conferred by this subsection is in addition to any arrest authority under other laws. The Secretary, with the approval of the Attorney General, shall issue guidelines to implement this subsection

Aug. 1, 1946 (357)
TITLE 42. THE PUBLIC HEALTH AND WELFARE • CHAPTER 23: DEVELOPMENT AND CONTROL OF ATOMIC ENERGY • DIVISION A: ATOMIC ENERGY • SUBCHAPTER XIII: GENERAL AUTHORITY OF COMMISSION

42 USC § 2278a. Trespass upon Commission installations;

The Gist: The Atomic Energy Commission can regulate firearms at any commission facility. Such regulations must be posted. Anyone willfully violating such regulations may be fined. If the violation is at a site that is fenced or enclosed by a roof, wall, floor or other structural barrier, the violator may be fined and imprisoned.

Issuance and posting of regulations; penalties for violation
(a) The Commission is authorized to issue regulations relating to the entry upon or carrying, transporting, or otherwise introducing or causing to be introduced any dangerous weapon, explosive, or other dangerous instrument or material likely to produce substantial injury or damage to persons or property, into or upon any facility, installation, or real property subject to the jurisdiction, administration, or in the custody of the Commission. Every such regulation of the Commission shall be posted conspicuously at the location involved.
(b) Whoever shall willfully violate any regulation of the Commission issued pursuant to subsection (a) of this section shall, upon conviction thereof, be punishable by a fine of not more than $1,000.
(c) Whoever shall willfully violate any regulation of the Commission issued pursuant to subsection (a) of this section with respect to any installation or other property which is enclosed by a fence, wall, floor, roof, or other structural barrier shall be guilty of a misdemeanor and upon conviction thereof shall be punished by a fine of not to exceed $5,000 or to imprisonment for not more than one year, or both.

Aug. 1, 1946 (191)
TITLE 42. THE PUBLIC HEALTH AND WELFARE • CHAPTER 23: DEVELOPMENT AND CONTROL OF ATOMIC ENERGY • DIVISION A: ATOMIC ENERGY • SUBCHAPTER XVII: ENFORCEMENT OF CHAPTER

42 USC § 2456. Permission to use firearms

The Gist: The officers and employees of the National Aeronautics and Space Administration may be authorized to carry firearms. Certain contractors and subcontractors of NASA may be authorized to carry firearms.

The Administrator may direct such of the officers and employees of the Administration as he deems necessary in the public interest to carry firearms while in the conduct of their official duties. The Administrator may also authorize such of those employees of the contractors and subcontractors of the Administration engaged in the protection of property owned by the United States and located at facilities owned by or contracted to the United States as he deems necessary in the public interest, to carry firearms while in the conduct of their official duties.

July 29, 1958 (91)
TITLE 42. THE PUBLIC HEALTH AND WELFARE • CHAPTER 26: NATIONAL SPACE PROGRAM • SUBCHAPTER I: GENERAL PROVISIONS

42 USC § 2456a. Arrest authority

The Gist: Employees, contractors and subcontractors of NASA, who are authorized to carry firearms, may make arrests in connection with their official duties.

Under regulations to be prescribed by the Administrator and approved by the Attorney General of the United States, those employees of the Administration and of its contractors and subcontractors authorized to carry firearms under section 2456 of this title may arrest without warrant for any offense against the United States committed in their presence, or for any felony cognizable under the laws of the United States if they have reasonable grounds to believe that the person to be arrested has committed or is committing such felony. Persons granted authority to make arrests by this section may exercise that authority only while guarding and protecting property owned or leased by, or under the control of, the United States under the administration and control of the Administration or one of its contractors or subcontractors, at facilities owned by or contracted to the Administration.

Nov. 17, 1988 (141)
TITLE 42.   THE PUBLIC HEALTH AND WELFARE • CHAPTER 26: NATIONAL SPACE PROGRAM •
SUBCHAPTER I: GENERAL PROVISIONS

42 USC § 3751. Description of drug control and system improvement grant program

The Gist: The Director of the Bureau of Justice Assistance may grant money to states to improve their criminal justice systems in a variety of ways. One of these is to treat violent 16- and 17-year olds as adults if they use firearms in armed robbery, aggravated battery, criminal sexual penetration or drive-by shootings.

(b) Grants to States and units of local government; purposes of grants
The Director of the Bureau of Justice Assistance (hereafter in this subchapter referred to as the "Director") is authorized to make grants to States, for the use by States and units of local government in the States, for the purpose of enforcing State and local laws that establish offenses similar to offenses established in the Controlled Substance Act (21 U.S.C. 801 et seq.) and to improve the functioning of the criminal justice system with emphasis on violent crime and serious offenders. Such grants shall provide additional personnel, equipment, training, technical assistance, and information systems for the more widespread apprehension, prosecution, adjudication, and detention and rehabilitation of persons who violate these laws, and to assist the victims of such crimes (other than compensation), including—
(23) programs that address the need for effective bindover systems for the prosecution of violent 16- and 17-year-old juveniles in courts with jurisdiction over adults for the crimes of—
(D) armed robbery when armed with a firearm;
(E) aggravated battery or assault when armed with a firearm;
(F) criminal sexual penetration when armed with a firearm; and
(G) drive-by shootings as described in section 36 of Title 18

Nov. 18, 1988 (208)
TITLE 42. THE PUBLIC HEALTH AND WELFARE • CHAPTER 46: JUSTICE SYSTEM IMPROVEMENT •
SUBCHAPTER V: BUREAU OF JUSTICE ASSISTANCE GRANT PROGRAMS

42 USC § 3759. Improvement of criminal justice records

> The Gist: States which receive funds from the Bureau of Justice Assistance are required to allocate a portion of the funds to improve their criminal justice records, to comply with background check requirements of the Brady Law, unless their records are adequate.

(a) Percentage allocation of funds
Subject to subsection (d), of this section, each State which receives funds under section 3756 of this title in a fiscal year shall allocate not less than 5 percent of such funds to the improvement of criminal justice records.

(b) Includible improvements
The improvement referred to in subsection (a) of this section shall include—

(1) the completion of criminal histories to include the final dispositions of all arrests for felony offenses:

(2) the full automation of all criminal justice histories and fingerprint records:

(3) the frequency and quality of criminal history reports to the Federal Bureau of Investigation; and

(4) the improvement of State record systems and the sharing with the Attorney General of all of the records described in paragraphs (1), (2), and (3) of this subsection and the records required by the Attorney General under section 103 of the Brady Handgun Violence Prevention Act, for the purpose of implementing that Act.

(4) <Note: two paragraphs "4" were enacted.> the improvement of State record systems and the sharing of all of the records described in paragraphs (1), (2), and (3) and the child abuse crime records required under the National Child Protection Act of 1993 <42 USC § 5119 et seq.> with the Attorney General for the purpose of implementing the National Child Protection Act of 1993 <42 USC § 5119 et seq.>.

(c) Guidelines
The Director, in consultation with the Director of the Bureau of Justice Statistics, shall establish guidelines for the fulfillment of the requirements specified in subsections (a) and (b) of this section.

(d) Expenditures unwarranted in light of quality of criminal justice records
In accordance with such guidelines as the Director shall issue and on the request of a State, the Director may—

(1) waive compliance with subsection (a) of this section by such State; or

(2) authorize such State to reduce the minimum amount such State is required to allocate under subsection (a) of this section: if the Director, in the discretion of the Director, finds that the quality of the State's criminal justice records does not warrant expending the amount allocated under subsection (a) of this section.

Nov. 29, 1990 (364)
TITLE 42: THE PUBLIC HEALTH AND WELFARE • CHAPTER 46: JUSTICE SYSTEM IMPROVEMENT • SUBCHAPTER V: BUREAU OF JUSTICE ASSISTANCE GRANT PROGRAMS • PART A: DRUG CONTROL AND SYSTEM IMPROVEMENT GRANT PROGRAM

42 USC § 3760. Purposes <Byrne grants>

> The Gist: Congress and the President agreed to provide federal funds, through the Byrne Discretionary Grant program, to private gun-safety trainers for educating the general public. Covers education and training programs for "the lawful and safe ownership, storage, carriage, or use of firearms," including the use of secure gun storage or safety devices. Such funds are prohibited for advocating gun control.

(a) In general
The purpose of this subpart is to provide additional Federal financial assistance to public or private agencies and private nonprofit organizations for purposes of—

(1) undertaking educational and training programs for—
(A) criminal justice personnel; and
(B) the general public, with respect to the lawful and safe ownership, storage, carriage, or use of firearms, including the provision of secure gun storage or safety devices;
(2) providing technical assistance to States and local units of government;
(3) undertaking projects which are national or multijurisdictional in scope and which address the purposes specified in section 3752 of this title; and
(4) providing financial assistance to public agencies and private nonprofit organizations for demonstration programs which, in view of previous research or experience, are likely to be a success in more than one jurisdiction.
(b) Grants and contracts
In carrying out this subpart, the Director is authorized to make grants to, or enter into contracts with non-Federal public or private agencies, institutions, or organizations or individuals to carry out any purpose specified in section 3751(b) of this title and is authorized to make grants to, or enter into contracts with, those persons and entities to carry out the purposes specified in subsection (a)(1)(B) of this section in accordance with subsection (c) of this section. The Director shall have final authority over all funds awarded under this subpart.
(c) Firearm safety education grants
(1) In accordance with this subsection, the Director may make a grant to, or enter into a contract with, any person or entity referred to in subsection (b) of this section to provide for a firearm safety program that, in a manner consistent with subsection (a)(1)(B) of this section, provides for general public training and dissemination of information concerning firearm safety, secure gun storage, and the lawful ownership, carriage, or use of firearms, including the provision of secure gun storage or safety devices.
(2) Funds made available under a grant under paragraph (1) may not be used (either directly or by supplanting non-Federal funds) for advocating or promoting gun control, including making communications that are intended to directly or indirectly affect the passage of Federal, State, or local legislation intended to restrict or control the purchase or use of firearms.
(3) Except as provided in paragraph (4), each firearm safety program that receives funding under this subsection shall provide for evaluations that shall be developed pursuant to guidelines that the Director of the National Institute of Justice of the Department of Justice, in consultation with the Director of the Bureau of Justice Assistance and recognized private entities that have expertise in firearms safety, education and training, shall establish.
(4) With respect to a firearm safety program that receives funding under this section, the Director may waive the evaluation requirement described in paragraph (3) if the Director determines that the program—
(A) is not of a sufficient size to justify an evaluation; or
(B) is designed primarily to provide material resources and supplies, and that activity would not justify an evaluation.

Oct. 21, 1998 (505)
TITLE 42. THE PUBLIC HEALTH AND WELFARE • CHAPTER 46: JUSTICE SYSTEM IMPROVEMENT • SUBCHAPTER V: BUREAU OF JUSTICE ASSISTANCE GRANT PROGRAMS • PART B: DISCRETIONARY GRANTS • SUBPART 1 - GRANTS TO PUBLIC AND PRIVATE ENTITIES

42 USC § 3796ee—4. Allocation and distribution of funds

> The Gist: Federal grant money is available for developing alternative methods of punishment for young offenders (rather than traditional methods of imprisonment and probation). In awarding such a grant, the Attorney General must consider whether a state requires school suspension and revoking driving privileges for juveniles caught with guns illegally on school grounds.

(e) Consideration

Notwithstanding subsections (a) and (b) of this section, in awarding grants under this subchapter, the Attorney General shall consider as a factor whether a State has in effect throughout such State a law or policy that requires that a juvenile who is in possession of a firearm or other weapon on school property or convicted of a crime involving the use of a firearm or weapon on school property—

(1) be suspended from school for a reasonable period of time and

(2) lose driving license privileges for a reasonable period to time.

Sept. 13, 1994 (94)

TITLE 42. THE PUBLIC HEALTH AND WELFARE • CHAPTER 46: JUSTICE SYSTEM IMPROVEMENT • SUBCHAPTER XII-F: CERTAIN PUNISHMENT FOR YOUNG OFFENDERS

42 USC § 3796ii-2. Definition <Historical Note>

The Gist: For the purposes of this subchapter, a *violent offender* included anyone convicted, or only charged, with a crime if the person at the time carried, possessed or used a firearm. (This subchapter deals with grants by the U.S. Attorney General to state, local and Indian authorities for programs related to substance-abuse treatment.) Such funds were not available to programs that accepted violent offenders, thus limiting the federal government's powers, and has been repealed.

42 USC § 5653. Research, demonstration, and evaluation functions of Institute

The Gist: The head of the National Institute for Juvenile Justice and Delinquency Prevention may help states identify chronic, serious, violent juvenile offenders who commit firearms crimes and other offenses.

(a) The Administrator, acting through the National Institute for Juvenile Justice and Delinquency Prevention, is authorized to—

(5) encourage the development and establishment of programs to enhance the States' ability to identify chronic serious and violent juvenile offenders who commit crimes such as rape, murder, firearms offenses, gang-related crimes, violent felonies, and serious drug offenses

Oct. 12, 1984 (56)

TITLE 42. THE PUBLIC HEALTH AND WELFARE • PART C: NATIONAL INSTITUTE FOR JUVENILE JUSTICE AND DELINQUENCY PREVENTION • CHAPTER 72: JUVENILE JUSTICE AND DELINQUENCY PREVENTION • SUBCHAPTER II: PROGRAMS AND OFFICES

42 USC § 5662. Special studies and reports

The Gist: One of the objectives of a study that the National Institute for Juvenile Justice and Delinquency Prevention is required to make is to find out if juveniles can get firearms, how juveniles use them, and how firearms are used against juveniles.

(b) Pursuant to 1992 amendments

(6)(A) Not later than 180 days after November 4, 1992, the Administrator shall begin to conduct a study and continue any pending study of the incidence of violence committed by or against juveniles in urban and rural areas in the United States.

(B) The urban areas shall include—

(i) the District of Columbia;
(ii) Los Angeles, California;
(iii) Milwaukee, Wisconsin;
(iv) Denver, Colorado;
(v) Pittsburgh, Pennsylvania;
(vi) Rochester, New York; and
(vii) such other cities as the Administrator determines to be appropriate.
(C) At least one rural area shall be included.
(D) With respect to each urban and rural area included in the study, the objectives of the study shall be—
(iii) to determine the accessibility of firearms, and the use of firearms by or against juveniles

Nov. 18, 1988 (133)
TITLE 42. THE PUBLIC HEALTH AND WELFARE • PART C: NATIONAL INSTITUTE FOR JUVENILE JUSTICE AND DELINQUENCY PREVENTION • CHAPTER 72: JUVENILE JUSTICE AND DELINQUENCY PREVENTION • SUBCHAPTER II: PROGRAMS AND OFFICES

42 USC § 7270a. Guards for Strategic Petroleum Reserve facilities

> The Gist: Employees, contractors and subcontractors of the Dept. of Energy may carry firearms while protecting the Strategic Petroleum Reserve.

Under guidelines prescribed by the Secretary and concurred with by the Attorney General, employees of the Department of Energy and employees of contractors and subcontractors (at any tier) of the Department of Energy, while discharging their official duties of protecting the Strategic Petroleum Reserve (established under part B of title I of the Energy Policy and Conservation Act <42 USC § 6231 et seq.>) or its storage or related facilities or of protecting persons upon the Strategic Petroleum Reserve or its storage or related facilities, may—
(1) carry firearms, if designated by the Secretary and qualified for the use of firearms under the guidelines

Oct. 25, 1988 (107)
TITLE 42. THE PUBLIC HEALTH AND WELFARE • CHAPTER 84: DEPARTMENT OF ENERGY • SUBCHAPTER VI: ADMINISTRATIVE PROVISIONS • PART C: GENERAL ADMINISTRATIVE PROVISIONS

Title 43 • Public Lands

43 USC § 1733. Enforcement authority

> **The Gist:** The Dept. of the Interior must issue regulations concerning the use of public lands. Using public lands in violation of the regulations is illegal. When the Dept. needs assistance in enforcing rules about public land, it must contract with local law enforcement officials to the maximum extent feasible. Such officials are authorized to carry firearms. Also, the uniformed desert ranger force in the California Desert Conservation area are authorized to carry firearms.

(a) Regulations for implementation of management, use, and protection requirements; violations; criminal penalties

The Secretary shall issue regulations necessary to implement the provisions of this Act with respect to the management, use, and protection of the public lands, including the property located thereon. Any person who knowingly and willfully violates any such regulation which is lawfully issued pursuant to this Act shall be fined no more than $1,000 or imprisoned no more than twelve months, or both. Any person charged with a violation of such regulation may be tried and sentenced by any United States magistrate designated for that purpose by the court by which he was appointed, in the same manner and subject to the same conditions and limitations as provided for in section 3401 of Title 18.

(b) Civil actions by Attorney General for violations of regulations; nature of relief; jurisdiction

At the request of the Secretary, the Attorney General may institute a civil action in any United States district court for an injunction or other appropriate order to prevent any person from utilizing public lands in violation of regulations issued by the Secretary under this Act.

(c) Contracts for enforcement of Federal laws and regulations by local law enforcement officials; procedure applicable; contract requirements and implementation

(1) When the Secretary determines that assistance is necessary in enforcing Federal laws and regulations relating to the public lands or their resources he shall offer a contract to appropriate local officials having law enforcement authority within their respective jurisdictions with the view of achieving maximum feasible reliance upon local law enforcement officials in enforcing such laws and regulations. The Secretary shall negotiate on reasonable terms with such officials who have authority to enter into such contracts to enforce such Federal laws and regulations. In the performance of their duties under such contracts such officials and their agents are authorized to carry firearms; execute and serve any warrant or other process issued by a court or officer of competent jurisdiction, make arrests without warrant or process for a misdemeanor he has reasonable grounds to believe is being committed in his presence or view, or for a felony if he has reasonable grounds to believe that the person to be arrested has committed or is committing such felony; search without warrant or process any person, place, or conveyance

according to any Federal law or rule of law; and seize without warrant or process any evidentiary item as provided by Federal law. The Secretary shall provide such law enforcement training as he deems necessary in order to carry out the contracted for responsibilities. While exercising the powers and authorities provided by such contract pursuant to this section, such law enforcement officials and their agents shall have all the immunities of Federal law enforcement officials.

(2) The Secretary may authorize Federal personnel or appropriate local officials to carry out his law enforcement responsibilities with respect to the public lands and their resources. Such designated personnel shall receive the training and have the responsibilities and authority provided for in paragraph (1) of this subsection.

(d) Cooperation with regulatory and law enforcement officials of any State or political subdivision in enforcement of laws or ordinances

In connection with the administration and regulation of the use and occupancy of the public lands, the Secretary is authorized to cooperate with the regulatory and law enforcement officials of any State or political subdivision thereof in the enforcement of the laws or ordinances of such State or subdivision. Such cooperation may include reimbursement to a State or its subdivision for expenditures incurred by it in connection with activities which assist in the administration and regulation of use and occupancy of the public lands.

(e) Uniformed desert ranger force in California Desert Conservation Area; establishment; enforcement of Federal laws and regulations

Nothing in this section shall prevent the Secretary from promptly establishing a uniformed desert ranger force in the California Desert Conservation Area established pursuant to section 1781 of this title for the purpose of enforcing Federal laws and regulations relating to the public lands and resources managed by him in such area. The officers and members of such ranger force shall have the same responsibilities and authority as provided for in paragraph (1) of subsection (c) of this section.

(f) Applicability of other Federal enforcement provisions

Nothing in this Act shall be construed as reducing or limiting the enforcement authority vested in the Secretary by any other statute.

(g) Unlawful activities

The use, occupancy, or development of any portion of the public lands contrary to any regulation of the Secretary or other responsible authority, or contrary to any order issued pursuant to any such regulation, is unlawful and prohibited.

Oct. 21, 1976 (780)
TITLE 43. PUBLIC LANDS • CHAPTER 35: FEDERAL LAND POLICY AND MANAGEMENT • SUBCHAPTER III: ADMINISTRATION

Title 44 • Public Printing and Documents

44 USC § 317. Special policemen

> The Gist: Employees of the Government Printing Office may be authorized to carry and use firearms.

The Public Printer or his delegate may designate employees of the Government Printing Office to serve as special policemen to protect persons and property in premises and adjacent areas occupied by or under the control of the Government Printing Office. Under regulations to be prescribed by the Public Printer, employees designated as special policemen are authorized to bear and use arms in the performance of their duties; make arrest for violations of laws of the United States, the several States, and the District of Columbia; and enforce the regulations of the Public Printer, including the removal from Government Printing Office premises of individuals who violate such regulations. The jurisdiction of special policemen in premises occupied by or under the control of the Government Printing Office and adjacent areas shall be concurrent with the jurisdiction of the respective law enforcement agencies where the premises are located.

July 31, 1970 (145)

TITLE 44. PUBLIC PRINTING AND DOCUMENTS • CHAPTER 3: GOVERNMENT PRINTING OFFICE

44 USC § 1510. Code of Federal Regulations

> The Gist: Many federal requirements concerning firearms are not enumerated in law, but are issued as regulations by various government agencies. The regulations are not technically laws, since they are not enacted by Congress, but are authorized by law, and have the force of law—which means that a violation can require fines and prison sentences. Anyone who looks at this book and might conclude that there really aren't that many federal laws, must keep in mind that in many cases these laws are merely *enabling legislation*, and that the real body of work exists in the monumental federal regulations these laws authorize.

The Office of the Federal Register is charged with the responsibility of publishing the entire body of federal regulations as the Code of Federal Regulations (CFR). Among the more significant portions of the CFR, with respect to firearms, are the regulations of the Bureau of Alcohol, Tobacco, Firearms and Explosives (found in Title 27); the Internal Revenue Service (in Title 26); the Federal Aviation Administration (Title 14); Parks, Forests and Public Property (Title 36) and many more. There are 50 titles in the full CFR set. Federal firearms licensees are typically more involved with

> CFR requirements on a day-to-day basis than they are with the actual federal statutes.

(a) The Administrative Committee of the Federal Register, with the approval of the President, may require, from time to time as it considers necessary, the preparation and publication in special or supplemental editions of the Federal Register of complete codifications of the documents of each agency of the Government having general applicability and legal effect, issued or promulgated by the agency by publication in the Federal Register or by filing with the Administrative Committee, and are relied upon by the agency as authority for, or are invoked or used by it in the discharge of, its activities or functions, and are in effect as to facts arising on or after dates specified by the Administrative Committee.

(b) A codification published under subsection (a) of this section shall be printed and bound in permanent form and shall be designated as the "Code of Federal Regulations." The Administrative Committee shall regulate the binding of the printed codifications into separate books with a view to practical usefulness and economical manufacture. Each book shall contain an explanation of its coverage and other aids to users that the Administrative Committee may require. A general index to the entire Code of Federal Regulations shall be separately printed and bound.

(c) The Administrative Committee shall regulate the supplementation and the collation and republication of the printed codifications with a view to keeping the Code of Federal Regulations as current as practicable. Each book shall be either supplemented or collated and republished at least once each calendar year.

(d) The Office of the Federal Register shall prepare and publish the codifications, supplements, collations, and indexes authorized by this section.

(e) The codified documents of the several agencies published in the supplemental edition of the Federal Register under this section, as amended by documents subsequently filed with the Office and published in the daily issues of the Federal Register, shall be prima facie evidence of the text of the documents and of the fact that they are in effect on and after the date of publication.

(f) The Administrative Committee shall prescribe, with the approval of the President, regulations for carrying out this section.

(g) This section does not require codification of the text of Presidential documents published and periodically compiled in supplements to Title 3 of the Code of Federal Regulations.

Oct. 22, 1968 (383)

TITLE 44. PUBLIC PRINTING AND DOCUMENTS • CHAPTER 15. FEDERAL REGISTER AND CODE OF FEDERAL REGULATIONS

Title 49 • Transportation

49 USC § 114. Transportation Security Administration

> The Gist: A new federal police force is authorized under the
> Transportation Security Administration. Employees designated as TSA law
> enforcement officers may carry firearms, at the Attorney General's
> discretion, subject to department guidelines approved by the AG, and
> under the AG's deadly force policy.

(q) Law Enforcement Powers—
(1) In General—The Under Secretary may designate an employee of the Transportation Security Administration to serve as a law enforcement officer.
(2) Powers—While engaged in official duties of the Administration as required to fulfill the responsibilities under this section, a law enforcement officer designated under paragraph (1) may—
(A) carry a firearm;
(3) Guidelines On Exercise Of Authority—The authority provided by this subsection shall be exercised in accordance with guidelines prescribed by the Under Secretary, in consultation with the Attorney General of the United States, and shall include adherence to the Attorney General's policy on use of deadly force.
(4) Revocation Or Suspension Of Authority—The powers authorized by this subsection may be rescinded or suspended should the Attorney General determine that the Under Secretary has not complied with the guidelines prescribed in paragraph (3) and conveys the determination in writing to the Secretary of Transportation and the Under Secretary.
Nov. 19, 2001 (157)
TITLE 49. TRANSPORTATION • SUBTITLE I: DEPARTMENT OF TRANSPORTATION • CHAPTER 1: ORGANIZATION

49 USC § 5103. General regulatory authority

> The Gist: The Dept. of Transportation identifies hazardous materials,
> which includes explosives, and regulates the transportation of these
> substances.

(a) Designating material as hazardous.—The Secretary of Transportation shall designate material (including an explosive, radioactive material, etiologic agent, flammable or combustible liquid of solid, poison, oxidizing or corrosive material, and compressed gas) or a group or class of material as hazardous when the Secretary decides that transporting the material in commerce in a particular amount and form may pose an unreasonable risk to health and safety or property.
(b) Regulations for safe transportation.—
(1) The Secretary shall prescribe regulations for the safe transportation of hazardous material in intrastate, interstate, and foreign commerce. The regulations—

(A) apply to a person—
(i) transporting hazardous material in commerce;
(ii) causing hazardous material to be transported in commerce; or
(iii) manufacturing, fabricating, marking, maintaining, reconditioning, repairing, or testing a packaging or a container that is represented, marked, certified, or sold by that person as qualified for use in transporting hazardous material in commerce; and
(B) shall govern safety aspects of the transportation of hazardous material the Secretary considers appropriate.
(2) A proceeding to prescribe the regulations must be conducted under section 553 of title 5, including an opportunity for informal oral presentation.

Jan. 3, 1975 (189)
TITLE 49. TRANSPORTATION • SUBTITLE III: GENERAL AND INTERMODAL PROGRAMS • CHAPTER 51: TRANSPORTATION OF HAZARDOUS MATERIAL

49 USC § 5117. Exemptions and exclusions

> The Gist: This section describes exemptions that exist or that may be applied for concerning the transportation of hazardous materials. The laws of this chapter (Chapter 51) do not prohibit or regulate transporting firearms or ammunition for personal use, or prohibit transporting firearms or ammunition in commerce.

(a) Authority to exempt.—(1) As provided under procedures prescribed by regulation, the Secretary of Transportation may issue an exemption from this chapter or a regulation prescribed under section 5103(b), 5104, 5110, or 5112 of this title to a person transporting, or causing to be transported, hazardous material in a way that achieves a safety level—
(A) at least equal to the safety level required under this chapter; or
(B) consistent with the public interest and this chapter, if a required safety level does not exist.
(2) An exemption under this subsection is effective for not more than 2 years and may be renewed on application to the Secretary.
(b) Applications.—When applying for an exemption or renewal of an exemption under this section, the person must provide a safety analysis prescribed by the Secretary that justifies the exemption. The Secretary shall publish in the Federal Register notice that an application for an exemption has been filed and shall give the public an opportunity to inspect the safety analysis and comment on the application. This subsection does not require the release of information protected by law from public disclosure.
(c) Applications to be dealt with promptly.—The Secretary shall issue or renew the exemption for which an application was filed or deny such issuance or renewal within 180 days after the first day of the month following the date of the filing of such application, or the Secretary shall publish a statement in the Federal Register of the reason why the Secretary's decision on the exemption is delayed, along with an estimate of the additional time necessary before the decision is made.
(d) Exclusions.—(1) The Secretary shall exclude, in any part, from this chapter and regulations prescribed under this chapter—
(A) a public vessel (as defined in section 2101 of title 46);
(B) a vessel exempted under section 3702 of title 46 from chapter 37 of title 46; and
(C) a vessel to the extent it is regulated under the Ports and Waterways Safety Act of 1972 (33 U.S.C. 1221 et seq.).
(2) This chapter and regulations prescribed under this chapter do not prohibit—
(A) or regulate transportation of a firearm (as defined in section 232 of title 18), or ammunition for a firearm, by an individual for personal use; or
(B) transportation of a firearm or ammunition in commerce.

(e) Limitation on authority.—Unless the Secretary decides that an emergency exists, an exemption or renewal granted under this section is the only way a person subject to this chapter may be exempt from this chapter.

July 5, 1994 (430)

TITLE 49. TRANSPORTATION • SUBTITLE III: GENERAL AND INTERMODAL PROGRAMS • CHAPTER 51: TRANSPORTATION OF HAZARDOUS MATERIAL

49 USC § 40113. Administrative

> The Gist: The Transportation Dept. and the Federal Aviation Administration have broad powers and discretion to regulate transportation, conduct investigations, set standards and procedures and more. This section does not, however, prohibit or regulate the transportation of personal firearms or ammunition.

(a) General authority.—The Secretary of Transportation (or the Administrator of the Federal Aviation Administration with respect to the aviation safety duties and powers designated to be carried out by the Administrator) may take action the Secretary or Administrator, as appropriate, considers necessary to carry out this part, including conducting investigations, prescribing regulations, standards, and procedures, and issuing orders.

(b) Hazardous material.—In carrying out this part, the Secretary has the same authority to regulate the transportation of hazardous material by air that the Secretary has under section 5103 of this title. However, this subsection does not prohibit or regulate the transportation of a firearm (as defined in section 232 <civil disorder> of title 18) or ammunition for a firearm, when transported by an individual for personal use.

July 5, 1994 (126)

TITLE 49. TRANSPORTATION • PART A: AIR COMMERCE AND SAFETY • SUBPART I: GENERAL • CHAPTER 401: GENERAL PROVISIONS

49 USC § 44901. Screening passengers and property

> The Gist: The Dept. of Transportation is required to deploy armed law enforcement personnel at every airport screening location, to ensure passenger safety and national security.

(g) Deployment of Armed Personnel.—

(1) In General.—The Under Secretary shall order the deployment of law enforcement personnel authorized to carry firearms at each airport security screening location to ensure passenger safety and national security.

Nov. 19, 2001 (36)

TITLE 49. TRANSPORTATION • SUBTITLE VII: AVIATION PROGRAMS • PART A: AIR COMMERCE AND SAFETY • SUBPART III: SAFETY • CHAPTER 449: SECURITY • SUBCHAPTER 1: REQUIREMENTS

49 USC § 44903. Air transportation security

> The Gist: In this section, law enforcement personnel includes anyone with an official badge (or similar sign of authority), authorized to carry firearms, and with a police-power-of-arrest that meets the Federal Aviation Administration's standards. A person who carries out air transportation security duties may be authorized to carry firearms.

A new category of arms was introduced into federal law here in 2001; "less-than-lethal weapons" for temporarily incapacitating persons. A Statute at Large authorized a National Institute of Justice examination of what already exists and might be used by flight deck (cockpit) crews. If the Dept. finds a suitable option, it may authorize issuing such weapons along with guidelines and training in their allowable use.

Added in 2002, an airline's request to arm its pilots with less-than-lethal weapons must get a response from the Transportation Dept. within 90 days.

<**Statute at Large** follows, from P.L. 107-71, Nov. 19, 2001>
"SEC. 126. Less-Than-Lethal Weaponry For Flight Deck Crews.
(a) National Institute Of Justice Study—The National Institute of Justice shall assess the range of less-than-lethal weaponry available for use by a flight deck crewmember temporarily to incapacitate an individual who presents a clear and present danger to the safety of the aircraft, its passengers, or individuals on the ground and report its findings and recommendations to the Secretary of Transportation within 90 days after the date of enactment of this Act."

(a) Definition.—In this section, "law enforcement personnel" means individuals—
(1) authorized to carry and use firearms;
(2) vested with the degree of the police power of arrest the Administrator of the Federal Aviation Administration considers necessary to carry out this section; and
(3) identifiable by appropriate indicia of authority.
(d) Authorizing individuals to carry firearms and make arrests.—
With the approval of the Attorney General and the Under Secretary of State, the Secretary of Transportation may authorize an individual who carries out air transportation security duties—
(1) to carry firearms
(h) Authority to Arm Flight Deck Crew With Less-Than-Lethal Weapons—
(1) In General—If the Under Secretary, after receiving the recommendations of the National Institute of Justice, determines, with the approval of the Attorney General and the Secretary of State, that it is appropriate and necessary and would effectively serve the public interest in avoiding air piracy, the Secretary may authorize members of the flight deck crew on any aircraft providing air transportation or intrastate air transportation to carry a less-than-lethal weapon while the aircraft is engaged in providing such transportation.
(2) Usage—If the Under Secretary grants authority under paragraph (1) for flight deck crew members to carry a less-than-lethal weapon while engaged in providing air transportation or intrastate air transportation, the Under Secretary shall—
(A) prescribe rules requiring that any such crew member be trained in the proper use of the weapon; and
(B) prescribe guidelines setting forth the circumstances under which such weapons may be used.
(i) Short-Term Assessment and Deployment of Emerging Security Technologies and Procedures.—
(3) Request Of Air Carriers To Use Less-Than-Lethal Weapons.—If, after the date of enactment of this paragraph, the Under Secretary receives a request from an air carrier for authorization to allow pilots of the air carrier to carry less than lethal weapons, the Under Secretary shall respond to that request within 90 days.

July 5, 1994 (313)
TITLE 49. TRANSPORTATION • SUBTITLE VII: AVIATION PROGRAMS • PART A: AIR COMMERCE AND SAFETY • SUBPART III: SAFETY • CHAPTER 449: SECURITY • SUBCHAPTER 1: REQUIREMENTS

49 USC § 44917. Deployment of Federal Air Marshals

> The Gist: The Dept. of the Transportation may make agreements with other official federal, state or local agencies to have armed officers of those agencies, while on board a flight of an air carrier, prepared to assist federal air marshals. The Dept. must establish procedures to notify the marshals of any armed or unarmed law enforcement officers on the aircraft.

(a) In General—The Under Secretary of Transportation for Security under the authority provided by section 44903(d)—

(6) may enter into agreements with Federal, State, and local agencies under which appropriately-trained law enforcement personnel from such agencies, when traveling on a flight of an air carrier, will carry a firearm and be prepared to assist Federal air marshals;

(7) shall establish procedures to ensure that Federal air marshals are made aware of any armed or unarmed law enforcement personnel on board an aircraft

Nov. 19, 2001 (83)

TITLE 49. TRANSPORTATION • SUBTITLE VII: AVIATION PROGRAMS • PART A: AIR COMMERCE AND SAFETY • SUBPART III: SAFETY • CHAPTER 449: SECURITY • SUBCHAPTER 1: REQUIREMENTS

49 USC § 44918. Crew training

> The Gist: Airline crews must receive classroom and hands-on situational training in self-defense techniques. The use of firearms is neither included nor prohibited, and several of the conditions (e.g., "use of protective devices assigned to crew members" "use of available items aboard the aircraft for self-defense" "methods to subdue and restrain an attacker") may allow such use. The new training programs may be developed by the private sector.

(a) In General—Not later than 60 days after the date of enactment of the Aviation and Transportation Security Act, the Administrator of the Federal Aviation Administration, in consultation with the Under Secretary of Transportation for Security, appropriate law enforcement, security, and terrorism experts, representatives of air carriers and labor organizations representing individuals employed in commercial aviation, shall develop detailed guidance for a scheduled passenger air carrier flight and cabin crew training program to prepare crew members for potential threat conditions.

(b) Program Elements—The guidance shall require such a program to include, at a minimum, elements that address the following:

(1) Determination of the seriousness of any occurrence.

(2) Crew communication and coordination.

(3) Appropriate responses to defend oneself.

(4) Use of protective devices assigned to crew members (to the extent such devices are required by the Administrator or Under Secretary).

(5) Psychology of terrorists to cope with hijacker behavior and passenger responses.

(6) Live situational training exercises regarding various threat conditions.

(7) Flight deck procedures or aircraft maneuvers to defend the aircraft.

(8) Any other subject matter deemed appropriate by the Administrator.

(c) Updates—

(1) In General—The Under Secretary shall update the training guidance issued under subsection (a) from time to time to reflect new or different security threats and require air carriers to revise their programs accordingly and provide additional training to their flight and cabin crews.

(2) Additional Requirements—In updating the training guidance, the Under Secretary, in consultation with the Administrator, shall issue a rule to—
(A) require both classroom and effective hands-on situational training in the following elements of self defense:
(i) recognizing suspicious activities and determining the seriousness of an occurrence;
(ii) deterring a passenger who might present a problem;
(iii) crew communication and coordination;
(iv) the proper commands to give to passengers and attackers;
(v) methods to subdue and restrain an attacker;
(vi) use of available items aboard the aircraft for self-defense;
(vii) appropriate and effective responses to defend oneself, including the use of force against an attacker;
(viii) use of protective devices assigned to crew members (to the extent such devices are approved by the Administrator or Under Secretary);
(ix) the psychology of terrorists to cope with their behavior and passenger responses to that behavior;
(x) how to respond to aircraft maneuvers that may be authorized to defend against an act of criminal violence or air piracy;
(F) ensure that no person is required to participate in any hands-on training activity that that person believes will have an adverse impact on his or her health or safety.
(3) Responsibility Of Under Secretary—
(A) Consultation—In developing the rule under paragraph (2), the Under Secretary shall consult with law enforcement personnel and security experts who have expertise in self-defense training, terrorism experts, and representatives of air carriers, the provider of self-defense training for Federal air marshals, flight attendants, labor organizations representing flight attendants, and educational institutions offering law enforcement training programs.

Nov. 19, 2001 (490)
TITLE 49. TRANSPORTATION • SUBTITLE VII: AVIATION PROGRAMS • PART A: AIR COMMERCE AND SAFETY • SUBPART III: SAFETY • CHAPTER 449: SECURITY • SUBCHAPTER 1: REQUIREMENTS

49 USC § 44921. Federal Flight Deck Officer Program

The Gist: Arm The Pilots, round two. One year after a hasty and unproductive effort to arm airline pilots (P.L. 107-71 Sec. 128, repealed), another effort is made here under the Homeland Security Act, replacing the former section. This takes the approach that a pilot can volunteer to be deputized as a federal agent, known as Federal Flight Deck Officers (FFDO), and then qualify to bear arms aboard the aircraft. Cargo pilots were added to the plan in 2003.

Contrary to the popular "Arm the Pilots" title, this law is not about arming pilots, it is about deputizing pilots, and arming the deputies.

The fundamental difference between arming a civilian pilot, and turning the civilian into a government agent as a deputy, is important for those who monitor the condition of the Second Amendment. Arming civilians, or letting them arm themselves, was unacceptable to the government in the context of air travel. The deputizing scheme implemented here provides an alternative, maintaining the full control of those in power. No "right" is conferred, and the permission to bear arms can be summarily revoked by the authorities.

Cargo pilots are to be treated "equitably" with respect to passenger pilots for access to training that would qualify them for FFDO status. Pilots per se may not be armed. Only an FFDO may be armed under this law. The total elimination of the Second Amendment in this context is not addressed—it is simply wiped out without comment.

A huge range of issues are identified for study and resolution, including for example: the type of firearm and ammo to be used; placement of the gun in the cockpit to ensure both its security and easy retrieval; firearm retention; analysis of the risk of catastrophic aircraft failure from gunfire to controls or sensitive areas of the craft (the results are classified); accidental discharge reporting and repercussions; interaction between air marshals, the pilot, crew and other persons; pilot selection and training; storage and transit of guns between flights and when pilots go off site; notifying security staff when pilots or others are authorized to be armed; guidelines on use of lethal force; and anything else the authorities deem necessary.

Pilots with military and law enforcement backgrounds are to get preference in the selection process. Although guns will be provided, pilots may buy their own. Participating pilots are not eligible for compensation from the government for their services as FFDOs. Limited liability is provided for airlines, the pilots and the government, for use or failure to use the firearms. Air carriers are prohibited from pressuring or forbidding their pilots from volunteering for the program, firing them for participating, or refusing to let them pilot aircraft. Years after passage, administrative wrangling has prevented all but a small fraction of pilot applicants from qualifying.

Preemption: Whenever necessary to participate in the program, pilots may carry firearms in any state and from one state to another.

Authority to carry outside the United States may be arranged, in consultation with the Secretary of State. Congress states that arming the pilots does not replace the need for air marshals.

The cargo pilot amendment included a Sense of Congress statement, omitted during the codification process, that said: "It is the sense of Congress that members of a flight deck crew of a cargo aircraft should be armed with a firearm or taser to defend the cargo aircraft against an attack by terrorists that could result in the use of the aircraft as a weapon of mass destruction or for other terrorist purposes."

(a) Establishment—The Under Secretary of Transportation for Security shall establish a program to deputize volunteer pilots of air carriers providing air transportation or intrastate air transportation as Federal law enforcement officers to defend the flight decks of aircraft of such air carriers against acts of criminal violence or air piracy. Such officers shall be known as "Federal flight deck officers".
(b) Procedural Requirements—
(1) In General—Not later than 3 months after the date of enactment of this section, the Under Secretary shall establish procedural requirements to carry out the program under this section.
(2) Commencement Of Program—Beginning 3 months after the date of enactment of this section, the Under Secretary shall begin the process of training and deputizing pilots who are qualified to be Federal flight deck officers as Federal flight deck officers under the program.
(3) Issues To Be Addressed—The procedural requirements established under paragraph (1) shall address the following issues:

(A) The type of firearm to be used by a Federal flight deck officer.
(B) The type of ammunition to be used by a Federal flight deck officer.
(C) The standards and training needed to qualify and requalify as a Federal flight deck officer.
(D) The placement of the firearm of a Federal flight deck officer on board the aircraft to ensure both its security and its ease of retrieval in an emergency.
(E) An analysis of the risk of catastrophic failure of an aircraft as a result of the discharge (including an accidental discharge) of a firearm to be used in the program into the avionics, electrical systems, or other sensitive areas of the aircraft.
(F) The division of responsibility between pilots in the event of an act of criminal violence or air piracy if only 1 pilot is a Federal flight deck officer and if both pilots are Federal flight deck officers.
(G) Procedures for ensuring that the firearm of a Federal flight deck officer does not leave the cockpit if there is a disturbance in the passenger cabin of the aircraft or if the pilot leaves the cockpit for personal reasons.
(H) Interaction between a Federal flight deck officer and a Federal air marshal on board the aircraft.
(I) The process for selection of pilots to participate in the program based on their fitness to participate in the program, including whether an additional background check should be required beyond that required by section 44936(a)(1).
(J) Storage and transportation of firearms between flights, including international flights, to ensure the security of the firearms, focusing particularly on whether such security would be enhanced by requiring storage of the firearm at the airport when the pilot leaves the airport to remain overnight away from the pilot's base airport.
(K) Methods for ensuring that security personnel will be able to identify whether a pilot is authorized to carry a firearm under the program.
(L) Methods for ensuring that pilots (including Federal flight deck officers) will be able to identify whether a passenger is a law enforcement officer who is authorized to carry a firearm aboard the aircraft.
(M) Any other issues that the Under Secretary considers necessary.
(N) The Under Secretary's decisions regarding the methods for implementing each of the foregoing procedural requirements shall be subject to review only for abuse of discretion.
(4) Preference—In selecting pilots to participate in the program, the Under Secretary shall give preference to pilots who are former military or law enforcement personnel.
(5) Classified Information—Notwithstanding section 552 of title 5 but subject to section 40119 of this title, information developed under paragraph (3)(E) shall not be disclosed.
(6) Notice to Congress—The Under Secretary shall provide notice to the Committee on Transportation and Infrastructure of the House of Representatives and the Committee on Commerce, Science, and Transportation of the Senate after completing the analysis required by paragraph (3)(E).
(7) Minimization Of Risk—If the Under Secretary determines as a result of the analysis under paragraph (3)(E) that there is a significant risk of the catastrophic failure of an aircraft as a result of the discharge of a firearm, the Under Secretary shall take such actions as may be necessary to minimize that risk.
(c) Training, Supervision, And Equipment—
(1) In General—The Under Secretary shall only be obligated to provide the training, supervision, and equipment necessary for a pilot to be a Federal flight deck officer under this section at no expense to the pilot or the air carrier employing the pilot.
(2) Training—
(A) In General—The Under Secretary shall base the requirements for the training of Federal flight deck officers under subsection (b) on the training standards applicable to Federal air marshals; except that the Under Secretary shall take into account the differing roles and responsibilities of Federal flight deck officers and Federal air marshals.
(B) Elements—The training of a Federal flight deck officer shall include, at a minimum, the following elements:

(i) Training to ensure that the officer achieves the level of proficiency with a firearm required under subparagraph (C)(i).

(ii) Training to ensure that the officer maintains exclusive control over the officer's firearm at all times, including training in defensive maneuvers.

(iii) Training to assist the officer in determining when it is appropriate to use the officer's firearm and when it is appropriate to use less than lethal force.

(C) Training In Use Of Firearms—

(i) Standard—In order to be deputized as a Federal flight deck officer, a pilot must achieve a level of proficiency with a firearm that is required by the Under Secretary. Such level shall be comparable to the level of proficiency required of Federal air marshals.

(ii) Conduct Of Training—The training of a Federal flight deck officer in the use of a firearm may be conducted by the Under Secretary or by a firearms training facility approved by the Under Secretary.

(iii) Requalification—The Under Secretary shall require a Federal flight deck officer to requalify to carry a firearm under the program. Such requalification shall occur at an interval required by the Under Secretary.

(d) Deputization—

(1) In General—The Under Secretary may deputize, as a Federal flight deck officer under this section, a pilot who submits to the Under Secretary a request to be such an officer and whom the Under Secretary determines is qualified to be such an officer.

(2) Qualification—A pilot is qualified to be a Federal flight deck officer under this section if—

(A) the pilot is employed by an air carrier;

(B) the Under Secretary determines (in the Under Secretary's discretion) that the pilot meets the standards established by the Under Secretary for being such an officer; and

(C) the Under Secretary determines that the pilot has completed the training required by the Under Secretary.

(3) Deputization By Other Federal Agencies—The Under Secretary may request another Federal agency to deputize, as Federal flight deck officers under this section, those pilots that the Under Secretary determines are qualified to be such officers.

(4) Revocation—The Under Secretary may, (in the Under Secretary's discretion) revoke the deputization of a pilot as a Federal flight deck officer if the Under Secretary finds that the pilot is no longer qualified to be such an officer.

(e) Compensation—Pilots participating in the program under this section shall not be eligible for compensation from the Federal Government for services provided as a Federal flight deck officer. The Federal Government and air carriers shall not be obligated to compensate a pilot for participating in the program or for the pilot's training or qualification and requalification to carry firearms under the program.

(f) Authority To Carry Firearms—

(1) In General—The Under Secretary shall authorize a Federal flight deck officer to carry a firearm while engaged in providing air transportation or intrastate air transportation. Notwithstanding subsection (c)(1), the officer may purchase a firearm and carry that firearm aboard an aircraft of which the officer is the pilot in accordance with this section if the firearm is of a type that may be used under the program.

(2) Preemption—Notwithstanding any other provision of Federal or State law, a Federal flight deck officer, whenever necessary to participate in the program, may carry a firearm in any State and from 1 State to another State.

(3) Carrying Firearms Outside United States—In consultation with the Secretary of State, the Under Secretary may take such action as may be necessary to ensure that a Federal flight deck officer may carry a firearm in a foreign country whenever necessary to participate in the program.

(g) Authority To Use Force—Notwithstanding section 44903(d), the Under Secretary shall prescribe the standards and circumstances under which a Federal flight deck officer may use, while the program under this section is in effect, force (including lethal force) against an individual in the defense of the flight deck of an aircraft in air transportation or intrastate air transportation.

(h) Limitation On Liability—

(1) Liability Of Air Carriers—An air carrier shall not be liable for damages in any action brought in a Federal or State court arising out of a Federal flight deck officer's use of or failure to use a firearm.

(2) Liability Of Federal Flight Deck Officers—A Federal flight deck officer shall not be liable for damages in any action brought in a Federal or State court arising out of the acts or omissions of the officer in defending the flight deck of an aircraft against acts of criminal violence or air piracy unless the officer is guilty of gross negligence or willful misconduct.

(3) Liability Of Federal Government—For purposes of an action against the United States with respect to an act or omission of a Federal flight deck officer in defending the flight deck of an aircraft, the officer shall be treated as an employee of the Federal Government under chapter 171 of title 28, relating to tort claims procedure.

(i) Procedures Following Accidental Discharges—If an accidental discharge of a firearm under the pilot program results in the injury or death of a passenger or crew member on an aircraft, the Under Secretary—

(1) shall revoke the deputization of the Federal flight deck officer responsible for that firearm if the Under Secretary determines that the discharge was attributable to the negligence of the officer; and

(2) if the Under Secretary determines that a shortcoming in standards, training, or procedures was responsible for the accidental discharge, the Under Secretary may temporarily suspend the program until the shortcoming is corrected.

(j) Limitation On Authority Of Air Carriers—No air carrier shall prohibit or threaten any retaliatory action against a pilot employed by the air carrier from becoming a Federal flight deck officer under this section. No air carrier shall-—(1) prohibit a Federal flight deck officer from piloting an aircraft operated by the air carrier, or

(2) terminate the employment of a Federal flight deck officer, solely on the basis of his or her volunteering for or participating in the program under this section.

(k) Applicability—

(1) Exemption—This section shall not apply to air carriers operating under part 135 of title 14, Code of Federal Regulations, <cargo pilots> and to pilots employed by such carriers to the extent that such carriers and pilots are covered by section 135.119 of such title or any successor to such section.

(2) Pilot Defined—The term "pilot" means an individual who has final authority and responsibility for the operation and safety of the flight or any other flight deck crew member.

(3) All-Cargo Air Transportation—In this section, the term "air transportation" includes all-cargo air transportation.

(b) Conforming Amendments—

(1) Chapter Analysis—The analysis for such chapter is amended by inserting after the item relating to section 44920 the following: "44921. Federal flight deck officer program.".

(2) Flight Deck Security—Section 128 of the Aviation and Transportation Security Act (Public Law 107-71) is repealed.

(c) Federal Air Marshal Program—

(1) Sense Of Congress—It is the sense of Congress that the Federal air marshal program is critical to aviation security.

(2) Limitation On Statutory Construction—Nothing in this Act, including any amendment made by this Act, shall be construed as preventing the Under Secretary of Transportation for Security from implementing and training Federal air marshals.

Nov. 25, 2002 (2,052)
TITLE 49: TRANSPORTATION • SUBTITLE VII: AVIATION PROGRAMS • PART A: AIR COMMERCE AND SAFETY • SUBPART III: SAFETY • CHAPTER 449: SECURITY • SUBCHAPTER 1: REQUIREMENTS

49 USC § 44944. Voluntary Provision of Emergency Services

The Gist: The Dept. of Transportation is required to implement a program that permits law enforcement, firefighting and medical authorities to provide emergency services aboard commercial flights during emergencies.

This section does not change Dept. regulations on possession of firearms in aircraft or related facilities, and does not authorize possession in aircraft or facilities not authorized under those regulations.

Yes, that's not completely clear. In addition, it was removed by staff during codification, and exists only in the original public law as a Statute at Large; making this a rare example where the statutory language itself has no visible implication of a nexus to firearms. It is a gun law, but doesn't say so.

(a) Program for Provision of Voluntary Services—
(1) Program—The Under Secretary of Transportation for Transportation Security shall carry out a program to permit qualified law enforcement officers, firefighters, and emergency medical technicians to provide emergency services on commercial air flights during emergencies.

<Statute at Large>
"(c) Construction Regarding Possession Of Firearms—Nothing in this section may be construed to require any modification of regulations of the Department of Transportation governing the possession of firearms while in aircraft or air transportation facilities or to authorize the possession of a firearm in an aircraft or any such facility not authorized under those regulations."

Nov. 19, 2001 (103)

TITLE 49. TRANSPORTATION • SUBTITLE VII: AVIATION PROGRAMS • PART A: AIR COMMERCE AND SAFETY • SUBPART III: SAFETY • CHAPTER 449: SECURITY • SUBCHAPTER II: ADMINISTRATION AND PERSONNEL

49 USC § 46303. Carrying a weapon

The Gist: A person who has a concealed dangerous weapon available in an aircraft is liable to the federal government for a $10,000 civil fine. The proper authorities are exempt.

Note that when this bill (P.L. 103-272) was codified, as is often the case, the words of Congress were changed by the people doing the codification. Notes on those changes are available in this instance, and are provided here to illustrate the nature of this process of rewriting the statutes after they are enacted.

"In subsection (a), the words "deadly or" and "which shall be recoverable in a civil action brought in the name of the United States" are omitted as surplus. In subsection (b)(1), the words "imposed under" are substituted for "provided for in" for consistency. In subsection (b)(2), the words "imposed or compromised" are substituted for "The amount of such penalty when finally determined or fixed by order of the Board, or the amount agreed upon in compromise" to eliminate unnecessary words. In subsection (c)(1), the words "State or political subdivision of a State" are substituted for "municipal or State government" for consistency in the revised title and with other titles of the United States Code. The words "or required" are omitted as surplus."

(a) Civil Penalty.—An individual who, when on, or attempting to board, an aircraft in, or intended for operation in, air transportation or intrastate air transportation, has on or about the individual or the property of the individual a concealed dangerous weapon that is or would be accessible to the individual in flight is liable to the United States Government for a civil penalty of not more than $10,000 for each violation.
(b) Compromise and Setoff.—
(1) The Secretary of Transportation may compromise the amount of a civil penalty imposed under subsection (a) of this section.
(2) The Government may deduct the amount of a civil penalty imposed or compromised under this section from amounts it owes the individual liable for the penalty.
(c) Nonapplication.—This section does not apply to—
(1) a law enforcement officer of a State or political subdivision of a State, or an officer or employee of the Government, authorized to carry arms in an official capacity; or
(2) another individual the Administrator of the Federal Aviation Administration by regulation authorizes to carry arms in an official capacity.

July 5, 1994 (183)
TITLE 49. TRANSPORTATION • CHAPTER 463: PENALTIES • SUBPART IV-ENFORCEMENT AND PENALTIES

49 USC § 46505. Carrying a weapon or explosive on an aircraft

The Gist: A special definition of a firearm is created in subsection (a) for this section only. Bringing or attempting to bring a concealed dangerous weapon on board an aircraft used in air transportation, so that the weapon would be available in flight, is illegal. Putting or attempting to put a loaded firearm on such an aircraft, in property that would not be available to passengers in flight, is illegal. Exceptions are made for the proper authorities. This section does not apply to a person transporting an unloaded firearm, in baggage that is inaccessible during flight, if the air carrier was notified of the presence of the weapon. The penalty under (b) was increased from one year to 10, and under (c) from five to 15, in 1996.

(a) Definition.—In this section, "loaded firearm" means a starter gun or a weapon designed or converted to expel a projectile through an explosive, that has a cartridge, a detonator, or powder in the chamber, magazine, cylinder, or clip.
(b) General criminal penalty.—An individual shall be fined under title 18, imprisoned for not more than 10 years, or both, if the individual—
(1) when on, or attempting to get on, an aircraft in, or intended for operation in, air transportation or intrastate air transportation, has on or about the individual or the property of the individual a concealed dangerous weapon that is or would be accessible to the individual in flight;
(2) has placed, attempted to place, or attempted to have placed a loaded firearm on that aircraft in property not accessible to passengers in flight; or
(3) has on or about the individual, or has placed, attempted to place, or attempted to have placed on that aircraft, an explosive or incendiary device.
(c) Criminal penalty involving disregard for human life.—An individual who willfully and without regard for the safety of human life, or with reckless disregard for the safety of human life, violates subsection (b) of this section, shall be fined under title 18, imprisoned for not more than 15 years, or both.
(d) Nonapplication.—Subsection (b)(1) of this section does not apply to—

(1) a law enforcement officer of a State or political subdivision of a State, or an officer or employee of the United States Government, authorized to carry arms in an official capacity;

(2) another individual the Administrator of the Federal Aviation Administration by regulation authorizes to carry a dangerous weapon in air transportation or intrastate air transportation; or

(3) an individual transporting a weapon (except a loaded firearm) in baggage not accessible to a passenger in flight if the air carrier was informed of the presence of the weapon.

July 5, 1994 (317)

TITLE 49. TRANSPORTATION • SUBTITLE VII: AVIATION PROGRAMS • PART A: AIR COMMERCE AND SAFETY • SUBPART IV: ENFORCEMENT AND PENALTIES • CHAPTER 465: SPECIAL AIRCRAFT JURISDICTION OF THE UNITED STATES

49 USC § 80302. Prohibitions

> The Gist: An NFA weapon in violation of NFA weapon laws (which begin at 26-5801) is contraband. It's illegal to use an aircraft, vehicle or ship to transport, conceal, possess, buy, sell or transfer contraband.

(a) Definition.—In this section, "contraband" means—

(2) a firearm involved in a violation of chapter 53 of the Internal Revenue Code of 1986 (26 U.S.C. 5801 et seq.);

(b) Prohibitions.—A person may not—

(1) transport contraband in an aircraft, vehicle, or vessel;

(2) conceal or possess contraband on an aircraft, vehicle, or vessel; or

(3) use an aircraft, vehicle, or vessel to facilitate the transportation, concealment, receipt, possession, purchase, sale, exchange, or giving away of contraband.

July 5, 1994 (78)

TITLE 49. TRANSPORTATION • SUBTITLE X: MISCELLANEOUS • CHAPTER 803: CONTRABAND

49 USC App. § 2404. Authority to make arrests; carrying of firearms; patrol by Park Police

> The Gist: Employees of the Dept. of Transportation may be authorized to make arrests, under certain conditions, at Washington National Airport. Anyone authorized to make such arrests may also be authorized to carry firearms.

(a) The Secretary, and any Department of Transportation employee appointed to protect life and property on the airport, when designated by the Secretary, is hereby authorized and empowered

(1) to arrest under a warrant within the limits of the airport any person accused of having committed within the boundaries of the airport any offense against the laws of the United States, or against any rule or regulation prescribed pursuant to this subchapter;

(2) to arrest without warrant any person committing any such offense within the limits of the airport, in his presence; or

(3) to arrest without warrant within the limits of the airport any person whom he has reasonable grounds to believe has committed a felony within the limits of the airport.

(b) Any individual having the power of arrest as provided in subsection (a) of this section may carry firearms or other weapons as the Secretary may direct or by regulation may prescribe.

June 29, 1940 (155)

TITLE 49. TRANSPORTATION • SUBCHAPTER I: WASHINGTON NATIONAL AIRPORT

49 USC App. § 2428. Authority to make arrests; carrying of firearms; patrol by Park Police; deposit of collateral by person charged with violation

> The Gist: Employees of the Dept. of Transportation may be authorized to make arrests, under certain conditions, at Dulles International Airport. Anyone authorized to make such arrests may also be authorized to carry firearms.

(a) The Secretary, and any Department of Transportation employee appointed to protect life and property on the airport, when designated by the Secretary, is hereby authorized and empowered

(1) to arrest under a warrant within the limits of the airport any person accused of having committed within the boundaries of the airport any offense against the laws of the United States, or against any rule or regulation prescribed pursuant to this subchapter;

(2) to arrest without warrant any person committing any such offense within the limits of the airport, in his presence; or

(3) to arrest without warrant within the limits of the airport any person whom he has reasonable grounds to believe has committed a felony within the limits of the airport.

(b) Any individual having the power of arrest as provided in subsection (a) of this section may carry firearms or other weapons as the Secretary may direct or by regulation may prescribe.

Sept. 7, 1950 (155)

TITLE 49. TRANSPORTATION • SUBCHAPTER II: WASHINGTON DULLES INTERNATIONAL AIRPORT

Title 50 • War and National Defense

50 USC § 403f. General authorities of Agency

> **The Gist:** The Director of the Central Intelligence Agency can authorize personnel to carry firearms. This authorization is limited, within the United States, to protecting classified materials, firearms training, and protecting CIA facilities, current and former staff and their immediate families, defectors and their immediate families, and other people in the United States under Agency auspices.

(a) In general—
In the performance of its functions, the Central Intelligence Agency is authorized to—
(4) Authorize personnel designated by the Director to carry firearms to the extent necessary for the performance of the Agency's authorized functions, except that, within the United States, such authority shall be limited to the purposes of protection of classified materials and information, the training of Agency personnel and other authorized persons in the use of firearms, the protection of Agency installations and property, and the protection of current and former Agency personnel and their immediate families, defectors and their immediate families, and other persons in the United States under Agency auspices:

June 20, 1949 (108)
TITLE 50. WAR AND NATIONAL DEFENSE • CHAPTER 15: NATIONAL SECURITY • SUBCHAPTER I: COORDINATION FOR NATIONAL SECURITY

50 USC § 403j. Central Intelligence Agency; appropriations; expenditures

> **The Gist:** The Central Intelligence Agency may spend its funds on firearms and ammunition, without regard to laws or regulations that otherwise control government spending.

(a) Notwithstanding any other provisions of law, sums made available to the Agency by appropriation or otherwise may be expended for purposes necessary to carry out its functions, including—
(1) personal services, including personal services without regard to limitations on types of persons to be employed, and rent at the seat of government and elsewhere; health-service program as authorized by law (5 U.S.C. 7901); rental of news-reporting services; purchase or rental and operation of photographic, reproduction, cryptographic, duplication and printing machines, equipment and devices, and radio-receiving and radio-sending equipment and devices, including telegraph and teletype equipment; purchase, maintenance, operation, repair, and hire of passenger motor vehicles, and aircraft, and vessels of all kinds; subject to policies established by the Director, transportation of officers and employees of the

Agency in Government-owned automotive equipment between their domiciles and places of employment, where such personnel are engaged in work which makes such transportation necessary, and transportation in such equipment, to and from school, of children of Agency personnel who have quarters for themselves and their families at isolated stations outside the continental United States where adequate public or private transportation is not available; printing and binding; purchase, maintenance, and cleaning of firearms, including purchase, storage, and maintenance of ammunition; subject to policies established by the Director, expenses of travel in connection with, and expenses incident to attendance at meetings of professional, technical, scientific, and other similar organizations when such attendance would be a benefit in the conduct of the work of the Agency; association and library dues; payment of premiums or costs of surety bonds for officers or employees without regard to the provisions of section 14 of Title 6; payment of claims pursuant to Title 28; acquisition of necessary land and the clearing of such land; construction of buildings and facilities without regard to sections 259 and 267 of Title 40; repair, rental, operation, and maintenance of buildings, utilities, facilities, and appurtenances; and

(2) supplies, equipment, and personnel and contractual services otherwise authorized by law and regulations, when approved by the Director.

(b) The sums made available to the Agency may be expended without regard to the provisions of law and regulations relating to the expenditure of Government funds; and for objects of a confidential, extraordinary, or emergency nature, such expenditures to be accounted for solely on the certificate of the Director and every such certificate shall be deemed a sufficient voucher for the amount therein certified.

June 20, 1949 (405)
TITLE 50. WAR AND NATIONAL DEFENSE • CHAPTER 15: NATIONAL SECURITY • SUBCHAPTER I: COORDINATION FOR NATIONAL SECURITY

50 USC App. § 2411. Enforcement

> The Gist: Employees of the Dept. of Commerce Office of Export Enforcement may be authorized to carry firearms.

(a) General authority

(3)(B) The Secretary may designate any employee of the Office of Export Enforcement of the Department of Commerce to do the following in carrying out enforcement authority under this Act [sections 2401 to 2420 of this Appendix]:

(i) Execute any warrant or other process issued by a court or officer of competent jurisdiction with respect to the enforcement of the provisions of this Act [sections 2401 to 2420 of this Appendix].

(ii) Make arrests without warrant for any violation of this Act [sections 2401 to 2420 of this Appendix] committed in his or her presence or view, or if the officer or employee has probable cause to believe that the person to be arrested has committed or is committing such a violation.

(iii) Carry firearms in carrying out any activity described in clause (i) or (ii).

Sept. 29, 1979 (138)
TITLE 50. WAR AND NATIONAL DEFENSE • ACT: EXPORT REGULATION

STATUTES AT LARGE

Statutes are easy to find, carefully numbered and indexed, used frequently by lawyers and courts. "Statutes-at-Large" have a tendency to become lost from view, especially over time.

When Congress enacts a new bill, all the words become a "Public Law." It gets a two-part number—the current session of Congress (which is the 109th in 2005), and a sequential number for each new enactment. Thus, P.L. 90-618, the Gun Control Act of 1968, was the 618th law passed in the 90th Congress. Recent enactments can be found online using the National Directory at gunlaws.com, and through other web-based or library resources. Older ones must be hunted down in libraries.

Often, only a few parts of a public law become numbered statutes, and increase the size of the laws "on the books" (that is, the official U.S. Code, the main body of this book). A public law can be hundreds of thousands of words long, but the statutes from it may be a tiny fraction of that. This creates a handful of complications in measuring the law by word count, as we do. For example, a public law may merely direct a change to an existing statute, like changing a time period from 10 to 15 years. The public law uses a dozen words to say this, but the word count of the statute is unchanged.

Public laws include many temporary or non-statutory components, such as annual funding appropriations, requests for reports to Congress, directives to various parts of government, statements of purpose or policy, new hires, additional equipment, rules for training and supplies, and more. As Michael Anthony has noticed however, there is a distinct tendency to obscure portions of new laws that limit or control the government, or protect the rights of individuals, by keeping them hidden among the statutes at large.

This "Anthony" effect is troubling, especially when it tends to loosen control of the government by the people. If a law does not restrict a citizen's rights or impose obligations on citizens, or grant power over citizens to government, then chances are good it will become a statute at large. A classic example was the expiration of the so-called assault-weapon law. The law, with myriad restrictions, was a numbered statute. The sunset provision, that eliminated this law, was an unnumbered statute at large.

Some statutes at large relate directly to specific numbered federal laws. For example, the funding and controls over the Brady law relate to, belong with, and appear in this book next to that law, numbered 18 USC §922(s) and (t).

Others are more general in nature and do not neatly fit at any particular spot among the statutes.

For example, Congress had prohibited the Clinton administration from making private contracts with gun manufacturers, in an effort to circumvent certain laws. The so-called Smith Amendment (it was not actually even given a name) was added at the last minute as a statute at large, in a funding bill of more than 400,000 words, to prevent the FBI from its announced plans of taxing gun sales, using the NICS background check system as a vehicle. It also prohibited funding the NICS system if it did not destroy the records of legal gun owners.

The Smith Amendment restricts the government, does not obligate citizens, is a very important law, and has no logical place within the main text of *Gun Laws of America*. We have decided to accumulate most such sections below, in chronological order. They formerly appeared as part of periodic updates inserted at the end of the book (through our fourth edition).

Some statutes at large would simply take up space here and not further the goals of this book. Mainly, these are annual funding provisions for BATFE, the FBI and others. Allocations from ten years ago, that expired nine years ago, provide little to merit inclusion, so they are accumulated online at gunlaws.com, and not presented here. In contrast, funding for reports and research that affects gun ownership are included, since those results are meaningful even if old, and if not noted here, might be lost to the public debate. We have used our best judgment on including what seemed relevant, and providing the rest online.

P.L. 104-132 (1996). Sec. 503. Report To Congress On Thefts Of Explosive Materials From Armories.

> The Gist: The Attorney General and Secretary of Defense must study and submit a report to Congress concerning firearm, ammunition and explosives thefts from national armories. The report is due within six months (by Oct. 24, 1996).

(a) STUDY- The Attorney General and the Secretary of Defense shall jointly conduct a study of the number and extent of thefts from military arsenals (including National Guard armories) of firearms, explosives, and other materials that are potentially useful to terrorists.

(b) REPORT TO THE CONGRESS- Not later than 6 months after the date of enactment of this Act, the Attorney General and the Secretary of Defense shall jointly prepare and transmit to the Congress a report on the findings of the study conducted under subsection (a).

P.L. 104-132 (1996). Sec. 732. Marking, Rendering Inert, And Licensing Of Explosive Materials.

> The Gist: Gunpowder is excluded from a Treasury Dept. study of taggants and explosives.

(a) STUDY-
(1) IN GENERAL- Not later than 12 months after the date of enactment of this Act, the Secretary of the Treasury (referred to in this section as the `Secretary') shall conduct a study of--
(A) the tagging of explosive materials for purposes of detection and identification;
(B) the feasibility and practicability of rendering common chemicals used to manufacture explosive materials inert;
(C) the feasibility and practicability of imposing controls on certain precursor chemicals used to manufacture explosive materials; and
(D) State licensing requirements for the purchase and use of commercial high explosives, including--
(i) detonators;
(ii) detonating cords;
(iii) dynamite;
(iv) water gel;
(v) emulsion;
(vi) blasting agents; and
(vii) boosters.
(2) EXCLUSION- No study conducted under this subsection or regulation proposed under subsection (e) shall include black or smokeless powder among the explosive materials considered.

P.L. 104-132 (1996). Sec. 806. Commission On The Advancement Of Federal Law Enforcement.

> The Gist: Federal authorities are to study law enforcement standards for the use of deadly force.

(a) ESTABLISHMENT- There is established a commission to be known as the `Commission on the Advancement of Federal Law Enforcement' (hereinafter in this section referred to as the `Commission').
(b) DUTIES- The Commission shall review, ascertain, evaluate, report, and recommend action to the Congress on the following matters:
(1) The Federal law enforcement priorities for the 21st century, including Federal law enforcement capability to investigate and deter adequately the threat of terrorism facing the United States.
(2) In general, the manner in which significant Federal criminal law enforcement operations are conceived, planned, coordinated, and executed.
(3) The standards and procedures used by Federal law enforcement to carry out significant Federal criminal law enforcement operations, and their uniformity and compatibility on an interagency basis, including standards related to the use of deadly force.
(4) The investigation and handling of specific Federal criminal law enforcement cases by the United States Government and the Federal law enforcement agencies therewith, selected at the Commission's discretion.
(5) The necessity for the present number of Federal law enforcement agencies and units.
(6) The location and efficacy of the office or entity directly responsible, aside from the President of the United States, for the coordination on an interagency basis of the operations, programs, and activities of all of the Federal law enforcement agencies.
(7) The degree of assistance, training, education, and other human resource management assets devoted to increasing professionalism for Federal law enforcement officers.
(8) The independent accountability mechanisms that exist, if any, and their efficacy to investigate, address, and to correct Federal law enforcement abuses.
(9) The degree of coordination among law enforcement agencies in the area of international crime and the extent to which deployment of resources overseas diminishes domestic law enforcement.

(10) The extent to which Federal law enforcement agencies coordinate with State and local law enforcement agencies on Federal criminal enforcement operations and programs that directly affect a State or local law enforcement agency's geographical jurisdiction.

(11) Such other related matters as the Commission deems appropriate.

P.L. 104-132 (1996). Sec. 809. Assessing And Reducing The Threat To Law Enforcement Officers From The Criminal Use Of Firearms And Ammunition.

> The Gist: The Treasury Dept. and the Attorney General are to conduct a study of law enforcement officer deaths and serious injuries, for the last decade, including: 1–felonies and accidents; 2–shootings; 3–identifying whether handguns used handgun or rifle ammo, if rifles used handgun or rifle ammo, and if shotguns were used; 4–officers shot with their own firearms or with other officers' firearms and 5–instances where a bullet-resistant vest or helmet was penetrated by armor-piercing ammunition. In addition the study must consider whether current strategies and body armor are sufficient for criminal encounters, and recommend increases in body armor that would provide more protection.
>
> The ammunition part of the study includes: 1–determining the most popular calibers based on quantities sold; 2–identifying common uses for the most popular ammunition, according to industry, sporting organizations and law enforcement; 3–determining the popular calibers for civilian defense and sporting uses that would be affected if they were banned to the public, if those calibers can pierce minimum-level vests.
>
> The study must take input from interested parties and report to Congress in one year (from April 24, 1996). An open-ended funding appropriation is provided.

(a) The Secretary of the Treasury, in conjunction with the Attorney General, shall conduct a study and make recommendations concerning--

(1) the extent and nature of the deaths and serious injuries, in the line of duty during the last decade, for law enforcement officers, including:

(A) those officers who were feloniously killed or seriously injured and those that died or were seriously injured as a result of accidents or other non-felonious causes;

(B) those officers feloniously killed or seriously injured with firearms, those killed or seriously injured with, separately, handguns firing handgun caliber ammunition, handguns firing rifle caliber ammunition, rifles firing rifle caliber ammunition, rifles firing handgun caliber ammunition and shotguns;

(C) those officers feloniously killed or seriously injured with firearms, and killings or serious injuries committed with firearms taken by officers' assailants from officers, and those committed with other officers' firearms; and

(D) those killed or seriously injured because shots attributable to projectiles defined as `armor piercing ammunition' under section 921(a)(17)(B) (i) and (ii) of title 18, United States Code, pierced the protective material of bullet resistant vests and bullet resistant headgear;

(2) whether current passive defensive strategies, such as body armor, are adequate to counter the criminal use of firearms against law officers; and

(3) the calibers of ammunition that are--

(A) sold in the greatest quantities;

(B) their common uses, according to consultations with industry, sporting organizations and law enforcement;

(C) the calibers commonly used for civilian defensive or sporting uses that would be affected by any prohibition on non-law enforcement sales of such ammunition, if such ammunition is capable of penetrating minimum level bullet resistant vests; and

(D) recommendations for increase in body armor capabilities to further protect law enforcement from threat.

(b) In conducting the study, the Secretary shall consult with other Federal, State and local officials, non-governmental organizations, including all national police organizations, national sporting organizations and national industry associations with expertise in this area and such other individuals as shall be deemed necessary. Such study shall be presented to Congress twelve months after the enactment of this Act and made available to the public, including any data tapes or data used to form such recommendations.

(c) There are authorized to be appropriated for the study and recommendations such sums as may be necessary.

P.L. 104-132 (1996). Sec. 821. Research And Development To Support Counterterrorism Technologies.

> The Gist: Up to $10 million may be spent by the National Institute of Justice in 1997 to develop ways to combat terrorism, including developing ways to detect firearms.

There are authorized to be appropriated to the National Institute of Justice Office of Science and Technology not more than $10,000,000 for fiscal year 1997, to--

(1) develop technologies that can be used to combat terrorism, including technologies in the areas of--

(A) detection of weapons, explosives, chemicals, and persons;

(B) tracking;

(C) surveillance;

(D) vulnerability assessment; and

(E) information technologies;

(2) develop standards to ensure the adequacy of products produced and compatibility with relevant national systems; and

(3) identify and assess requirements for technologies to assist State and local law enforcement in the national program to combat terrorism.

P.L. 104-208 (1997). Sec. 113. General Provisions--Department of Justice <Taggant Study>

> The Gist: Five experts to be appointed by the National Academy of Sciences are authorized by Congress to study tagging black and smokeless gunpowders, for detection and identification. The study must cover whether tracers in powders will: 1–pose a risk to human life or safety; 2–help law enforcement; 3–harm the quality and performance of powders for any lawful use; 4–harm the environment, and 5–cost more than it's worth. In addition, the panel must project: 1–the cost to make tagged powders; 2–the cost to regulate the system; 3–the cost and effects on consumers; 4–the effect on consumer demand for ammunition; 5–how hard it would be for terrorists to evade taggants, and 6–if taggants could be evaded by using basic chemicals to make gunpowders.
>
> The panel must consult on this study with all interested government and national organizations, and with individuals as deemed necessary. The

report is due on Sept. 30, 1997, is available to the public, and Congress places no constraints on funding for the study.

Section 732 of Public Law 104-132 (110 Stat. 1303; 18 U.S.C. 841 note) is amended--
(2) by adding at the end the following new subsection:
``(f) Special Study.--
``(1) In general.--Notwithstanding subsection (a) <deals with high-tech detection of terrorist explosive devices>, the Secretary of the Treasury shall enter into a contract with the National Academy of Sciences (referred to in this section as the `Academy') to conduct a study of the tagging of smokeless and black powder by any viable technology for purposes of detection and identification. The study shall be conducted by an independent panel of 5 experts appointed by the Academy.
``(2) Study elements.--The study conducted under this subsection shall--
``(A) indicate whether the tracer elements, when added to smokeless and black powder--
``(i) will pose a risk to human life or safety;
``(ii) will substantially assist law enforcement officers in their investigative efforts;
``(iii) will impair the quality and performance of the powders (which shall include a broad and comprehensive sampling of all available powders) for their intended lawful use, including, but not limited to the sporting, defense, and handloading uses of the powders, as well as their use in display and lawful consumer pyrotechnics;
``(iv) will have a substantially adverse effect on the environment;
``(v) will incur costs which outweigh the benefits of their inclusion, including an evaluation of the probable production and regulatory cost of compliance to the industry, and the costs and effects on consumers, including the effect on the demand for ammunition; and
``(vi) can be evaded, and with what degree of difficulty, by terrorists or terrorist organizations, including evading tracer elements by the use of precursor chemicals to make black or other powders; and
``(B) provide for consultation on the study with Federal, State, and local officials, non-governmental organizations, including all national police organizations, national sporting organizations, and national industry associations with expertise in this area and such other individuals as shall be deemed necessary.
``(3) Report and costs.--The study conducted under this subsection shall be presented to Congress 12 months after the enactment of this subsection and be made available to the public, including any data tapes or data used to form such recommendations. There are authorized to be appropriated such sums as may be necessary to carry out the study.''.

P.L. 104-208 (1997). Disease Control, Research, and Training <CDC Advocacy Ban>

The Gist: Congress prohibits The Centers for Disease Control and Prevention from spending certain public funds to advocate or promote gun control. Other funding sources are not covered, and the term *advocate* is not defined.

Provided further, That none of the funds made available for injury prevention and control at the Centers for Disease Control and Prevention may be used to advocate or promote gun control.

P.L. 104-208 (1997). Salaries and Expenses <BATF Funding Controls>

The Gist: This law places controls on the Bureau of Alcohol, Tobacco and Firearms. Congress prohibits the Treasury Dept., under which the BATF operates, from spending any of its allocated funds on: 1–consolidating or centralizing the firearms records of FFLs; 2–changing 27 CFR 178.118 (deals with importing curios and relics); 3–changing the "curios and relics" definition in 27 CFR 178.11; 4–removing anything from ATF 5300.11 (the curios and relics list); 5–investigating or acting on applications for relief from federal firearm disabilities for individuals; 6–providing ballistics imaging equipment to certain local authorities unless they agree to pay for or return it; 7–electronically retrieving data, by name or any personal identification code, from the firearms records of out-of-business FFLs. Congress authorizes the use of Treasury Dept. funds to investigate or act on applications for relief from federal firearms disabilities for corporations.

It would seem, since Congress specifically acted to limit activity by the bureaucracy through funding restrictions, that each subsequent allocation will need to include similar restrictions, or the bureaucracy might conclude that the restrictions no longer apply if not specifically mandated.

Provided further, That no funds appropriated herein shall be available for salaries or administrative expenses in connection with consolidating or centralizing, within the Department of the Treasury, the records, or any portion thereof, of acquisition and disposition of firearms maintained by Federal firearms licensees: Provided further, That no funds appropriated herein shall be used to pay administrative expenses or the compensation of any officer or employee of the United States to implement an amendment or amendments to 27 CFR 178.118 or to change the definition of "Curios or relics" in 27 CFR 178.11 or remove any item from ATF Publication 5300.11 as it existed on January 1, 1994: Provided further, That none of the funds appropriated herein shall be available to investigate or act upon applications for relief from Federal firearms disabilities under 18 U.S.C. 925(c): Provided further, That such funds shall be available to investigate and act upon applications filed by corporations for relief from Federal firearms disabilities under 18 U.S.C. 925(c): Provided further, That no funds in this Act may be used to provide ballistics imaging equipment to any State or local authority who has obtained similar equipment through a Federal grant or subsidy unless the State or local authority agrees to return that equipment or to repay that grant or subsidy to the Federal Government: Provided further, That no funds available for separation incentive payments as authorized by section 663 <concerning severance pay> of this Act may be obligated without the advance approval of the House and Senate Committees on Appropriations: Provided further, That no funds under this Act may be used to electronically retrieve information gathered pursuant to 18 U.S.C. 923(g)(4) by name or any personal identification code.

P.L. 105-277 (1998). H11058 Salaries And Expenses, United States Attorneys

The Gist: Provides $1 billion in funding to the U.S. Attorney's office, with $2.3 million of it for new gun-law enforcement personnel in Philadelphia and in Camden County. This program is known as Project Exile.

This material is identified by its page number in the House Congressional Record for Oct. 19, 1998, the date the conference committee set the final language for this bill (two days before it became law), since it is the only numbering available.

For necessary expenses of the Offices of the United States Attorneys, including intergovernmental and cooperative agreements, $1,009,680,000;

Provided further, That $2,300,000 shall be used to provide for additional assistant United States attorneys and investigators to serve in Philadelphia, Pennsylvania, and Camden County, New Jersey, to enforce Federal laws designed to prevent the possession by criminals of firearms (as that term is defined in section 921(a) of title 18, United States Code), of which $1,500,000 shall be used to provide for those attorneys and investigators in Philadelphia, Pennsylvania, and $800,000 shall be used to provide for those attorneys and investigators in Camden County, New Jersey.

In addition, $80,698,000, <applies to the full $1 billion in funding> to be derived from the Violent Crime Reduction Trust Fund, to remain available until expended for such purposes.

P.L. 105-277 (1998). H11060 Violent Crime Reduction Programs, State and Local Law Enforcement Assistance

The Gist: Provides $2.4 billion funding for anti-crime programs, including $45 million to upgrade state criminal records systems, as part of the Brady NICS background check system, and to help states connect to the federal system.

For assistance (including amounts for administrative costs for management and administration, which amounts shall be transferred to and merged with the `Justice Assistance' account) authorized by the Violent Crime Control and Law Enforcement Act of 1994 (Public Law 103-322), as amended (`the 1994 Act'); the Omnibus Crime Control and Safe Streets Act of 1968, as amended (`the 1968 Act'); and the Victims of Child Abuse Act of 1990, as amended (`the 1990 Act'), $2,369,950,000, to remain available until expended, which shall be derived from the Violent Crime Reduction Trust Fund;

of which $45,000,000 shall be for grants to upgrade criminal records, as authorized by section 106(b) of the Brady Handgun Violence Prevention Act of 1993, as amended, and section 4(b) of the National Child Protection Act of 1993;

P.L. 105-277 (1998). H11075 SEC. 621. <Prohibiting NICS Gun Tax & Requiring Record Destruction>

The Gist: **The Smith Amendment.** This is the language added at the last minute to the Omnibus Bill, to prevent the FBI from taxing the sale of firearms, using the NICS background check system for the purpose. It also prohibits funding the operation of NICS if it doesn't destroy the information it collects about private gun owners. The section is inserted awkwardly in the original bill in the middle of an unrelated section on Korean steel imports.

None of the funds appropriated pursuant to this Act or any other provision of law may be used for
(1) the implementation of any tax or fee in connection with the implementation of 18 U.S.C. 922(t);

(2) any system to implement 18 U.S.C. 922(t) that does not require and result in the destruction of any identifying information submitted by or on behalf of any person who has been determined not to be prohibited from owning a firearm.

P.L. 105-277 (1998). H11174 Federal Law Enforcement Training Center Salaries and Expenses

> The Gist: Provides funding for federal law enforcement shooting matches and awards, and other training for federal police.

For necessary expenses of the Federal Law Enforcement Training Center, as a bureau of the Department of the Treasury, including
the conducting of and participating in firearms matches and presentation of awards;

P.L. 105-277 (1998). H11175 Bureau of Alcohol, Tobacco and Firearms. Salaries and Expenses

> The Gist: Funding for ATF. Includes 812 new vehicles, funding for the Youth Crime Gun Interdiction Initiative, funds to pay for citizens' attorney's fees in the event they win a suit over wrongly confiscated guns, federal payments to local police for cooperating in ATF operations, a prohibition on taking duties away from ATF, funds for the National Tracing Center, a prohibition against consolidating or centralizing FFL records in the Treasury Dept., a prohibition against changing the definitions or lists of curio and relic firearms, a prohibition against funding any appeals for relief from federal firearms disability for citizens, permission to spend funds for appeals for relief from federal firearms disabilities for corporations, requirements on police ballistics equipment provided by federal authorities, and a prohibition on electronic retrieval systems for out-of-business FFL records.

For necessary expenses of the Bureau of Alcohol, Tobacco and Firearms, including purchase of not to exceed 812 vehicles for police-type use, of which 650 shall be for replacement only, and hire of passenger motor vehicles; hire of aircraft; services of expert witnesses at such rates as may be determined by the Director; for payment of per diem and/or subsistence allowances to employees where an assignment to the National Response Team during the investigation of a bombing or arson incident requires an employee to work 16 hours or more per day or to remain overnight at his or her post of duty; not to exceed $15,000 for official reception and representation expenses; for training of State and local law enforcement agencies with or without reimbursement, including training in connection with the training and acquisition of canines for explosives and fire accelerants detection; and provision of laboratory assistance to State and local agencies, with or without reimbursement; $541,574,000, of which $2,206,000 shall not be available for obligation until September 30, 1999; of which $27,000,000 may be used for the Youth Crime Gun Interdiction Initiative; of which not to exceed $1,000,000 shall be available for the payment of attorneys' fees as provided by 18 U.S.C. 924(d)(2); and of which $1,000,000 shall be available for the equipping of any vessel, vehicle, equipment, or aircraft available for official use by a State or local law enforcement agency if the conveyance will be used in joint law enforcement operations with the Bureau of Alcohol, Tobacco and Firearms and for the payment of overtime salaries, travel, fuel, training, equipment, and other similar costs of State and local law enforcement personnel, including sworn officers and support personnel, that are incurred in joint operations with the Bureau of Alcohol, Tobacco and Firearms: *Provided,* That no funds made available by this or any other

Act may be used to transfer the functions, missions, or activities of the Bureau of Alcohol, Tobacco and Firearms to other agencies or Departments in fiscal year 1999: *Provided further,* That of the funds made available, $4,500,000 shall be made available for the expansion of the National Tracing Center: *Provided further,* That no funds appropriated herein shall be available for salaries or administrative expenses in connection with consolidating or centralizing, within the Department of the Treasury, the records, or any portion thereof, of acquisition and disposition of firearms maintained by Federal firearms licensees: *Provided further,* That no funds appropriated herein shall be used to pay administrative expenses or the compensation of any officer or employee of the United States to implement an amendment or amendments to 27 CFR 178.118 or to change the definition of `Curios or relics' in 27 CFR 178.11 or remove any item from ATF Publication 5300.11 as it existed on January 1, 1994: *Provided further,* That none of the funds appropriated herein shall be available to investigate or act upon applications for relief from Federal firearms disabilities under 18 U.S.C. 925(c): *Provided further,* That such funds shall be available to investigate and act upon applications filed by corporations for relief from Federal firearms disabilities under 18 U.S.C. 925(c): *Provided further,* That no funds in this Act may be used to provide ballistics imaging equipment to any State or local authority who has obtained similar equipment through a Federal grant or subsidy unless the State or local authority agrees to return that equipment or to repay that grant or subsidy to the Federal Government: *Provided further,* That no funds under this Act may be used to electronically retrieve information gathered pursuant to 18 U.S.C. 923(g)(4) by name or any personal identification code.

P.L. 105-277 (1998). H11187 SEC. 646. <In-Transit Relief for Firearms Importers>

> The Gist: When the President directed the Treasury Dept. to outlaw the importation of certain types of firearms and accessories, on April 6, 1998, a number of U.S. firms were caught with legal products they ordered and paid for, but were now impounded by Customs. To compensate them for the "taking" of their property, Congress approved payment to the firms, and took title to the goods.

Notwithstanding any other provision of law, the Secretary of the Treasury is authorized to, upon submission of proper documentation (as determined by the Secretary), reimburse importers of large capacity military magazine rifles as defined in the Treasury Department's April 6, 1998 "Study on the Sporting Suitability of Modified Semiautomatic Assault Rifles", for which authority had been granted to import such firearms into the United States on or before November 14, 1997, and released under bond to the importer by the U.S. Customs Service on or before February 10, 1998: *Provided,* That the importer abandons title to the firearms to the United States: *Provided further,* That reimbursements are submitted to the Secretary for his approval within 120 days of enactment of this provision. In no event shall reimbursements under this provision exceed the importers cost for the weapons, plus any shipping, transportation, duty, and storage costs related to the importation of such weapons.

Money made available for expenditure under 31 U.S.C. section 1304(a) in an amount not to exceed $1,000,000 shall be available for reimbursements under this provision: *Provided,* That accepting the compensation provided under this provision is final and conclusive and constitutes a complete release of any and all claims, demands, rights, and causes of action whatsoever against the United States, its agencies, officers, or employees arising from the denial by the Department of the Treasury of the entry of such firearms into the United States. Such compensation is not otherwise required by law and is not intended to create or recognize any legally enforceable right to any person.

P.L. 105-277 (1998). H11187 SEC. 655.
<Pawn Broker NICS Glitch Fix>

> The Gist: NICS created an awkward situation in the case of pawn brokers who are FFLs. When a broker takes a gun as collateral, a NICS check must be completed before returning the gun to its original owner (or anyone else). If an owner fails the NICS check, the broker is in the untenable position of either confiscating private property, or illegally returning the gun to its owner. This section allows pawn brokers to make a NICS check when taking the collateral, which the law otherwise prohibits, but leaves unresolved what the broker should do after taking possession and doing the paperwork to make the check. NICS is not required to notify local authorities, but pawn brokers must tell local law enforcement if a customer is denied by NICS, within 48 hours. A NICS check when the collateral is redeemed is also required.

None of the funds appropriated pursuant to this Act or any other provision of law may be used for any system to implement section 922(t) of title 18, United States Code, unless the system allows, in connection with a person's delivery of a firearm to a Federal firearms licensee as collateral for a loan, the background check to be performed at the time the collateral is offered for delivery to such licensee: *Provided,* That the licensee notifies local law enforcement within 48 hours of the licensee receiving a denial on the person offering the collateral: *Provided further,* That the provisions of section 922(t) shall apply at the time of the redemption of the firearm.

P.L. 105-277 (1998). H11250 SEC. 1101. Short Title.
<Replacement of Arms Control and Disarmament Agency by State Dept.>

> The Gist: The statutes that follow eliminate the United States Arms Control and Disarmament Agency, and place most of its functions and responsibilities with the State Dept., as part of a general reorganization of certain foreign services. The State Dept. assumes the remnants of Cold War policy generally referred to as nuclear disarmament and non-proliferation.

This subdivision may be cited as the "Foreign Affairs Agencies Consolidation Act of 1998".

P.L. 105-277 (1998). H11250 SEC. 1102. Purposes.
<Replacement of Arms Control and Disarmament Agency by State Dept.>

> The Gist: The reasons for replacing The United States Arms Control and Disarmament Agency with the State Dept. are spelled out. They are generally described as administrative and economic in nature, and to preserve the mission and skills of the agency, along with several others.

The purposes of this subdivision are—
(1) to strengthen—
(A) the coordination of United States foreign policy; and
(B) the leading role of the Secretary of State in the formulation and articulation of United States foreign policy;

(2) to consolidate and reinvigorate the foreign affairs functions of the United States within the Department of State by—
(A) abolishing the United States Arms Control and Disarmament Agency, the United States Information Agency, and the United States International Development Cooperation Agency, and transferring the functions of these agencies to the Department of State while preserving the special missions and skills of these agencies;

P.L. 105-277 (1998). H11250 SEC. 1201. Effective Date.
<Replacement of Arms Control and Disarmament Agency by State Dept.>

> The Gist: The United States Arms Control and Disarmament Agency is abolished on April 1, 1999.

This title, and the amendments made by this title, shall take effect on the earlier of—
(1) April 1, 1999; or
(2) the date of abolition of the United States Arms Control and Disarmament Agency pursuant to the reorganization plan described in section 1601.

P.L. 105-277 (1998). H11250 SEC. 1211. Abolition of United States Arms Control and Disarmament Agency.

> The Gist: The United States Arms Control and Disarmament Agency is abolished.

The United States Arms Control and Disarmament Agency is abolished.

P.L. 105-277 (1998). H11250 SEC. 1212. Transfer of Functions to Secretary of State.

> The Gist: As of March 31, 1999, the State Dept. assumes all functions of The United States Arms Control and Disarmament Agency.

There are transferred to the Secretary of State all functions of the Director of the United States Arms Control and Disarmament Agency, and all functions of the United States Arms Control and Disarmament Agency and any office or component of such agency, under any statute, reorganization plan, Executive order, or other provision of law, as of the day before the effective date of this title.

P.L. 106-398 (2000). Sec. 826. Requirement To Disregard Certain Agreements In Awarding Contracts For The Purchase Of Firearms Or Ammunition.

> The Gist: The Clinton administration, in an effort to limit gun ownership, had entered a contractual arrangement with British-owned Smith and Wesson, to limit availability of its firearms to the general public. In exchange, S&W was promised preferential treatment from the Dept. of Defense when it acquired firearms or ammunition. This created conditions by contract that Congress was unwilling to implement by law. The following language was enacted to prevent S&W, or any other gun or ammunition maker or vendor, from getting such lucrative preferences, removing the incentive for such an arrangement.

In accordance with the requirements contained in the amendments enacted in the Competition in Contracting Act of 1984 (title VII of division B of Public Law 98-369; 98 Stat. 1175), the Secretary of Defense may not, in awarding a contract for the purchase of firearms or ammunition, take into account whether a manufacturer or vendor of firearms or ammunition is a party to an agreement under which the manufacturer or vendor agrees to adopt limitations with respect to importing, manufacturing, or dealing in firearms or ammunition in the commercial market.

P.L. 107-296 (2002). Sec. 1404. Commercial Airline Security Study.

The Gist: The Transportation Secretary shall study the numbers of armed officials who may be aboard aircraft, and how they might be staggered to provide the best coverage.

(a) STUDY- The Secretary of Transportation shall conduct a study of the following:
(1) The number of armed Federal law enforcement officers (other than Federal air marshals), who travel on commercial airliners annually and the frequency of their travel.
(5) The feasibility of staggering the flights of such officers to ensure the maximum amount of flights have a certified trained Federal officer on board.

P.L. 108-7 (2003). Sec. 753. <Armed agriculture agents.>

The Gist: The "Consolidated Appropriations Resolution, 2003," a huge budget bill, in typical fashion contains assorted unrelated gun law, all of it in the form of Statutes at Large. Annual funding allotments for firearms and ammunition for various agencies is not included here, along with various non-permanent gun-related law enforcement programs. See P.L. 108-7 online for these temporary measures.

The Secretary of Agriculture is authorized to permit employees of the United States Department of Agriculture to carry and use firearms for personal protection while conducting field work in remote locations in the performance of their official duties.

The Secretary of Agriculture is authorized to permit employees of the United States Department of Agriculture to carry and use firearms for personal protection while conducting field work in remote locations in the performance of their official duties.

P.L. 108-7 (2003). 1st Sec. 616. <Brady restraints.>

The Gist: No funds in this budget may be used for placing any tax or fee on the implementation of the Brady law (implying that authorities cannot charge for using the background check system to complete retail gun sales; they had indicated a desire to do so when the system was first set up). Funds may also not be used to implement Brady if its background check records are not destroyed, in an unspecified time frame, on approved sales.

Note: The inclusion of this language in a funding bill implies that such limitations are not recognized by law. As such, every funding bill in the future must contain similar restraining language, or the authorities will likely consider themselves free to use their budgets to implement the actions banned here. This provides a door for a future administration to simply omit these limitations and thus implement the banned activities. The activities are generally considered highly detrimental to the right to keep and bear arms.

None of the funds appropriated pursuant to this Act or any other provision of law may be used for:
(1) the implementation of any tax or fee in connection with the implementation of 18 U.S.C. 922(t); and
(2) any system to implement 18 U.S.C. 922(t) that does not require and result in the destruction of any identifying information submitted by or on behalf of any person who has been determined not to be prohibited from owning a firearm.

P.L. 108-7 (2003). Sec. 644. <Release of records>

The Gist: No funds in this budget may be used to respond to requests for records related to explosion and fire investigations, FFL documents, or FFL investigations. See note in P.L. 108-7 Sec. 616.

No funds appropriated under this Act or any other Act with respect to any fiscal year shall be available to take any action based upon any provision of 5 U.S.C. 552 <public records requests> with respect to records collected or maintained pursuant to 18 U.S.C. 846(b), 923(g)(3) or 923(g)(7), or provided by Federal, State, local, or foreign law enforcement agencies in connection with arson or explosives incidents or the tracing of a firearm, except that such records may continue to be disclosed to the extent and in the manner that records so collected, maintained, or obtained have been disclosed under 5 U.S.C. 552 prior to the date of the enactment of this Act.

P.L. 108-7 (2003). Div. J—Title 1. <BATF Prohibitions>

The Gist: No funds in this budget may be used for 1–Centralizing the firearm sales records of FFLs; 2–Changing the firearm Curios and Relics list or definitions from what it was on Jan. 1, 1994; 3–Acting upon requests for relief from firearms disabilities, except for corporations; 4–electronically retrieving records of FFLs who are out of business, whose paperwork has been collected and stored. See note in P.L. 108-7 Sec. 616.

Provided, That no funds appropriated herein shall be available for salaries or administrative expenses in connection with consolidating or centralizing, within the Department of the Treasury, the records, or any portion thereof, of acquisition and disposition of firearms maintained by Federal firearms licensees: Provided further, That no funds appropriated herein shall be used to pay administrative expenses or the compensation of any officer or employee of the United States to implement an amendment or amendments to 27 CFR 178.118 or to change the definition of "Curios or relics" in 27 CFR 178.11 or remove any item from ATF Publication 5300.11 as it existed on January 1, 1994: Provided further, That none of the funds appropriated herein shall be available to investigate or act upon applications for relief from Federal firearms disabilities under 18 U.S.C. 925(c): Provided further, That such funds shall be available to investigate and act upon applications filed by corporations for relief from Federal firearms disabilities under 18 U.S.C. 925(c): Provided further, That no funds under this Act may be used to electronically retrieve information gathered pursuant to 18 U.S.C. 923(g)(4) by name or any personal identification code.

P.L. 108-7 (2003). Div. G, Title II. <CDC "gun-control advocacy" ban>

> The Gist: None of the funds in this budget may be used by the Centers for Disease Control to promote gun control, and undefined term. See note in P.L. 108-7 Sec. 616.

Provided further, That none of the funds made available for injury prevention and control at the Centers for Disease Control and Prevention may be used, in whole or in part, to advocate or promote gun control

P.L. 108-7 (2003). 1st Sec. 515. <Conventional ammunition>

> The Gist: The President can commit funds for conventional ammunition, with respect to the Arms Export Control Act, without prior notice to Congress.

Provided, That the President shall not enter into any commitment of funds appropriated for the purposes of section 23 of the Arms Export Control Act for the provision of major defense equipment, other than conventional ammunition, or other major defense items defined to be aircraft, ships, missiles, or combat vehicles, not previously justified to Congress or 20 percent in excess of the quantities justified to Congress unless the Committees on Appropriations are notified 15 days in advance of such commitment

About Alan Korwin

Alan Korwin, author of three books and co-author of seven others, is a full-time freelance writer, consultant and businessman with a twenty-five-year track record. He is a founder and two-term past president of the Arizona Book Publishing Association, which has presented him with its Visionary Leadership award, named in his honor, the Korwin Award. He has received national awards for his publicity work as a member of the Society for Technical Communication, and is a past board member of the Arizona chapter of the Society of Professional Journalists.

Working with American Express, Mr. Korwin wrote the executive-level strategic plan that defined its worldwide telecommunications strategy for the 1990s; he wrote the business plan that raised $5 million in venture capital and launched SkyMall; he did the publicity for Pulitzer Prize cartoonist Steve Benson's fourth book; and he had a hand in developing ASPED, Arizona's economic strategic plan. Korwin's writing appears often in a wide spectrum of local and national publications.

Korwin turned his first book, *The Arizona Gun Owner's Guide,* into a self-published best-seller, now in its 21st edition. With his wife Cheryl he operates Bloomfield Press, which has grown into the largest producer and distributor of gun-law books in the country. It is built around seven books he has completed on the subject including the unabridged guide *Gun Laws of America,* an expanding line of related items, and countless radio and TV appearances. His 10th book is *Supreme Court Gun Cases.*

Alan Korwin is originally from New York City, where his clients included IBM, AT&T, NYNEX and others, many with real names. He is a pretty good guitarist and singer, with a penchant for parody (his last band was The Cartridge Family). In 1986, finally married, he moved to the Valley of the Sun. It was a joyful and successful move.

About Michael P. Anthony

Michael P. Anthony is a Phoenix-based trial lawyer with more than 28 years of experience in criminal, civil and military law. He is admitted to practice before the United States Supreme Court, the Ninth Circuit Court of Appeals, the U.S. Court of Military Appeals, U.S. District Court of Arizona and the Supreme Courts of Texas and Arizona.

Mr. Anthony has more than eight years of experience in the Air Force, exercising responsibilities in law enforcement, circuit defense council, civil rights investigations and as a squadron commander.

Mr. Anthony has lectured and published instructional materials in the fields of criminal and civil law, and regarding the lawful use of deadly force. He was directly involved in the drafting and passage of Arizona's concealed-weapons statute in 1994, and has developed training materials for accredited concealed-carry classes in that state. Michael Anthony is certified by the Arizona Dept. of Public Safety to provide legal and judgmental-shooting training in any certified concealed-weapons program in Arizona, and trains certified instructors on legal matters for Arizona's CCW programs. He served for over ten years on the Phoenix Police Dept. Use of Force Review Board, Disciplinary Review Board and Oral Examinations Board.

During his legal career, Mr. Anthony has done trial work in nine states, for clients ranging from Ford, Jeep, International Harvester and the Resolution Trust Corporation to small businesses and individuals, in civil and criminal matters. He is a partner in one of the oldest law firms in Arizona, Carson Messinger Elliott Laughlin & Ragan, P.L.L.C., in Phoenix, where he concentrates on civil litigation and civil appeals.

Originally from Oklahoma, Mr. Anthony settled in Arizona in 1980. He is actively involved in lecturing and teaching about firearms, firearms safety, firearms laws, firearms liability issues and the use of firearms by law-abiding citizens.

IMPORTANT BOOKS FOR AMERICAN GUN OWNERS

NATIONAL GUN LAWS
"It doesn't make sense to own a gun and not know the rules."

GUN LAWS OF AMERICA Every federal gun law on the books, with plain-English summaries

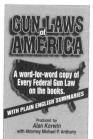

by Alan Korwin with Michael P. Anthony, 352 pgs., $19.95. Like a complete gun-law library in your hand! The first and only *unabridged* compilation of federal gun law—everything Congress has done on guns and the right to arms, and **every law is clearly described in plain English!** Covers citizens, dealers, collectors, Militia, National Guard, manufacturers, global disarmament, "proper" authorities, free training ammo, the lost national right to carry, National Transport Guarantee, much more. Good laws, bad laws, 70 pages of juicy intro, and the plain-English summaries make it so easy. You'll pick it up again and again. Settles arguments big time. Widely endorsed.
"Outstanding"—former Arizona Attorney General Bob Corbin.

SUPREME COURT GUN CASES Every key case, & plain-English

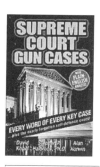

analysis by David Kopel, Stephen P. Halbrook, Ph.D., Alan Korwin, $24.95. More than 90 Supreme Court gun cases demolish the myths that they've said little and you have no rights. The key 44 cases are unedited, the rest carefully excerpted. Every case has a plain-English gist, and 1,000 fascinating passages are highlighted. In a landmark essay, Kopel finds that, "Supreme Court opinions dealing with the 2nd Amendment come from almost every period in the Court's history, and almost all of them assume or are consistent with the proposition that the 2nd Amendment is an individual right." Groundbreaking, superb reference. Also in hardcover, $49.95.

Traveler's Guide to the Firearm Laws of the 50 States

by Attorney J. Scott Kappas, 60 pgs., $12.95. Because you are subject to arrest for simply traveling from state to state with a personal firearm, some sort of guide has been badly needed for years. This excellent book covers all the basics for armed travel: vehicles, glove box, open carry, permits, loaded or not, weapon types, even Canada and Mexico and more. An indispensable tool if you want to travel armed and know the basic rules at the next state line. Before you pack your bags and go, get and read this book.
Includes the Nationwide CCW Reciprocity List!

LICENSED TO CARRY Guide to 30 "Shall Issue" States'

Concealed-Carry Laws by Greg Jeffrey, 74 pgs., $19.95. Shows each state's requirements for eligibility, background checks, training, permitted weapons, permit forms, waiting periods, reciprocity, penalties for unlicensed carry, who issues the license, cost, renewal fees, prohibited places and more. Packed with charts and graphs comparing how your rights are managed and restricted from state to state, then ranked for strictness in seven categories. Includes the number of licenses issued and revoked.

BLOOMFIELD PRESS
The nation's leading publisher and provider of gun-law books.
gunlaws.com • 1-800-707-4020
Founded 1988

PERSONAL SAFETY   Try some of these all-time classics.

"It's better to avoid an attack than to survive one."

In The Gravest Extreme (Ayoob) 132 pgs. $12.95. Widely recognized as the definitive work on the use of deadly force. This former law enforcement officer describes what you actually face in a lethal confrontation, a criminal's mindset, gun-fight tactics, judicial system's view on self-defense cases, more. Dispels the myths, truly excellent—**a must for any armed household & especially CCW permit holders.** Ayoob has written for most major gun magazines for decades.

The Truth About Self-Protection (Massad Ayoob) 418 pgs. $7.95. Get the facts on every aspect of personal safety, from evasive driving to planting cactus by your windows. **Lifesaving techniques** will help keep you, your family and your possessions safe, prepare you for defense if it becomes absolutely necessary, and guide you in buying lethal and less-than-lethal goods, from locks to firearms. Very big on crime-avoidance techniques.

Gun-Proof Your Children (Masaad Ayoob) 52 pgs. $4.95. One of the world's leading experts on lethal-force issues, this father of two shares his thoughts and very practical ideas on gun safety for kids in a classic short booklet. Also includes a primer on handguns for the novice. Here is a parent's guide that **does not advocate avoidance,** and instead proposes that knowledge should trump ignorance, and that education is the best choice.

You and The Police (Boston T. Party) 128 pgs. $16.00. If you're like most people, you don't have a clue what to do if you're stopped by the police. This book tells you how to handle a stop with dignity, and reviews the rights you do and do not have. What should you say or do if a peace officer wants to search your car, or if you're arrested? **Can you talk your way out of a ticket?** What are the limits on warrantless searches, and how can you respond to intimidation? If self defense is important to you, then so is this book.

Armed & Female (Paxton Quigley) 284 pgs. $5.99. Read about the tough decisions of a former activist in the anti-rights movement, who finally chose the victor over victim psychology. Features lessons she learned through extensive study, research and personal work. Compelling reading, packed with thought-provoking ideas and advice. The author is now a leading firearms trainer in Beverly Hills. **A great gift for a woman you know.**

Principles of Personal Defense (Col. Jeff Cooper) 44 pgs. $14. Hard-boiled wisdom from "The Father of the Modern Techniques of Shooting." His 7 principles are stark and brutal (Alertness, Decisiveness, Aggressiveness, Speed, Coolness, Ruthlessness and Surprise). **Too much for the squeamish.** An instant, violent counterattack is a total surprise to most criminals, legally justified if your life is in danger, and in a mortal struggle, Cooper says, "The perfect fight is one that is over before the loser really understands what is going on."

Stressfire—Gunfighting Tactics for Police (Massad Ayoob) 150 pgs. $11.95. Heavy-duty reading for advanced students and those who want the deepest understanding of lethal confrontations and how to survive a deadly encounter. Ayoob pours on the experience and techniques that make him a sought-after world-class expert, in a real page-turner. Not for the faint of heart, it will make you think. You may be able to shoot straight, but can you "clear" a house?

No Second Place Winner (Jordan) 114 pgs. $14.95. Unique discussion of armed response by a man who made it his trade. Jordan worked the U.S. Border Patrol of the old days and lived to tell about it. He became one of the deadliest shots of modern times. In an easy going style he describes with chilling clarity what it takes to win gun fights. "Be first or be dead... there are no second place winners." Filled with draw-and-shoot techniques, wonderful B&W stop-action photos.

Boston's Gun Bible (Boston T. Party) 848 pgs. $28. Astounding compendium of everything for the modern gun owner. Starts with legalities of gun use, safe handling, self defense, tactics and training. Covers weapons for fighting—combat handguns and battle rifles of most makers, info on caliber and cartridge types. Even covers reliable pre-1899 guns. Ideas for women, and how best to obtain everything you need. Wraps up with superb section on civilian disarmament forces, who's doing what, and ways to defend your rights. Great essays on courage and preparing for the worst while working to avoid it.

The Concealed Handgun Manual (Chris Bird) 416 pgs. $21.95. One of the standards for people who keep or carry guns for self defense. Bird has 40 years experience as a handgunner on 3 continents, and is a former crime reporter. Detailed accounts of self-defense incidents, latest info on laws and licenses, but the bulk of the book is packed with the nitty gritty on picking and packing a gun, advanced shooting technique, street-wise tactics, how to see trouble coming and avoid it. What to expect after you have shot someone.

The Good Citizen's Handbook (J.M. Trontz) 140 pgs. $12.95. Lessons from civics, scouting, even government guides from decades ago. Real wisdom from before America's values were debased. With drawings of wholesome lifestyles from 1920s to 1950s, here is what made America great—the dignity, courtesy, values we stood for. Re-awakens long-forgotten goals and ideals— penmanship matters, a good little boy doesn't talk back, Jr. Rifleman's Code of Conduct (Rule #9): "I will seek the advice of better marksmen than myself."

DEFENDING YOUR RIGHTS and POLITICAL REALITY
"It's not about winning a debate or being right. It's about convincing the other guy."

How To Win Friends And Influence People (Carnegie) 276 pgs. $7.50. The first, and still best book of its kind. Protecting your rights is not just about facts. If you win all your gun debates, you're losing. You don't want to win debates, you want to win friends and influence people. This wonderful book shows you how. 12 Ways To Win People To Your Way Of Thinking; 9 Ways To Change People Without Arousing Resentment; 6 Ways To Make People Like You. Powerful people skills.

Getting To Yes—Negotiate Agreement Without Giving In (Fisher & Ury) 200 pgs. $14. Based on the Harvard Negotiation Project, these groundbreaking principles are the heart of the most effective persuasion, will make you more effective with anti-rights advocates, legislators, bureaucrats. Tells you how to negotiate successfully with people who are more powerful, refuse to play by the rules, or resort to dirty tricks. Don't get angry or taken, get results.

Confrontational Politics (Sen. Richardson) 136 pgs. $9.95. The BS you see in government seems unexplainable but isn't: "Politics works, just not the way you think it does." State Senator Richardson lays out what really goes on, and you'll grasp the truth right away. His insider view clears the fog—politics follows simple rules and patterns you can manipulate. One of those rare books that is all meat.

That Every Man Be Armed (Stephen P. Halbrook) 274 pgs. $19.95. Answers the questions about intent of the 2nd Amendment. With 1,300 footnotes, Halbrook quotes sheaves of original documents of our founders. There may be confusion in America today, but there wasn't any back then. The title is from Patrick Henry, "The whole object is that every man be armed. Everyone who is able may have a gun." Henry's peers make similarly unambiguous remarks, removing all doubt.

More Guns, Less Crime (John R. Lott, Jr.) 324 pgs. $12. The classic. Lott, a scholar at Yale, became famous for it—a statistically sound, scientifically valid analysis of every American county, which found gun ownership lowers crime. He published the data, and other scholars confirmed the results. Anti-gun bigots hate this book because it shows gun ownership, specifically the right to carry, helps reduce crime.

The Samurai, The Mountie, and The Cowboy (David B. Kopel) 470 pgs. $35.
Hardcover. Kopel compares gun policy and gun laws of Japan, Canada, England, New Zealand, Switzerland, Jamaica, Australia and the U.S., then contrasts the cultures, social values, safety and relative freedom of these countries. **The best guide to foreign gun laws**; also shows how "gun control" disguises true causes of crime, gives deep appreciation of why America is the linchpin of freedom on planet Earth.

The Worst-Case Scenario Survival Handbook (Piven & Borgenicht) 176 pgs. $14.95.
Survival experts provide illustrated, step-by-step instructions on what you need to do in dire straights: How to take a punch; How to deliver a baby in a taxi; How to jump from a moving car; How to stop a car with no brakes; How to escape killer bees; How to treat a bullet or knife wound; How to use a defibrillator; How to do a tracheotomy; How to land the plane and more!

The Gun Control Debate: You Decide (Lee Nisbet, Ph.D., Editor) 580 pgs. $20. Using selections from historians, criminologists, social scientists, public health specialists, and jurists, Nisbet provides in-depth analysis of central issues involved in the gun debate. By providing a set of critical-thinking questions, and examples from experts on those very points, you can evaluate gun-control issues more deeply than is possible from the news media's portrayal of the issue.

Parliament of Whores (P.J. O'Rourke) 236 pgs. $12. "A lone humorist attempts to explain the entire U.S. government." Lighten up with this #1 National Bestseller, and gain refreshing insight into the foibles of the government you seek to change. With countless examples and piercing wit, America's outrageous humorist tears apart the tyrants who foist all that crud on you lowly peasants, bringing a perspective to things you can get no other way. He makes you laugh out loud.

Armed: New Perspectives on Gun Control (Kleck, Kates Jr.) 360 pgs. $27. Street wisdom says guns cause numerous child deaths, owners endanger themselves more than criminals, and legal consensus says the 2nd Amendment doesn't support an individual right to arms. These faulty assumptions are refuted by legal and criminological evidence. Sums up policy implications of reducing violence, effectiveness of defensive gun use, covert prohibitionist agenda, more.

Guns: Who Should Have Them? (David B. Kopel , Editor) 475 pgs. $32. Hardcover. Each chapter, by experts in law, criminology, medicine, psychiatry, and feminist studies, addresses a major gun-rights issue, and shows "gun control" is deflecting attention from true causes of crime—breakdown of the family; failed social welfare programs; and increasing hopelessness among male youths, especially in inner cities. "An intellectual tour-de-force." –Critical Review

Lost Rights, The Destruction of American Liberty (James Bovard) 408 pgs. $16.95.
How bad is it? Here's a virtual catalog of government abuse, incompetence, dishonesty and outright oppression. Highly researched and well documented. A full section on guns, but also taxes, seizures, police, subsidies, petty dictators, free speech, more. The only way many agencies measure their "public service" is by the number of citizens they harass, hinder, restrain or jail.

Hologram of Liberty (Kenneth W. Royce) 246 pgs. $19.95. Its premise and conclusion is stark and new, yet it makes so much sense it gave me chills. Why is Congress out of control, central government so large and powerful, and the public so increasingly subservient to the federal boot? Because, contrary to what you were taught, the Founding Fathers designed it that way. Cuts straight against the grain yet accurately describes the gritty reality around us.

"Grandpa Jack" Series (Aaron Zelman & others) 24 pgs. each, only $3 each, get all 7 for $15, save $6! Illustrated booklets tear up myths and make a case a child can see. Order by name: Gun Control Kills Kids, Can You Get a Fair Trial In America, Gun Control Is Racist, U.N. Is Killing Your Freedom, Will Gun Control Make You Safer?, It's Common Sense To Use Our Bill Of Rights, and their latest: Do Gun Prohibitionists Have A Mental Problem?

BLOOMFIELD PRESS gunlaws.com

DVDs PROVIDE A BRAVE NEW WORLD OF EDUCATION
"Firearm tactics and techniques are best seen and heard."

ADVANCED CONCEALED CARRY, FASTER, MORE ACCURATELY
$34.95 list, our price only $29.95. The followup to the basic concealed-carry program. Includes deep concealment techniques and real gunfight survival tools, including shooting on the move, the five-step draw method, and popular methods of carry and concealment with popular modern handguns. 110 minutes.

ADVANCED SELF–DEFENSE SHOOTING TACTICS & TECHNIQUES
$34.95 list, our price only $29.95. Designed for more experienced shooters, learn to shoot on the move what to expect at 3, 7, 10 yards and beyond. Practice techniques help you learn quickly. Then learn to shoot while moving away from an adversary, a crucial survival skill for gunfights. 60 minutes.

A WOMAN'S GUIDE TO FIREARMS
$24.95 list, our price only $21.95. Host Gerald McRaney (TV's "Major Dad") leads you through a step-by-step programs designed with women in mind. Helps reduce fear some women feel when learning about firearms, makes you comfortable with new skills. Thorough how-to video includes careful instruction from two champion shooters. 60 minutes.

BASIC SELF–DEFENSE HANDGUN USE & SAFETY
$34.95 list, our price only $29.95. Experts Bill Wilson, Ken Hackathorn and Lenny Magill take you through the shooting basics of grip, stance, sight alignment, trigger pull; Weaver and Isosceles stances and interesting variations too. Preparation for real life situations, info on self defense, dry fire practice you can do at home. 60 minutes.

CONCEALED CARRY TECHNIQUES AND SECRETS OF THE PROS
$24.95 list, our price only $21.95. How to select, wear and draw from more than 40 different concealment methods. Think you know how to carry? Wait till you see some of the options you've never thought about, which may be right for you. Includes an incredible display of draw and shoot from concealed carry, a mind-opening experience. 110 minutes.

HANDGUN BASICS FOR SELF DEFENSE AND TARGET SHOOTING
$34.95 list, our price only $29.95. Perfect for the newcomer, learn about handling and shooting revolvers and semi-auto pistols. Easy-to-follow info on how the guns work, safety, loading and unloading, at-home self defense, and a review of the most popular models and ammo for basic home use. 90 minutes.

HOUSE CLEARING & CORNERING TACTICS & TECHNIQUES
$39.95 list, our price only $34.95. Important pointers on self-defense include how to handle close quarters at home, when blind corners and exposure to possible gun fire is critical. What do you do if you know a burglar has broken into your home? What are the smart moves that will leave you the victor and safe? Advanced, for experienced shooters. 60 min.

The Massad Ayoob Video Series—Most people will never in their lives see real-life footage of tactical instruction like this. Ayoob, world-renowned, has produced recordings that truly stand out.

JUDICIOUS USE OF DEADLY FORCE

In this video, police captain Massad Ayoob, generally recognized as the leading authority on use of deadly weapons by civilians in self defense, goes beyond his book, "In the Gravest Extreme" to deal from the ground up in the core principles of law, ethics, and tactics of using lethal force. Ideal for the instructor or attorney, and vital for the citizen who keeps or carries a loaded gun. 130 min. $34.95 list, our price only $29.95.

LFI HANDGUN SAFETY

Seen by every Lethal Force Institute student before training begins. Ayoob pulls no punches showing how old-fashioned "Manuals of Arms" set the stage for accidents, and demonstrating the safest, most modern techniques of loading, unloading, drawing, and handling revolvers and semiautomatics. This is the video LFI grads bring back to their gun clubs on special order... now available to the gun-owning public. Warning: occasional four-letter word vulgarities underscore the deadly seriousness of the topic. 55.min $34.95 list, our price only $29.95.

CUTE LAWYER TRICKS Ayoob reveals the slick side of "the suits" and how to prevail in court. Available again at last. 30 min. Call for info.

ALWAYS SOMETHING GOOD AT GUNLAWS.COM
Visit our site for the classics — and books you won't find elsewhere!

NATION OF COWARDS

Essays on the Ethics of Gun Control, by Attorney Jeff Snyder, $14.95. These are simply some of the most brilliant essays ever written on this subject. The title essay has become globally famous. The rest are as good or better. His basic premise is that you alone own your life, and that it is unethical, immoral, politically corrupt to entrust your right to your life to someone else, or to abdicate the tools needed to protect yourself and your loved ones. People who would ban these rights, or encourage you to abandon them, even if they believe they are doing good, are the worst kind of cowards and represent the opposite of American values.

Police books for the public:
TERRORISM PREVENTION & RESPONSE

by Cliff Mariani, $16.95. Police are rapidly developing tactical plans, emergency protocols, new approaches to intelligence and information, as the War on Terror ramps up. An inside view of the mindsets and plans, it will change your thinking and planning for "asymmetrical threats." Key agency contacts, antiterrorism checklists, crucial mass-emergency response information, extended discussion of the nature of the enemies, detecting activity, types of threats, illicit money handling, the real effect of the color warnings, evacuation plans, much more.

POLICE OFFICER'S RESPONSE GUIDE TO CRIMES IN PROGRESS

by Nate Tanguay, $34.95. Model your own defensive responses on police expertise. Here are effective strategies for more than 60 different calls, including hit-and-runs, assaults, suicides, riots, rape/sexual assaults, gunshot/stab wounds, kidnappings, hostage situations, domestic violence, drunk drivers, gangs, armed suspects, cults, more. Summarizes what police have found from countless incidents, no fluff, right down to evidence collection—critical for winning cases (and self defense) later.

Who can bear arms? Where are guns forbidden?
When can you shoot to kill?

STATE-BY-STATE GUN LAWS
"If you knew all your rights you might demand them."

The books Bloomfield Press is famous for! Only $14.95 each! An astounding level of detail on state gun laws, *all presented in plain English,* cross-referenced to the actual statutes reprinted in the back. Gun owners, trainers and schools all use our guides, you should too—get the straight scoop on your state gun laws. You get the laws for owning, buying, selling, carrying and using firearms; deadly force and self defense, carry licenses, reciprocity, special weapons, gun safety, kid and school laws, transport, federal laws... the most complete coverage for your state's handling of the 2nd Amendment to the Constitution. Perfect if you have a carry license, widely endorsed, easy to use and really fun to read. Takes the mystery out of owning guns! You have a right to know your laws.

PLUS—Gun-Owner Guides from Other Publishers:

Massachusetts
$18.50

Missouri
$23.95

Minnesota
$24.95

Montana
$12.95

New Jersey
$24.95

Prices Vary

New Mexico
$8.00

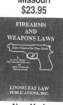
New York
$31.95

Nevada
$17.90

Tennessee
$14.95

Utah
$18.76

Washington
$9.95

Order these books by the name of the state. MI, OH & VT too! Check with us for your state!

Order our books on the web, or by mail, email, fax or phone!

1. By mail, send us your name, address & phone number on a piece of paper;
2. List the books you want to own, and the price of each;
3. Send check or money order payable to Bloomfield Press, and include S&H:
   (S&H = $4 for 1 book, $5 for 2, $6 up to 6 books, call for larger orders).
4. If ordering by credit card, include your card number and expiration date.
   It's Easy! WE WELCOME YOUR TELEPHONE AND FAX ORDERS
   MasterCard, Visa and Discover accepted.   **AZ residents add 8.1% sales tax.**
   Retail orders are shipped by USPS. **Prices, like life, are subject to change without notice.**

DEALERS: Contact us for wholesale orders!
Great for your customers, and your rights, and your bottom line.

Published by

BLOOMFIELD PRESS